CONTROVERSIES IN MACROECONOMICS: GROWTH, TRADE AND POLICY

I dedicate this volume to my parents, Margaret and Graham, with thanks for all that they have given me.

CONTROVERSIES IN MACROECONOMICS
GROWTH, TRADE AND POLICY

Edited by
HUW DAVID DIXON
University of York

First published 2000

2 4 6 8 10 9 7 5 3 1

Blackwell Publishers Ltd
108 Cowley Road
Oxford OX4 1JF
UK

Blackwell Publishers Inc.
350 Main Street
Malden, Massachusetts 02148
USA

British Library Cataloguing in Publication Data
A CIP catalogue record for this book is available from the British Library.

Library of Congress Cataloging-in-Publication Data
Controversies in macroeconomics : growth, trade, and policy / edited by
   Huw David Dixon.
         p.   cm.
   Includes bibliographical references and index.
   ISBN 0-631-21585-9 (alk. paper). — ISBN 0-631-21586-7 (pbk : alk. paper)
   1. Macroeconomics.   2. Economic development.   3. Commercial policy.
   4. Economic policy.   I. Dixon, Huw David.
   HB172.5.C658   2000
   339—dc21   99-33935
                                                                   CIP

Typeset in 10 on 12 pt. Baskerville by Ace Filmsetting Ltd, Frome, Somerset
Printed in Great Britain by MPG Books, Bodmin, Cornwall

This book is printed on acid-free paper.

CONTENTS

AUTHORS

JONAS AGELL is Professor of Economics at Uppsala University. He was previously a research fellow at the Institute for International Economic Studies, Stockholm University, after completing his PhD in 1986. His research interests are public economics and macroeconomics. He has published articles on these issues in many journals. He is the coauthor of *Does Debt Management Matter?* (Oxford University Press) and *Incentives and Redistribution in the Welfare State* (Macmillan).

PHILIP ARESTIS is Professor of Economics at the University of East London. He completed his PhD in 1976, and has also taught at the Universities of Surrey and Cambridge (Department of Extra-Mural Studies) and Greenwich University (where he was Head of the Economics Division). His research interests are in the areas of Macroeconomics, Monetary Economics, Applied Econometrics, Political Economy and Applied Political Economy. He has published or edited more than 20 books, has contributed to numerous edited books, and he has published more than 200 papers in academic journals.

Professor KYLE BAGWELL of Columbia University was born in 1961 and educated at the Southern Methodist University before doing his PhD at Stanford. He has published over 30 papers on industrial organisation, trade theory, game theory and public finance.

ANDREW B. BERNARD is Associate Professor of Economics at the Yale School of Management. He was an undergraduate at Harvard University and then studied at Stanford University where he received his PhD in 1991. Professor Bernard taught in the economics department at MIT before moving to Yale in 1997. Professor Bernard specialises in studying the role of international trade in promoting long-run growth for both firms and countries. His research on the interaction of exports and productivity has been featured in *The Wall Street Journal, Nikkei, Fortune,* and *Business Week.*

JAGDISH BHAGWATI, Arthur Lehman Professor of Economics and Professor of Political Science at Columbia University, was born in 1934 and raised in India. He attended Cambridge University where he graduated and then studied at MIT and Oxford, returning to India in 1961 as Professor of Economics at the Indian Statistical Institute. He returned to MIT in 1968, leaving it twelve years later as the Ford International Professor of Economics to join Columbia. Professor Bhagwati has also served as Economic

Policy Advisor to Director-General, GATT (1991–1993). Professor Bhagwati has published more than two hundred articles and forty volumes. Regarded as one of the foremost international trade theorists of his generation, he has also made contributions to development theory and policy, public finance, immigration, and to the new theory of political economy.

PANICOS DEMETRIADES is Professor of Financial Economics at South Bank University, London. Born in Cyprus, in 1959, he received his university education in the UK at the Universities of Essex and Cambridge. He returned to Cyprus in 1985 and worked in the Central Bank for several years before returning to the UK, where he served as lecturer then reader at the University of Keele until 1997. He has written extensively on financial liberalisation and economic growth, with emphasis on developing economies. He has acted as consultant for the World Bank and the African development Bank, as a speaker for the Economic Development Institute of the World Bank. He also acted as Advisor to the Cyprus Co-operative Central Bank on issues relating to financial liberalisation.

HUW D. DIXON is Professor at York University (UK). Born in 1958, he studied at Oxford University where he obtained his PhD in 1985. He has published over 50 papers in research journals and books. He has been involved in editing the *Review of Economic Studies*, the *Journal of Industrial Economics* and the Controversies section of the *Economic Journal*. Dixon's research areas include the macroeconomics of imperfect competition, oligopoly theory, learning and bounded rationality

After sitting-in and dropping-out of a science degree in 1971 and spending ten years as a community worker in Wales, STEVE DOWRICK completed an undergraduate degree in economics at the University of Cambridge and a PhD at the University of Warwick. His early research was on union bargaining and industrial relations. More recently he has studied economic growth and convergence. Most recently still, a joint research project with John Quiggin has proposed and implemented a solution to 'the index number problem' in making meaningful international comparisons of real GDP levels and standards of living. He is currently Professor of Economics and Head of the Department of Economics at the Australian National University in Canberra where he lives in sunshine with his partner and their two daughters.

STEVEN N. DURLAUF is Professor of Economics at The University of Wisconsin-Madison. He obtained his BA in 1980 from Harvard and PhD in 1986 from Yale. He is a former Economics Program Director of the Santa Fe Institute. A Fellow of the Econometric Society, his research interests lie in the areas of macroeconomics and econometrics.

WILFRED J. ETHIER is currently Professor of Economics at the University of Pennsylvania. He is currently editor of the *International Economic Review*. He obtained his PhD in 1970 from Rochester University. He has published widely in the field of trade theory and policy.

ROBERT H. FRANK is Goldwin Smith Professor of Economics, Ethics, and Public Policy at

Cornell University. His most recent book, *Luxury Fever*, examines the causes and consequences of the recent surge in conspicuous consumption. An earlier book, *The Winner-Take-All Society*, was named to Business Week's Ten Best Books list in 1995, and has been translated into six languages.

MAXWELL J. FRY was born in 1944 and obtained his PhD at the LSE in 1970. He is currently Professor of Banking at the Birmingham Business School, previously being at the University of California Irvine. He is also currently Director of the Centre of Central Bank Studies at the Bank of England. He has written extensively on the subjects of banking, finance and development.

ODED GALOR is Professor of Economics at Brown University and currently editor of *The Journal of Economic Growth*. He has written widely on many aspects of growth, including income distribution, migration, wage inequality, trade and poverty traps.

Professor DAVID GREENAWAY, born in 1952, has been at the University of Nottingham since 1987. He is a Professor of Economics, Director of the Centre for Research on Globalisation and Labour Markets and has been a Pro-Vice-Chancellor since 1994. His research interests lie primarily in international trade policy, economic development and European integration. He has published widely in academic journals and a number of books. He has been a consultant to the World Bank, UNIDO, UNCTAD, European Commission, GATT, UNECE and HM Treasury. He is Chair of the Panel for Economics and Econometrics in the 2001 Research Assessment Exercise in the UK, a Member of the Council of ESRC and a Member of the Armed Forces Pay Review Body.

MAGNUS HENREKSEN is a Research Fellow at The Research Institute of Industrial Economics, Stockholm. Born in 1958, he obtained his BA and PhD at the University of Gothenburg. His research interests include entrepreneurship, economic growth, public finance, stabilization policy, international finance, technical change, structural change, and (open economy) macroeconomics.

CHARLES I. JONES is assistant Professor at Stanford University. He was an undergraduate at Harvard and completed his PhD at MIT in 1993. He has researched and published on the sources of long-run growth and international differences in growth.

WALTER KORPI is Professor of social policy at the Swedish Institute for Social Research, Stockholm University. Educated at Stockholm University (where he obtained his degree in 1966), he has been a visiting scholar at Columbia University, University of Wisconsin at Madison, and University of Mannheim (Germany). He has researched and published on comparative analyses of welfare state developments in the Western countries, income inequality, poverty, political economy and economic growth.

ANNE O. KRUEGER is Herald L. and Caroline L. Ritch Professor of Humanities and Science in the Economics Department, Director of the Center for Research on Economic Development and Policy Reform, and Senior Fellow at the Hoover Institution at Stanford University. She is a Distinguished Fellow and Past President of the American Economic

Association, a member of the National Academy of Sciences, and a Fellow of the Econometric Society and the American Academy of Arts and Sciences. She is a Senior Research Associate of the National Bureau of Economic Research, and Co-Director of the NBER series on East Asian economics. She received her PhD at the University of Wisconsin in 1958 and taught at the University of Minnesota and at Duke University and served as Vice President, Economics and Research at the World Bank from 1982 through 1986 prior to joining the Stanford faculty in 1993. She is currently a member of the National Commission on US Trade Policy. Her current research interests include policy reform in developing countries, trade policy and economic development and political economy of US trade policy. She has written many articles and books, including *Political Economy of Economic Reform in Developing Countries* (MIT Press).

SAJAL LAHIRI was born in 1950 in the Indian state of West Bengal. He obtained all his degrees (BStat, MStat and PhD) from the Indian Statistical Institute, Calcutta. Before coming to the University of Warwick as a postdoctoral research fellow in 1977, he worked for a year at the Indian Planning Commission. In 1978, he joined the University of Essex where he is currently Professor of Economics. He has held visiting positions in USA, Australia, Japan and Denmark. His initial research interest was in the area of development planning, and for the last 15 years or so he has been working in the areas of international trade and development economics. He has published over 50 articles in academic journals and is one of the editors of the *Review of Development Economics*.

WYN MORGAN, Senior Lecturer in Economics at the University of Nottingham, was born in 1964. He took his undergraduate degree at the University of Exeter before gaining a PhD from the University of Nottingham in 1991. He was appointed Lecturer in Economics at the University of Nottingham in 1990. He has published in a range of areas including liberalisation and growth, commodity and futures markets, food economics and agricultural policy. Research output includes thirteen refereed journal articles, three books and seven contributions to edited works.

Professor YEW-KWANG NG was born in 1942 in Malaysia. He graduated with a BCom from Nanyang University (Singapore) in 1966 and a PhD from Sydney University in 1971. He holds a personal chair at Monash University (Melbourne) and is a fellow of the Academy of Social Sciences in Australia. He has published more than a hundred refereed articles in economics and a dozen in biology, mathematics, philosophy, and psychology, and about a hundred articles in the popular press. Books published include *Welfare Economics* (1979), *Mesoeconomics: A Micro-Macro Analysis* (1986), *Social Welfare and Economic Policy* (1990), *Specialization and Economic Organization* (1993, with X. Yang), *Increasing Returns and Economic Analysis*, ed. (1998, with K. Arrow and X. Yang), *Efficiency, Equality, and Public Policy: With a Case for Higher Public Spending* (London: Macmillan, forthcoming).

WILLIAM D. NORDHAUS is the A. Whitney Griswold Professor of Economics at Yale University, New Haven, Connecticut, USA. He was born in Albuquerque, New Mexico (which is part of the USA). He completed his undergraduate work at Yale University and received his PhD in Economics in 1967 from MIT. From 1977 to 1979, he was a Member of the US President's Council of Economic Advisers. He is a member and senior advisor of the Brookings Panel on Economic Activity, Washington, DC and is a Fellow of the American Academy of Arts and Sciences. Professor Nordhaus is current or past editor of a number of scientific journals and has served on the executive committees of the American Economic Association and the Eastern Economic Association. His research has focused on economic growth and natural resources, as well as the question of the extent to which resources constrain economic growth, with pioneering work beginning in the 1970s on the economics of global warming. Professor Nordhaus has also undertaken studies in wage and price behaviour, augmented national accounting, the political business cycle, productivity, and the costs and benefits of regulation.

JOSE A. OCAMPO was born in Colombia in 1952 and has been Executive Secretary of the Economic Commission for Latin America and the Caribbean (ECLAC), since January 1988. He took his BA in Economics and Sociology at Notre Dame and his PhD from Yale in 1976. He has previously held positions in the Colombian government as Minister of Finance and Public Credit, Minister of Agriculture and Minister of Planning.

ANDREW J. OSWALD was born in 1953. He is professor of Economics at Warwick University, and taught previously at Oxford and LSE, and in the USA at Dartmouth and Princeton. His research has been mainly on the labour market and on the economics of well-being. The book *The Wage Curve*, jointly written with David Blanchflower, was published by MIT Press in 1994. It won Princeton University's Lester Prize. Other recent awards include the Medal of the University of Helsinki in 1995 and best-article-of-the-year in the 1996 journal *Applied Psychology*.

Professor ARVIND PANAGARIYA received a Master's degree in Economics at Rajasthan University in India where he also taught for one year. He received his PhD from Princeton University in 1978 when he joined the Maryland faculty. He has spent the years 1989–93 at the Policy Research Department of the World Bank studying and writing on a variety of trade policy issues. His principal area of research is trade theory and policy. He has written on topics such as economies of scale and trade, smuggling and trade, trade policy reform, the political economy of uniform tariffs and regional integration. He has published many articles and, in 1993, his book *New Dimensions of Regional Integration* (Cambridge University Press).

DANNY T. QUAH is Professor of Economics at the London School of Economics and Political Science (LSE) and Director of the Technology and Growth Programme at LSE's Centre for Economic Performance. He serves on the Academic Panels of the Treasury and the Office for National Statistics in the UK. In July 1998, the Andrew W. Mellon Foundation awarded him a grant for continued study of the weightless economy and the economics of information technology. Quah's academic research has been further supported by awards from the British Academy, the Economic and Social Research Council, and the MacArthur Foundation. Quah has made contributions in a number of areas, ranging from time-series econometrics, business cycles, inflation, and international income inequality to, most recently, technology and economic growth.

XAVIER X. SALA-I-MARTIN is currently Professor of Economics at Columbia University and Universitat Pompeu Fabra. He obtained his undergraduate economics degree from the Autonomous University of Barcelona and his PhD from Harvard in 1990. Previously, he was an associate Professor at Yale. He is an associate editor of the *Journal of Economic Growth*. His research interests include various aspects of growth: empirical studies of convergence, technological diffusion, human capital and investment, social security, money and inflation.

AJIT SINGH, an Indian economist who graduated from Punjab University and obtained his PhD at the University of California, Berkeley, has been teaching economics at Cambridge University since 1965. He is currently Professor of Economics at the University and Senior Fellow at Queens' College, Cambridge. Between 1970 and 1994, he was Director of Studies in Economics at Queens'. He has been a senior economic adviser to the governments of Mexico and Tanzania and a consultant to various UN developmental organisations, including the World Bank, the ILO, UNCTAD and UNIDO. His essay, 'How do developing country corporations finance their growth?' was awarded a $5000 prize and Bronze medal in the Amex Awards Competition, 1994.

ROBERT W. STAIGER is associate professor at the University of Wisconsin-Madison, which he joined in 1993. He obtained his PhD from the University of Michigan in 1985. He has researched widely in the field of international economics.

LANCE TAYLOR is the Arnhold Professor of International Cooperation and Development Department of Economics, New School for Social Research, New York New School for Social Research. Born in 1940, his first degree was at California Institute of Technology and his PhD from Harvard in 1968. He spends most of his time teaching, doing applied research, and proffering policy advice in developing countries; the balance he devotes to trying to understand how their economies work. He has published many articles on the topic of development and transition, in particular the role of markets and liberalisation in the development process.

PETER WRIGHT became a member of staff at the University of Nottingham in 1993, after completing his Doctorate at the University of Warwick. He is a lecturer in Labour Economics and a Research Fellow in the Leverhulme Centre for Research on Globalisation and Labour Markets. His research interests lie primarily in the area of labour market adjustment, and he has worked in both open and closed economy frameworks. His work has been both theoretical and applied. He has published a range of papers including articles in the *Economic Journal, The European Journal of Political Economy, Economic Development and Cultural Change, The Journal of International Trade and Economic Development and World Development*.

PREFACE

William D. Nordhaus

Controversies are hardly new to economics. What is their source? You might think that controversies are sparked either by burning political issues or by analytical questions of high import. That reading would misjudge the crucial ingredients of a controversy. It takes three to sustain a controversy: two people sufficiently taken with their points of view to argue and someone who is looking for entertainment and is willing to listen. None of these requires that the topic of importance be of any durable value, just as family arguments need not be about anything more important than the fair allocation of garbage disposition.

There is evidently a market failure in the provision of high-quality controversies in economics. We should therefore be grateful for the good judgment of *The Economic Journal* and the inspired editorship of Huw Dixon in providing a journal that would serve as *agent provocateur* and serve up an audience for the controversies in these pages.

While economists can dispute anything, most serious controversies have a key component – usually they touch on core myths and religious beliefs of the guild. To some economists, no single issue is more sacred than the belief in the sanctity of the market mechanism. Question the role of the market, or of the market distribution of income, and you have the formula for arousing controversy.

Take the example of the lighthouse, which has been the subject of a storm of controversies in the area of a public good. The role of government in providing lighthouse services was articulated by economists such as John Stuart Mill, Henry Sedgwick and Alfred Pigou. When the theory of public goods and the severe difficulties with the market provision of pure public goods was rigorously developed in the 1950s, lighthouses were put forth as a signal example of a public good. In our 15th edition of *Economics*, Paul Samuelson and I stated the standard view of lighthouses as a public good as follows (Samuelson and Nordhaus, 1994):

> Lighthouses are a typical example of a public good provided by government. They save lives and cargos. But lighthouse keepers cannot reach out to collect fees from ships; nor, if they could, would it serve an efficient social purpose for them to exact an economic penalty on ships who use their services. The light can be provided most efficiently free of charge, for it costs no more to warn 100 ships than to warn a single ship of the nearby rocks.

This view became 'controversial' when Ronald Coase (1974) reviewed the history of lighthouses in England and Wales and determined that these had indeed been *privately* provided. He noted that lighthouses operated profitably under patents purchased from the Crown and with 'light duties' levied on ships that were presumed to benefit from the lighthouses. From this history, Coase (1974, p. 375) concluded that 'contrary to the belief of many economists, a lighthouses service can be provided by private enterprise'. Some have even concluded that lighthouses are not public goods.

The lighthouse controversy is typical in that it involves semantic confusion, a selective reading of history and unwarranted extrapolation. The essence of a public good is its non-rivalry in consumption and its non-excludability. However, a 'public' good is not necessarily publicly provided. It may be provided by no one. Moreover, just because it is privately provided does not indicate that it is efficiently provided or that a pure market mechanism exists to finance private lighthouses. Rather, the English example shows the interesting case where, *if* provision of the public good can be tied to another good or service (in that case, vessel tonnage), and *if* the government gives private persons the right to collect what are essentially taxes, then an alternative mechanism for *financing* the public good can be found. Such an approach would work poorly where the fees could not be easily tied to tonnage, such as in international channels; and it would not work at all if the government refused to privatize the right to collect light duties on shipping.

We can pursue the question of the market response to navigational dangers by examining the American case, where the government does not tie lighthouse provision to a private financing mechanism. In the US, Congress believed that navigational aids should be government provided. Indeed, one of the first acts of the first Congress, and America's first public-works law, provided that 'the necessary support, maintenance, and repairs of all lighthouse, beacons, [and] buoys . . . shall be defrayed out.of the Treasury of the United States'. Among Alexander Hamilton's duties as Secretary of the Treasury was the personal supervision of navigational aids.

However, Congress was slow to invest in navigational aids, and the interesting question arises as to what happened in dangerous waters in the absence of navigational aids. A fascinating case is that of the Florida reef, which lies astride the heavily used channel Southeast of Florida. This is one of the most treacherous waters in the world, with a 200-mile reef lying submerged a few feet below the surface in the prime hurricane track of the Atlantic Ocean, and was prime territory for storm, shipwreck and piracy.

There were no lighthouses in Florida until 1825, and no private-sector lighthouses were ever apparently built in this area. The market did respond vigorously to the perils, however. What arose from the private sector was a thriving 'wrecking' industry. Wreckers were ships that lurked near the dangerous reefs waiting for an unfortunate boat to become disabled. The wreckers would then appear, offer their help in saving lives and cargo, tow the boat into the appropriate port, and then claim a substantial part of the value of the cargo. Wreckers were the major industry of south Florida in the mid-nineteenth century and made Key West the richest town in America at that time (For historical details on lighthouses and wrecking in Florida, see Love (1998) and Viele (1996).

While wreckers probably had positive value added, they provided none of the public-good attributes of lighthouses and other navigational aids. Indeed, because many cargoes were insured, there was significant moral hazard involved in navigation. Connivance between wreckers and captains was often suspected as a way of enriching both, at the expense of owners and insurance companies. It was only when the US Lighthouse Service, financed by general revenues, began to build lighthouses through the Florida channel that the public goods were provided – and the wreckers were gradually put out of business.

I recount these details partly to restore the good name of lighthouses and of public goods. However, the history also illustrates how a controversy that involves the core beliefs of economics can start and be sustained. Lighthouses are hardly a central issue of public finance today, and indeed they have been largely replaced by global positioning systems (GPSs), which are also a public good provided free by the government. But examples like this can set economists' adrenaline pumping.

The pages that follow illustrate how controversies arise when issues touch the core beliefs of economics. Whether the issue is free trade, Keynesian activism versus monetarist rules or the welfare state, readers here will be treated to applications of fine rhetoric at the service of central economic problems. Whatever the outcome of these debates, of one thing we can be assured: fascinating and important controversies in economics will be with us as long as scarcity itself.

References

Coase, R. (1974). The lighthouse in economics. *Journal of Law and Economics*, 357–76.
Love D. (1998). *Lighthouses of the Florida Keys*, Sarasota, Florida: Pineapple Press.
Samuelson, P. A. and Nordhaus, W. D. (1994). *Economics*, 15th edn. New York: McGraw-Hill.
Viele, J. (1996). *The Florida Keys: A History of The Pioneers*, Sarasota, Florida: Pineapple Press.

ACKNOWLEDGEMENTS

I would like to thank the many people who have made the controversies section a success over the years: the contributors too numerous to mention, the people with whom I have discussed possible controversies, the people who have suggested possible topics, the staff at the *Economic Journal* office (Caroline Dearden and Kathy Crocker in particular) and last but not least the two editors of the *Economic Journal* during my period (John Hey and Mike Wickens) for their help and support.

To produce this book, I must thank the *Royal Economic Society* for giving its permission for these articles to be reprinted in this collection. Also, the team at Blackwells (Al Bruckner and Katie Byrne) were always very helpful and efficient, not least in reminding me what had to be done! Thanks to Rimawan Pradiptyo for compiling the index.

The following articles were reprinted with the permission of the *Royal Economic Society*:

On the convergence and divergence of growth rates: An introduction, Steven N. Durlauf, *Economic Journal*, 1996, 106 (July), 1016–18.

The classical approach to convergence of growth analysis, Xavier X. Sala-i-Martin, *Economic Journal*, 1996, 106 (July), 1019–36.

Technology and convergence, Andrew B. Bernard and Charles I. Jones, *Economic Journal*, 1996, 106 (July), 1037–44.

Twin peaks: growth and convergence in models of distribution dynamics, Danny T. Quah, *Economic Journal*, 1996, 106 (July), 1045–55.

Convergence? Inferences from theoretical models, Oded Galor, *Economic Journal*, 1996, 106 (July), 1056–69.

Trade liberalisation and growth: An introduction, Huw D. Dixon, *Economic Journal*, 1998, 108 (September), 1511–12.

Why trade liberalisation is good for growth, Anne O. Krueger, *Economic Journal*, 1998, 108 (September), 1513–22.

Trade liberalisation in developing economies: modest benefits but problems with productivity growth, macro prices, and income distribution, Jose A. Ocampo and Lance Taylor, *Economic Journal*, 1998, 108 (September), 1523–46.

Trade reform, adjustment and growth: what does the evidence tell us?, David Greenaway, Wyn Morgan and Peter Wright, *Economic Journal*, 1998, 108 (September), 1547–61.

Regionalism versus multilateralism: introduction, Sajal Lahiri, *Economic Journal*, 1998, 108 (July), 1126–7.

Trading preferentially: theory and policy, Jagdish Bhagwati, David Greenaway and Arvind Panagariya. *Economic Journal*, 1998, 108 (July), 1128–48.

The new regionalism, Wilfred J. Ethier, *Economic Journal*, 1998, 108 (July), 1149–61.

Will preferential agreements undermine the multilateral trading system? Kyle Bagwell and Robert W. Staiger, *Economic Journal*, 1998, 108 (July), 1162–82.

Finance and development: editorial note, Huw D. Dixon, *Economic Journal*, 1997, 107 (May), 752–3.

In favour of financial liberalisation, Maxwell J. Fry, *Economic Journal*, 1997, 107 (May), 754–70.

Financial liberalisation, stockmarkets and economic development, Ajit Singh, *Economic Journal*, 1997, 107 (May), 771–82.

Financial development and economic growth: assessing the evidence, Philip Arestis and Panicos Demetriades, *Economic Journal*, 1997, 107 (May), 773–99.

Economics and happiness: introduction, Huw D. Dixon, *Economic Journal*, 1997, 107 (November), 1812–14. (Amended for this publication).

Happiness and economic performance, Andrew J. Oswald, *Economic Journal*, 1997, 107 (November), 1815–31.

The frame of reference as a public good, Robert H. Frank, *Economic Journal*, 1997, 107 (November), 1832–47.

A case for happiness, cardinalism and interpersonal comparability, Yew-Kwang Ng, *Economic Journal*, 1997, 107 (November), 1848–58.

Traditional productivity estimates are asleep at the (technological) switch, William D. Nordhaus, *Economic Journal*, 1997, 107 (September), 1548–59.

Economists, the welfare state and growth: the case of Sweden: editorial note, Huw D. Dixon, *Economic Journal*, 1996, 106 (November), 1725–6.

Eurosclerosis and the sclerosis of objectivity: on the role of values among economic policy experts, Walter Korpi, *Economic Journal*, 1996, 106 (November), 1727–46.

Sweden's relative economic performance: lagging behind or staying on top?, Magnus Henreksen, *Economic Journal*, 1996, 106 (November), 1747–59.

Why Sweden's welfare state needed reform, Jonas Agell, *Economic Journal*, 1996, 106 (November), 1760–71.

Swedish economic performance and Swedish economic debate: A view from outside, Steve Dowrick, *Economic Journal*, 1996, 106 (November), 1772–9.

INTRODUCTION

Huw D. Dixon

While economists in general have found much to agree about in microeconomics, the field of macroeconomics has always been one prone to controversy. Ever since Keynes slugged it out with his critics in the 1930s, there has been heated debate. Growth has become one of the hottest topics in macroeconomics since the mid-1980s. As Lucas has said, once you start thinking about it you can think of little else.

For this volume, I have selected some of the controversies in macroeconomics published over the period 1996–1998 in the *Economic Journal's* controversy section, with particular focus on the issue of *economic growth*. Each controversy consists of a brief introduction, summarizing the main issues, followed by papers in which leading researchers in the field put forward their own point of view on the topic in a manner which is accessible to the general economist. The way the economics profession works nowadays, many of these debates are carried on 'behind closed doors' in academic journals in a technical style which is often open only to the specialist researcher. This volume aims to bring these debates into the open.

The subject of economic growth has raised many issues in the last decade or so. Six particular issues and questions are covered in this volume:

- Do growth rates converge? If two economies start from different initial positions (e.g. one rich and one poor), will the differences tend to diminish over time (the economies converge) or will the differences persist or even grow (the economies diverge)?
- Is trade liberalization good for growth? Should we encourage free trade in all circumstances, or are there some cases where some protection can be good for growth?
- Should trade liberalization take the form of establishing freer trade in specific regions (such as the EU or the North American free-trade zone), or is a global approach necessary?
- Is financial liberalization good for growth? The International Monetary Fund (IMF) has long been pressing the idea that financial liberalization is a 'good thing'. However, what is the evidence for this?
- Is economic growth desirable? Does it make people happier? Much of economics assumes that anything that increases measured GNP is a 'good thing'. However, does the evidence back this up?

- Does the welfare state reduce growth? The issue of welfare state reform is high on the agenda in Europe and elsewhere: many believe that it can reduce growth and reduce economic performance, but is this supported by the evidence?

Since each controversy itself has an introduction, I shall not seek to survey or outline the individual controversies themselves here. Rather, I shall look at two things: the nature of controversy in economics and the impetus behind the founding of the *Controversies* section in the *Economic Journal*. These should very much be seen as a personal perspective, in which I have erred on the side of boldly stating my views rather than careful scholarship, as seems appropriate in this volume.

1 WHAT DO ECONOMISTS ARGUE ABOUT?

It is often said of economists that if you have three economists in a room, then you will find four opinions. Why do economists argue, and what do they argue about? Clearly, this latter question is a very big question and raises many issues that are general to any area of human understanding: people disagree and argue about many things and indeed almost anything. However, in the case of macroeconomics, I believe that we can usefully simplify matters into three major levels or sources of disagreement:

- The extent to which economists adhere to the *laissez-faire*[1] view that the market gets things right (or as right as possible)
- The appropriate model that best describes the economy
- The relative importance in practice of different factors within a model

Of course, in any one debate, all three of these sources are often present and interact: for example, take the issue of anti-trust regulation. A person who is relatively *laissez faire* in outlook will tend to think that the competitive model is most appropriate and that the market imperfections that do exist are not important in magnitude. However, it is useful to divide these different levels, at least at the conceptual level, when we read a particular controversy.

2 WORLD-VIEWS AND SPECTACLES

If you wear sunglasses, then the world becomes a darker place. Green-tinted glasses make the world look green. Economists have different perspectives or world-views that act like spectacles and that shade how they look at any problem. In the field of macro-economics (and indeed any policy relevant field of economics), there are traditionally two dominant views on policy: *laissez-faire* and interventionist. I will outline a brief sketch (caricature) of these views.

---

[1] The term *laissez faire* is traditionally associated with free trade: there should be no restrictions to free trade in the form of tariff or non-tariff barriers. However, in a wider context, it denotes a general belief that the market is best left to its own devices in most or all areas.

- *Laissez-faire:* the free-market works!

  In macroeconomics, the *laissez-faire* view is associated with the Classical/neo-Classical or New-Classical view. Economists wearing these spectacles tend to think of the economy as a (more or less) well functioning competitive free-market economy. The First Fundamental Theorem of Welfare Economics says that such an economy should be 'efficient' in the technical sense of Pareto optimality. According to this type of economist, the free-market pretty much gets most things right and the role of government is limited to ensuring that markets can operate freely, and perhaps intervening where there are clear and major market failures (due for example to externalities or public goods).

  Indeed, in the extreme free-market view, government intervention or regulation of markets is seen as a last resort. Far from being the disembodied, almost divine, 'social planner' that can intervene to rectify any problem (however slight) in the functioning of markets, the government is a very imperfect tool. It is itself subject to economic influences (lobbying), the need for re-election (in democracies), while regulatory bodies and bureaucracies are difficult to control. Indeed, government intervention in markets often has a lot of unintended side-effects that may be counterproductive. It is the government that has the health warning, while the free market is presumed innocent until proven guilty.

- *Interventionist:* the free market works, but . . .

  The second view has no generic label, but in the macroeconomic field it is certainly linked to the adjective 'Keynesian'. Economists with these spectacles see markets as being inherently imperfect to some significant extent. The free market will get things wrong if left to its own devices. There is some disagreement over whether the government can do much about it, but the question of regulation or some form of intervention is certainly on the menu as a possibility to be given serious consideration. However, the interventionist has a basic lack of trust about the free market and believes that its outcome can be, at best, efficient but unjust and, at worst, both inefficient and unjust. Even perfectly functioning markets need not get the question of equity and the distribution of income right (it is Pareto optimal to share a cake so that one person has everything and the rest nothing). When there is market power or dominance, imperfect information and other imperfections, the free market can yield highly undesirable outcomes. In this case, the efficient operation of the economy may require some sort of intervention to avoid these imperfect outcomes.

Of course, the extreme *laissez-faire* view is held by few, although free-market ideologues are certainly an important political policy pressure group, on both sides of the Atlantic and around the world.[2] Likewise, most interventionists would accept that there is no real alternative to the market to achieve the bulk of economic organization in an economy.[3]

---

[2] Occasionally, they are even elected to run the economy, as in the Thatcher/Reagan years.
[3] Although it is worth noting in the 1990s that in previous decades (1950–1970) the degree of intervention in some highly successful western economies was considerable, e.g. France, Japan and Sweden.

Hence one can say that the real debate is really along a continuum: the question is one of extent. How much should the government intervene and how should this best be done? For example, Mankiw and Romer (1991, p.3) state in their collection of *New Keynesian* papers that

> . . . new Keynesian economists not necessarily believe that active government policy is desir-able. Because the theories developed . . . emphasise market imperfections, they usually imply that the unfettered market reaches inefficient equilibria. Thus these models show that government intervention can potentially improve the allocation of economic resources. Yet whether the government should intervene in practice is a more difficult question that entails political as well as economic judgements. Many of the traditional arguments against active stabilisation policy, such as long and unpredictable lags with which policy works, may remain valid even if one is persuaded by new Keynesian economics.

Thus Mankiw and Romer are equivocal about intervention despite their belief that market imperfections are central to understanding the economy.

Three of the controversies in this volume have this divergence at their heart: does 'liberalization' stimulate or encourage growth. This general theme is explored in the specific arena of financial liberalization, trade liberalization and the reform of the welfare state. In all three cases, there is a clearly defined *laissez-faire* view that little or no intervention and regulation as possible. However, as is clear from the controversies, the arguments for and against this position take place on a variety of fronts and, at the end of the day, even the evidence is difficult to interpret unambiguously.

The importance of history in determining which view is more or less popular is clear. The experience of the depression in the 1930s and the success of the highly interventionist post-war reconstruction in Western Europe meant that most eco-nomists until the mid-1970s were interventionist in instinct. The revival of *laissez-faire* economics started in the 1970s with the world slow-down in growth. It reached its fulfilment in the 1980s with the two icons of free-market economics in Britain and the USA, Prime Minister Thatcher and President Reagan. Privatization and de-regulation became the buzz words of the 1980s, while the international bodies such as the IMF and World Bank tried to foist these reforms on otherwise unwilling coun-tries. Others simply imitated what seemed like a successful policy, if only as a political strategy to reduce taxes.

This seemed to have reached its zenith in 1990 when the Soviet Union collapsed: for many it symbolized the triumph of the free market over the state as an economic organizer.

However, the pendulum is perhaps swinging back. Privatization never really worked well, and has created many unforeseen problems: regulating a privatized monopoly is not an easy thing to achieve, particularly as in most countries there is little tradition in anti-trust law and regulation.[4] While hordes of western consultants and advisers to the

---

[4] Indeed, the USA is the exception: in a wave of anti big-business Populist sentiment the Sherman Act was passed in 1890. Hence, the USA has a century-old tradition of anti-trust litigation and an army of lawyers who make money out of conducting cases under this legislation. In contrast, most of the rest of the world actively encouraged cartels and restrictive practices until the 1960s. Most countries (includ-ing the UK) still lack effective anti-trust legislation.

ex-Soviet sphere encouraged the instant dismantling of the planning system, this has had disastrous consequences in the short run. At the time of writing (1998), the transition is still to yield growth in the ex Soviet Union. One can only compare this to the great success of China, which has instead gone for a gradualist and highly regulated transition, being possibly the most successful large economy in the 1990s. Most of Europe is in recession while the Far East has faced financial collapse. This will no doubt foster a return to more Keynesian macroeconomics and interventionist policies: we will have to wait and see.

3 EVIDENCE

Even though economists might agree on the basic framework, they might disagree on the practical importance of different forces at work. For example, economic theory says that demand curves can slope up or down: in the case of an inferior good, the *income effect* of a price-rise is positive and may outweigh the *substitution effect*. It is an empirical question of whether this happens often and for significant classes of goods. I think that most economists would agree that Giffen goods are a rarity. However, let us take a more controversial case: do labour supply curves slope up or down? In this case, even for normal goods, the income and substitution effects of a wage increase work in different directions. It is simply an empirical question of which will dominate. However, it has important consequences: for example, will people work harder if income taxes are cut (the substitution effect dominates) or less (the income effect dominates)?

Many disagreements are about the relative importance of different factors in a particular phenomenon. For example, financial liberalization has many effects: some good for growth and some bad. The key issue is which of these tends to predominate in practice. To answer this, we need to look at some evidence. If you do not take the extreme *laissez-faire* view, then really much depends on what you think to be the important elements in practice. For example, while the world might not be perfectly competitive, is the imperfect competition that is present a *significant* deviation from perfect competition or not?

Unfortunately, the evidence is rarely conclusive. To test a hypothesis, it is necessary to choose a data set, to formulate a statistical model and framework to estimate the economic model. There are different statistical/econometric methodologies about how to go about this.[5] At a first stage, there is the testing of the model against the data: is it acceptable as a null hypothesis? A second stage is to test competing models: this is often not undertaken, and is often inconclusive. At each stage, decisions need to be made that are open to debate. The results of empirical evaluation and testing are often not decisive in convincing people that they are wrong in what they believe; indeed, it is very difficult to convince some people that they are wrong using *any* evidence, let alone econometric evidence. For many economists, the process of empirical testing is so imperfect that they prefer to rely on theory alone to inform their views. Certainly, there are few examples of economic theories that have been abandoned solely because

[5] For time-series econometrics, some of the issues are debated in the *Controversy* on modelling the long run in econometrics, *Economic Journal* January 1997.

of the evidence:[6] evidence plays a role in shifting opinion in the profession, but only a very selective role. If only economists could test their theories in laboratories![7]

The controversy on the convergence of growth rates is largely an empirical one. There are different theories that predict different types of convergence, and the issue is to determine which one works the best. The controversy on happiness and economic growth is also empirical. However, it really turns on what data you use. The authors in this controversy all argue that you should base your judgement on changes in well-being or happiness over time on questionnaire and survey data – data that is not usually used by economists. Many more conventional economists would prefer to rely on measures of welfare based on GNP statistics rather than answers to survey questions. If you believe the survey evidence, however, it casts doubt on the very desirability of economic growth itself. This raises big issues for policy makers and economists alike, which are explored by the papers in this volume.

4 CONTROVERSIES AND THE ADVANCE OF ECONOMICS

It is important that economists argue about things. Of course, an economist should be forced to develop his or her views and, if possible, to find evidence to back it up. However, this sort of process is fairly weak. When we develop a theory, we tend to use it to interpret the world (it is a bit like sunglasses): we tend to focus upon evidence that confirms our beliefs, and we ignore or play down evidence to the contrary. Nobody likes to be wrong or to have to change their fundamental beliefs; on the economic consequences of cognitive dissonance[8] see Akerlof and Dickens (1982).

Argumentation forces an economist to confront and answer to other economists. Other economists will often represent different theories, put emphasis on different evidence or interpret existing evidence differently. The need to persuade others places constraints on what can become generally accepted. Of course, an individual may continue to believe something despite what others believe: however, a belief can only become *widespread* in the economics profession if it has some sort of reasonable foundation. The interplay of debate ensures that there is a constant process of going through arguments, sifting through evidence, looking at new ideas and new evidence. Over time, we can but hope the ideas that become widespread among economists are reasonable and appropriate. The process of argumentation ensures that this is the case.

---

[6] It is always possible to recast a theory ('generalize' it) so that it can conform more closely to the facts. A theory is only abandoned when this process of generalization results in a ramshackle theory and a simpler alternative comes along.

[7] Some people have interpreted certain decisive historical events as almost experiments: for example, the Thatcher years or the Vietnam war. However, the essence of experimental methodology is that experiments can be repeated and the design developed over time. Thatcher and Vietnam only happened once, so our ability to evaluate their effects is limited and inconclusive.

[8] Cognitive dissonance occurs when there is a conflict between what you believe and what you see. For example, at various times Messianic groups have predicted the imminent end of the world: a classic case of cognitive dissonance occurs when the end of the world fails to materialize at the appointed time. It is amazing how many people prefer to stick to their beliefs come what may: 'Do not adjust your mind, reality is at fault'.

The fact that many controversies remain unresolved does not necessarily mean that there is no progress. Rather, it is like a tug-of-war. The truth lies in between the two teams (points of view): the process of debate determines some sort of equilibrium that reflects a mid-point. As outlined earlier, few people adopt the most extreme views: to some extent, we are all eclectic and middle of the road. However, we come at problems from different directions and try to pull other people towards us. Different types of evidence become salient or important at different times and so lead to shifts of emphasis. For example, with a few hyper-inflationary exceptions, significant inflation was a rarity in peacetime before 1970: economists had tended to ignore it. During the 1970s and 1980s, inflation was significant in many OECD countries, and inflation and inflationary expectations became a major concern of economists. By the late 1990s, inflation is already looking like a phenomenon of the past: the 1970s and 1980s were as much a Dark Age aberration for inflation as the 1950s and 1960s were a golden age of high employment in Europe.

The controversies published in this volume provide excellent examples of this process. They allow the reader to understand the main positions and points of view in each topic, as well giving the evidence in most cases. In each case, we have the leading researchers in their fields arguing for their own personal point of view. It is now for you, the reader, to decide who offers the best arguments and which viewpoint convinces you.

5 THE *CONTROVERSIES* SECTION OF THE *ECONOMIC JOURNAL*

All of the papers contained in this volume appeared in the *Controversies* section of the *Economic Journal*. It might be of interest to some readers to understand what the objectives of this section were and how it came about.

The proposal for a controversies section originated in the then Editor, John D. Hey. He put a proposal to the executive of the *Royal Economic Society (RES)* to obtain permission to enlarge the size of the *Economic Journal* to include this section.[9] The proposal itself generated some controversy, but was accepted by the executive, with the enthusiastic support of David Hendry, the then President of the *RES*. I was asked to be the founding editor of this section, an offer I was eager to accept.

Why have a new *Controversies* section? The view was taken that there was a lack of open controversy in much of economics. This may sound a surprising thing to say, but there are strong pressures on academic economists to avoid direct and open controversy.

The source of these pressures is the need to publish in peer reviewed journals. This is a powerful constraint on both what you write and, just as importantly, how you write it. I do not want to sound critical of the anonymous referring process used by most journals: as Winston Churchill said of democracy, it is the worst system available, until you consider the alternatives. However, however admirable the system may be in general, it certainly influences the way economists write.

---

[9] This permission was necessary merely because of the extra cost.

For most journals, there is a 10 per cent acceptance rate: the decision to publish is taken by the editor(s) on the basis of reports by anonymous referees (usually written by one or two fellow academic economists). To avoid offending referees, it is often the case that authors will try to tone down their real beliefs and opinions for fear of offending potential referees – the very people whom the author might believe to be in error. A bigoted referee is unlikely to recommend acceptance unless the author at least agrees with him/her, is his/her friend, or perhaps has cited him/her with due respect. Even if the referee does not recommend to the editor that the author should be rejected, he/she may recommend that revisions are made. Authors sometimes include opinions to which they do not subscribe simply to satisfy a hostile referee. Thus, caution is often a necessary evil if authors are to succeed in the publication game and hence reap the rewards of professional advancement and make their ideas known.

However, while the anonymous refereeing system breeds a tendency to eclecticism and a toning down of opinions, the story does not end there. There are other pressures as well: the need to derive 'significant results' and the need to write short papers. Turning first to length: most journal editors will put pressure on authors to make their papers shorter. Thus, in the refereeing process, it is quite common for papers to adopt a very compressed exposition. Steps in the argument are missed out or skated over rapidly, and methods are not explained. Indeed, in some journals, theoretical articles have been published which omit all proofs! These pressures mean that, often, articles are only accessible to the specialist in that area and not to the general reader. Some articles are almost like detective stories, where to reach the result, you need to reconstruct what the author did from what are often skimpy evidence and pointers in the published paper. One of the first victims in this condensed journal style is the clearly stated opinion of the author.

Finally, there is a requirement by journals for significant results. Most journals would not seriously consider publishing a paper which does not contain some 'new' result that is, in some way, significant. This rules out certain types of papers that might be useful in themselves: for example, a simple pedagogic reinterpretation or exposition of existing results and opinion pieces. The recognition of the need for new outlets to overcome this has been around for some time: this was presumably the impetus behind the *American Economics Association* to launch the *Journal of Economic Perspectives*.

So, in starting the new *Controversies* section, we wanted to encourage a new way of writing.

- The papers were to be accessible to the general economist, not just the specialist researcher. Preferably, papers should be understandable by any graduate economist and preferably undergraduate economists as well.
- Papers were to be written in a way that clearly expressed the opinion of the author. We wanted authors to *argue* for their own point of view.
- The papers need not contain any new results: rather, we were seeking the accumulated wisdom of experts in their fields and of leading younger researchers.

There was the additional practical aim of persuading the most distinguished authors to write. This would be good for the journal's circulation and would ensure that the new section was well received. However, there is the problem that the best people are also often the busiest and the ones least in need of an extra publication (since they would already be well published). In addition, there is also a potential incentive problem with invited papers. Once an author is invited, it is difficult to reject the manuscript: hence there is little incentive for the author to supply a high quality manuscript, because he/she knows that it will be accepted. When I invited people to contribute, I sent a style guideline, and awaited the result. In practice, I was very pleasantly surprised. As you can see from the contents page of this volume, many of the leading researchers in their fields were happy and willing to contribute to the controversies section. Moreover, the pieces were well written and certainly controversial (although some more controversial than others – old habits die hard).

I think that the reason for the section's success was that economists welcomed the opportunity to be able to express their opinions in the controversies format.

The current volume draws together six of the best controversies published in the *Economic Journal*. The success of the section indicates that there is a demand for papers in this style. In particular, these papers are useful to students at both the undergraduate and the graduate level, as well as to researchers who would like to keep in touch with what is happening in areas outside their own. In the case of all but one controversy, they appear exactly as in the *Economic Journal*. In the case of the controversy 'Economics and Happiness', I added an additional paper from another controversy (Bill Nordhaus's) and hence slightly rewrote the introduction.

I hope that you, the reader, will find this collection both informative and enjoyable.

References

Akerlof, G. and Dickens, W. (1982). The economic consequences of cognitive-dissonance. *American Economic Review*, 72(3), 307–19.

Mankiw G. and Romer D. (1991). *New Keynesian Economics*, MIT Press.

Part 1

ON THE CONVERGENCE AND DIVERGENCE OF GROWTH RATES

INTRODUCTION

Steven N. Durlauf

The resurgence of interest in economic growth, spurred by the seminal theoretical contributions of Romer (1986) and Lucas (1988) on endogenous growth mechanisms, has generated a lively empirical literature. This literature has primarily focused on the so-called convergence hypothesis. While the convergence hypothesis can be formalised in a number of ways (see Bernard and Durlauf, 1996), roughly speaking the hypothesis asserts that differences in contemporaneous *per capita* income between any pair of economies will be transitory so long as the two economies possess identical technologies, preferences and population growth rates. By implication, the effects of initial stocks of human and physical capital on *per capita* output differences will be transitory, so long as these other factors are accounted for.

The convergence hypothesis speaks to one of the critical economic motivations of the endogenous growth literature – namely the persistence of *per capita* income differences across countries. In the original Romer and Lucas formulations, initial differences could grow without bound over time due to spillover effects which generate social increasing returns; Jones and Manuelli (1990) showed how to obtain similar results for convex technologies without spillovers. In formulations such as Azariadis and Drazen (1990), it was shown that spillovers could create multiple, locally stable steady states.

Interestingly, while the bulk of the new theoretical literature on growth has focused on models which generate divergence across economies with very different initial conditions, the bulk of their empirical writings, exemplified by Barro (1991) and Mankiw et al. (1992), have found evidence that economies with low initial incomes tend to grow faster than economies with high initial incomes, after controlling for rates savings and population growth. This finding has been treated as evidence of convergence, and has generally been taken as evidence that the neoclassical growth model pioneered by Solow (1956) is consistent with observed growth patterns; by implication, these studies have been taken as evidence against a range of endogenous growth models. These empirical studies have in turn generated an opposing literature (examples include Durlauf and Johnson (1995) and Quah (1996*a,b*)) which argues, using alternative econometric methods, that the pattern of cross-country growth is inconsistent with convergence and thus is consistent with a variety of endogenous growth mechanisms.

This collection of papers is designed to elucidate the differing perspectives on convergence. Each paper identifies a particular feature of the convergence hypothesis and related it to the existing literature. As will be clear, these alternate perspectives on convergence may be explained by a combination of differences in (1) the definition of convergence, (2) the class of theoretical growth models of interest, and (3) the econometric method for studying cross-sections.

Xavier Sala-i-Martin in 'The Classical Approach to Convergence Analysis' provides a summary and defence of the cross-section regression approach which has been most popular in empirical work. In particular, Sala-i-Martin argues that a negative coefficient on initial income in a cross-section regression of growth rates which includes a set of controls is a robust feature for a wide array of data sets, ranging from the Summers–Heston (1991) panel of 110 countries to US states. Sala-i-Martin further argues that this conditional convergence parameter is approximately 2 per cent per year, regardless of the data set. This is taken as strong evidence supporting the convergence hypothesis. Interestingly, this paper focuses more on the robustness of the conditional convergence finding than its economic interpretability.

Each of the other papers in this collection challenges some aspect of the convergence hypothesis, either from the perspective of econometrics or economic theory. In 'Technology and Convergence', Andrew Bernard and Charles Jones argue that empirical analyses of convergence have overemphasised the role of capital accumulation in generating convergence at the expense of the diffusion of technology. Bernard and Jones argue that, under the assumption of a Cobb–Douglas technology, it is possible to demonstrate the existence of substantial technology gaps across OECD countries. These gaps are particularly evident when one considers sectoral productivity differences. Bernard and Jones suggest that little evidence exists for the convergence of manufacturing technologies over time (at least since 1970), and therefore question the conventional convergence claim.

Danny Quah, in 'Twin Peaks: Growth and Convergence in Models of Distribution Dynamics', describes an alternative approach to studying the evolution of a population of economies. Quah argues that the behaviour of any such population needs to be studied as the evolution of an entire distribution, rather than through a cross-section regression which looks for average behaviour in the cross-section. Such a consideration is particularly important if one is interested in the behaviour of very poor versus very rich economies, for example. Quah outlines a number of ways of studying the evolution of cross-sections, and concludes that conventional convergence findings can mask the presence of convergence clubs and the polarisation of a population into rich and poor.

Finally, 'Convergence? Inferences from Theoretical Models' by Oded Galor considers the econometric predictions of various theoretical growth models. Galor demonstrates how for a wide range of plausible and interesting economic specifications, multiple locally stable steady states in output levels can exist. Interestingly, such multiplicity can occur even in absence of those spillovers or nonconvexities which are at the heart of the initial papers on endogenous growth. Each of the models considered exhibits convergence clubs. Galor argues that the concentration on linear cross-section regressions is thus misplaced. This argument thus reinforces Quah's paper and is in turn reinforced by Bernard and Durlauf (1996) which shows how data exhibiting club convergence can spuriously produce conditional convergence.

Each of these papers provides a valuable statement of a school of thought on convergence, and to some extent, of economic growth more generally. At the same time, the divergence of perspectives in these papers indicates why empirical and theoretical work on growth continues to be an important and lively enterprise.

References

Azariadis, C. and Drazen, A. (1990). 'Threshold externalities and economic development.' *Quarterly Journal of Economics*, vol. 105, pp. 501–26.

Barro, R. (1991). 'Economic growth in a cross section of countries.' *Quarterly Journal of Economics*, vol. 106, pp. 407–44.

Bernard, A. and Durlauf, S. (1996). 'Interpreting tests of the convergence hypothesis.' *Journal of Econometrics*, forthcoming.

Durlauf, S. and Johnson, P. (1995). 'Multiple regimes and cross-country growth behavior.' *Journal of Applied Econometrics*, vol. 10, pp. 365–84.

Jones, L. and Manuelli, R. (1990). 'A convex model of equilibrium growth.' *Journal of Political Economy*, vol. 98, pp. 1008–38.

Lucas, R. (1988). 'On the mechanics of economic development.' *Journal of Monetary Economics*, vol. 22, pp. 3–42.

Mankiw, N. G., Romer, D. and Weil, D. (1992). 'A contribution to the empirics of economic growth.' *Quarterly Journal of Economics*, vol. 107, pp. 407–37.

Quah, D. (1996a). 'Convergence empirics with (some) capital mobility.' *Journal of Economic Growth*, forthcoming.

Quah, D. (1996b). 'Aggregate and regional disaggregate fluctuations.' *Empirical Economics*, forthcoming.

Romer, P. (1986). 'Increasing returns and long run growth.' *Journal of Political Economy*, vol. 94, pp. 1002–37.

Solow, R. (1956). 'A contribution to the theory of economic growth.' *Quarterly Journal of Economics*, vol. 70, pp. 65–94.

Summers, R. and Heston, A. (1991). 'The Penn World Table (Mark 5): An expanded set of international comparisons, 1950–1988.' *Quarterly Journal of Economics*, vol. 106, pp. 327–68.

1

THE CLASSICAL APPROACH TO CONVERGENCE ANALYSIS*

Xavier X. Sala-i-Martin

The concepts of σ-convergence, absolute β-convergence and conditional β-convergence are discussed in this paper. The concepts are applied to a variety of data sets that include a large cross-section of 110 countries, the sub-sample of OECD countries, the states within the United States, the prefectures of Japan, and regions within several European countries. Except for the large cross-section of countries, all data sets display strong evidence of σ-convergence and absolute β-convergence. The cross-section of countries exhibits σ-divergence and conditional β-convergence. The speed of conditional convergence, which is very similar across data sets, is close to 2 per cent per year.

Will relatively poor economies remain poor for many generations? Will the rich countries of the year 2100 be the same countries that are relatively rich today? Is the degree of income inequality across economies increasing or falling over time? The importance of these questions, which lie at the heart of the convergence debate, is obvious to anyone interested in general worldwide welfare.

Even though economists have been interested in these issues for many decades, it was not until the end of the 1980s that the convergence debate captured the attention of mainstream macroeconomic theorists and econometricians. In addition to the inherent importance of the questions dealt with, the reason for this sudden increase in interest was two-fold. First, the existence of convergence across economies was proposed as the main test of the validity of modern theories of economic growth. Moreover, estimates of the speeds of convergence across economies (to be more precisely defined in a later section) were thought to provide information on one of the key parameters of growth theory: the share of capital in the production function (see the discussion in section 3). For this reason, growth theorists started paying close attention to the evolution of the convergence debate. Second, and perhaps more importantly, a data set on internationally comparable GDP levels for a large number of countries became available in the mid 1980s.[1] This new data set allowed empirical economists to compare GDP levels across a large number of countries, and to look at the evolution of these levels over time, a necessary feature for the study of the convergence hypothesis.

In this paper I shall discuss the classical approach to convergence analysis. I call this

* I thank Paul Cashin, Michelle Connolly and Tornarà A. Serrica-i-Plena for useful comments.
[1] The University of Pennsylvania project was originally started in the 1960s by A. Kravis and was finished by Allan Heston and Robert Summers (see Summers and Heston (1991)).

the classical approach because it was the first methodology to be used in the literature and because it uses the traditional techniques of classical econometrics, a feature that is shared by some, but not all, of the alternative approaches. Perhaps more importantly, like classical art, it is the basis of reference and target of criticism of all other methodologies, and it has survived the challenges of more modern and 'surrealist' movements.[2]

The rest of the paper is organised as follows. Section 1 introduces two useful definitions of convergence and highlights their similarities and differences. Section 2 analyses some evidence on convergence using a sample of 110 economies. In section 3, I interpret the above evidence in light of the neoclassical model and introduce the concept of conditional convergence. Section 4 applies the concept of conditional convergence to the sample of 110 countries. Section 5 provides evidence on convergence for a number of regional data sets. I conclude in section 6.

1 DEFINITIONS OF CONVERGENCE

Two main concepts of convergence appear in the classical literature. They are called β-convergence and σ-convergence.[3] We say that *there is absolute β-convergence if poor economies tend to grow faster than rich ones.*[4] Imagine that we have data on real *per capita* GDP for a cross-section of economies. Let $\gamma_{i,t,t+T} \equiv \log\ (y_{t\infty,\ t+T}/y_{i,t})/T$ be economy i's annualised growth rate of GDP between t and $t + T$, and let $\log\ (y_{i,t})$ be the logarithm of economy i's GDP *per capita* at time t. If we estimate the following regression

$$\gamma_{i,t,t+T} = a - \beta\log\ (y_{i,t}) + \varepsilon_{i,t} \tag{1}$$

and we find $\beta > 0$, then we say that the data set exhibits absolute β-convergence.

The concept of σ-convergence can be defined as follows: *a group of economies are converging in the sense of σ if the dispersion of their real per capita GDP levels tends to decrease over time.* That is, if

$$\sigma_{t+T} < \sigma_t \tag{2}$$

where σ_t is the time t standard deviation of $\log\ (y_{i,t})$ across i. The concepts of σ- and absolute β-convergence are, of course, related. If we take the sample variance of $\log\ (y_{i,t})$ from (1) (note that the growth rate is the difference between $\log\ (y_{i,t+T})$ and $\log$

---

[2] Quah (1996) proposes a new way of telling a good empirical technique from a bad one, which is summarised by the following statement: 'if I can find a set of questions (no matter how unrelated to your initial query) that your research technique cannot address, then your technique is useless and mine becomes extremely useful . . . *even if my technique cannot answer those questions either*'. Notice that the strict application of this methodology would render all empirical techniques (with the possible exception of Quah's) both useless and extremely useful (see Salvador Dali (1965) for a description of a similar methodology applied to surrealist double images).

[3] This terminology was first introduced in Sala-i-Martin (1990).

[4] In section 3, I will introduce the important concept of *conditional β-convergence.*

$(y_{i,t})$ divided by T), we will get a relation between σ_t and σ_{t+T} which depends on β. Intuitively, we can see that if the GDP levels of two economies become more similar over time, it must be the case that the poor economy is growing faster. As an illustration, Fig. 1 displays the behaviour of the log of GDP *per capita* (log (GDP)) for two economies over time. Imagine that we observe the data at two discrete intervals, t and $t + T$. Economy A starts out being richer than economy B, there is an initial distance or dispersion between the two levels of income. In Panel a, the growth rate of economy A is smaller (actually negative) than the growth rate of economy B between times t and $t + T$ and, therefore, we say that there is β-convergence. Moreover, because the dispersion of log (GDP) at $t + T$ is smaller than at time t, we also say that there is σ-convergence. Note that it is impossible for the two economies to be closer together at $t + T$ without having the initially poor economy (in this case economy B) growing faster. In other words, *a necessary condition for the existence of σ-convergence is the existence of β-convergence.*

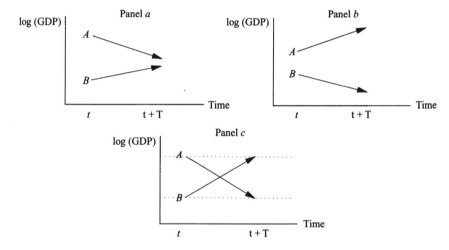

Fig. 1 The relation between σ and β-convergence

Moreover, it is natural to think that when an initially poor economy grows faster than a rich one, then the levels of GDP *per capita* of the two economies will become more similar over time. In other words, *the existence of β-convergence will tend to generate σ-convergence.* Panel a in Fig. 1 is an example where β-convergence exists and is associated with σ-convergence. Panel b provides an example where the lack of β-convergence (the initially rich economy grows faster) is associated with the lack of σ-convergence (the distance between economies increases over time). Hence, it would appear that the two concepts are identical. However, at least theoretically, it is possible for initially poor countries to grow faster than initially rich ones, without observing that the cross-sectional dispersion falls over time. That is, we could find β-convergence without finding σ-convergence. In Panel c, I have constructed an example where the initially poor economy (B) grows faster than the initially rich (A), so there is β-convergence. However, the growth rate of *B* is so much larger than the growth rate of *A* that, at time $t + T$, *B* is richer than *A*. In fact, the example is such that, at time $t + T$, the distance between *A* and *B* is the same as it was at time t (except that now the rich economy is *B*). Hence, the dispersion between these two economies has not fallen, so there is no σ-convergence. In fact I could have constructed the example so that the dispersion at $t + T$ was larger than at t. In that case there would have been σ-divergence despite there being β-convergence. It follows that β-convergence, although necessary, is not a sufficient condition for σ-convergence.

The reason why the two concepts of convergence may not always show up together is that they capture two different aspects of the world. σ-convergence relates to whether or not the cross-country distribution of world income shrinks over time. β-convergence, on the other hand, relates to the mobility of different individual economies within the given distribution of world income. Panels *a* and *b* are examples where the movements of the various economies over time change the final distribution of income. Panel *c*, on the other hand, is an example where there is mobility within the distribution, but the distribution itself remains unchanged.[5]

2 CROSS-COUNTRY EVIDENCE

Maddison (1991) provided data on GDP levels across 13 rich countries starting in 1870. These data were constructed following the methodology of the United Nations' International Comparison Project (ICP) so, in principle, the data across countries can be compared and are, therefore, suitable for use in the analysis of convergence. The main disadvantage of these data is that they are available for rich countries only, a problem that almost proved fatal to early students of convergence. Using Maddison's data, Baumol (1986) documented the existence of cross-country convergence. He found that convergence was especially strong after World War II. This evidence, however, was quickly downplayed by Romer (1986) and DeLong (1988), on the grounds of *ex-post* sample selection bias: by working with Maddison's data set of nations which were industrialised *ex-post* (that is, by 1979), those nations that did not converge were excluded from the sample, so convergence

---

[5] This possibility led some economists (most prominently Quah (1993)) to criticise the classical approach on three grounds. First they suggested that classical analysts were confusing the two concepts of convergence. Secondly, they argued that the only meaningful concept of convergence was that of σ. Finally, they said that the concept of β-convergence conveyed no interesting information about σ-convergence (or about anything else) so it should not be studied. Needless to say that the three points were not entirely correct. First, classical analysts were well aware of the distinction from the very beginning (see for example Easterlin (1960), Sala-i-Martin (1990) and Barro and Sala-i-Martin (1992)). In fact, that is why they made the distinction in the first place! Secondly, the intra-distributional mobility (reflected in β) is at least as interesting as the behaviour of the distribution itself (reflected in σ). In fact, it could even be argued that if mobility was very high, the evolution of σ would be uninteresting. Surprisingly, Quah (1994, 1996) highlights the importance of intra-distributional mobility in the context of stochastic Kernel estimators. Finally, β provides information about σ to the extent that any necessary condition does – the fact that the two phenomena tend to appear together in most data sets seems to support this view.

in Baumol's study was all but guaranteed. As soon as Maddison's data set was expanded to include countries that appeared rich *ex-ante* (that is, by 1870) the evidence for convergence quickly disappeared (DeLong, 1988 and Baumol and Wolff, 1988).

An obvious solution to the sample selection problem was to analyse a larger set of countries. This is where the newly created Summers–Heston data set came in handy, as it comprised GDP levels for more than one hundred countries. However, unlike Maddison's project, where the time series dimension of the data was quite large, 1960 is the first year for which the Summers–Heston data are available. Hence, by using the Summers–Heston data set analysts could study a broader set of countries, but at the cost of a much shorter time span. In Fig. 2 I display the behaviour of the dispersion of GDP *per capita* for the set of 110 countries for which I have data in all years between 1960 and 1990. Note that the dispersion, σ, increases steadily from $\sigma = 0.89$ in 1960 to $\sigma = 1.12$ in 1980. The cross-country distribution of world income has become increasingly unequal: we live in a world where economies have diverged in the sense of σ over the last 30 years.

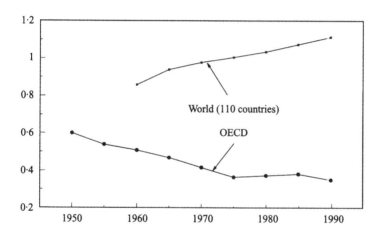

Fig. 2 Dispersion of GDP across 110 countries

Fig. 3 analyses the existence of β-convergence across the same set of 110 economies. On the horizontal axis, I display the log of GDP *per capita* in 1960. On the vertical axis, I depict the growth rate between 1960 and 1990. The figure shows that the relation between growth and the initial level of GDP is not negative. In fact, the slope of the regression line (also shown in the fig.) is positive, although the fit is far from impressive.

In order to quantify the lack of convergence across these 110 countries, I estimate the following equation

$$\gamma_{i,t,t+T} = a - b \log (y_{i,t}) + \varepsilon_{i,t,t+T} \tag{3}$$

Table 1 reports the estimated speed of convergence, β, for a variety of data sets

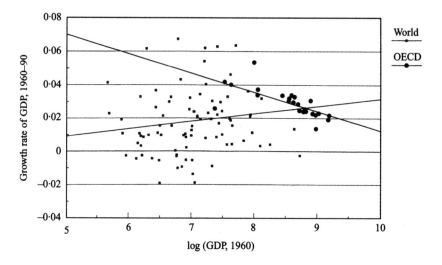

Fig. 3 Convergence across countries, 1960–90

under three different setups.[6] The first row relates to the large sample of 110 countries. The first column refers to the estimate of β when a single equation is estimated for the whole time period and no other explanatory variable is included. Each box in this table contains four numbers. The first one is the estimate of β. The number just below (in parentheses) is its standard error. To its right, we have the adjusted R^2 of the regression and below the R^2, the standard error of the regression. The estimated speed of convergence for the cross-section of 110 countries is negative, $\beta = -0.004$ (S.E. = 0.002), so the relation between growth and initial income is positive as shown in Fig. 3. The R^2 is 0.04 and the standard error of the regression is 0.0176. During this period of 30 years, therefore, poor economies did not grow faster than rich ones. The set of 110 countries in the world did not converge in the sense of β.

3 INTERPRETATION OF THESE FINDINGS IN THE LIGHT OF MODELS OF ECONOMIC GROWTH: ABSOLUTE VERSUS CONDITIONAL CONVERGENCE

The lack of convergence across countries is an interesting finding on various grounds. It says that, in our world, the degree of cross-country income inequality not only fails to disappear, but rather tends to increase over time (σ-divergence). It also suggests that countries which are predicted to be richer a few decades from now are the same countries

---

[6] If one estimates the linear equation (3), then the speed of convergence can be computed by using the formula $b = (1 - e^{-\beta T})/T$, where T is the length of time between two observations (that is, if we regress the growth rate of GDP between 1960 and 1985, then T is 25). Instead of estimating the linear relation (3) and using this formula to compute the speed, β, we can estimate a nonlinear least squares (NLS) relation directly. The direct estimation of NLS delivers standard errors for the speed of convergence directly. In this paper, I report the estimates of β (and not b) and its standard errors.

Table 1 Estimates of the speeds of β-convergence for a variety of data sets

| Data set | Long-run single regression* | | | | Panel estimates* |
	Absolute convergence (1)		Conditional convergence (2)		Conditional convergence (3)
World 110 countries (1960–90)	−0.004	0.04	0.013	0.46	0.025
	(0.002)	[0.0176]	(0.004)	[0.0134]	(0.0028)
OECD countries (1960–90)	0.014	0.48	0.029	0.78	–
	(0.003)	[0.0062]	(0.008)	[0.0050]	–
United States 48 states (1880–1990)	0.021	0.89	0.017	0.89	0.022
	(0.0003)	[0.0015]	(0.002)	[0.0015]	(0.002)
Japan 47 prefectures (1955–90)	0.019	0.59	0.019	0.59	0.031
	(0.003)	[0.0027]	(0.004)	[0.0027]	(0.004)
Europe total 90 regions (1950–90)†	0.015	0.51	0.015	0.52	0.018
	(0.002)	[0.0030]	(0.002)	[0.0030]	(0.003)
Germany (11 regions)	0.014	0.56	0.014	0.55	0.016
	(0.006)	[0.0028]	(0.005)	[0.0027]	(0.006)
United Kingdom (11 regions)	0.020	0.62	0.030	0.61	0.029
	(0.008)	[0.0021]	(0.007)	[0.0021]	(0.009)
France (21 regions)	0.016	0.55	0.016	0.55	0.015
	(0.005)	[0.0023]	(0.004)	[0.0022]	(0.003)
Italy (20 regions)	0.010	0.46	0.010	0.46	0.016
	(0.003)	[0.0033]	(0.003)	[0.0031]	(0.003)
Spain (17 regions) (1955–87)	0.021	0.63	0.023	0.63	0.019
	(0.005)	[0.0042]	(0.007)	[0.0040]	(0.005)

* The regressions use nonlinear least squares to estimate equations of the form:

$$(1/T) \ln (y_{it}/y_{i,t-T}) = a - [\ln (y_{i,t-T})] (1 - e^{-\beta T}) (1.T) + \text{'other variables'}$$

where $Y_{i,t-T}$ is the *per capita* income in country or region i at the beginning of the interval divided by the overall CPI. T is the length of the interval; 'other variables' are regional dummies and sectoral variables that hold constant temporary shocks that may affect the performance of a region in a manner that is correlated with the initial level of income.

Each column contains four numbers. The first one is the estimate of β. Underneath it, in parentheses, its standard error. To its right, the adjusted R^2 of the regression and below the R^2, the standard error of the regression. The constant, regional dummies and/or structural variables are not reported in the Table

The coefficients for Europe total include one dummy for each of the eight countries.

Columns 1 and 2 report the value of β estimated from a single cross section using the longest available data. Column 1 reports the coefficient when the only variable held constant is the initial level of income. Column 2 reports the value of β estimated when additional variables are held constant.

Column 3 reports the panel estimates when all the subperiods are assumed to have the same coefficient β. This estimation allows for time effects. For most countries, the restriction of β being constant over the subperiods cannot be rejected (see Barro and Sala-i-Martin (1995)).

† The regressions for Europe total allow each country to have its own constant term.

that are rich today (β-divergence). These findings may be used by economists or politicians to devise international institutions which may work to overturn this sombre tendency.

These findings were also seen by growth theorists, in the mid-1980s as evidence against the neoclassical model of Ramsey (1928), Solow (1956), Swan (1956), Cass (1965), and Koopmans (1965), and as support for their new models of endogenous growth. The intuition behind this conclusion is the following: the assumption of diminishing returns to capital implicit in the neoclassical production function has the prediction that the rate of return to capital (and therefore its growth rate) is very large when the stock of capital is small and *vice versa*. If the only difference across countries is their initial levels of capital, then the prediction of the neoclassical growth model is that countries with little capital will be poor and will grow faster than rich countries with large capital stocks, so there will be cross-country β-convergence. Since the model does not predict the type of overshooting displayed in Panel *c* of Fig. 1, the prediction of β-convergence will tend to be associated with a reduction in cross-economy dispersion of income over time, i.e. σ-convergence.

More precisely, consider a neoclassical model with a Cobb–Douglas production function

$$Y_{i,t} = A_i\, K_{i,t}^a L_{i,t}^{1-a}$$

where $Y_{i,t}$ is economy i's aggregate output at time t, $K_{i,t}$ and $L_{i,t}$ are the stock of capital and labour in that economy respectively, and A_i is the level of technology. Following Solow (1956) and Swan (1956), suppose that the saving rate in this economy is constant (the key results do not depend on this assumption) and that the rate of depreciation of K is δ, the rate of population growth is n and the rate of productivity growth is x. The dynamic equation that characterises the behaviour of economy i over time says that capital accumulation is the difference between overall savings and effective depreciation. If we log-linearise this dynamic equation around the steady state, we find that the growth rate of economy i between periods t and $t + T$ is given by (3). Moreover, given this production function, the parameter β is exactly equal to

$$\beta = (1 - a)\ (\delta + n + x) \qquad (4)$$

where a is again the capital share in the production function.[7] Since, according to the neoclassical model, $0 < a < 1$, the prediction is that $\beta > 0$. In other words, the neoclassical model predicts convergence.

This prediction contrasts with the implications of the first generation of models of endogenous growth (see, for example, Romer (1986) and Rebelo (1991)). These models rely on the existence of externalities, increasing returns and the lack of inputs that cannot be accumulated.[8] The key point of these new models is the absence of dimin-

---

[7] See Barro and Sala-i-Martin (1995, Chapter 1) for a derivation of this result. See also Chapter 2 of the same book for the extension of this result to the optimising version of the neoclassical model first developed in Ramsey (1928).

[8] Labour, which is not purposely accumulated in the neoclassical model, is often substituted with human capital, the stock of which increases in accordance with the investment decisions of private agents.

ishing returns to capital (the concept of capital should be understood in a broad sense that includes human capital), so these models do not exhibit the neoclassical model's convergence property. In terms of equation (4), the one sector models of endogenous growth are similar to the neoclassical model except that, in the former, a has a value of 1. Note that if $a = 1$, equation (4) then says that the speed of convergence should be β = 0. For this reason, in the mid-1980s, the lack of convergence across countries was seen as evidence against the neoclassical model and in favour of the new models of endogenous growth.[9]

3.1 The absolute convergence fallacy and the concept of conditional convergence

The argument that the neoclassical model predicts that initially poor countries will grow faster than initially rich ones relies heavily on the key assumption that *the only difference across countries lies in their initial levels of capital.* In the real world, however, economies may differ in other things such as their levels of technology, A_i, their propensities to save, or their population growth rates. If different economies have different technological and behavioural parameters, then they will have different steady state and the above argument (developed by the early theorists of endogenous growth) will be flawed. The intuition can be captured by a simple two-economy example. Imagine that the first economy is poor but is in the steady state. Accordingly, its growth rate is zero. The second economy is richer, but has a capital stock below its steady-state level. The model predicts that its growth rate is positive and, therefore, will be larger than the growth rate of the first economy, even though the first economy is poorer! What the model says is that, as the capital stock of the growing economy increases, its growth rate will decline and go to zero as the economy reaches its steady state. Hence, the prediction of the neoclassical model is that the growth rate of an economy will be positively related to the distance that separates it from its own steady state. This concept is known in the classical literature[10] as *conditional β-convergence*. To facilitate the distinction, the concept of β-convergence as discussed above is sometimes called *absolute convergence*. Only if all economies converge to the *same steady state* does the prediction that poor economies should grow faster than rich ones holds true. This is because with common steady states, initially poorer economies will be unambiguously farther away from their steady state. In other words, the conditional convergence and the absolute convergence hypotheses coincide, only if all the economies have the same

---

[9] Equation (4) is interesting for another reason. The parameters δ, n and x can be estimated fairly accurately. Hence, if we have an estimate of β, we will indirectly have an estimate of the capital share a. This particular parameter is very important because the first generation of models of endogenous growth highlighted the importance of physical capital externalities and the existence of human capital. This meant that the traditional way to compute the capital share by using income shares was incorrect. Since the exact size of the externalities was unknown and the fraction of labour that could be accumulated in the form of human capital was also unknown, the relevant capital share (whose size was seen as crucial from a theoretical point of view) remained unknown. Equation (4) says that the convergence literature can provide an indirect way to say something about the size of a.

[10] See Sala-i-Martin (1990), Barro and Sala-i-Martin (1992) and Mankiw et al. (1992).

steady state. Since the neoclassical model predicts conditional convergence, the evidence on absolute convergence discussed in the previous section says little about the validity of the model in the real world.

To test the hypothesis of conditional convergence one has to, somehow, hold constant the steady state of each economy. Classical analysts have tried to hold the steady state constant in two different ways. The first one is by introducing variables that proxy for the steady state in a regression like (1) or (3). In other words, instead of estimating (1) or (3) one estimates

$$\gamma_{i,t,t+T} = a - b\log(y_{i,t}) + \psi\mathbf{X}_{i,t} + \varepsilon_{i,t,t+T} \tag{5}$$

where $\mathbf{X}_{i,t}$ is a vector of variables that hold constant the steady state of economy i, and $b = (1 - e^{-\beta T})/T$. If the estimate of β is positive once $\mathbf{X}_{i,t}$ is held constant, then we say that the data set exhibits *conditional β-convergence*. In Section 4 I will use this first approach to condition the data.

The second way to hold constant the steady state is to restrict the convergence study to sets of economies for which the assumption of similar steady states is not unrealistic. For example, because we think that the technology, institutions, and tastes of most African economies are very different from those of Japan or the United States, the assumption that these economies converge to a common steady state is not realistic. However, the technological and institutional differences across regions within a country or across 'similar' countries (for example, those of the OECD) are probably smaller. Hence, we may want to look for absolute convergence within these sets of 'more similar' economies. This second approach is used in Section 5.

4 CONDITIONAL CONVERGENCE (1): MULTIPLE REGRESSION ANALYSIS

The concept of conditional β-convergence defined above suggests the estimation of a multiple regression like (5). If the neoclassical model is correct and the vector $\mathbf{X}$ successfully holds constant the steady state, we should find a positive b (and therefore a positive β). The key, therefore, is to find variables that proxy for the steady state, and economic theory should guide our search for such variables. Different growth models suggest different variables. The strict version of the Solow–Swan model, for example, says that the steady state depends on the level of technology, A, the saving rate, and the parameters δ, n, and x. A broad interpretation of 'technology' would allow A to capture various types of distortions (public or otherwise), political variables, etc. Following Barro (1991), a large literature has estimated equations like (5). In this literature, more than 50 variables have been used in this type of analysis (and found to be significant in at least one regression).[11] The key point for our purposes here is that, once some variables that can proxy for the steady state are held constant, the estimate of β

---

[11] See for example, Mankiw et al. (1992), Levine and Renelt (1992) and Barro and Sala-i-Martin (1995, chapter 12).

becomes significantly positive, as predicted by the neoclassical theory. This finding is robust to the exact choice of $\mathbf{X}$.[12] For example, columns 2 and 3 of Table 1 report the estimate of β when additional variables are held constant. In this particular case, the primary and secondary school enrolments, the saving rate, and some political variables are used as the vector $\mathbf{X}$. Note that, unlike column 1, the estimate of β for the 110 countries (row one of Table 1) is now positive and significant, $\beta = 0.013$ (s.e. $= 0.004$). Column 3 divides the sample period 1960–90 into two subperiods and estimates β by restricting it to be the same across subperiods. The estimated β is now 0.025 (s.e. $= 0.003$) which is, again, significantly positive.

The conclusion is that the sample of 110 countries in the world displays conditional β-convergence. Furthermore, the estimated speed of conditional convergence is close to 2 per cent per year. I should re-emphasise, however, that this does not mean that poor economies grow faster or that the world distribution of income is shrinking. These are phenomena captured by the concepts of *absolute β-convergence* and σ-convergence and, in this sense, the set of economies diverges unambiguously. What this evidence says is that economies seem to approach some long-run level of income which is captured by the vector of variables $\mathbf{X}$, and the growth rate falls as the economy approaches this long-run level.

5 CONDITIONAL CONVERGENCE (2): REGIONAL EVIDENCE

The second method for 'holding constant the steady state' is to analyse sets of economies that appear similar to the researcher so that the assumption of a common steady state is reasonable. For example, the OECD economies and regions within countries could be considered as similar *ex-ante*. The neoclassical theory that guided our analysis suggests that, if it is true that these sets of economies are similar, we should find that these data sets display absolute β-convergence as well as σ-convergence. If evidence of absolute β-convergence is to be found anywhere, it will be in these data sets.[13]

5.1 OECD economies

Figs. 2 and 3 also display the convergence behaviour of a subset of the world sample: the OECD countries. In Fig. 2, I plot the cross-sectional dispersion of GDP *per capita* for these economies starting in 1950.[14] The key message of this Fig. is that there was an

---

[12] The existence of convergence is less strong during the 1980s, a phenomenon that holds true for almost all data sets analysed in this paper. See Levine and Renelt (1992) for some evidence on this point.

[13] These data sets include economies that are open in the sense that capital flows across regional or national boundaries. Thus, evidence on convergence cannot be directly interpreted in the light of the closed economy neoclassical growth model. Barro et al. (1995) amend the neoclassical model to allow for *partial* capital mobility. They show that this version of the neoclassical model predicts the same type of transitional dynamics as the strict closed economy version. Hence, it is satisfactory to look at these data sets through the lenses of the closed-economy neoclassical growth model.

[14] The reason for starting in 1950 is that data are available for all 24 OECD economies in 1950. This is not true for the 110 countries that constitute the world data set.

overall downward trend in dispersion between 1950 and 1990, interrupted only during the period from 1975 to 1985.

Fig. 3 also highlights the differential behaviour of OECD economies (which are denoted by black dots). For these countries, the relation between growth and the initial level of income is significantly negative as depicted, in Fig. 3, by the downward-sloping regression line. OECD economies have thus also converged in the sense of β. The exact estimate of the speed of absolute β-convergence can be found in the second row of Table 1. When no other variables are held constant, the estimated speed of convergence is $\beta = 0.014$ (s.e. $= 0.003$). Hence, OECD economies exhibit absolute β-convergence. When additional conditioning variables are held constant (column 2 in Table 1), the estimated β is 0.029 (s.e. $= 0.008$). Hence, the estimated speed of convergence across OECD economies is close to 2 per cent per year.[15]

Dowrick and N'guyen (1989) add to this evidence by using various measures of productivity. They show that, not only do GDP levels *per capita* converge across OECD economies, but so do the levels of productivity.

5.2 The states of the United States

The third row of Table 1 shows estimates of equation (3) for 48 US states for the period 1880 to 1990.[16] The first and second columns report the estimate for a single long sample (1880–1990). Column 1 uses the initial level of income as the only explanatory variable. The estimated speed of convergence is $\beta = 0.021$ (s.e. $= 0.0003$). The good fit ($R^2 = 0.89$) can be appreciated by looking at Fig. 4, which is a scatter plot of the average growth rate of income *per capita* between 1880 and 1990 versus the log of income *per capita* in 1880. Column 2 includes some additional explanatory variables such as the share of agriculture and mining in total income as well as some regional dummies. These variables have little effect on the estimates of β over the long run. The point estimate in this case is 0.017 (s.e. $= 0.0026$).

The third column reports the estimated β when the overall sample period is divided into sets of 10 year pieces (20 years for 1880 to 1900 and 1900 to 1920). I restrict the estimate of β over time, but allow for time fixed-effects. I also hold constant the shares of income originating in agriculture and industry to proxy for sectoral shocks that affect growth in the short run. The restricted point estimate of β is 0.022 (s.e. $= 0.002$). Thus, the estimated speed of convergence across states of the United States is similar to that of OECD economies: about 2 per cent per year. Fig. 5 shows an overall downward trend in the cross-sectional standard deviation for the log of *per capita* personal income net of transfers for 48 U.S. states from 1880 to 1992. The fall in dispersion was interrupted during the 1920s (a period of large declines in agricultural prices which hurt the poorer agricultural states) and the 1980s.

---

[15] The existence of classical measurement error could deliver a negative relation between growth and the initial level of income. Barro and Sala-i-Martin (1992) show that this is an unlikely explanation for the finding of β-convergence. Measurement error, on the other hand, cannot explain the existence of σ-convergence, unless one argues that the size of the error falls over time.

[16] See Easterlin (1960) and Barro and Sala-i-Martin (1992, 1995, chapter 11).

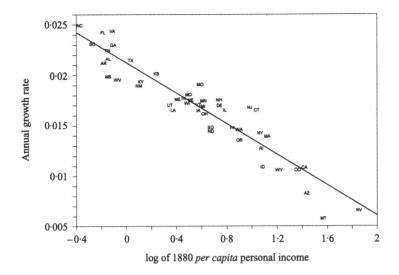

Fig. 4 Convergence of personal income across US states: 1880 personal income and income growth from 1880 to 1990

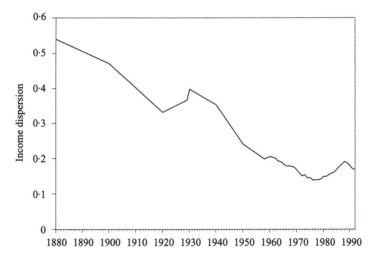

Fig. 5 Dispersion of personal income across US states, 1880–1992

5.3 Japanese prefectures

The fourth row of Table 1 reports similar estimates for 47 Japanese prefectures for the period 1955–87.[17] As for the United States, the first and second columns correspond to

---

[17] See Barro and Sala-i-Martin (1995, chapter 11) and Shioji (1995).

a single regression for the entire sample period which, in the case of Japan, is 1955–90. Column 1 estimates β with the initial level of income as the sole explanatory variable. The estimated coefficient is 0.019 (s.e. = 0.003). Column 2 adds some sectoral variables (such as the fraction of income originating in agriculture or industry), but they do not affect the estimated β. The estimates reported in Table 1 use data starting in 1955 because income data by sector are not available before that date. Income data, however, are available from 1930. If we use the 1930 data, the estimated speed of convergence would be 0.027 (s.e. = 0.003). The good fit can be appreciated in Fig. 6. The evidently strong negative correlation between the growth rate from 1930 to 1990 and the log of *per capita* income in 1930 confirms the existence of absolute β-convergence across the Japanese prefectures.

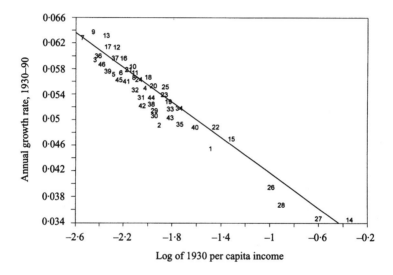

Fig. 6 Convergence of personal income across Japanese prefectures 1930 income and income growth 1930–90

To assess the extent to which there has been σ-convergence across prefectures in Japan, Fig. 7 shows that the dispersion of personal income increased from 0.47 in 1930 to 0.63 in 1940. After 1940, the cross-prefectural dispersion decreased dramatically until 1978 and it increased slightly afterwards. Note that Japan shares with the United States and the set of OECD economies the phenomenon of σ-divergence during a decade that starts somewhere in the mid-1970s.

5.4 European regions

Rows 5 to 10 in Table 1 refer to β-convergence across regions within five European countries (Germany, France, the United Kingdom, Italy, and Spain).[18] The fifth row

---

[18] See Barro and Sala-i-Martin (1995, chapter 11). See also Dolado et al. (1994) for a careful study of the Spanish case.

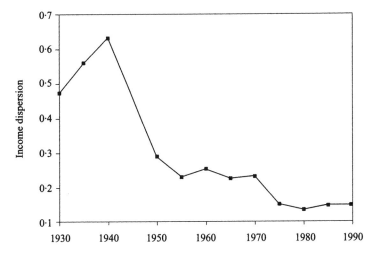

Fig. 7 Dispersion of personal income across Japanese prefectures 1930–90

relates to the estimate of β for a sample of 40 years, 1950–90, when the speeds of convergence are restricted across the 90 regions of the 5 countries and over time. The estimate does, however, allow for country fixed-effects. The estimated β is 0.015 (s.e. = 0.002). The third column shows that the panel estimates of β is 0.031 (s.e. = 0.004). Again, these estimates lie in the neighbourhood of the 2 per cent per year found in the other data sets.

Fig. 8 shows the results on β-convergence visually. The values shown are all measured

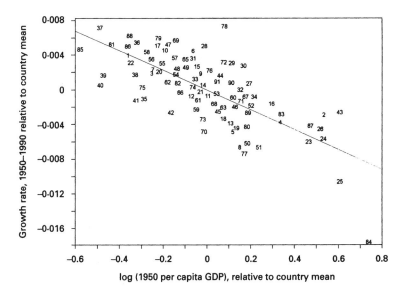

Fig. 8 Growth rate from 1950 to 1990 versus 1950 per capita GDP for 90 regions in Europe

relative to the means of the respective countries. The figure shows the type of negative relation that is familiar from our earlier discussion of the U.S. states and Japanese prefectures. The correlation between the growth rate and the log of initial *per capita* GDP in Fig. 5 is − 0.72. Because the underlying numbers are expressed relative to own-country means, the relation in Fig. 8 pertains to β-convergence within countries rather than between countries, and corresponds to the estimates reported in column 1 of Table 1.

Separate estimates for the long sample for each of the five countries are reported in columns 1 and 2 for the next five rows. The estimates range from 0.010 (s.e. = 0.003) for Italy to 0.030 (s.e. = 0.007) for the United Kingdom. The restricted panel estimates for the individual countries are reported in column 3. It is interesting to note that the individual point estimates are all close to 0.020 or 2 per cent per year. They range from 0.015 for France to 0.029 for the United Kingdom.

Fig. 9 shows the behaviour of σ_t for the regions within each country. The countries are always ranked, from highest to lowest, as Italy, Spain, Germany, France, and the United Kingdom. The overall pattern shows declines in σ_t over time for each country, although little net change has occurred since 1970 for Germany and the United Kingdom. In particular, the rise in σ_t from 1974 to 1980 for the United Kingdom – the only oil producer in the European sample – likely reflects the effects of oil shocks.

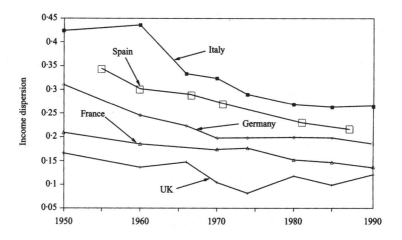

Fig. 9 Dispersion of GDP *per capita* within five European countries

5.5 Other countries

The empirical research on convergence across regions within a country is now substantial. The main conclusion of most of the studies is that there is regional convergence, and that the speed of convergence is close to 2 per cent per year (some countries display faster and some countries display slower speed of convergence, but it always lies close to the 2 per cent). Among others, the countries studied are Canada (see Coulombe and Lee (1993)), Australia (see Cashin (1995)), India (see Cashin and Sahay (1995)), Sweden (see Persson (1994)), Austria and Germany (see Keller (1994)).

6 CONCLUSIONS

There are four main lessons to be gained from the classical approach to convergence analysis. First, the cross-country distribution of world GDP between 1960 and 1990 did not shrink, and poor countries have not grown faster than rich ones. Using the classical terminology, in our world there is no *σ-convergence* and there is no *absolute β-convergence*. Secondly, holding constant variables that could proxy for the steady state of the various economies, the same sample of 110 economies displays a negative partial correlation between growth and the initial level of GDP, a phenomenon called *conditional β-convergence*. The estimated speed of conditional convergence is close to 2 per cent per year. Thirdly, the sample of OECD economies converge in an absolute sense at a speed which is also close to 2 per cent per year. The sample of countries displays σ-convergence over the same period. However, the process of σ-convergence did seem to stop for about a decade somewhere in the mid-1970s. Fourth, the regions within the United States, Japan, Germany, the United Kingdom, France, Italy, Spain, and other countries display absolute and conditional *β*-convergence, as well as σ-convergence. Interestingly, the estimated speed of convergence is, in all cases, close to 2 per cent per year. As for the OECD economies, within most of these countries the process of σ-convergence also seemed to stop for about a decade somewhere in the mid-1970s.

I would like to finish this paper with four thoughts about these results. First, we have seen that something strange happened in the mid-1970s all over the world: the process of σ-convergence in most data sets that displayed σ-convergence stopped for about a decade. In other words, income inequality within the countries studied, increased for a while. Secondly, the speed of convergence, *β*, has been estimated to be within a narrow range centring on 2 per cent per year ($\beta = 0.02$). Although this is a very robust and strongly significant finding, I would like to emphasise that a speed of 2 per cent per year is very small. For example, it suggests that it will take 35 years for half of the distance between the initial level of income and the steady state level to vanish. This is quite slow. Thirdly, the estimate of $\beta = 0.02$ and equation (4) can be used to provide estimates of the relevant capital share, *a*. If we let $x = 0.02$ (the rate of productivity growth must be equal to the long-run growth rate of an economy, which is close to 0.02), $n = 0.01$ (the estimated rate of population growth in recent decades), and $\delta = 0.05$ (this rate of depreciation is more controversial; 0.05 corresponds to the rate of depreciation for the overall stock of structures and equipment for the United States), then the capital share implied by the estimated $\beta = 0.02$ is $a = 0.75$. This capital share is larger than the traditional $a = 0.30$ estimated under the assumptions of perfectly competitive economies with no externalities and no human capital. A value of $a = 0.75$ suggests that, even though the neoclassical model is qualitatively consistent with the data, from a quantitative point of view, it tends to predict too high a speed of conditional convergence. For the model to be consistent with the slow speed of 2 per cent per year, it needs to be amended so that the relevant capital share is larger. Finally, in this paper I followed the classical convergence literature and analysed the empirical results in the light of the neoclassical model. The reason is that, as I said in the text, early theorists of endogenous growth proposed the absence of absolute *β*-convergence as the main evidence in favour of their models and against neoclassical growth. The introduction of the concept of conditional convergence showed that the neoclassical model is consistent with the data, so it can be a useful framework to guide the convergence literature. However, this is not to say that no other models may be consistent with the existence of convergence. As an example, it can be shown that a model of endogenous growth and technological diffusion (which, in Quah's terminology, make the distinction between growth and convergence effects) can predict an equation exactly like (4) (see Barro and Sala-i-Martin (1995, chapter 8)).

References

Barro, Robert J. (1991). 'Economic growth in a cross section of countries.' *Quarterly Journal of Economics*, vol. 106, no. 2 (May), pp. 407–43.

Barro, Robert J. and Sala-i-Martin, Xavier (1992). 'Convergence.' *Journal of Political Economy*, vol. 100, no. 2 (April), pp. 223–51.

Barro, Robert J. and Sala-i-Martin, Xavier (1995). *Economic Growth*. Boston MA: McGraw Hill.

Barro, Robert J., Mankiw, N. Gregory and Sala-i-Martin, Xavier (1995). 'Capital mobility in neoclassical models of growth. *American Economic Review*, vol. 85, no. 5, pp. 103–15.

Baumol, William J. (1986). 'Productivity growth, convergence, and welfare: what the long-run data show.' *American Economic Review*, vol. 76, no. 5 (December), pp. 1072–85.

Baumol, William J. and Wolff, E. (1988). 'Productivity growth, convergence, and welfare: reply.' *American Economic Review*, vol. 78, no. 5 (December), pp. 1195–9.

Cashin, Paul (1995). 'Economic growth and convergence across the seven colonies of Australasia: 1861–1991.' *Economic Record*, vol. 71, pp. 128–40.

Cashin, Paul and Sahay, Ratna (1995). 'Internal migration, center-state grants, and economic growth in the states of India.' *International Monetary Fund Working Paper* 95/75, Washington, DC.

Cass, David (1965). 'Optimum growth in an aggregative model of capital accumulation.' *Review of Economic Studies*, vol. 32, no. 91 (July), pp. 233–40.

Coulombe, S. and Lee, F. C. (1993). 'Regional economic disparities in Canada.' Unpublished paper, University of Ottawa, July.

Dali, Salvador (1965). 'The critical-paranoic method and the diary of a genius.' *Departament de Publications de la Generalital de Catalunya* (translated to English by Richard Howard).

DeLong, J. Bradford (1988). 'Productivity growth, convergence, and welfare: comment.' *American Economic Review*, vol. 78, no. 5 (December), pp. 1138–54.

Dolado, Juan, Gonzalez-Paramo, J. M. and Roldan, J. M. (1994). 'Convergencia economica entre provincias Españolas.' *Moneda y Credito*, no. 1998.

Dowrick, Steve and N'guyen, Duc Tho (1989). 'OECD comparative economic growth 1950–85; catch-up and convergence. *American Economic Review*, vol. 79, no. 5 (December), pp. 1010–30.

Easterlin, Richard A. (1960). 'Regional growth of income: long-run tendencies.' In *Population Redistribution and Economic Growth, United States, 1870–1950*. (eds. Simon Kuznets, Ann Ratner Miller, and Richard A. Easterlin). II: *Analyses of Economic Change*, Philadelphia: The American Philosophical Society.

Keller, Wolfgang (1994). 'On the relevance of conditional convergence under diverging growth paths. The case of east and west German regions, 1955–1988.' Mimeographed, Yale University, November.

Koopmans, Tjalling C. (1965). 'On the concept of optimal economic growth.' In *The Econometric Approach to Development Planning*, Amsterdam: North Holland.

Levine, Ross and Renelt, David (1992). 'A sensitivity analysis of cross-country growth regressions.' *American Economic Review*, vol. 82, no. 4 (September), pp. 942–63.

Maddison, Angus (1991). *Dynamic Forces in Capitalist Development.* Oxford: Oxford University Press.

Mankiw, N. Gregory, Romer, David and Weil, David N. (1992). 'A contribution to the empirics of economic growth.' *Quarterly Journal of Economics*, vol. 107, no. 2 (May), pp. 407–37.

Quah, Danny (1993). 'Galton's fallacy and tests of the convergence hypothesis.' *Scandinavian Journal of Economics*, vol. 95, no. 4, pp. 427–43.

Quah, Danny (1994). 'Empirics for economic growth and convergence.' Unpublished manuscript, London School of Economics, September.

Quah, Danny (1996). 'Twin Peaks: growth and convergence in models of distribution dynamics.' *Economic Journal* (this issue).

Persson, Joakim (1994). 'Convergence in per capita income and migration across the Swedish counties 1906–1990' (mimeo). University of Stockholm.

Ramsey, Frank P. (1928). 'A mathematical theory of saving.' *Economic Journal*, vol. 38, December, pp. 543–59.

Rebelo, Sergio (1991). 'Long run policy analysis and long run growth.' *Journal of Political Economy*, October, vol. 94, pp. 1002–37.

Romer, Paul (1986). 'Increasing returns and long run growth.' *Journal of Political Economy*, June, vol. 99, pp. 500–21.

Sala-i-Martin, Xavier (1990). 'On growth and states' Ph.D. Dissertation, Harvard University.

Shioji, Etsuro (1995). 'Regional growth in Japan.' Working paper no. 138. Universitat Pompeu Fabra, October.

Solow, Robert M. (1956). 'A contribution to the theory of economic growth.'. *Quarterly Journal of Economics*, vol. 70, pp. 65–94.

Summers, Robert and Heston, Alan (1991). 'The Penn World Table (Mark 5): an expanded set of international comparisons, 1950–1988.' *Quarterly Journal of Economics*, vol. 106, no. 2 (May), pp. 327–68.

Swan, Trevor W. (1956). 'Economic growth and capital accumulation.' *Economic Record*, vol. 32, no. 63 (November), pp. 334–61.

2
TECHNOLOGY AND CONVERGENCE

Andrew B. Bernard and Charles I. Jones

The empirical convergence literature envisages a world in which the presence or lack of convergence is a function of capital accumulation. This focus ignores a long tradition among economic historians and growth theorists which emphasises technology and the potential for technology transfer. We suggest here that this neglect is an important oversight: simple models which incorporate technology transfer provide a richer framework for thinking about convergence. Empirically, differences in technologies across countries and sectors appear to match differences in labour productivity and to exhibit interesting changes over time.

The debate over convergence has lost its way. From its initial concerns about the paths of output for poorer nations, it has become mired down in a debate about 2 per cent per year convergence rates and their robustness or lack thereof. In spite of work showing that convergence itself is not sufficient to distinguish among important alternative growth models, two lines of thought remain dominant in the convergence debate: that which believes convergence is a robust phenomenon and signals the primacy of the neoclassical growth model and the dominant roles of aggregate capital accumulation in determining relative output levels and growth rates, and that which is sceptical of the worldwide convergence finding and focuses on the possibility of multiple steady states and output paths for similarly endowed countries. However, regardless of the camp one aligns with, both sides have remained fixated on the role of capital, either physical or human, in determining long-run outcomes.

This is perhaps best seen in the oft-cited work of Mankiw et al. (1992) who aim to explain both cross-country differences in output levels and growth rates with a Solow-style growth model in which countries have identical exogenous rates of technological change. The exercise is one of pushing the simple model of capital accumulation to its logical limit, adding only a second capital type when the estimated factor share for physical capital seems too large. Barro and Sala-i-Martin (1992) and Barro et al. (1995) argue from a similar perspective.[1]

Almost completely forgotten by the empirical literature is the role of technology. Technology, at best, is allowed to index differences in an initial multiplicative factor, and all economies are assumed to accumulate technology at the same rate. In such a capital-based world, differences in growth rates stem from differences in capital accu-

---

[1] A notable early exception to this characterisation is Dowrick and N'guyen (1989) who examine the convergence of total factor productivity in the OECD.

mulation. Technological choices, through adoption and accumulation, are completely assumed away in explaining both relative output levels and growth rates, hence convergence. To the extent that the adoption and accumulation of technologies is important for convergence, the empirical convergence literature to date is misguided.

Section 1 of this paper makes the simple observation that technology is featured prominently in almost every other analysis of economic growth except for the convergence literature. Economic historians, technologists, and advocates of the 'new' growth theory all emphasise the importance of technology for understanding growth, development and convergence. In Section 2, we consider the meaning of technology in the production function and argue for a broader definition of technology than is traditionally recognised in the analysis of the production function. Section 3 summarises some evidence on convergence in labour productivity and technology and argues that the evolution of technology is an important driving force behind convergence in the OECD. Finally, Section 4 offers our view of where the literature should go in the future.

1 WHAT HAPPENED TO TECHNOLOGY?

The focus on capital accumulation in the recent empirical literature ignores a long tradition among economic historians and technologists and lags behind much of the 'new' growth theory. Economic historians have long emphasised the importance of technological progress as a driving force behind economic growth and as one of the key advantages associated with Gerschenkron's 'relative backwardness' (Gerschenkron, 1952; Abramovitz, 1986). For example, 'innovation-sharing' was one of the primary explanations cited by Baumol (1986) for the convergence he documented among advanced economies. Rosenberg (1982) cautions that technological backwardness may not be unambiguously beneficial, but he nevertheless highlights the prominence of technology transfer in the history of economic growth:

> Francis Bacon observed almost 400 years ago that three great mechanical inventions – printing, gunpowder, and the compass – had 'changed the whole face and state of things throughout the world; the first in literature, the second in warfare, the third in navigation'. What Bacon did not observe was that none of these inventions, which so changed the course of human history, had originated in Europe, although it was from that continent that their worldwide effects began to spread. Rather, these inventions represented successful instances of technology transfer . . . (p. 245).

The current omission of technology from the empirical literature on convergence also runs counter to the emphasis of the 'new' growth theory. Initially, of course, the empirical convergence literature was read partially as a rejection of the constant returns to accumulable factors associated with the 'AK'-style endogenous growth models. Virtually all of the new 'new' growth theory, however, focuses instead on the importance of endogenising technological change, distinct from capital accumulation, in order to understand economic growth. Technology transfer is then logically a potential force behind convergence. This avenue has been emphasised by Romer (1993) and his 'idea gaps', as well as 25 in more traditional analysis by Grossman and Helpman (1991), and Parente and Prescott (1994), among others.

2 WHAT IS TECHNOLOGY?

Since we do not intend to settle the ongoing debates about the most appropriate growth modelling strategy, we will make our points within the context of a constant returns Solow growth model without necessarily endorsing it. Suppose the aggregate production function is given by

$$Y_i = K_i^{a_i}(A_i L_i)^{1-a_i} \Rightarrow y_i = A_i^{1-a_i} k_i^{a_i} \tag{1}$$

where lower case letters denote *per capita* quantities and the factor weights, a_i, and the levels of labour-augmenting technological change, A_i, are allowed to vary across countries. The variation in A across countries needs no further explanation. The variation in a though, may appear slightly strange. Traditionally, technology is represented as a single labour-augmenting factor in the production function. However, in the general F (K, L, t) production function, there is no reason to think that technology need enter multiplicatively. The notion of technology we argue for here is broadened to include the exponents of the production function: two economies with the same K, L, and even A will produce different quantities of output if the as differ. Economically, we can interpret this difference as arising from the heterogeneity of goods that are produced within an economy. Such heterogeneity may be particularly important if we examine the convergence of productivity at the sectoral level, for example, rather than aggregate level.

Accumulation takes place in both capital and labour-augmenting technology. Net capital accumulation is a constant fraction of output

$$\dot{K}_i = s_i Y_i - \delta_i K_i \tag{2}$$

For the growth rate of technology in country i, we make the simplest assumption possible regarding technology transfer to illustrate the results:

$$\frac{\dot{A}_i}{A_i} = \xi_i \left(\frac{A_w}{A_i}\right) \tag{3}$$

where ξ_i indexes the ability of a country to adopt the most productive labour-augmenting technology, A_w, which is assumed to grow exogenously at rate $g \equiv \xi_w$. One can solve this differential equation to find that the steady state technology ratios are given by

$$\frac{A_i}{A_w} = \frac{\xi_i}{\xi_w} \tag{4}$$

As usual, steady state growth rates for output *per capita* and the capital–labour ratio for each country will equal the growth of the world labour-augmenting technology

$$g_{y_i} = g_{k_i} = g_{A_i} = g \tag{5}$$

Relative steady state levels of output *per capita* in this framework depend on more than just the relative savings rates, depreciation rates and population growth rates. They also hinge upon the ability of countries to adopt the frontier, level of technology and on the aggregate factor shares:

$$\frac{y_i^*(t)}{y_{us}^*(t)} = \frac{\xi_i}{\xi_{us}} \cdot \frac{\left(\dfrac{s_i}{n_i + g + \delta_i}\right)^{a_i/(1-a_i)}}{\left(\dfrac{s_{us}}{n_{us} + g + \delta_{us}}\right)^{a_{us}/(1-a_{us})}} \tag{6}$$

In this framework, we allow technology to vary across countries, both because of differential abilities to adopt the leading technology (or because different amounts of resources are devoted to such adoption) and because product and industry composition varies across countries. This leads to a world in which similar steady states outcomes are the exception rather than the rule. Countries that are good adapters fare well. The mix of products and the ability to reap from the efforts of others determine the relative positions of countries in the long-run, even if they have similar population growth rates and investment rates. One could also derive the rates at which countries converge to their own steady state in this model, and it should be obvious that the result will depend on the parameters of the technology transfer equation in addition to the parameters of the production function.

3 SOME FACTS

Our simple theoretical framework suggests that differences in technologies across countries can have important implications for the convergence, or lack thereof, of labour productivity. In this section, we review some empirical evidence from Bernard and Jones (1994 *a*, *b*) supporting the hypothesis that there are important differences in technology across countries.

Fig. 1 compares the cross-country dispersion in labour productivity to the cross-country dispersion in technology for fourteen OECD economies.[2] Results are displayed for total industry and for the manufacturing sector. Here, the measure of technology, Total Technological Productivity (TTP), incorporates variation in both *A* and *a* across countries. It is thus a complete measure of technology.[3]

Two results are immediately apparent from the figure. First, there is substantial variation in technology across countries, which is roughly the same order of magnitude

[2] The data are from the OECD's Intersectoral Database, and the countries included are the United States, Canada, Japan, Germany, France, Italy, the United Kingdom, Australia, the Netherlands, Belgium, Denmark, Norway, Sweden and Finland.

[3] Bernard and Jones (1994*a*) discuss this measure in detail. Essentially, it represents the amount of output produced by an economy with a specified quantity of capital and labour. The numbers reported are calculated using the median capital–labour ratio in 1970.

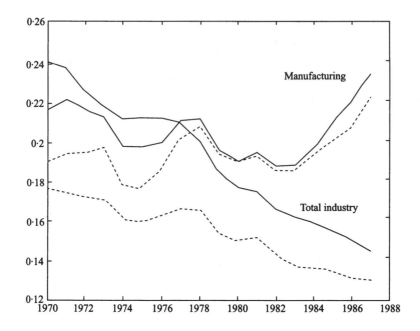

Fig. 1 Cross-country dispersion in Y/L and TTP

Note: Solid line = Y/L; dashed line = TTP. Cross-country dispersion is measured as
the standard deviation of the natural log of productivity

as the variation in labour productivity. In 1987, the standard deviation of the log of labour productivity is about 0.14 for total industry, and the dispersion of technology is about 0.13. For manufacturing, the two numbers are 0.24 for Y/L and 0.22 for technology. Secondly, the change in the dispersion of labour productivity over time corresponds closely to the change in the dispresion of technology. For total industry, both measures decline over time, with the decline in the dispersion of labour productivity (from about 0.24 in 1970 to 0.14 in 1987) being slightly more than the decline for TTP (from about 0.18 in 1970 to 0.13 in 1987). For manufacturing, however, both measures exhibit a pronounced lack of convergence and even suggest the presence of an increase in dispersion during the 1980s. The figure suggests that understanding changes in technology may be important for explaining the change in the dispersion of labour productivity over time. It also suggests that the convergence evidence may vary in interesting and informative ways across sectors.

   Figs 2 and 3 examine the changing dispersion of technology in more detail by breaking TTP into its components. Fig. 2 examines changes in the labour-augmenting part of technology A. The figure shows a substantial decline in dispersion for total industry over the 1970s and 1980s, while the pattern for manufacturing is less clear. In the context of the simple model that we outlined before, the results for total industry are consistent with some kind of technology transfer, while the results for manufacturing suggest that technology transfer may be less than automatic.

   Fig. 3 illustrates the dispersion in the factor weights that is present in the data. For

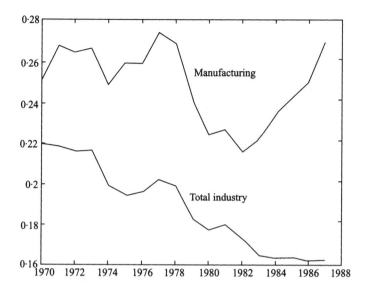

Fig. 2 Cross-country dispersion in '*A*'
Note: Cross-country dispersion is measured as the standard deviation of the natural log of productivity.

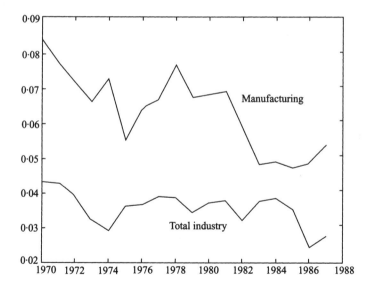

Fig. 3 Cross-country dispersion in '*a*'
Note: Cross-country dispersion is measured as the standard deviation of the labour share of GDP.

the purpose of this analysis, we assume that the factor share of income for labour corresponds to its weight in the production function.[4] Another indication of this variation is indicated by the average factor shares over the period 1970–87. For total industry, the variation is relatively small: the averages for the labour share range from a minimum of 0.61 in Australia and West Germany to a maximum of 0.68 in Denmark and Sweden. In contrast, for manufacturing there is substantial variation: ranging from 0.57 in Japan to 0.79 in the United Kingdom. The figure also indicates little change in the dispersion of factor shares for total industry and some decline in dispersion for manufacturing, particularly in the 1980s.

4 WHERE DO WE GO FROM HERE?

For the theoretical and empirical reasons outlined here, we think that future work on convergence should focus much more carefully on technology. Why do countries have different levels of technology? How do technologies change over time? How do we measure technology – is it sufficient to simply consider a labour-augmenting technology factor or are other differences in the production function important? How much of the convergence that we observe is due to convergence in technology versus convergence in capital labour ratios?

A second theme of this paper is that these questions become even more important, and other interesting questions arise, when one considers convergence at the sectoral level rather than the aggregate level. Both for data quality concerns and for theoretical reasons one might be interested in examining convergence in the manufacturing sector. For example, most R & D and international trade occurs in this sector. Yet when one examines the convergence question in this sector, the results look very different from the aggregate results: there is little or no convergence in either labour productivity or technological productivity in the manufacturing sector since the 1970s. Moreover, differences in technology (both in the As and the αs) are particularly important in this sector.

This evidence suggests to us that important forces underlying economic growth and the convergence or lack of convergence of labour productivity remain unaddressed by the empirical growth literature. Recent advances in endogenising technological change have the potential to illuminate these issues, but so far the empirical literature has refrained from exploiting these advances.

References

Abramovitz, M. (1986). 'Catching up, forging ahead and falling behind.' *Journal of Economic History*, vol. 46, pp. 385–406.

Barro, R. J. and Sala-i-Martin, X. (1992). 'Convergence.' *Journal of Political Economy*, vol. 100, pp. 223–51.

Barro, R. J., Mankiw, N. and Sala-i-Martin, X. (1995). 'Capital mobility in neoclassical models of growth.' *American Economic Review*, vol. 85, pp. 103–15.

---

[4] This assumption would be valid under perfect competition and constant returns to scale.

Baumol, W. J. (1986). 'Productivity growth, convergence and welfare: what the long-run data show.' *American Economic Review*, vol. 76, pp. 1072–85.

Bernard, A. B. and Jones, C. I. (1994*a*). 'Comparing apples to oranges: productivity, convergence, and measurement across industries and countries.' M.I.T. Working Paper no 94–12.

Bernard, A. B. and Jones, C. I. (1994*b*). 'Productivity across industries and countries: time series theory and evidence.' *Review of Economics and Statistics*, February, 1996 forthcoming.

Dowrick, S. and N'guyen, D. (1989). 'OECD comparative economic growth 1950 85: catch-up and convergence.' *American Economic Review*, vol. 79, pp. 1010–30.

Gerschenkron, A. (1952). 'Economic backwardness in historical perspective.' In *The Progress of Underdeveloped Areas*. (ed. B. F. Hoselitz). Chicago: University of Chicago Press.

Grossman, G. M. and Helpman, E. (1991). *Innovation and Growth in the Global Economy*. Cambridge: MA: M.I.T. Press.

Mankiw, N., Romer, D. and Weil, D. (1992). 'On the empirics of economic growth.' *Quarterly Journal of Economics*, vol. 107, pp. 407–38.

Parente, S. L. and Prescott, E. C. (1994). 'Barriers to technology adoption and development'. *Journal of Political Economy*, vol. 102, pp. 298–321.

Romer, P. (1993). 'Idea gaps and object gaps in economic development.' *Journal of Monetary Economics*, vol. 32, pp. 543–73.

Rosenberg, N. (1982). *Inside the Black Box: Technology and Economics*. New York: Cambridge University Press.

3

TWIN PEAKS: GROWTH AND CONVERGENCE IN MODELS OF DISTRIBUTION DYNAMICS

Danny T. Quah

Convergence concerns poor economies catching up with rich ones. At issue is what happens to the cross sectional distribution of economies, not whether a single economy tends towards its own steady state. It is the latter, however, that has preoccupied the traditional approach to convergence analysis. This paper describes a body of research that overcomes this shortcoming in the traditional approach. The new findings – on persistence and stratification; on the formation of convergence clubs; and on the distribution polarising into twin peaks of rich and poor – suggest the relevance of a class of theoretical ideas, different from the production-function accounting traditionally favoured.

Conventional analyses of economic growth and convergence address one natural set of questions. What is the contribution of physical capital to output? Knowing this allows us to understand or explain patterns of growth by pointing to rates of capital accumulation. How quickly can poor countries catch up with richer ones? What factors aid this convergence? Appreciating these gives us perspective on the relative levels of development that we observe across different countries, and insight into how poor countries can improve their circumstances.

There is a traditional approach to answering such questions: estimate a cross-section regression of growth rates on income levels, possibly including other variables on the right hand side of that regression. In this reasoning, the levels coefficient informs on both capital's contribution to output and the rate at which poor economies catch up with those richer. (Whether this catch up occurs is known as the *convergence hypothesis.*) Such an equation relating growth rates and levels takes on added significance when we recall that it can be derived from theoretical growth models. This traditional approach thus seems doubly blessed. It sheds light on important economic questions; it dovetails neatly with theoretical reasoning. This is the standard that all empirical analysis strives for; what, in this traditional approach, could be controversial?

This paper argues that conventional analyses miss altogether key aspects of economic growth and convergence. The reason is the following. One dimension of growth is the mechanism by which agents in an economy push back technological and capacity constraints; this increases aggregate output. When the mechanism works spectacularly well, we consider the economy a growth success. Such economic progress is germane to rich countries, just as it is to poor ones – there need be no distinction between them.

A different dimension of growth, however, is the mechanism that determines the relative performance of rich and poor economies: does growth in poorer economies lead to their catching up with the richer ones? Here, one wants to know if economic progress occurs differently in poorer economies than it does in richer ones.

The two mechanisms – pushing back and catching up – are related, but logically distinct: one can occur without the other. For brevity, I will refer to the first as a *growth* mechanism, and the second as a *convergence* mechanism. As with all such taxonomies, the distinction is imperfect, but, we will see, is better than nothing. Taking the distinction seriously means, temporarily, divorcing the convergence hypothesis from issues of any one country's productivity performance. What is important for convergence is how economies perform relative to each other, not how a single economy performs relative to its own history. Obviously, both growth and convergence mechanisms matter: to make progress in understanding, however, the details of one are usefully abstracted away to focus on the other.

This paper argues that a key shortcoming of the traditional approach is that it fails to distinguish these two dimensions of economic growth. Theoretical and empirical statements made about one are taken, inappropriately, to apply to the other. Consequently, theoretical insights recognising the distinction are unavailable in the standard approach.

I will describe below a body of newer empirical research that repairs this shortcoming. This work models directly the dynamics of the cross-section distribution of countries. In doing so, it uncovers regularities fundamentally different from those in conventional analyses. This research provides evidence on persistence and stratification; on the formation of convergence clubs; and on the cross-section distribution polarising into twin peaks of rich and poor.

Such regularities raise intriguing questions. What economic structures produce these dynamics? What mechanisms determine club formation and membership? Is it only those already-rich economies that converge towards each other, leaving the poor to form a different convergence club? What features of cross-country interaction generate polarisation and stratification? When physical capital flows more freely from one part of the world to another, does that lead to a spreading out of the distribution – so that the rich get richer and the poor, poorer? Or, does the opposite happen, and the poor have opportunity to become richer than those previously rich? In addressing these questions, the researcher is led to draw on fresh theoretical ideas, in ways hidden to the traditional approach. Thus, these distribution dynamics empirics not only repair the failure in the traditional approach to represent reality accurately, they also generate new theories on economic growth and convergence.

The discussion below concentrates on income distributions across countries. It directly applies, however, to convergence and growth in other economic units as well. Thus, the criticisms of the traditional approach extend readily. They imply that the traditional approach cannot at all address the concerns of policy-makers interested in regional development, economic and geographical redistribution, and comparative economic performance. Instead, revealing analysis must be found elsewhere – possibly in extensions of the models of distribution dynamics described below.

The goal of the rest of this paper is to flesh out the points just made. The paper is not intended as a broad survey of all possible criticisms of the traditional approach. Rather, the coverage is selective. Section 1 highlights those aspects of conventional analyses relevant to the current discussion. Section 2 describes that class of newer empirical findings that use distribution dynamics, and indicates the theoretical issues raised in such work. Section 3 concludes.

1 THE TRADITIONAL APPROACH

Traditional empirical analyses of growth and convergence derive from an elegant theoretical insight. This is that, in many growth models, equilibrium growth rates can be shown to be related to income levels through physical capital's relative contribution to national income (Barro and Sala-i-Martin, 1992; Romer, 1994; Sala-i-Martin, 1995; 1996). Developed explicitly, this insight gives a 'convergence equation' with growth on the left-hand side, explained by – among other things – income levels on the right.

In this reasoning, the cross-country correlation between growth rates and income levels is doubly interesting. It sheds light on the rate at which poor economies catch up with rich ones. Simultaneously, it informs on physical capital's importance for growth. Estimated on a wide range of data, this correlation implies a stable uniform rate of convergence equal to 2 per cent a year. Thus, while the poor do eventually catch up with the rich, the speed with which this happens is low: only half the gap between rich and poor is closed in 35 years. Moreover, the implied contribution of physical capital to aggregate output is high – much higher than suggested by factor income shares in national income accounts.

The second of these implications raises a puzzle: if it is physical capital that is driving growth, why is it not being properly compensated by the market? This basic question has motivated research on externalities and endogenous technological progress (Romer, 1990). Such research seeks to explain the observed empirical regularities on convergence rates and capital's factor income share. At the same time, it resolves deep theoretical subtleties in the theory of economic equilibrium with non-rival commodities.

In the taxonomy given earlier, such analyses provide powerful insights on the growth mechanism. However, whether they help us understand the convergence mechanisms hinges on auxiliary assumptions. What is the nature of interaction across different countries? Are currently leading economies always the first to push back technology frontiers, and does new technology then always filter passively to poorer economies? Are there costs of adoption that lead to leap-frogging, where it is the temporarily follower economies that jump to being leader, because they find it easier to exploit new discoveries? Or, do persistent advantages accrue to the leader, richer countries, simply by virtue of their already being leader and richer? Do poorer economies need to overcome poverty-trap barriers before they can hope to catch up with richer ones?

Traditional cross-section regressions on the 'convergence equation' can address none of these issues. That they are revealing to the coefficient of physical capital in a production function is just that, no more and no less. Such exercises, while using dynamic information creatively, are part of a time-honoured practice in production-function accounting, and might be usefully compared to empirical analyses like those in Griliches and Ringstad (1971). However, in the absence of auxiliary assumptions, they give no insight on whether poor countries are catching up with rich ones.

I show below that all the different possibilities relating rich and poor, described two paragraphs above, are consistent with a 'stable uniform 2 per cent rate of convergence' – as estimated from the traditional convergence equation. Thus, a negative correlation between growth rates and levels says nothing about the poor catching up with the rich.[1] Contrary to claims made elsewhere, traditional empirics are completely silent on the important convergence dimension in economic growth.

To see this, I need to make explicit some ideas – empirical and theoretical – on the dynamics of large cross sections. We turn to this next.

2 DISTRIBUTION DYNAMICS

This section develops models of distribution dynamics to study the convergence hypothesis.[2]

Fix a year – say t – and consider the then-extant empirical distribution of *per capita* incomes across countries. Suppose that the density of that distribution is as plotted, at time t, in Fig. 1. That density shows some rich countries in the upper part of the distribution; a majority of middle-income countries in the middle part of the distribution; and some poor countries, in the lower.

There is a density for each year: Fig. 1 plots, at $t + s$, the density at some date in the future from t. As drawn, two suggestive classes of features of Fig. 1 should be noted. The first class constitutes the *location, shape,* and other external characteristics of the distributions at different times: these can, in general, fluctuate. The second comprises the *intra-distribution* dynamics, or churning-like behaviour – indicated by arrows in Fig. 1 – when individual economies transit from one part of the distribution to another. We consider these different features in turn.

Fig. 1 has drawn the income distribution at $t + s$ to be bimodal or twin-peaked: in the picture, there is a group of the rich, collecting together; a group of the poor, collecting together; and a middle-income class, vanishing.[3] There is no *a priori* reason for this. The $t + s$ distribution might well have been unimodal, and tightly concentrated at a single point: then, the researcher could, with some confidence, say the originally poor at t had, by $t + s$, attained equal footing with the originally rich. The researcher might even want to call that catching up.[4]

---

[1] Sometimes, evidence on that negative correlation comes only with additional conditioning, hence the term '*conditional convergence*'. Sometimes, in the traditional approach, that evidence is buttressed also with evidence on cross-sectional standard deviations. While this last is marginally helpful, it remains potentially misleading: the next section shows why. As for conditional convergence, even in the best of all possible scenarios, all it could show is whether each country converges to its own steady state, different from that of other countries. It is a complete puzzle to me how this can be interesting for whether the poor are catching up with the rich.

[2] Emphases on the empirics of distribution characteristics and dynamics appeared earlier in the personal income distribution literature, e.g., Atkinson (1976) and Shorrocks (1978).

[3] Why say 'twin peaks' rather than just 'bimodal', or make up the word 'twin-peakedness' rather than simply use 'bimodality'? Despite having more letters, the former contain fewer syllables.

[4] Something like this must be what European Commission policy makers have in mind when they talk about achieving cohesion or equity across rich and poor regions in Europe.

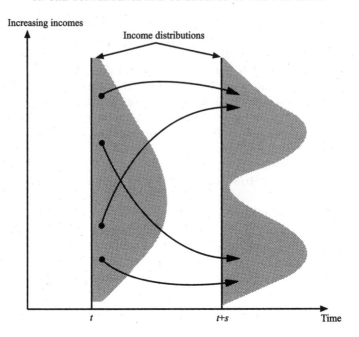

Fig. 1 Twin-peaks distribution dynamics

If time $t + s$ is within the researcher's data sample, then a hypothesised tendency towards twin-peakedness can be examined directly from observed data. If, however, time $t + s$ is beyond the available sample, then a model is needed before the researcher can reach a conclusion on this.

Is the twin-peakedness drawn in Fig. 1 more than just whimsy and artistic licence? Below, I describe empirical techniques to study this. The quick answer is that the world cross-section of countries does show such tendencies. There is even evidence that twin-peakedness can already be observed for $t + s$ within current data samples. However, twin-peakedness will certainly not be seen if all the researcher does is calculate means, standard deviations, third moments, and so on, of the cross-section distributions.

Turn now to intra-distribution dynamics. It does not take a high-tech econometrician to note that, in the world, there are some rich countries that have remained rich for long periods of time, and, similarly, that there are some poor countries that have remained poor. Casual observation also readily comes up with examples of rich countries that have transited to being relatively poor; poor countries, to relatively rich; and groups of countries, beginning at similar levels of development, eventually diverging, with some becoming richer, and others, poorer. (Korea and the Philippines are the usual examples for the last.) Put briefly, one sees a broad range of intra-distribution dynamics.

Next consider the intra-distribution arrows drawn in Fig. 1. Just as cross-sectional standard deviations give no insight on potential twin-peakedness in the distribution, they say nothing either about churning within the cross-section. Understanding these intra-distribution dynamics, however, would inform on the dynamics of the poor catching up with the rich. It would inform on the poor stagnating within poverty traps; on the poor overtaking those previously rich; and on convergence club dynamics – subgroups or clubs forming, with member countries converging towards each other, and diverging away from different clubs. It would shed light on possibilities for the poorest 5 per cent of the cross section catching up with the richest 5 per cent; and on whether global development takes multi-tier forms. Intra-distribution dynamics include information on switches in ranks – the leading country falling to seventeenth position, or *vice versa* – but, more than that, they also include information on the distance traversed when such switches happen.

I have just described some characteristics of (cross-country income) distribution dynamics that will be of interest in discussing convergence. Formalising this description offers two payoffs: first, precise statistical quantification; second, theoretical analysis based on economic ideas.

The simplest useful model of distribution dynamics is one where a stochastic difference equation describes the evolution of the sequence of distributions. Let F_t denote the time t cross-country income distribution. Associated with each F_t is a probability measure λ_t, where

$$\forall\, y \in \mathbb{R}: \lambda_t\,([-\infty, y]) = F_t\,(y)$$

A stochastic difference equation describing distribution dynamics is then

$$\lambda_t = T^*\,(\lambda_{t-1},\, u_t), \quad \text{integer } t \tag{1}$$

where $\{u_t:$ integer $t\}$ is a sequence of disturbances, and T^* is an operator mapping the Cartesian product of probability measures with disturbances to probability measures. (Needless to say, the first-order specification in (1) is just a convenience for the discussion. Nothing substantive hinges on it, and the model easily generalises to higher-order dynamics.)

Since our concerns include intra-distribution dynamics, (1) has to record more than just means and standard deviations – or more generally – of a finite set of moments of the distribution sequence $\{F_0, F_1, \ldots \}$. Equation (1) takes values that are measures, rather than just scalars or finite-dimensioned vectors, and thus differs from the typical time-series model.

The structure of T^* reveals if dynamics like those in Fig. 1 occur. Estimated from observed data, T^* allows empirical quantification of those dynamics. Economic hypotheses restrict T^* in particular ways: they therefore provide predictions on how λ_t and thus the distributions F_t, can evolve over time.

Just as in time-series analysis, the researcher might seek to understand T^* by its 'impulse response function': set the disturbances u to zero, and run the difference equation forwards.

$$T^*\,(\lambda_{t+s-1}, 0) = T^*\,(T^*\,(\lambda_{t+s-2}, 0), 0)$$
$$\vdots$$
$$= T^*\,(T^*\,(T \ldots (T^*\,(\lambda_t, 0), 0) \ldots 0), 0) \tag{2}$$

with the result being a proxy for λ_{t+s}. Then, convergence in country incomes to equality might be represented by (2) tending, as $s \to \infty$, towards a degenerate point mass. Alternatively, the world polarising into rich and poor might be represented by (2) tending towards a two-point measure: the implied limit distribution F_{t+s}, $s \to \infty$, would then be bimodal or twin-peaked. More generally, stratification into different convergence clubs might manifest in (2) tending towards a multi-point, discrete measure, or equivalently, a multi-modal distribution. How quickly a given initial distribution, F_0, evolves into the limiting distribution, F_{t+s}, $s \to \infty$, can be read off T^*'s (spectral) structure.

Finally, T^* also contains information on intra-distribution dynamics. Exploiting that structure, one can quantify the likelihood of the poor catching up with the rich, and characterise the (random) occurrence times for such events.

In summary, studying T^* informs on all the interesting issues in convergence analysis. What then does empirical evidence – the Summers–Heston (1991) data – tell us about T^* and Fig. 1? Desdoigts (1994), Lamo (1995), Paap and van Dijk (1994), and Quah (1993a, b; 1996a) take the approach of estimating – in some form – the operator T^*. Some of this work views estimating T^* as an exercise in nonparametric analysis, others, in semi-parametrics; yet others take discretisations of λ, whereupon T^* becomes just a stochastic matrix. The important insight driving these methods is not a technical one, say, of greater flexibility in estimating a 'convergence equation' regression. Rather, it is that all these methods provide a global, entire picture of what happens with incomes across countries. For cross-country data, all the research just mentioned find T^* having features that imply 'twin-peaks' dynamics.[5] Estimated T^*s indicate that clustering or clumping together of country incomes – convergence club behaviour – occurs eventually. Estimated T^*s reveal precise descriptions of events where economies, initially starting out close together, diverge over time towards either of the twin peaks. Thus, the empirical evidence shows all the features hypothesised in Fig. 1.

Durlauf and Johnson (1995) side-step analysing T^* directly. Instead, they estimate cross section regressions, but allow the regression to 'adapt' subsamples, depending on data realisations. This innovative empirical technique permits consistently uncovering local basins of convergence. Durlauf and Johnson find evidence for the kind of multimodal behaviour depicted in Fig. 1. They interpret their findings as multiple regimes; in the distribution-dynamics framework here, multiple regimes and multi-modality are indistinguishable.

Bianchi (1995) takes yet a third approach to studying twin-peakedness. As in Durlauf and Johnson (1995), Bianchi eschews dealing directly with T^*. Actually, he goes even further, and considers each distribution F_t, in isolation, ignoring dynamic information. Bianchi estimates each F_t non-parametrically, and then applies to each a bootstrap test for multi-modality. He finds that in the early part of the sample (the early 1960s), the data show unimodality. However, by the end of the sample (the late 1980s) the data reject unimodality in favour of bimodality. Since Bianchi imposes less structure in his analysis – nowhere does he consider T^* dynamics – one can reasonably guess that his

---

[5] Ben-David (1994) takes a different approach, but with end results that have the same interpretation.

findings are more robust to possible misspecification. Here again, twin-peakedness manifests.

It is obvious that calculating standard deviations or any other moment of the cross section distribution can show nothing about twin-peaks dynamics. The cross-section correlation between growth rates and income levels reveals even less, its interpretation plagued by a version of Galton's Fallacy.[6] However, operator T^* *can* shed light on that seductive intuition – the poor growing faster and thereby catching up, with the rich – that growth-on-levels regressions wish to exploit. Quah (1996a) calculates, from an estimated T^*, the probability density of passage times from poor parts of the income distribution to rich parts.[7] He finds that although growth miracles – the Hong Kongs, the South Koreas, and the Singapores – can happen with reasonable positive probability, the passage time from the bottom 5 per cent percentile to the top, given the magnitude of the gap extant, averages in the hundreds of years. Thus, persistence and immobility characterise the world cross section of country incomes.

(Although their being stated with T^*-induced preciseness is new with the body of research that I have just summarised, all such empirical facts have long been used informally in work such as Lucas (1988, 1993)).

What new economic ideas do these distribution dynamics suggest? These dynamics draw attention towards the nature of cross-country interactions – although, to be clear, not entirely away from production function accounting. They suggest that an appropriate test of economic ideas about the convergence hypothesis will come from looking at implications on how the entire cross-section distribution evolves, not from studying the behaviour of a single, representative economy.

A theoretical model of distribution dynamics – in generational earnings – was developed by Loury (1981). Many of those technical modelling ideas apply here as well, although the current emphasis on clustering and coalition formation across individual elements of the distribution is novel. This focus on cross-sectional grouping does, however, mesh with recent econometric research (Brock and Durlauf, 1995; Manski, 1993).

That particular economic features – threshold externalities, capital market imperfection, heterogeneity, country size, club formation – might produce 'twin peaks' dynamics across countries can be seen in theoretical models in Azariadis and Drazen (1990), Galor and Zeira (1993), Quah (1995b, 1996a), and Tamura (1992). Quah (1995b, 1996a) most closely relates the theoretical message in these papers to empirical analysis.

The theoretical model in Quah (1995b) describes economic forces that determine coalition or convergence club formation. That model shows why 'conditional convergence' in the traditional approach can be misleading: when different convergence clubs form, factor inputs (e.g. human capital) and social characteristics (e.g., democracy) will endogenously align around values determined by each country's conver-

---

[6] This connection is made in Friedman (1992) and Quah (1993b, 1996b). Quah (1996b also details why no combination of β-convergence and σ-convergence (in the terminology of Barro and Sala-i-Martin (1992) and Sala-i-Martin (1995, 1996)) can provide a satisfactory work-around.

[7] Durlauf and Johnson (1994) have studied similar phenomena in the dynamics of personal income distribution.

gence club. Conditioning on such 'explanatory variables' leads the researcher using the traditional approach to conclude, erroneously, that it is those variables that determine a country's economic position. By contrast, in the model, it is the factors deciding club membership that determine everything. The traditional researcher never finds those, and incorrectly attributes growth and convergence to factor inputs and social characteristics. Moreover, because in that traditional approach, the researcher only estimates a cross-section regression, he sees only the behaviour of the (conditional) representative economy. He will never detect the multi-peakedness that arises in the cross-country distribution.

Similar lessons manifest in the model in Quah (1996a). Here, it is varying degrees of capital market imperfection that lead to twin-peaks dynamics in the model. In the traditional approach, the researcher might simply proxy the capital market imperfectness by interest rates, say. However, in the model, all countries eventually have equal rates of return for borrowing and investment. The traditional researcher, therefore, never finds out the reason why twin-peaks dynamics occur – not that he ever even realises their presence. Moreover, the model predicts that every country converges (in a univariate sense) to its own steady state at an identical rate shared by all other countries. The traditional researcher then finds exactly a globally stable, constant rate of 'convergence' in the traditional conditional convergence regression. Such a finding, however, sheds no light on the actual distribution dynamics occurring.

3 CONCLUSION

With hindsight, the key point in this paper is obvious. Convergence concerns poor economies catching up with rich ones. What one wants to know here is, what happens to the entire cross sectional distribution of economies, *not* whether a single economy is tending towards its own, individual steady state. However, it is the latter that has preoccupied the traditional approach. Proposed fixes to that approach (e.g., the increased emphasis on σ-convergence in Sala-i-Martin (1995) continue to miss the principal important features of economic growth and convergence.

Such criticisms would be merely idle if there were no alternative empirics that appropriately address the key issues relevant to convergence analysis. This paper has described a rich and growing body of research that does exactly that. The new findings reported here – on persistence and stratification; on the formation of convergence clubs; on the distribution polarising into twin peaks of rich and poor – suggest the relevance of a class of theoretical ideas, different from the production-function accounting favoured by the traditional approach. It might, ultimately, be those factors that are important for growth, not just crudely boosting the inputs in a neoclassical production function.

Many issues remain to be researched in this alternative approach. The empirical analyses of distribution dynamics can be substantially refined: Quah (1995a, c) explore some ways to do this. Theoretical models for cross-country, or more general social, interaction (e.g., Benabou (1995); Brock and Durlauf (1995); Quah (1995b), among many others) provide new insights on how economies evolve – and, in turn, generate intriguing new predictions to be studied empirically.

References

Atkinson, Anthony B. (1970). 'On the measurement of inequality.' *Journal of Economic Theory*, vol. 2(3), pp. 244–63 (September).

Azariadis, Costas and Drazen, Allan (1990). 'Threshold externalities in economic development.' *Quarterly Journal of Economics*, vol. 105 (2), pp. 501–26 (May).

Barro, Robert J. and Sala-i-Martin, Xavier (1992). 'Convergence.' *Journal of Political Economy*, vol. 100 (2), pp. 223–51 (April).

Ben-David, Dan (1994). 'Convergence clubs and diverging economies.' Working paper 922, Centre for Economic Policy Research, London (February).

Benabou, Roland (1995). 'Heterogeneity, stratification, and growth: macroeconomic implications of community structure and school finance.' Working paper, Economics Department, New York University (March).

Bianchi, Marco (1995). 'Testing for convergence: a bootstrap test for multimodality.' Working paper, Bank of England (May).

Brock, William A. and Durlauf, Steven N. (1995). 'Discrete choice with social interactions.' Working paper, University of Wisconsin, Madison (April).

Desdoigts, Alan (1994). 'Changes in the world income distribution: a nonparametric approach to challenge the neoclassical convergence argument.' PhD thesis, European University Institute, Florence (June).

Durlauf, Steven N. and Johnson, Paul (1994). 'Nonlinearities in intergenerational income mobility.' Working paper, University of Wisconsin, Economics Department.

Durlauf, Steven N. and Johnson, Paul (1995). 'Multiple regimes and cross-country growth behavior.' *Journal of Applied Econometrics*, vol. 10. (Forthcoming).

Friedman, Milton (1992). 'Do old fallacies ever die?'. *Journal of Economic Literature*, vol. 30 (4), pp. 2129–32 (December).

Galor, Oded and Zeira, Joseph (1993). 'Income distribution and macroeconomics.' *Review of Economic Studies*, vol. 60 (1), pp. 35–52 (January).

Griliches, Zvi and Ringstad, Vidar (1971). *Economies of Scale and the Form of the Production Function*, Amsterdam: North-Holland.

Lamo, Ana R. (1995). 'Cross-section distribution dynamics.' Ph.D thesis, London School of Economics, London. (In progress).

Loury, Glenn C. (1981). 'Intergenerational transfers and the distribution of earnings.' *Econometrica*, vol. 49 (4), pp. 843–67 (July).

Lucas, Robert E. Jr. (1988). 'On the mechanics of economic development.' *Journal of Monetary Economics*, vol. 22 (3), pp. 3–42 (June).

Lucas, Robert E. Jr. (1993). 'Making a miracle.' *Econometrica*, vol. 61 (2), pp. 251–71 (March).

Manski, Charles F. (1993). 'Identification of endogenous social effects: the reflection problem.' *Review of Economic Studies*, vol. 60 (3), pp. 531–42 (July).

Paap, Richard and van Dijk, Herman K. (1994). 'Distribution and mobility of wealth of nations.' Working paper, Tinbergen Institute, Erasmus University (October).

Quah, Danny (1993a). 'Empirical cross-section dynamics in economic growth.' *European Economic Review*, vol. 37 (2/3), pp. 426–34 (April).

Quah, Danny (1993b). 'Galton's fallacy and tests of the convergence hypothesis.' *The Scandinavian Journal of Economics*, vol. 95 (4), pp. 427–43 (December).

Quah, Danny (1995a). 'Coarse distribution dynamics for convergence, divergence, and polarization.' Working paper, Economics Department, London School of Economics (July).

Quah, Danny (1995b). 'Ideas determining convergence clubs.' Working paper, Economics Department. London School of Economics (August).

Quah, Danny (1995c). 'International patterns of growth: II. Persistence, path dependence, and sustained take-off in growth transition.' Working paper, Economics Department, London School of Economics (June).

Quah, Danny (1996*a*). 'Convergence empirics across economies with (some) capital mobility.' *Journal of Economic Growth*, vol. 1 (1), pp. 95–124 (March).

Quah, Danny (1996*b*). 'Empirics for economic growth and convergence.' *European Economic Review*. (Forthcoming).

Romer, Paul M. (1990). 'Endogenous technological change.' *Journal of Political Economy* vol. 98 (5, Part 2), pp. S71–102 (October).

Romer, Paul M. (1994). 'The origins of endogenous growth.' *Journal of Economic Perspectives* vol. 8 (1), pp. 3–22 (Winter).

Sala-i-Martin, Xavier (1995). 'The classical approach to convergence analysis.' Working Paper 117, Universitat Pompeu Fabra, Barcelona (June).

Sala-i-Martin, Xavier (1996). 'Regional cohesion: evidence and theories of regional growth and convergence.' *European Economic Review* (Forthcoming).

Shorrocks, Anthony F. (1978). 'The measurement of mobility.' *Econometrica*, vol. 46 (5), pp. 1013–24 (September).

Summers, Robert and Heston, Alan (1991). 'The Penn World Table (Mark 5): an expanded set of international comparisons, 1950–1988.' *Quarterly Journal of Economics*, vol. 106 (2), pp. 327–68 (May).

Tamura, Robert (1992). 'Efficient equilibrium convergence: heterogeneity and growth.' *Journal of Economic Theory*, vol. 58(2), pp. 355–76 (December).

4

CONVERGENCE? INFERENCES FROM THEORETICAL MODELS*

Oded Galor

This essay suggests that the convergence controversy may reflect, in part, differences in perception regarding the viable set of competing testable hypotheses generated by existing growth theories. It argues that in contrast to the prevailing wisdom, the traditional neoclassical growth paradigm generates the club convergence hypothesis as well as the conditional convergence hypothesis. Furthermore, the inclusion of empirically significant variables such as human capital, income distribution, and fertility in conventional growth models, along with capital markets imperfections, externalities, and non-convexities, strengthens the viability of club convergence as a competing hypothesis with conditional convergence.

The convergence hypothesis has been the subject of intense controversy in the past few years. The controversy has been largely empirical, focusing primarily on the validity of three competing hypotheses:

1 The *absolute convergence hypothesis* – per capita incomes of countries converge to one another in the long-run independently of their initial conditions.[1]
2 The *conditional convergence hypothesis* – per capita incomes of countries that are identical in their structural characteristics (e.g. preferences, technologies, rates of population growth, government policies, etc.) converge to one another in the long-run independently of their initial conditions.[2]
3 The *club convergence hypothesis* (polarisation, persistent poverty, and clustering)[3] – per capita incomes of countries that are identical in their structural characteristics converge to one another in the long-run provided that their initial conditions are similar as well.[4]

---

* I wish to thank Costas Azariadis, Daniel Tsiddon, David Weil, and Joseph Zeira for helpful discussions.
[1] See Romer (1986), Lucas (1988), and Barro (1991) for conclusive evidence against the hypothesis.
[2] See Barro (1991), Mankiw et al. (1992), and Barro and Sala-i-Martin (1995) for supporting cross-country evidence for the conditional convergence hypothesis. Note, however, that this evidence is to a large extent consistent with the club convergence hypothesis as well.
[3] See Durlauf and Johnson (1995) and Quah (1996) for supporting evidence for the club convergence hypothesis.
[4] That is, countries converge to one another if their initial conditions are in the basin of attraction of the same steady-state equilibrium.

This essay contributes to the convergence debate from a theoretical viewpoint. It suggests that the prevailing controversy may reflect, in part, differences in perception regarding the viable set of testable hypotheses that existing theories of economic growth could generate. An empirical resolution of the convergence debate therefore necessitates a better understanding of the range of competing testable hypotheses generated by plausible growth models.

The essay analyses a variety of theories that have led to the existing controversy, examining their robustness and plausibility. In particular, in light of the existing range of inferences that growth theory offers, the essay attempts to assess the justification for the current hegemony of the conditional convergence hypothesis. It argues that the existing domination of the conditional convergence hypothesis may be attributed partly to insufficient familiarity with its theoretical non-robustness. Contrary to prevailing wisdom, the traditional neoclassical growth paradigm generates both the conditional convergence hypothesis and the club convergence hypothesis. Furthermore, inclusion of empirically significant variables such as human capital, income distribution, and fertility, in conventional growth models, along with capital markets imperfections, externalities, and non-convexities, strengthens the viability of club convergence as a competing hypothesis with conditional convergence.

The origin of the current debate is in the absolute convergence hypothesis, which suggests that *per capita* incomes of countries converge to one another in the long run independently of initial conditions. Since an economy's long-run equilibrium depends on its structural characteristics (e.g. technologies, preferences, population growth, government policy, factor market structure, etc.) absolute convergence requires convergence in structural characteristics across countries. Not surprisingly, therefore, the absolute convergence hypothesis has been refuted in recent empirical studies based on cross-country regressions (e.g. Barro (1991)) and the evolution of the distribution of income across nations (e.g. Quah (1996)).[5] Ironically, however, despite the fact that the neoclassical growth model does not generate the absolute convergence hypothesis, the empirical rejection of this hypothesis was one of the prime factors that led some of the originators of the endogenous growth literature to reject the neoclassical growth model as a framework for the study of economic growth. As argued however by Barro (1991), Mankiw, et al. (1992), and Barro and Sala-i-Martin (1995), the neoclassical growth model leads to the conditional convergence hypothesis rather than to the absolute one, and thus rejection of the absolute convergence hypothesis naturally does not imply rejection of the neoclassical growth model.

The conditional convergence hypothesis suggests that among countries that are similar in preferences, technologies, rates of population growth, government policies, etc. the lower the levels of output *per capita* the higher the growth rates. Thus, countries that are similar in all respects except for their initial level of output *per capita* are expected to converge to the same steady-state level of output *per capita* and hence to

---

[5] The presence of convergence in a sub-sample of countries selected according to their proximity in initial or terminal conditions (e.g. Baumol (1986)), does not provide empirical support for the absolute convergence hypothesis, but rather to the conditional and club convergence hypotheses (see De Long (1988)).

one another. Transitory shocks in this scenario affect the income ranking of an economy in the short-run, but do not have a lasting effect. The conditional convergence hypothesis is intimately related to the notion that each economy is characterised by a unique, globally stable, (non-trivial) steady-state equilibrium. Hence countries that are identical in their fundamentals (and therefore in their dynamical systems) converge to one another regardless of their initial conditions (see Fig. 1). Clearly, if the dynamical

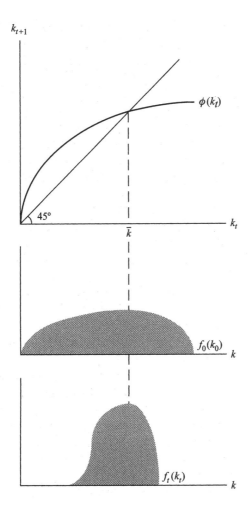

Fig. 1 Conditional convergence

system were characterised by multiple locally stable steady-state equilibria, a (conditional) club convergence hypothesis rather than a conditional convergence hypothesis would emerge. That is, countries that are similar in their structural characteristics converge to the same steady-state equilibrium if their initial *per capita* output levels are similar as well (see Fig. 2).[6] Transitory shocks in this scenario may affect the economic performance of a country permanently.

   The assessment of the two competing hypotheses is therefore nearly isomorphic to the examination of the plausibility of scenarios in which an economic system is characterised by a unique and globally stable, steady-state equilibrium rather than by multiple, locally stable steady-state equilibria.

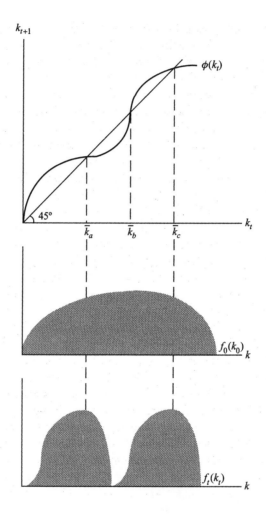

Fig. 2 Club convergence

[6] Clearly, 'similar initial *per capita* output' is a rather arbitrary term. Countries that are close to one another and are on different sides of an unstable steady-state equilibrium will diverge from one another. A more precise, but somewhat less tangible terminology would be that countries with similar fundamentals that are in the same basin of attraction to a given steady-state equilibrium will converge in the long run.

This essay traces the theoretical origin of the conditional convergence hypothesis within the prominent neoclassical growth frameworks of the one-sector growth model and the one-sector overlapping-generations model. It demonstrates that, indeed, given the neoclassical specifications, the conditional convergence hypothesis emerges as the sole hypothesis of the growth model (Solow, 1956) as well as the optimal growth model (Ramsey, 1928).[7] The economy is characterised by a unique (non-trivial) steady-state equilibrium and its growth rate declines as the economy evolves towards this stationary equilibrium. In the overlapping-generations model, in contrast, conditional convergence shares the stage with club convergence, unless additional restrictions beyond the neoclassical ones are imposed on preferences and technologies.

It is customarily argued that the source of conditional convergence is the assumption about diminishing marginal productivity of factors of production. That is, as the economy grows and the capital–labour ratio increases, the marginal productivity of capital declines and consequently saving and capital accumulation increase at decreasing rates. In the one-sector growth model, the neoclassical *per capita* production function is strictly concave in the capital–labour ratio. Saving, which is assumed to be a constant fraction of aggregate output (due to the implicit homogeneity of individuals), is therefore a strictly concave function of the capital–labour ratio as well. Hence, the evolution of the capital–labour ratio is characterised by a unique globally stable steady-state equilibrium, and conditional convergence emerges as the sole hypothesis generated by the model.

However, if heterogeneity is permitted across individuals, the dynamical system of the Solow growth model could be characterised by multiple steady-state equilibria and (conditional) club convergence would become a viable testable hypothesis despite diminishing marginal productivity of capital. Heterogeneity in factor endowments may cause saving rates out of interest income to differ from saving rates out of wage income. Specifically, if saving is a constant fraction of the wage share in output (rather than the entire income), since wages are not necessarily a concave function of the capital–labour ratio, there may be a region over which saving is a convex function of the capital–labour ratio. The growth rate may not be monotonically decreasing in the capital–labour ratio despite the neoclassical production technology, the economic system may be characterised by multiple steady-state equilibria, and club convergence may become a viable hypothesis as well.

As to the conventional one-sector overlapping-generations model, since saving in this model is inherently a function of the wage share in total output, and since the wage share is not necessarily a concave function of the capital–labour ratio, the growth rate may not be a monotonically decreasing function of the capital–labour ratio. As established in Galor and Ryder (1989) and Azariadis (1996), the economic system may be characterised by multiple steady-state equilibria and both club convergence and conditional convergence may emerge as viable hypotheses.[8]

---

[7] Due to the deterministic nature of these models the income ranking of countries is unaffected in the convergence process. A stochastic version of the growth model will generate conditional convergence as well as ranking reversals.

[8] In contrast to prevailing wisdom, the one-sector growth model and the one-sector overlapping-generations model may share an identical dynamical system and thus the possibility for multiple steady-state equilibria and club convergence (see section 1).

In sharp contrast to the existing conventional wisdom, even in the austere neoclassical growth models, multiplicity of steady-state equilibria is consistent with the neoclassical paradigm. Club convergence is perfectly consistent with constant returns to scale and diminishing marginal productivity, and it cannot be excluded *a priori* in a non-increasing returns to scale environment. Moreover, adding realism to the one-sector neoclassical growth models will result in an increase in the dimensionality of the economy's dynamical system. The range of parameters that lead to multiple steady-state equilibria would be augmented and the conditional club convergence hypothesis would rest on a more plausible set of assumptions.[9]

Once the neoclassical growth models are augmented so as to capture additional empirically significant elements such as human capital, income distribution, and fertility, along with capital market imperfections, externalities, non-convexities, and imperfectly competitive market structures, club convergence emerges under broader plausible configurations. The incorporation of human capital formation into basic growth models provides an environment in which club convergence is a viable theoretical hypothesis under plausible scenarios. Countries that are identical in their structural characteristics but differ in their initial level or distribution of human capital may cluster around different steady-state equilibria in the presence of social increasing returns to scale from human capital accumulation (e.g. Lucas (1988) and Azariadis and Drazen (1990)), capital market imperfections (e.g. Galor and Zeira (1993)), parental and local effects in human capital formation (e.g. Benabou (1996), Durlauf (1996), and Galor and Tsiddon (1994)), imperfect information (e.g. Tsiddon (1992)) and non-convex production function of human capital (e.g. Becker et al. (1990)).

The introduction of heterogeneous agents into growth models provides a channel through which income distribution affects economic growth. A large number of theoretical studies have documented the importance of initial conditions with respect to the distribution of income for the evolution of economies and their steady-state behaviour. Countries that are similar in their structural characteristics and in their initial level of output *per capita*, but differ in their initial distribution of income may cluster around different steady-state equilibria (e.g. Galor and Zeira (1993), Aghion and Bolton (1996), Benabou (1996), Durlauf (1996), and Quah (1996)).

The endogenisation of fertility decision provides an additional plausible framework that generates the club convergence hypothesis. Countries that are identical in their fundamentals and differ in their initial level of physical capital or human capital may cluster around different steady-state equilibria in terms of output *per capita* and fertility rate (e.g. Barro and Becker (1989), Becker et al. (1990)'s non-convex model, and Galor and Weil (1996)'s convex economy).

Finally, sectoral and technological complementarities, along with a non-competitive market structure or non-convexities, may generate multiple steady-state equilibria due to aggregate demand spillovers (e.g. Murphy et al. (1989) and Durlauf (1993)). Thus,

---

[9] For instance, in a two-sector overlapping-generations model in which a distinction is made between consumption goods and investment goods (Galor, 1992), multiplicity of steady-state equilibria occurs in a neoclassical CRS framework under a less restrictive set of assumptions than those required in the one-sector model.

countries that are identical in their fundamentals but differ in their initial level of output per-capita may cluster around different steady-state equilibria.

1 THE ROBUSTNESS OF CONDITIONAL CONVERGENCE IN NEOCLASSICAL GROWTH MODELS

This section traces the theoretical origin of the conditional convergence hypothesis within the prominent neoclassical growth frameworks of the one-sector growth model and the one-sector overlapping-generations model. It analyses the robustness of the hypothesis and examines critical assumptions for the emergence of this hypothesis within these frameworks of analysis. Contrary to conventional wisdom, it demonstrates that the presence of multiple steady-state equilibria and thus club convergence is consistent with the neoclassical paradigm in general and with constant returns to scale and diminishing marginal productivity in particular.

1.1 The neoclassical one-sector growth model

Given the specifications of the neoclassical one-sector growth model the conditional convergence hypothesis emerges as the sole hypothesis. The economy is characterised by a unique, globally stable (non-trivial) steady-state equilibrium and its growth rate declines as the economy approaches this stationary equilibrium. However, the introduction of heterogeneous individuals may give rise to a non-monotonic evolution of the growth rate and multiplicity of steady-state equilibria.

Conditional convergence

Consider a world in which economic activity is performed over infinite discrete time.[10] In each period a single good is produced, using two factors – capital and labour – in the production process. The good can be either consumed or saved for future consumption. The endowment of labour at time $t+1$, is $L_{t+1} = (1 + n) L_t$, where $n \geqslant 0$ is the rate of population growth, and the endowment of capital at time $t+1$, is $K_{t+1} = (1 - \delta) K_t + S_t$, where S_t, is aggregate savings at time t, and $\delta \in (0,1)$ is the rate of capital depreciation. Production occurs within a period according to a constant return to scale neoclassical production technology, which is stationary across time. The output produced at time t, $Y_t = F(K_t, L_t) = L_t F(K_t/L_t, 1) \equiv L_t f(k_t)$, where $k_t \equiv K_t/L_t$ is the capital-labour ratio employed in production at time t.

The economy allocates a fraction $s \in (0, 1)$ of aggregate output in every period to saving, and the remaining fraction is consumed. The aggregate saving at time t, S_t is therefore $S_t = sY_t = sL_t f(k_t)$. The evolution of the capital–labour ratio from a given initial condition, k_0, is governed by the following non-linear dynamical system:

$$k_{t+1} = \frac{(1 - \delta) (k_t + sf(k_t))}{1 + n} \equiv \phi (k_t) \tag{1}$$

---

[10] The dynamical system of the growth model is described in a discrete time framework to facilitate comparability with the inherently discrete dynamical system of the overlapping-generations model.

As depicted in Fig. 1 (for positive initial conditions), the economy is characterised by a unique and globally stable nontrivial steady-state equilibrium, and its growth rate declines monotonically in the capital–labour ratio. Countries that are identical in their technology, population growth, depreciation rate, and saving rate, converge to the steady-state equilibrium $\bar{k}$ and hence to one another regardless of their initial level of output *per capita*. The evolution of the initial cross-country distribution of capital–labour ratio, f_0 (k_0), reflects conditional convergence.

Club convergence

Suppose that output *per capita* in the one-sector growth model, $f(k_t)$, is divided into a labour share and a capital share according to the marginal productivity of labour and capital. That is $f(k_t) = w(k_t) + r(k_t)k_t$ where $w(k_t) \equiv f(k_t) - f'(k_t)k_t$ and $r(k_t) \equiv f'(k_t)$. Suppose further that the saving rates from wage income, $s^w \in [0, 1]$, and interest income, $s^r \in [0, 1]$, differ.[11] It follows that the evolution of the capital–labour ratio is governed by the non-linear dynamical system:

$$k_{t+1} = \frac{(1-\delta)k_t + s^w f(k_t) + (s^r - s^w)f'(k_t) k_t}{1+n} \equiv \psi(k_t) \tag{2}$$

and a positive, steady-state equilibrium is therefore given by $\bar{k}$ such that

$$s^w[f(\bar{k})/\bar{k}] + (s^r - s^w)f'(\bar{k}) = n + \delta \tag{3}$$

As depicted in Fig. 2, and demonstrated in Galor (1996), the dynamical system may be characterised by multiple locally stable steady-state equilibria, and club convergence is a viable hypothesis. Multiplicity of stationary equilibria occurs if saving out of labour income is larger than that out of capital income (not implausible in a life-cycle configuration) and if production technology is either CES with low elasticity of substitution or a member of a class of non-CES production functions.[12] Countries with an initial k_0 in the interval $[0, \bar{k}^b)$ converge to the low steady-state equilibrium $\bar{k}^a$, whereas those with initial k_0 in the interval $[\bar{k}^0, \infty)$ converge to the higher steady-state equilibrium $\bar{k}^c$. Thus, the initial cross-country distribution of capital–labour ratio, $f_0(k_0)$, becomes gradually polarised.

Despite the neoclassical features of the model (e.g. constant returns to scale and diminishing marginal productivity of factors of production), the growth rate of the capital–labour ratio may not be monotonically decreasing in the capital–labour ratio: the economic system may be characterised by multiple steady-state equilibria, and club convergence is a viable hypothesis. Conditional convergence would emerge in this model if saving is assumed to be a constant fraction of total output rather than a fraction of some nonlinear function of output (e.g. the wage share and the capital share in total output). Since the *per capita* production function is strictly concave in the capital–labour ratio, saving would be a strictly concave function of the capital–labour

---

[11] Heterogeneity of factor endowments across individuals may lead to this outcome.
[12] Fig. 2 is drawn for a non-CES production technology.

ratio as well. The economy's dynamical system would be characterised by a unique, globally stable steady-state equilibrium and conditional convergence would emerge as the sole hypothesis of the model. However, if, due to heterogeneity, individuals' saving were a constant fraction of the wage share in output, rather than of the entire output, since wages are not necessarily a concave function of the capital–labour ratio, there might be a region in which saving would be a convex function of the capital–labour ratio despite the neoclassical characteristics of the production technology. Thus, the club convergence hypothesis may emerge.

1.2 The one-sector overlapping-generation model

Consider a perfectly competitive world in which economic activity is performed over infinite discrete time. In each period a single homogeneous good is produced using two factors – capital and labour – in the production process. In accordance with the one-sector growth model the endowment of labour at time $t + 1$, is $L_{t+1} = (1 + n) L_t$, where $n > -1$ is the rate of population growth, and the capital stock at time $t + 1$ is $K_{t+1} = S_t + (1 - \delta) K_t$, where $\delta \in [0, 1]$. Production occurs within a period according to a neoclassical constant returns to scale production technology, which is stationary across time. Producers operate in a perfectly competitive environment. Given the wage rate w_t and the rate of return to capital r_t at time t, producers' inverse demand for factors of production is $w_t = f(k_t) - f'(k_t) k_t \equiv w(k_t)$ and $r_t = f'(k_t) \equiv r(k_t)$.

In every period t, L_t individuals are born. Individuals are identical within as well as across time. Individuals live two periods. In the first period they work and in the second period they are retired. Individuals born at time t are characterised by their intertemporal utility function $u(c_t^t, c_{t+1}^t)$ defined over consumption during the first and the second periods of their life. The utility function is monotonic increasing and strictly quasi-concave, and old-age consumption is a normal good. In the first period of their lifetime individuals born at time t supply their unit-endowment of labour inelastically and allocate the resulting wage income between first-period consumption, c_t^t, and saving, s_t. That is, $s_t = w_t - c_t^t$. Savings earn the rate of return r_{t+1} in period $t + 1$ and enable individuals to consume during retirement. Second-period consumption of an individual of generation t, is therefore, $c_{t+1}^t = (1 + r_{t+1} - \delta) s_t$. The level of saving is chosen so as to maximise the intertemporal utility function:

$$s_t = s(w_t, r_{t+1}) = \text{argmax } u[w_t - s_t, (1 + r_{t+1} - \delta) s_t]$$

subject to, $0 \leq s_t \leq w_t$, where r_{t+1} is the rationally anticipated return to capital in the next period. Given (w_t, r_{t+1}), the properties of the utility function imply that $s(w_t, r_{t+1})$ exists and is unique.

The evolution of the capital–labour ratio from an initial level k_0 is governed by the non-linear dynamical system

$$k_{t+1} = \frac{s[w(k_t), r(k_{t+1})]}{(1 + n)} \tag{4}$$

If saving is a non-decreasing function of the interest rate, there exists a monotonic increasing single-valued function $\phi(k_t)$ such that $k_{t+1} = \phi(k_t)$.

The neoclassical restrictions on preferences and technology do not preclude multiple steady-state equilibria as follows from the potential non-monotonicity of $\phi''(k_t)$. Specifically, if preferences are log–linear, saving is a fixed fraction of wages and is therefore not necessarily a concave function of the capital–labour ratio. The growth rate may not be a monotonic decreasing function of the capital–labour ratio, and multiple steady-state equilibria could emerge (see Galor and Ryder (1989)).[13] Note that in this case the overlapping-generations model is identical to the Solow growth model for the case in which saving out of interest income equals zero. Fig. 1 depicts a dynamical system in which each economy is characterised by a unique, globally stable steady-state equilibrium and countries that are identical in their fundamentals would converge to this steady state regardless of initial conditions (i.e. the initial cross-country distribution of the capital–labour ratio, $f_0(k_0)$, contracts over time). Fig. 2 depicts a system in which each economy's dynamical system is characterised by two locally stable steady-state equilibria. Countries that are identical in their structural characteristics converge, provided that their initial conditions belong to the same basin of attraction. Thus, polarisation takes place in the world economy.

2 CLUB CONVERGENCE IN AUGMENTED GROWTH MODELS

This section demonstrates that the incorporation of empirically significant elements such as human capital, income distribution, and fertility into the basic neoclassical growth model, along with capital market imperfections, externalities, non-convexities, and imperfectly competitive market structures, strengthens the viability of the club convergence hypothesis.

2.1 Human capital

The incorporation of human capital formation into the basic models provides an environment in which club convergence is a viable hypothesis under a plausible set of assumptions. The introduction of social increasing returns to scale from human capital accumulation permits initial conditions with respect to human capital accumulation to dictate the ultimate fate of otherwise identical economies and to generate club convergence (e.g. Lucas (1988), and Azariadis and Drazen (1990)). In the presence of capital market imperfections along with some non-convexities in the production of human capital, club convergence emerges. Countries that are similar in their structural characteristics and in their initial levels of output and human capital *per capita*, but differ in their initial distribution of human capital, may cluster around different steady-state equilibria (e.g. Galor and Zeira (1993)). Parental and local effects in offsprings' human capital formation generate a role for the initial distribution of human capital in the determination of the steady-state equilibrium of otherwise identical

---

[13] Alternatively, multiplicity of steady-state equilibria may occur if saving is a non-homothetic function of the wage rate, or in the presence of subsistence level of consumption (see Azariadis (1996)).

economies (e.g. Benabou (1996), Durlauf (1996), and Galor and Tsiddon (1994)), and non-convexities in the production function of human capital generate club convergence based on the initial average level of human capital accumulation (e.g. Becker et al. (1990)).

2.2 Income distribution

As documented in recent empirical studies (e.g. Alesina and Rodrik (1994), Persson and Tabellini (1994), and Perotti (1996)), income distribution is a significant explanatory variable of economic growth. A large number of theoretical studies have documented the importance of the distribution of income for the evolution of economies and their steady-state behaviour. The presence of capital market imperfections, along with some fixed cost in the production of human capital or final goods, will generate the club convergence hypothesis according to which countries that are similar in their structural characteristics and in their initial levels of output *per capita*, but differ in their initial distribution of income, may cluster around different steady-state equilibria (e.g. Galor and Zeira (1993), Aghion and Bolton (1996), Benabou (1996), Durlauf (1996), and Quah (1996)). Income distribution may affect the long-run level of output even in the absence of capital market imperfections as long as the parental human capital is an input in the production of the offspring's human capital (Galor and Tsiddon, 1994).[14]

2.3 Endogenous fertility

The endogenisation of fertility decisions provides an additional plausible avenue for generating club convergence. As argued by Barro and Becker (1989), multiplicity of steady-state equilibria is feasible in a growth model with endogenous fertility. Becker et al. (1990) demonstrate that if the production of human capital is non-convex, and if the discount rate of future dynastic utilities declines with the number of offspring, the economy may be characterised by multiple steady-state equilibria and initial conditions with respect to the number of children as well as the level of human capital may dictate the economy's steady-state equilibrium. In a convex economy, Galor and Weil (1996) demonstrate that differences in comparative advantage between male and female may be a viable source of multiple steady-state equilibria. If capital complements women's labour input more than men's labour input and if consistent with empirical evidence an increase in women's relative wages decreases fertility then, a low capital–labour ratio leads to low relative wages for women and a high fertility rate. Thus, the low capital–labour ratio may persist. A high capital–labour ratio, in turn, leads to high relative wages for women, and a low fertility rate; the high capital–labour ratio may persist. Thus, countries that are identical in their fundamentals but differ in their initial level of physical capital may converge to different steady-state equilibria in terms of output *per capita* and fertility rates.

---

[14] In a related contribution, Benhabib and Rustichini (1996) demonstrate that in the presence of social conflict over the distribution of income, low initial level of wealth may persist due to its effect on the incentives for accumulation.

3 ROBUSTNESS OF CLUB CONVERGENCE

This section examines the robustness of the club convergence hypothesis in the presence of international capital movements and technological progress.

3.1 International capital mobility

The existence of perfect international capital movements eliminates the importance of initial conditions in neoclassical growth models in which the evolution of the economy is dictated uniquely by the evolution of the capital–labour ratio.[15] Thus, in light of the presence of some movements of capital across countries, one may view this observation as an element that weakens the club convergence hypothesis.[16] However, in more realistic settings, where the evolution of the economy is based upon the evolution of human capital as well as physical capital, international movements of capital will not resolve the dependency of an economy on initial conditions with respect to human capital. Hence, since human capital is not perfectly mobile across countries, and since the parental–environmental effects on human capital formation are immobile across families, club convergence remains a viable and plausible hypothesis. As documented in Galor and Zeira (1993), in the presence of capital market imperfections in the domestic economy, multiple steady-state equilibria will prevail despite perfect international capital movements; and as argued in Galor and Tsiddon (1994), perfect capital mobility does not preclude multiple steady-state equilibria in an environment where the parental effect is a factor in the offspring's production of human capital.

3.2 Technological progress and technological diffusion

Labour-augmenting technological progress does not affect the qualitative nature of dynamical systems in the neoclassical growth models, and the conditions that lead to a club convergence hypothesis remain intact. However, in some augmented growth models technological progress may turn a system, that under a given level of technology, is characterised by multiple locally stable steady-state equilibria, into one characterised by a unique globally stable steady-state equilibrium. Conditional convergence will be observed in these models in the long-run. Nevertheless, provided that for some technological level the system is characterised by multiple steady state equilibria, the transition to the long-run steady-state is associated with non-monotonic evolution of the distribution of income across countries (e.g. Galor and Tsiddon (1994)). Thus, convergence may be preceded by polarisation and clustering, and club convergence will be generated by these models in the medium run. As depicted in Fig. 3, given the

---

[15] However, if the production function exhibits locally increasing returns to scale, then a single interest rate may be associated with several wage rates and, despite perfect capital mobility, economies may experience persistent differences in output *per capita*.

[16] One may argue, however, that in light of the arguments raised by Lucas (1990), this effect is not very significant.

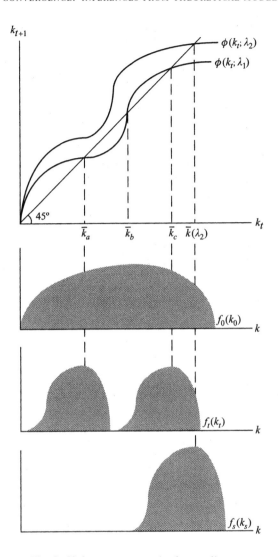

Fig. 3 Club convergence in the medium run

technological parameter λ_1, the dynamical system is characterised by multiple steady-state equilibria. However, technological progress increases the technological parameter to λ_2 and shifts the dynamical system upward. The dynamical system changes qualitatively and the number of non-trivial steady-state equilibria is reduced to one. Consequently, the cross-country distribution of capital–labour ratios evolves non-monotonically and polarisation in period t is followed by convergence as depicted for a later period, s.

4 CONCLUDING REMARKS

This essay suggests that the convergence controversy may reflect, in part, differences in perception regarding the viable set of testable hypotheses that existing theories of economic growth have generated. An empirical resolution of the debate therefore necessitates a better understanding of the range of competing testable hypotheses generated from plausible growth models. It is argued that the current hegemony of the conditional convergence hypothesis may be attributed in part to insufficient familiarity with its theoretical non-robustness. In contrast to conventional wisdom, the essay demonstrates that an economic system may be characterised by multiple steady-state equilibria and may thus lead to club convergence even in traditional neoclassical growth models that exhibit diminishing marginal productivity of capital and constant returns to scale. Furthermore, the inclusion of empirically significant variables such as human capital, income distribution, and fertility in conventional growth models, along with capital market imperfections, externalities and non-convexities, strengthens the viability of multiple steady-state equilibria and presents club convergence as a competing hypothesis with conditional convergence.

References

Aghion, P. and Bolton, P. (1996). 'A trickle-down theory of growth and development with debt-overhang.' *Review of Economic Studies* (forthcoming).

Alesina, A. and Rodrik, D. (1994). 'Distributive politics and economic growth.' *Quarterly Journal of Economics*, vol. 109, pp. 465–90.

Azariadis, C. (1996). 'The economics of development traps.' *Journal of Economic Growth* (forthcoming).

Azariadis, C. and Drazen, A. (1990). 'Threshold externalities in economic development.' *Quarterly Journal of Economics*, vol. 105, pp. 501–26.

Barro, R. J. (1991). 'Economic growth in a cross section of countries.' *Quarterly Journal of Economics*, vol. 106, pp. 407–44.

Barro, R. J. and Becker, G. S. (1989). 'Fertility choice in a model of economic growth.' *Econometrica*, vol. 57, pp. 481–501.

Barro, R. J. and Sala-i-Martin, X. (1995). *Economic Growth.* McGraw-Hill.

Baumol, W. (1986). 'Productivity growth, convergence and welfare.' *American Economic Review*, vol. 76, pp. 1072–85.

Becker, G. S., Murphy, K. M. and Tamura, R. (1990). 'Human capital, fertility, and economic growth.' *Journal of Political Economy*, vol. 98, pp. S12–37.

Benabou, R. (1996). 'Equity and efficiency in human capital investment: the local connection.' *Review of Economic Studies* (forthcoming).

Benhabib, J. and Rustichini, A. (1996). 'Social conflict and growth.' *Journal of Economic Growth*, vol. 1, pp. 125–42.

De Long, B. (1988). 'Productivity growth, convergence and welfare: Comment.' *American Economic Review*, vol. 78, pp. 1138–54.

Durlauf, N. S. (1993). 'Nonergodic economic growth.' *Review of Economic Studies*, vol. 60, pp. 349–67.

Durlauf, N. S. (1996). 'A theory of persistent income inequality.' *Journal of Economic Growth*, vol. 1, pp. 75–94.

Durlauf, N. S. and Johnson, P. (1995). 'Multiple regimes and cross country growth behaviour.' *Journal of Applied Econometrics* (forthcoming).

Galor, O. (1992). 'A two sector overlapping-generations model: a global characterization of the dynamical system.' *Econometrica*, vol. 60, pp. 1351–86.

Galor, O. (1996). 'Heterogeneity and club convergence in growth models.' Brown University.

Galor, O. and Ryder, H. E. (1989). 'Existence, uniqueness and stability of equilibrium in an overlapping-generations model with productive capital.' *Journal of Economic Theory*, vol. 49, pp. 360–75.

Galor, O. and Tsiddon, D. (1994). 'Human capital distribution, technological progress, and economic growth,' CEPR Working Paper No 971.

Galor, O. and Weil, D. N. (1996). 'The gender gap, fertility, and growth.' *American Economic Review* vol. 86 (June).

Galor, O. and Zeira, J. (1993). 'Income distribution and macroeconomics.' *Review of Economic Studies*, vol. 60, pp. 35–52.

Lucas, R. E. Jr. (1988). 'On the mechanics of economic development.' *Journal of Monetary Economics*, vol. 22, pp. 3–42.

Lucas, R. E. Jr. (1990). 'Why doesn't capital flow from rich to poor countries? *American Economic Review*, vol. 80, pp. 92–6.

Mankiw, N., Romer, D. and Weil, D. N. (1992). 'A contribution to the empirics of economic growth.' *Quarterly Journal of Economics*, vol. 107, pp. 407–37.

Murphy, K., Shleifer, A. and Vishny, R. (1989). 'Industrialization and the big push.' *Journal of Political Economy*, vol. 97, pp. 1003–26.

Perotti, R. (1996). 'Growth, income distribution and democracy: what the data says.' *Journal of Economic Growth* (forthcoming).

Persson, T. and Tabellini, G. (1994). 'Is inequality harmful for growth? Theory and evidence.' *American Economic Review*, vol. 84, pp. 600–21.

Quah, D. (1996). 'Convergence empirics across countries with (some) capital mobility.' *Journal of Economic Growth*, vol. 1, pp. 95–124.

Ramsey, F. P. (1928). 'A mathematical theory of savings.' *Economic Journal*, vol. 38, pp. 543–59.

Romer, P. M. (1986). 'Increasing returns and long-run growth.' *Journal of Political Economy*, vol. 94, pp. 1002–37.

Solow, R. (1956). 'A contribution to the theory of economic growth'. *Quarterly Journal of Economics*, vol. 70, pp. 65–94.

Tsiddon, D. (1992). 'A moral hazard trap to growth.' *International Economic Review*, vol. 33, pp. 299–322.

Part 2

Trade Liberalisation and Growth

INTRODUCTION

Huw D. Dixon

One of the most striking features of the economic environment of the past two decades has been the extent of trade liberalisation in developing countries. Around 100 countries in all parts of the globe have undertaken unilateral trade reforms of one form or another. Some of these have been voluntary, most have been promoted by the two key multilateral lending agencies, the World Bank and IMF. Both have lending programmes where loan advances are conditional on policy reform and trade policy is a favoured target. The reason for the emphasis on reform of trade policy is quite simple: a belief that liberalisation is conductive to growth. But is it?

In the first paper Anne Krueger argues that it most definitely is. She begins by explaining the close link between trade policy and overall development strategy and the follies of relying upon import substitution as a basis for industrialisation. Not only does this inflict static costs on the economy by way of resource misallocation but also dynamic costs through rising incremental capital: output ratios and exclusion from new technology. By contrast when trade policy is outer oriented the externalities and productivity enhancing benefits identified by new growth theory can be exploited. The transition from inward orientation to outward orientation can only be effected through liberalisation.

In the second paper Lance Taylor and Jose Antonio Campo challenge this view on the grounds that the standard neo-classical view is both incomplete and naïve. They argue that the standard microeconomic conditions which underpin the 'liberalisation leads to growth' position rarely hold in practice and once brings in increasing returns and productivity enhancing investment the standard case breaks down. Moreover, they also point out that standard liberalisation packages can have highly regressive effects. They conclude by arguing that it is a mistake to simply try to generalise from the Asian experience.

In the final paper David Greenway, Wyn Morgan and Peter Wright turn to the evidence. In reviewing previous work they point out its inconclusiveness and explain this by reference to the complications associated with empirically measuring liberalisation and the range of methodologies used in the literature. They try to 'encompass' the previous literature by estimating a new growth model on a large panel of developing countries, using a range of alternative methodologies for capturing trade liberalisation. The results are illuminating. They suggest that liberalisation does indeed impact favourably on growth but not in a wholly straightforward way. In particular, there may be a 'J curve' type of adjustment at work. Among other things this implies that previous work may have failed to capture the growth effect because it failed to model the dynamics adequately.

5
WHY TRADE LIBERALISATION IS GOOD FOR GROWTH*

Anne O. Krueger

There are three titles that might have been assigned for this paper: 1) Why Is Growth so Rapid with Outer-Oriented Trade Strategies?; 2) Do Countries with Outer-Oriented Trade Strategies Grow Faster? and 3) the one actually assigned. They are not the same. Of the three, the first is probably the most difficult to answer. The second is a factual question, and the empirical demonstration is straightforward (Sachs and Warner, 1995). The third, by focusing on trade liberalisation, implies that developing countries have highly restrictive trade regimes and thus asks if a move away from those regimes is good for growth. It is far easier to show why, especially over time, liberalising a restrictive trade regime is conducive to more rapid growth than it is to show why outer-oriented trade strategies have been so highly successful.

Trade strategies and development strategies are closely related, and it is useful to start by defining a few terms. An import-substitution (IS) industrialisation strategy was adopted by most developing countries in the years following the Second World War. In most cases those countries were then predominantly agricultural and exporters of primary commodities.

The belief then was that rapid industrialisation was the essential (if not the sole) feature of economic growth and that only by domestically producing goods then imported could developing countries industrialise.[1] Under IS, it was intended to provide protection to new industries during their developmental period until they could compete with their counterparts in industrialised countries. In practice, the IS strategy pulled most new resources into import-competing activites (with a number of negative consequences discussed later) and one result was that export earnings grew less rapidly than the demand for foreign exchange and usually less rapidly even than real GDP.

An almost universal policy response was then to impose restrictive import licensing in response to 'foreign exchange shortage'. The stated reasons for this were the need to 'conserve scarce foreign exchange' for 'essential' developmental needs. The outcome was, of course, a restrictive trade regime. For reasons to be discussed below, as IS strategies continued, trade regimes increased in restrictiveness and growth slowed.

Hence, to discuss trade liberalisation is to address the removal (or at least reduction)

* I am indebted to Philip Levy for helpful comments on an earlier draft of this paper.
[1] See Krueger (1997) and the references therein for a fuller statement of the logic behind the IS policies.

of incentives for IS industrialisation. And, because – again to be discussed below – growth spurred under an IS industrialisation strategy slows down over time, trade liberalisation is therefore associated with more rapid growth than the final phases of IS which precede it. It was and is in response to this phenomenon that trade liberalisation offers the only known way to escape from the ever-slowing growth rates of developing countries. Many liberalisation episodes in fact take place in response to economic crisis.[2]

By contrast, by the early 1960s a few then-developing countries[3] – most notably Korea, Taiwan, Hong Kong and Singapore – had abandoned import substitution and adopted outer-oriented trade strategies. The results were spectacularly rapid growth.

By outer-oriented is meant a trade strategy that is *not* biassing incentives in favour of import-competing industries and that provides roughly equal incentives to all exporting activities. Thus, an exporter shipping goods for $1 million of foreign exchange can expect to receive approximately the same amount of local currency regardless of the nature of the goods actually shipped.

It is important, in this regard, to note that outer-oriented does *not* mean more incentives for producing for export than for the domestic market. It does, however, imply relatively uniform across-the-board incentives for exports, and that the growth and industrialisation strategy relies on rapid growth of exports.

It should now be evident why the three questions differ. There is no doubt that the countries following outer-oriented strategies grew faster. Moreover, even among larger samples of countries, there is no question that more rapid growth of exports is associated with a more rapid rate of growth of real GDP.

There are, however, questions about why the East Asian economies grew more rapidly. These focus on issues such as whether productivity growth was more rapid in East Asia,[4] how much the government intervened in the market,[5] and other policies that were complementary to the outer-oriented trade strategy. It is for that reason that an article on why an outer-oriented trade strategy is so successful would be more difficult than one on why trade liberalisation is desirable. We know an outer-oriented trade strategy has led to more rapid growth, but there are arguments as to exactly why.

1 TRADE STRATEGIES AND DEVELOPMENT

Trade policy is integrally tied up with overall development strategy. Although we have learned through painful experience that productivity and output growth in agricul-

---

[2] See Little et al. (1996) and Michaely et al. (1993) and the individual studies on which they are based.
[3] These all had very low per capita incomes in the 1950s. Korea was estimated to have one of the lowest per capita incomes in Asia. Korea and Taiwan both followed policies of import substitution in the 1950s, and then changed to outer oriented trade policies in the 1960s. Singapore's history with regard to early trade strategy is somewhat more murky because it did not separate from Malaya until 1965. Hong Kong, of course, followed a laissez-faire policy continuously. The world Bank now classifies Korea, Hong Kong and Singapore as high-income countries. See World Bank (1997), pp. 214–5. Taiwan is not included in the Bank's *World Tables*, but has a higher per capita income than Korea.
[4] See Young, (1992) and (1994).
[5] See World Bank (1993) for one view.

ture, services, and manufacturing are all essential for growth, and that overemphasis on any subset of economic activities is almost certain to result in retarding the development process, the linkages between trade policy and development-cum-industrialisation strategy are crucial.

First, development does entail more rapid changes in economic structure (from agriculture to industry, from household production to market production, and so on) than does continuing growth in developed countries. Moreover, developing countries typically depend on imports for the preponderance of manufactured goods used domestically and are, at least in initial stages of development, highly specialised.[6] Consequently, there is even greater sensitivity to trade policy than in developed countries: protection of some industries, and especially high protection, will pull resources, and especially new resources, into those industries and out of disprotected industries. Thus, whereas an increase or decrease in protection in developed countries normally results in changes at the margin in the composition of output, in developing countries the structure of protection (or lack thereof) virtually determines the direction in which new resources are allocated and, in the context of low income countries, therefore the entire pattern of production, especially in manufacturing.

Second, developing countries have production patterns which are skewed toward labour-intensive services, agriculture, and manufacturing. In accordance with comparative advantage, they import most capital-intensive goods and services. Since the latter category includes many investment and intermediate goods, developing countries' growth is contingent upon their ability to import those goods and services. When, instead, they confront relatively slow growth of foreign exchange earnings, they substitute domestically produced goods at higher cost for these capital-intensive items. Not only does this substitution process pull resources out of labour-intensive areas (such as textiles and clothing) where comparative advantage resides, but it implies slower growth because a given fraction of national income saved implies a lower level of real investment as the prices of capital goods are higher.

Third, because people have such low per capita incomes, most developing countries' markets are relatively small, outside of food and housing. Protection of production activities in these small markets results in a dilemma: either the number of firms producing a given good must be very small, or the size of individual plants may well be below minimum efficient size. If the number of firms is very small, the absence of competition results in low-quality high-cost production over and above that resulting from comparative disadvantage as producers have monopoly or quasi-monopoly positions. If the number of firms is large, each one is producing on a very small scale with consequent higher costs. By contrast, a liberalised trade regime permits low-cost producers to expand their output well beyond that demanded in the domestic market. Whereas industrialisation based on protection of domestic industries thus results in ever-higher capital intensity of production (as the 'easy import substitution' phase is exhausted), the open trade regime permits enjoyment of constant returns to scale over a much wider range.[7]

Fourth, because import substitution policies pull new resources (and even existing

---

[6] This is both because of their factor endowment which typically lies well away from the world mean and also because of the small size of their domestic markets (discussed further below).
[7] See Ventura (1997) on this.

resources from agriculture) into import-substitution industries, export growth lags, if exports do not decline absolutely. Import substitution itself is import intensive, both because rising rates of investment in 'modern industries' have a high component of imported goods and because many IS industries rely on imports of intermediate goods and raw materials. Hence, the demand for foreign exchange for imports grows at a rate normally well in excess of GDP while the supply of foreign exchange from exports grows more slowly. The authorities have typically been reluctant to increase the price of foreign exchange, believing that doing so would make goods 'essential for development' more expensive. The result has been an ever-widening gap between the demand and the supply of foreign exchange at the prevailing official exchange rate. The authorities' response has been to move to ever more restrictive import licensing and exchange controls (the latter so that exporters will not be able to keep their earnings abroad) along with increasing black market activity and smuggling.[8] At some point, the negative effects were sufficiently undesirable that policy makers adopted a stabilisation programme. This resulted in a stop-go pattern of economic activity, itself with negative effects on the overall growth rate.[9]

Fifth, because of its centrality, decisions with respect to trade policy almost force a number of other policies. Import substitution regimes normally give bureaucrats considerable discretion either in determining which industries should be encouraged or in allocating scarce foreign exchange in a regime of quantitative restrictions. Open trade regimes force much greater reliance on the market, if for no other reason than that bureaucrats cannot very effectively force foreigners to accede to their edicts.

That, under import-substitution regimes, bureaucrats have control over import licensing implies great power over all producers, not only producers of tradables. It typically makes all foreign exchange scarce, thus inducing the imposition of additional regulations (to 'conserve scarce foreign exchange'). One consequence is a major temptation to corruption. Another is a belief that all producers are cheating (which may be true), which in turn leads to additional scrutiny of import licensing applications, delays in receiving needed imports, and other production inefficiencies.

Sixth, as import substitution continues, most regimes become increasingly complex. The costs of the regime, and the likely costs and benefits of alternative choices, become increasingly less transparent to decision-makers. Additional governmental resources become engaged in attempting to make the licensing system work, almost always to the detriment of other essential government functions, including the development of infrastructure.[10]

---

[8] The nominal exchange rate typically is altered at times of 'foreign exchange crisis', which happened to most countries periodically under import substitution. Those alterations were typically 'too little, too late', and, while providing for some liberalisation of trade regimes in the short run, did nothing to alter the underlying policy stance toward IS. Over the longer run, the restrictiveness of the trade regime increased. See Krueger (1978) for a discussion.

[9] See Diaz Alejandro (1978) for the argument.

[10] The inadequacy of transport and communications facilities in developing countries that have followed import-substitution policies is well known. The precise mechanisms that result in their inadequacy are not clear. It is evident, however, that – almost by definition – a liberalised trade regime cannot persist unless ports, roads, and communications are adequate to service a large and rapidly growing volume of trade. Bottlenecks become visible very quickly.

2 STATIC INEFFICIENCIES OF IMPORT SUBSTITUTION

Even if all that IS did was to misallocate resources and result in static inefficiency, the gains from liberalising might be sufficient so that the growth rate accelerated for a period of years. If, for example, the resource cost of static misallocations were 20% of GDP and it required 5 years after liberalisation to reallocate resources appropriately, the realised growth rate would be between 3 and 4 percentage points higher during the transition to the more efficient growth path because of gains in economic efficiency.

If, in fact, growth is at a standstill prior to the liberalisation effort, the apparent gain can be even greater.[11] Static sources of loss include the production cost of trade distortions, the losses associated with rent-seeking for import licenses and corruption, the losses associated with delays and other costs imposed by quantitative restrictions, and the losses associated with producers' monopoly positions in the domestic market.[12] The total far exceeds the production cost,[13] the trade theoretic measure defined as the difference in the international value added under existing incentives and that which could be achieved under a regime that more accurately reflected international marginal rates of substitution between goods.

3 DYNAMIC COSTS OF IS

However, it would appear that the dynamic losses under IS far outweigh the static losses. That is ironic, because the early arguments for IS always were based on the assertion that, while comparative advantage showed that free trade was superior from a 'static resource allocation' viewpoint, dynamic considerations (presumably derived from the infant industry notion) outweighed the static, and tilted the balance in favour of IS.

In practice, the outer-oriented trade strategies win the dynamic gains argument easily because IS strategies were and are associated with increasing costs and slowing growth over time.

There are a number of reasons for this, many of them emanating from phenomena already described. First of all, if a country embarks on an IS strategy, the 'easy' IS

---

[11] A large number of countries have reversed slow growth for a period of years after liberalisation. For example, the Turkish rate of economic growth in the 1956–58 period was about 2–3% annually. After liberalisation in 1958–60, growth averaged around 7% for the next 7 years. The same pattern was observed after the 1980 Turkish liberalisation. In Ghana, real GDP was declining at 1–2% annually prior to the 1984 structural adjustment programme began. It averaged around 5% a year for the next half decade or more.

[12] One frequently encounters the argument that countries cannot liberalise their trade regimes because they depend upon tariff revenues for support of their fiscal programmes. In fact, when quantitative restrictions and import prohibitions are the mechanisms by which excess demand is suppressed, there is scope for trade liberalisation accompanied by *increased* government revenue at lower rates of protection through tariffs or their QR-equivalents.

[13] See Johnson (1960) for a rigorous definition of the production costs of a tariff.

opportunities will likely be largely exploited first. These opportunities may lie relatively close to the country's comparative advantage.[14] As the IS proceeds and the 'easy' opportunities are already exploited, the new activities induced by protection would lie further away from comparative advantage. For developing countries with relative abundances of relatively unskilled labour, lying further away from comparative advantage means more human- and physical-capital using activities. This, in turn, means rising incremental capital–labour ratios. For a given savings and investment rate, that implies a declining rate of economic growth.

In addition to rising capital–labour ratios because new activities are more capital-using, the fact that the domestic market for many industrial commodities can be small further intensifies the problem. Once such relatively widely-consumed (at low income levels) items as shoes, clothing, and radios are produced, the size of the market for other manufactured goods can dwindle rapidly. Underutilised pieces of capital equipment (because either of indivisibilities or because of multiple products) also contribute to increasing incremental capital–output ratios and hence reduced growth rates.[15]

Other factors also contribute. The stop-go pattern, described above, clearly reduced growth rates. So, too, did increasing corruption and greater smuggling in response to larger black market premiums. One can even argue that the tension between the private sector and government officials rose over time.

In recent years, the focus on endogenous growth has pointed to another source of reduced growth rates under IS. It focuses on the opportunities for growth through use of ideas, and knowledge capital. Here, the argument is that imports provide domestic producers and consumers with new ideas (which are an externality) and that the restriction of imports (in response to lower export earnings) reduces the growth rate by reducing the rate at which people accumulate and use knowledge capital.[16]

To be sure, *anything* that is a property of trade that leads to an endogenous growth mechanism could equally well account for differences in growth rates between alternative trade strategies. It might be that exporters acquire more knowledge by their interaction with foreign buyers than do producers for the domestic market. Or learning by doing might take place more rapidly in export industries. But that countries whose economies are relatively more insulated from international trade do seem to fall behind in production techniques, quality, and other attributes of production associated with knowledge and new goods seems evident. It remains to determine how this source of growth might be quantified.

Finally, feedback mechanisms to policy makers under IS seem weaker than those under outer-oriented regimes. The obvious point is that the tariff equivalent of import quotas or prohibitions is not known. But there are others. With import licensing, policy makers are less sensitive to the degree of overvaluation of the exchange rate

---

[14] This appears empirically to have been roughly the pattern actually followed. However, in theory, a would-be producer, deciding upon which activity to undertake, would consider not only his costs relative to prices of imports, but also the degree of monopoly power he would attain. This latter would not necessarily be correlated with the excess of domestic production costs over world prices.

[15] In fact, developing countries' savings rates rose dramatically from the 1950s to the 1980s, while growth rates on average did not. See World Bank (1983).

[16] See Grossman and Helpman (1991).

than they are under outer-oriented trade regimes, where diminishing rates of export growth serve as a signal that things are not going well, and pressures rise from export interests (which relatively are more important and more influential than under IS) to adjust the exchange rate. The high costs of poor infrastructure are less evident than under a more open trade regime, and those costs spill over far beyond the tradable goods activities in an economy.

4 NEED FOR SUPPORTING POLICIES

While most countries liberalise from an initial situation that is sufficiently extreme so that gains are almost inevitable, trade policy does not operate in a vacuum. Other policies supporting trade liberalisation may be necessary and in any event can greatly increase the benefits.

The most obvious such policy pertains to exchange rate determination. The move from a regime in which quantitative restrictions have restrained foreign exchange expenditures to foreign exchange availability to one in which producers and consumers are to be free to choose at prevailing prices requires an adjustment of the nominal exchange rate. In fact, even if one moved from a regime in which there had been a uniform tariff of $x\%$ to one in which the tariff was $0.5x$, an alteration in the nominal exchange rate would be called for.[17]

There have been a number of instances where trade liberalisation was not accompanied by a change, or at least a meaningful change, in the nominal exchange rate. In such circumstances, excess demand for foreign exchange has once again emerged and the authorities must either adjust the exchange rate or reimpose quantitative restrictions. Until they do so, however, incentives for domestic production of import substitutes have fallen while there has been no increased incentive for production of exportables (whose price remains unchanged in domestic currency as long as the nominal exchange rate is unaltered) or for production of home goods. The result is often a period during which the level of economic activity declines. Such a period not only leads to output losses, but also to political pressures to reverse the liberalisation.

Often, too, other regulations are built into the system which buttress quantitative restrictions. If they are not removed when an attempt at import liberalisation is made, the entire effort can be thwarted.[18]

---

[17] Of course, as an alternative, one could always subject the domestic economy to deflation, but in most instances that would require a period of domestic recession until expectations as to the price level adjusted. It should be noted that removal of quantitative restrictions is in itself deflationary, but the additional imports accompanying the liberalisation would have to be financed by additional foreign exchange earnings, which must be induced by the exchange rate adjustment (or by an absolute drop in the price of nontradable goods as well as the domestic price of imports).

[18] An example will illustrate. In India in the mid-1980s, an effort was made to liberalise imports by removing licensing requirements under certain circumstances. But producers sometimes found that when they wanted, e.g. state government licenses to operate, they had to show their documents from national investment licensing officials, which in turn were contingent upon approval by the import authorities.

Beyond the policy mistakes which prevent accelerated growth from starting or persisting after liberalisation, there are a number of policies whose alteration can greatly enhance the gains. It was already mentioned that infrastructure inadequacies become glaringly apparent with an open trade regime. Often, the evidence has been sufficient to convince leaders that improvements must be made.

Other growth-inhibiting policies can also usefully be altered. These include, but are by no means limited to, labour market regulations, policies favouring procurement by public sector enterprises, reform of tax laws and/or administration, and changes in agricultural pricing policies.

In most instances, failure to address these issues results in smaller gains from trade liberalisation than would otherwise have occurred. But in extreme cases, policies may be so restrictive that little can happen before they, too, are altered.

5 WHAT DIFFERENCES ARE THERE BETWEEN TRADE LIBERALISATION AND OUTER-ORIENTED TRADE STRATEGY?

As stated at the outset, explaining why outer-oriented economies have achieved such high rates of economic growth is subject to considerable debate. Answers range all the way from high productivity growth (which might result from endogenous growth theoretic bases), to getting *all* the policies (not only prices) right, clever government intervention, to laissez-faire policies, to good luck.

That argument cannot be resolved here. But one can, at least, address the difference between simply liberalising the trade regime and moving to an outer-oriented trade policy. Liberalisation is, by definition, the action of making a trade regime less restrictive.

There are always benefits to liberalisation, although their size may depend on many things. But clearly one could not expect to achieve an outer-oriented trade regime simply by replacing quotas with tariffs[19] or increasing the size of quotas.

An outer-oriented trade strategy is one in which the development strategy itself is based on the growth of domestic economic activity in response to producer incentives that closely mirror international prices. As such, it is expected that rapid growth of industry will occur (as agricultural productivity rises) as producers find their best alternatives in the global economy. That means that policy makers must focus on delivering adequate transport and communications, permitting imports for exporters at world prices, and going well beyond simply the easing or removal of restrictions on imports. If one ignores the variance across commodities, one can define the bias of a trade regime as the extent to which the ratio of domestic prices of import-competing goods to their international prices relative to the ratio of the domestic prices of exportables relative to their international prices deviates from unity. An outer-oriented trade regime is one where the deviation is small, while an IS regime is one in which it is larger.

---

[19] The empirical evidence, however, is that efforts to replace quotas with tariff equivalents seems nonetheless to reduce protection. This was found in several of the countries reported upon in Krueger (1978), including Egypt and the Philippines.

Trade liberalisation clearly implies a reduction in the bias of the regime. Moving to an outer-oriented trade strategy implies moving to a very small, or even zero, deviation. Turkey liberalised the trade regime in 1958–60 and again in 1970. Turkey then moved to an outer-oriented trade strategy in 1980–3.

6 CONCLUSION

There is much still to be learned about trade liberalisation, the best means of achieving an outer-oriented trade regime, and the reasons for the very rapid growth that the outer-oriented economies have achieved. But the reason why trade liberalisation delivers more rapid growth is that IS, over time, becomes a failed strategy. As such, any significant degree of relaxation of restrictiveness can result in gains, unless there are other policies in effect in the economy that thwart their impact.

Trade liberalisation undertaken from a period of declining growth rates or even falling real GDP can normally lead to a period of growth above the rates previously realised. It cannot, however, lead to sustained growth at the sorts of high rates achieved by the truly outer-oriented economies unless policy makers adopt far reaching measures that effectively provide incentives within the tradables sector at world prices and thus an outer-oriented trade regime.

References

Diaz Alejandro, Carlos, (1978). *Foreign Trade Regimes and Economic Development: Colombia.* New York: Columbia University Press.

Grossman, Gene and Helpman, Elhanan (1991). Innovation and Growth in the World Economy. Cambridge, MA: MIT Press.

Johnson, Harry G., (1960). 'The cost of protection and the scientific tariff', *Journal of Political Economy,* vol 68, no. 4. August, pp. 327–45.

Krueger, Anne O., (1978). *Foreign Trade Regimes and Economic Development: Liberalisation Attempts and Consequences,* Lexington, MA: Ballinger Press.

Krueger, Anne O., (1997). 'Trade policy and economic development: how we learn', *American Economic Review,* vol. 87. no. 1, March, pp. 1–22.

Little. I. M. D., Cooper, Richard N., Corden, W. Max and Rajapatirana, Sarath., (1996). *Boom, Crisis, and Adjustment. The Macroeconomic Experience of Developing Countries.* Oxford and New York: Oxford University Press.

Michaely, Michael, Papageorgiou, Demetris and Choksi, Armeane M. (1993). *Lessons of Experience in the Developing World,* Volume 7 of Michaely et al, editors, *Liberalizing Foreign Trade,* Oxford: Basil Blackwell.

Sachs, Jeffrey and Warner, Andrew (1995). 'Economic Reform and the Process of Global Integration', Brookings Papers on Economic Activity, no. 1, pp. 1–118.

Ventura, Jaume, (1997). 'Growth and interdependence', *Quarterly Journal of Economics,* vol. 112(1), February, pp. 57–84.

World Bank, (1983). *World Development Report,* Oxford and New York: Oxford University Press.

World Bank, (1993). *The East Asian Miracle,* Oxford and New York: Oxford University Press.

World Bank, (1997). *World Development Report,* Oxford and New York: Oxford University Press.

Young, Alwyn, (1992). 'A tale of two cities: factor accumulation and technical change in Hong

Kong and Singapore', in (Olivier Blanchard and Stanley Fischer, eds), *NBER Macroeconomics Annual,* Cambridge MA: MIT Press, pp. 13–54.

Young, Alwyn, (1994). 'Lessons from East Asian NICs: a contrarian view', *European Economic Review.* vol. 38, no. 3–4. (April) pp. 964–73.

6

TRADE LIBERALISATION IN DEVELOPING ECONOMIES: MODEST BENEFITS BUT PROBLEMS WITH PRODUCTIVITY GROWTH, MACRO PRICES, AND INCOME DISTRIBUTION*

Jose A. Ocampo and Lance Taylor

Microeconomically, the case for liberalisation is dubious under increasing returns to scale and when firms can invest directly in productivity enhancement. Distributional effects of commercial policy changes can be regressive and large, but the 'rents' they generate can serve as a basis for effective policy intervention contingent on firms performance. Macroeconomically, the case of liberalisation rests on Say's Law, which is not always enforced. Recent combined current and capital market liberalisations have been associated with strong exchange rates and high interest rates and output and productivity growth have positive mutual feedbacks which liberalisation may well suppress.

Disentangling the effects of trade liberalisation in developing countries is no easy task. Recent moves toward deregulation have often been accompanied by macroeconomic stabilisation packages and removal of controls on international capital movements, and have had visible effects on income and wealth distributions. In any serious assessment the pure theory of international trade, open economy macroeconomics in its 'tropical' version, and a large dose of political economy must come in. To begin, it makes sense to review and criticise what received theory says about the determinants and outcomes of trade flows, first at the microeconomic and then at the macro level.

1 MICROECONOMICS

To this day, as Krueger's (1997) American Economic Association Presidential Address makes clear, the preferred defence of trade liberalisation invokes a general equilib-

* The authors write solely in their personal capacities, and acknowledge research support from the Center for Economic Policy Analysis, New School for Social Research.

rium model with constant or decreasing returns to scale, built upon the choices of individual agents interacting solely through the market. There is competition in the sense that the agents are price takers, rationally arriving at the usual marginal conditions. When they are partitioned into 'countries' by restrictions on their access to resources, standard notions of static comparative advantage emerge, with trade patterns determined by technology differences in Ricardian models and resource endowments in Heckscher–Ohlin. Insofar as this theory describes observed specialisations in trade, it applies best to sectors or countries in which traditional inputs such as natural resources and/or unskilled labour predominate. Or, to tell the story the other way, once such 'bargain' competitive advantages run out, their replacements in the form of infant import-substituting (IS) and export industries have to be created. Historically, in most countries both the private sector and the state have had a hand in this process.

1.1 Traditional arguments against trade interventions

Leaving aside such dynamic considerations for the moment, the argument for liberalisation in the static framework boils down to the second theorem of welfare economics, as Chakravarty and Singh (1988) make clear: any Pareto-optimal allocation can be realised as a competitive equilibrium in the presence of all-around 'convexity' provided that suitable lump-sum transfers can be arranged among all participants. Trade distortions imposed upon an otherwise competitive allocation create welfare (and presumably output) losses by driving it away from Pareto optimality.

This first line of defence of economic liberalism is not unbreached, as the whole world recognises. It is interesting to observe the back-up positions regarding scale economies, non-competitive market structures, and the magnitudes of liberalisation benefits that trade theorists have set up in recent decades.

With regard to decreasing costs of increasing returns to scale, the widely shared opinion is that they are ubiquitous in manufacturing and present in other sectors. The existence of such non-convexities invalidates the second welfare theorem and renders the existence of Walrasian equilibrium suspect. Young (1928) and Kaldor (1978) emphasised how increasing returns and cross-firm externalities can lead to cumulative growth processes and different patterns of specialisation across economies. At the industry and enterprise levels, changing 'advantage' is likely to be the rule, as suppliers' input prices shift and differential rates of productivity growth modify cost structures. To a degree, policy can guide such changes.[1]

---

[1] Amsden (1989) draws interesting comparisons among future East Asian miracle economies in the 1950s. At a financially sustainable nominal exchange rate, Hong Kong's wages were low enough to give the city-state an absolute advantage in garment production; for the first couple of decades the colony's rapid output growth was based squarely on cheap labour, its export markets 'protected' from incursion by other producers by pre-existing quota rights. Unlike Hong Kong, South Korea and Taiwan historically had specialised in textiles. With the technologies they had at hand, they could not compete, i.e. their yen-equivalent wage levels were *not* low enough to let them undersell Japan. Hence they initially had to subsidise the capital used in textile production (Amsden's famous recommendation to 'get prices wrong') and push for high productivity growth by hands-on industrial policy. In more recent times. South China's export boom has in many ways resulted from an amalgamation of the Hong Kong and Korea/Taiwan strategies.

The main response to decreasing costs on the part of mainstream 'new' trade theory has been to muffle the impact of scale economies by 'convexifying' assumptions, e.g. the Dixit–Stiglitz (1977) model of monopolistic competition in which firms' profitability gains from returns to scale are strictly limited by consumers' desires for product diversity. Protection to force big cost reductions from long product runs cannot pay off. It makes little sense to introduce one more yuppie automobile marque if its intended consumers' preferences for diversity are going to limit sales to an uneconomical 100,000 units per year.

The older literature on development economics, by contrast, recognised that there can be room for substantial benefits from establishing industries with scale economies, especially when transport costs and other factors drive wedges between border prices of imports and exports (Scitovsky, 1954). Moreover, 'local' project analysis undertaken with the current vector of relative prices is not an adequate guide for choosing investments which can radically switch cost structures.

Fig. 1 illustrates these points in a 'buy/make/sell' diagram for an industry open to foreign trade. The prices at which the commodity in question can be imported and exported are P_m and P_e respectively. The domestic supply curve for low levels of output

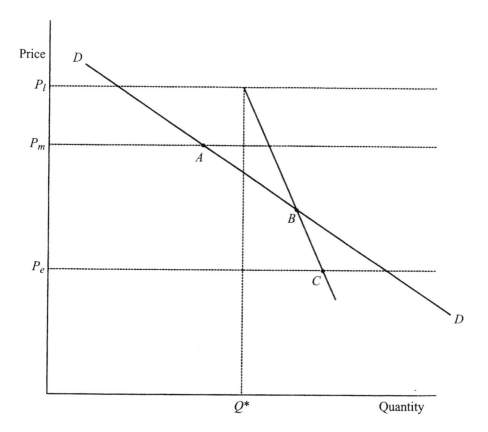

Fig. 1 The buy/make/sell decision in partial equilibrium

Q is flat – the price sticks at P_l. However, for levels of output above Q^*, an increasing returns technology becomes profitable (perhaps with a jump in Q as techniques shift), and the price falls along a downward-sloping supply curve.

For low levels of domestic demand along curve DD, the import price lies well below domestic production cost, and it makes no sense to import-substitute the good. Foreign products can satisfy local needs at point A. However, it is also in principle feasible to produce with decreasing costs at point B – instead of being bought, the good is made. To get from A to B, a non-marginal change is required. The private sector might or might not recognise and be capable of making the transition; the same is true of exporting in volume in the 'sell' option (another non-marginal change), with production at C. As discussed below, choices like those illustrated in the diagram open room for policies aimed at promoting both import substitution and export growth.

Intersectoral linkages can further complicate matters, especially for widely used intermediates such as metal products or chemicals. In the older development literature the need to attain minimum viable scales of operation was at the heart of Hirschman's (1958) recognition of the significance of cross-sectoral demand and supply linkages. His logic goes together well with Young's vision of the growth of an 'infant economy', a striking generalisation of the standard Mill–Bastable criteria to which the mainstream literature consistently adheres.

1.2 Effects of trade interventions in practice

To deal concretely with the issues raised by Young and Hirschman, one has to bring in imperfectly competitive market structures and the means by which firms operating in them can be induced to raise their productivity and reduce costs. Following Ocampo (1997), consider an established IS firm which may also have the possibility to export. It can cut its unit costs by investing T_C in improved technology, and enhance its ability to penetrate export markets by investing T_X (with both investment activities subject to decreasing returns to additional outlays).

Solving the firm's profit maximisation problem (details in the appendix) shows that it will undertake more T_C as the sum of its outputs for the domestic market (Q) and export (X) is greater, because the investment cost can be 'spread' over a bigger production run. If its costs are low enough to make exporting profitable, it will also choose a positive value for T_X. Fig. 2 depicts the situation for a pure IS firm for which exports are not profitable. The TT schedule shows that technological investment rises with the volume of output for the reason just given. Moreover, by reducing costs more investment permits higher output levels along the QQ curve. In such a situation, shifting QQ to the right by providing protection can help induce a productivity increase. Indeed, if the resulting cost reduction is strong enough the firm may be able to export, adding another positive feedback via X and T_X to Fig. 2's 'win-win' mutual crowding-in scenario.[2] As discussed later, at the macro level such phenomena can underlie sustained output growth *à la* Young and Kaldor.

---

[2] There is obviously room in the model for productivity enhancement by both import protection and export promotion. As discussed more fully below, they are not just symmetric and mutually offsetting, as in mainstream interpretations of South Korea's deployment of both sorts of interventions.

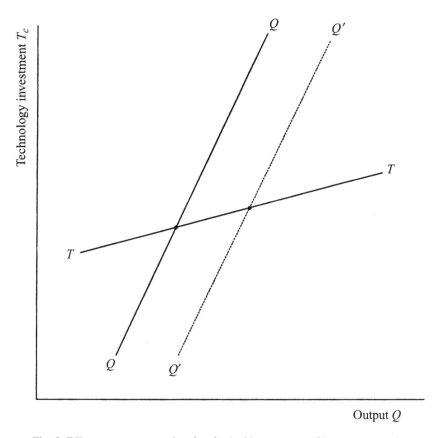

Fig. 2 Effects on output and technological investment of import protection

1.3 Little welfare triangles and big distributional shifts

If decreasing costs and crowding-in of productivity growth are assumed away or convexified into irrelevance, a second problem with the standard model emerges – the welfare losses associated with trade and other distortions do not signify. The negligible size (1 or 2% of the relevant output indicator, once off) of 'little triangle' welfare gains from liberalisation has been apparent ever since Harberger (1959) began cranking the numbers 40 years ago.[3] What has not been stressed in the literature, however, is that

---

[3] At times, computable general equilibrium models such as the one constructed ex ante to evaluate a Canada/US free trade agreement by Harris and Cox (1984) do generate large welfare gains from trade liberalisation under conditions of decreasing cost – the model's number for Canada was around 7% of GDP. However, as Hazeldine (1990) demonstrates, the results of the Harris–Cox exercise depend crucially on assumptions of very strong scale economies, facile entry and exit from monopolistically competitive industry, and high sensitivity of the national price level to the cost of competitive imports.

Continued on next page

the income transfers associated with liberalisation or imposition of regulation are measured by rectangles – not triangles – and can be large (Rodrik, 1994).

For example, consider the effects of an import quota in Fig. 3, which shifts the
supply curve faced by domestic consumers from *SS* to *S'S'* and corresponds to an
internal price *P* above the world price *P**. Removing the quota gives a 'triangle' welfare
gain of *BFG + CDE*, the difference between 'rectangle' overall gains of *ACDH* and losses
of *ABGH* to import-competing producers and *BCEF* to owners of the rights to the
quota. Such distributional effects of liberalisation programmes have recently emerged
as a major topic of debate.

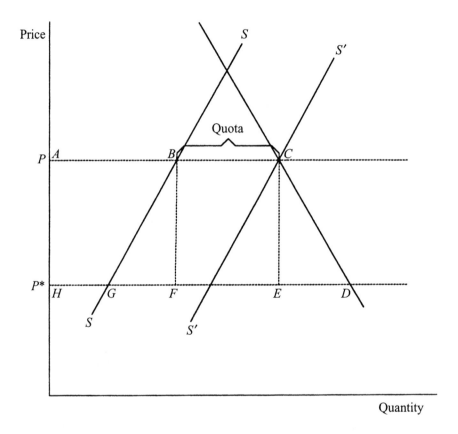

Fig. 3 Distributional effects of removing an import quota

Cutting protection then reduces national prices, drives out entrants who have 'crowded' into production and are operating at small, inefficient scales, and thereby generates decreasing costs. A positive
macroeconomic feedback through an appreciating exchange rate due to lower export prices stimu-
lates even more cost reductions and output growth. There is no reason to expect such a long chain of
consequences to work themselves out in practice.

1.4 Intersectoral distributional complications

In particular, much discussion has centred on two trade theory warhorses, the Stolper–Samuelson (1941) theorem and factor-price equalisation (Samuelson, 1948), applied to 'skilled' and 'unskilled' labour as opposed to the more traditional labour and capital. Following Wood (1994), there has been substantial debate about the Stolper–Samuelson proposition that trade liberalisation in advanced economies should benefit the input intensive in production of their exports, i.e. skilled labour. In developing countries, on the other hand, the unskilled should benefit. Discussion around the OECD attributes some part (say in the range of 10–20%) of that region's increasing wage inequality to trade effects, more to a 'skill twist' against low-paid workers induced by computerisation, and a significant part to a changing social perceptions of 'fair pay' and lagging aggregate demand (Howell et al. 1998). In developing economies, a distributional shift in favour of the low paid remains to be observed.

With regard to factor-price equalisation, the real question is whether the standing Heckscher–Ohlin hypothesis that all countries have access to the same technologies is even remotely correct. It is argued below that Verdoorn's (1949) Law is a crucial determinant of economy-wide productivity growth. Across sectors within an economy, it implies that labour productivity levels should converge, i.e. technologies differ between countries (Milberg, 1997). Even more damaging to the standard factor-price equalisation argument is the fact that recent moves toward (not just trade) liberalisation in developing countries have been associated with striking divergences in patterns of productivity growth overall (Pieper, 1997).

1.5 Rent-seeking and Austrian competition

The mainstream response to the existence of little triangle welfare losses from trade interventions has been to try to expand them in one way or another. There are two main, related lines of thought: rent-seeking and Austrian-style assertions about the powers of liberal policies to unleash entrepreneurship. We take up basic arguments here, postponing their empirical consideration to section 3.

In a competitive model, the real costs to society of economic actors trying to gain the rents generated by distortions were first pointed out by Tullock (1967) in a paper on 'The Welfare Costs of Tariffs, Monopoly, and Theft'. Presumably many more economic actors seek such income flows than gain them, while others have to pay for self- or social protection. All such efforts consume resources but do not produce 'goods'. In the case of theft, expenditures for alarms, security services, gated suburban enclaves, police, courts, and jails must greatly exceed the incomes received by the thieves.

In the trade and development literature while still assuming perfect competition, Krueger (1974) dropped monopoly and theft (private sector activities, largely) to focus on government interventions aimed at regulating trade, especially import quotas which generate rents as illustrated in Fig. 3. Numerous estimates of large welfare losses due to trade interventions have been made (e.g. deMelo and Robinson, 1982) but are difficult to accept at face value. If quotas cover only a fraction of imports and imports are a fraction of GDP, associated rents and rent-seeking outlays cannot be huge. More fundamentally, rents are a form of exploitation, a notion mainstream economists find difficult to swallow. Marxists, of course, have been trying to quantify exploitation for a long time. Even with great ingenuity – as in Baran and Sweezy (1966) – they rarely raise their estimates of surplus values to large fractions of GDP. The same seems likely to be true with regard to rents and even their pursuit.

If perfect competition is not present, further complications come in. Following the discussion in section 1.2 and anticipating the macro analysis of section 2, we mention just two. First, standard rent-seeking models suppose that tariffs or quotas always generate higher prices. But in fact, firms may take advantage of protection to build up a stable clientele by adjusting prices to bid up sales in Okun's (1981) 'customer markets'. If resources are not fully utilised or there is a binding external constraint, the additional income flows associated with a larger volume of sales (if they can be called 'rents' at all) do not generate welfare losses. The second point is that rents in the right hands may speed capital accumulation, as discussed more fully below. This possibility does not arise in standard trade theory models, which implicitly assume that all incomes (including rents) are consumed.

Austrian arguments concentrate on competition as a process instead of an exercise in comparative statics. Subject to one key reservation, the central point is that imperfect competition in all its forms – oligopolies, efficiency wages, externalities, indivisibilities, and so on – is doomed to disappear in some not very lengthy run. It will be undone by entrepreneurial forces. Through entry of firms into oligopolised markets, mark-ups will be driven toward zero. Unemployed workers will toil at low pay to bid down efficiency wages until every willing hand finds a job. Economic externalities or production indivisibilities will be 'internalised' through bargained market solutions until socially optimal marginal benefit = marginal cost equalities applies.[4]

The reservation, of course, is that ham-handed public interventions can frustrate even this process, blocking entrepreneurship and (more importantly) discouraging people from thinking in an entrepreneurial way. Far reaching liberalisation may break these barriers down and permit the economy to jump to a much faster pace of economic growth (or, in Schumpeterian terminology, to a vastly improved configuration of circular flow). Chile since the mid-1980s is often cited as proof for this assertion (Solimano, 1996). This story has an element of truth – scions of the present-day Chilean bourgeoisie are far more obsessed with profitable business undertakings than were their parents a generation past – but completely ignores the complicated history of the Chilean transition (Fanelli et al., 1992) and the inconvenient fact that exchange rate devaluation was much more important than import liberalisation in driving Chile's export success (Helleiner, 1995a).

---

[4] Empirical support for these assertions on the part of the Austrian school elite is rather casual. In fancy terminology, Austrian economists view the socioeconomic system as an evolutionary game in which the forces of entrepreneurship will finally prevail, leading to a socially optimal competitive resource allocation. However, no formal convergence proofs are offered. Hayek (1988) argued that the existence and benefits of a trend toward capitalism worldwide are demonstrated by the rapid expansion of the human population observed over the last two hundred years. The correlation exists, but the assertion of causality is more than most people can swallow.

1.6 Contingent interventions

A final point is that by making their pay-offs contingent on performance state interventions also can induce entrepreneurship. Two steps are required (Hikino and Amsden, 1994; Mohanty, 1996). One is to define the criteria on which contingency is based; East Asian experience suggests that export performance can serve, along with other indicators such as output growth, technological upgrading, etc.

Second, the state has to have leverage over firms, e.g. via control of allocated credits, so that non-performing recipients of publicly created rents can be chastised. Manipulation of 'rectangle' rents like those illustrated in Fig. 3 is the instrument at hand; the political question is whether the authorities can use it to discipline capital effectively. Circumstances are bound to vary with time and place. Neither interventionist nor liberalisation packages can be evaluated outside history, contrary to the main thrust of mainstream economic theory.

2 MACROECONOMICS

Macroeconomic considerations must also be brought in to assess the effects of trade liberalisation. We first take up a mainstream narrative, and then go on to implications of simultaneous liberalisation of the capital and trade accounts. The importance of the dynamics of aggregate productivity growth and how they can be influenced by policy are the closing themes.

2.1 Implications of Say's Law

True to its Walrasian roots, the standard model presupposes full employment of all resources (or Say's Law) and balanced trade, subject to existing restrictions on imports. If not all commodities are traded, the local currency/foreign currency exchange rate, e, serves as a relative price between traded and non-traded goods (Dornbusch, 1974, sets out a convenient model). It enters as the key variable in a 'symmetry' argument of the type originally advanced by Lerner (1936) which, on its own assumptions, shows that liberalising imports will promote export growth.

To see the details, assume that import protection is reduced, leading to an incipient trade deficit. To close the gap, imports must be pushed back down or exports up. If the exchange rate, e, adjusts to clear a current account imbalance (which may or may not be the case), then a higher (i.e. depreciated) value of e will stimulate production of exportables and import substitutes with resources transferred from the non-traded sector. In other words, liberalisation pays off in the form of faster export growth. The underlying Say's Law assumption assures that local resources can be deployed to produce *something* and balanced trade assures it will find an external market (Stanford, 1995). Historical observations of liberalisation experiences are rendered irrelevant by theory.

But what happens if resources are not automatically fully employed or if the country in question can borrow abroad? Then income as well as substitution effects of both trade liberalisation and exchange rate changes matter. They can easily be associated with output losses and a wider trade deficit. As Orchard and Stretton (1997) point out, these are two of the cases – structural unemployment and rising foreign debt – in which Adam Smith observed that protection can generate welfare gains. The other two (highlighted above) were industries with acquired rather than natural advantages, and with high cost production thresholds. Arguments in support of trade liberalisation have to overcome objections familiar from *The Wealth of Nations*.[5] They have not succeeded fully to date.

2.2 Capital market liberalisation

The next macro linkage that bears on the liberalisation debate is the fact that in many cases in the past decades, both the trade and capital accounts of the balance of payments have been deregulated simultaneously. The exchange rate is allowed (at least dirtily) to float, responding to developments in financial markets instead of imbalances in the current account. In countries where this package has been applied (more in Latin America and Asia than sub-Saharan Africa), almost uniformly a combination of a high local interest rate and a strong exchange rate has emerged, diluting whatever benefits concomitant trade liberalisation was supposed to bring and often leading to a balance of payments crisis in the medium run. It of interest to explore why this particular combination of macro prices has been so common. The answer is fairly complicated.

Uncovering it is not made easier by the fact that the standard portfolio balance model for 'home' and 'foreign' interest rates (say i and i^*) and the exchange rate (e) between the two countries has been treated incorrectly in the literature (Taylor, 1998). Two key misinterpretations stand out. First, when proper wealth accounts are derived from it, the model can be shown to determine only two of the variables just mentioned – not all three as has been assumed for the past 20 years. Second, devaluation reduces home and raises foreign wealth, contrary to the usual assumption.[6]

If stable asset market adjustment in response to interest rate changes is assumed in the short run, these wealth effects show directly that devaluation will lower home and increase foreign interest rates. With lower wealth induced by a higher value of e, home asset demands fall, so that i must decrease as well. The opposite occurs abroad. To take the discussion a step further (particularly when capital markets have been liberalised),

---

[5] Smith's reasoned defence of tariffs in certain circumstances appears in the latter part of Book IV, Chapter II of *The Wealth of Nations*.

[6] Standard presentations (Branson and Henderson, 1985; Isard, 1995) get these results wrong because they do not take into account the dependence of asset demands on wealth levels, and of the latter on the exchange rate. Substitution of reduced form expressions for home and foreign wealth into demand balances for national and foreign bonds and money and a little algebra show that each country has only one independent balance, so that there are two in the system. The wealth effects of devaluation cited in the text emerge from the reduced forms directly. The facts that devaluation can reduce both national wealth and real income (as in the contractionary devaluation literature *à la* Krugman and Taylor (1978)) tend to be underplayed in the formal economics literature, but in most countries do not escape the attention of the general public and its political representatives.

it makes sense to endogenise the exchange rate over time by bringing in an uncovered interest rate parity (UIP) differential equation of the form[7]

$$\frac{de}{dt} = e(i - i^*) = e\delta \tag{1}$$

in which for analytical simplicity myopic perfect foresight is invoked to set the actual equal to the expected rate of devaluation on the left-hand side.

In a stationary state, $i = i^*$ and $de/dt = 0$ at an initial exchange rate e. Now suppose that the home country permanently reduces its money supply, making i rise and i^* decline. At the ruling exchange rate, the right-hand side of (1) suddenly becomes positive. This sets up a well-defined initial value problem in de/dt and e.

Differentiating the right-hand side of (1) shows that $\delta (de/dt)/\delta e < 0$ unless asset preferences themselves are highly sensitive to changes in de/dt (that is, a condition of the form $e[\partial\delta/\delta (de/dt)] < 1$ is required). When stability applies, a simple dynamic process unfolds. If i exceeds i^*, the expected forward exchange rate will be high according to UIP. As the expected devaluation turns into reality, home wealth falls. Demand for home money goes down, and the interest rate differential narrows. The change in the exchange rate, de/dt, will go to zero at a new stationary value of e. Unlike most models incorporating perfect foresight, the one here does not require the use of jump variables and transversality conditions to demonstrate stability. Some might find the dynamics plausible on such grounds.

Turning to the effects of capital market liberalisation, an immediate question arises. If deregulation induces a shift in desired foreign portfolios toward the home market (the goal of the whole exercise in the first place), then its asset prices should rise or interest rates fall. Reversing the argument just presented, the home currency should begin to appreciate. This result is consistent with experience, but where do the high interest rates often observed in the wake of market liberalisation come from?

One possible explanation is that economic actors at home may pull back from the local market in a dynamic process. For example, the authorities might well tighten monetary policy in an attempt to keep the current account deficit under control. (In the Latin American context, inflation stabilisation would be a complementary objective.) If $D(i, e)$ is the deficit, their response could take the form

$$\frac{dM}{dt} = \beta \{D^t - D[i(e, M), e\} \tag{2}$$

where M is the money supply and D^t is a target level for D.

Equations (1) and (2) make up a simple dynamic system in e and M. In equation (2), $\partial(dM/dt)/\partial M < 0$ because a bigger money supply reduces the home interest rate,

---

[7] By way of derivation, if UIP holds then it should be true that $e(1 + i) = f(1 + i^*) - (e + \varepsilon) (1 + i^*)$, where e is the spot and f is the expected forward exchange rate with ε as the expected change. If the product term εi^* is negligible, then (1) follows immediately with myopic perfect foresight which sets $\varepsilon = de/dt$.

increases the external deficit via a higher level of economic activity, and makes international reserves decline. The exchange rate influences D directly and through i. If the direct effect dominates, then $\partial D/\partial e < 0$ and $\partial(dM/dt)\partial e > 0$, i.e. the monetary authorities think that a weaker exchange rate gives them room to raise growth of the money supply.

Fig. 4 illustrates a possible scenario, with the exchange rate schedule corresponding to $de/dt = 0$ and the money curve representing $dM/dt = 0$. An increase in foreign preferences for home assets shifts the exchange rate schedule to the left, i.e. a lower or more appreciated value of e is consistent with $de/dt = 0$ when external demands for local assets rise. For a given e, M has to go down to hold $dM/dt = 0$ in (2) when liberalisation happens; a reduction in the target trade deficit would accentuate this effect. As shown in Fig. 4, the outcome could be a new stationary state with a lower e and a level of M sufficiently reduced to raise i. Analysis of parameters would be necessary to give a definite result, but the uncomfortable high interest rate/strong currency combination is compatible with the present model. It does not provide a solid base for improved trade performance or investment to support economic growth.

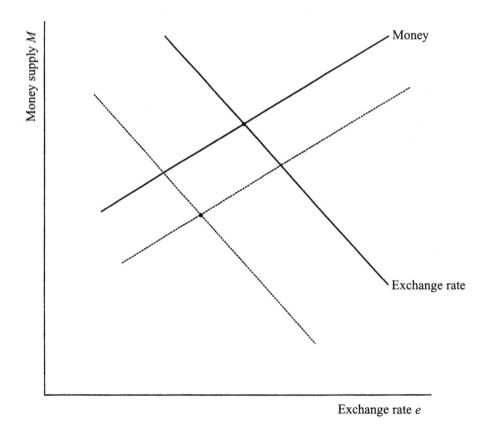

Fig. 4 Asset market adjustment to a switch in foreign preferences toward home assets ('capital market decontrol') accompanied by more restrictive monetary policy

What is worse, the continuing trade deficit can lead ultimately to a dynamically unstable situation, which can be characterised by an underestimation of risk as in a classic model by Frenkel (1983). At some point, the underestimation reverses, leading to massive capital outflow, devaluation, and stagflation. Mexico in 1994 and East Asia in 1997 are the most striking recent examples. The adverse effects of capital market liberalisation can easily overwhelm whatever small triangle benefits trade deregulation may bring.

2.3 Trade policy and productivity growth

The final macroeconomic questions to be addressed are long-term. It is well known that productivity growth[8] is far more important for the creation of income gains than the resource reallocations of static models, even with increasing returns. Productivity gains lead to a win–win set of dynamic interactions, of the sort already illustrated in Fig. 2.

On the one hand, more rapid output growth tends to speed up productivity increases, i.e.

$$\frac{d\xi}{dt} = f_\xi(\xi, g) \tag{3}$$

with first and second partial derivatives of f_ξ being negative and positive respectively (the former condition simply states that accelerations in productivity growth are not explosive). Rationales have been provided by authors as diverse as Verdoorn (1949), Okun (1962), and Kaldor (1978), as well as 'new' growth theorists.

Positive feedback emerges from a stimulating effect of ξ on g,

$$\frac{dg}{dt} = f_g(\xi, g) \tag{4}$$

in which the first and second partials of f_g are positive and negative respectively.

At least three channels have been emphasised by different schools of thought. First, technical change promotes investment and (by reducing costs) additional exports. Unless effective demand is strongly wage-led so that overall spending is held down in Luddite fashion by job losses associated with rising productivity (Taylor, 1991), the outcomes are greater capacity utilisation and faster output growth. Second, aggregate supply will expand more rapidly, as emphasised by mainstream growth theory. Finally, if the economy is constrained by foreign exchange along the lines emphasised by Chenery and Bruno (1962) and subsequent two- and three-gap models (Taylor, 1994), a supply effect through the relaxation of 'import compression' is added to demand growth from the exports and import substitution permitted by lower production costs.

---

[8] Productivity growth should be understood here as the 'residual' in traditional calculations, figured with respect to either labour or total factor inputs. It includes scale economies (both static and dynamic, as it is impossible to differentiate the effects of one from the other over time) but omits price shifts due to changing mark-ups over time.

Fig. 5 illustrates the effects of alternative policies in a diagram wherein the schedules along which $d\xi/dt = 0$ and $dg/dt = 0$ are represented by TT and GG respectively. The presentation is of course similar to the one Kaldor used in discussing his technical progress function, and is the obvious macroeconomic analog to the micro analysis of Fig. 2. Abstracting from the growth of the labour force, a long-run equilibrium at which $g = \xi$ and $dg/dt = d\xi/dt = 0$ emerges at the intersection of TT and GG; it will be stable if TT has the shallower positive slope.[9] One way to shift the equilibrium point is through protection to infant industries. When successful, it can stimulate technological investment, shifting the TT schedule upward in Fig. 5a. If output growth is limited by aggregate demand or available foreign exchange, GG will move to the right, raising both ξ and g.

Two potentially important offsetting factors should immediately be pointed out. If the infants produce capital or intermediate goods, adverse effects on user sectors due to more expensive or lower quality inputs have to be taken into consideration (that is, negative linkage effects due to increasing costs predominate).[10] Second, it may not be possible for the state to make the benefits of import protection contingent on perform-

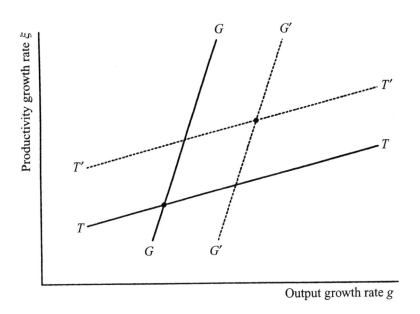

Fig. 5 (*a*) Infant industry protection or export promotion in mature IS industries

[9] One interpretation of endogenous growth theory is that TT is steeper than GG. Saddlepoint dynamics emerge around the point at which the curves cross, leading to ever-increasing or ever-decreasing rates of output and productivity growth. We leave such fireworks aside, preferring to concentrate on more traditional analysis of stable comparative dynamics.

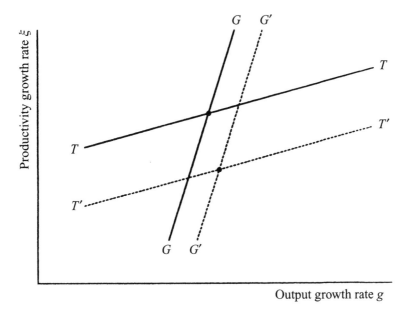

Fig. 5 (*b*) Increased protection to mature IS industries, with X-inefficiency and weak effects of growth

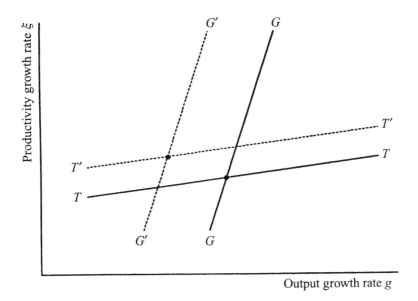

Fig. 5 (*c*) Import liberalisation with favourable productivity effects but adverse impacts on growth

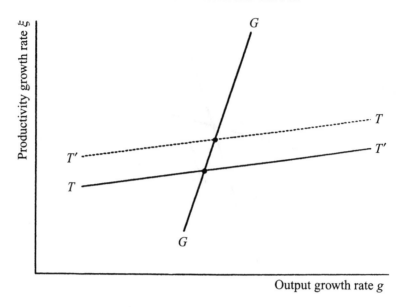

Fig. 5 (*d*) Devaluation with neutral long-run effects on aggregate demand

ance for well-ensconced 'mature' IS firms. Their non-competitive response to extra protection might be to reduce x-efficiency. Overall productivity growth could decline and aggregate demand and supply effects could be weak, as in Fig. 5*b*. As the diagram is drawn, economic growth does not slow but technological advancement falters.

In such circumstances, contingent incentives might be created through export promotion via subsidies or import liberalisation for intermediate inputs. The *TT* function could rise while export dynamism could shift *GG* to the right – we are back to Fig. 5*a*. This possibility of helping domestic firms overcome the fixed costs of breaking into external markets reflects the importance of an 'infant export industry' argument.

By contrast, an overall reduction of protection can cut back on economic growth. The effects on the *GG* function in a demand-or (especially) a foreign exchange-constrained economy are clearly adverse. Its leftward movement in Fig. 5*c* can be accompanied by an indeterminate shift in *TT*. Removing protection should ameliorate the negative effects of restricted competition on productivity growth in domestic markets, while export sectors can benefit from cheaper intermediate inputs (these are basically little triangle welfare gains). But viable infant industries may be strangled, while national firms' financial base for penetration of export markets is eroded. In Fig. 5*c*, the *TT* function shifts upward along neoclassical lines, but the leftward shift of the

---

[10] Taylor (1991) sets up a non-Say's Law growth model in which higher profitability in a sector producing intermediate goods resulting from *G* protection may or may not induce enough additional investment across sectors to raise the economy-wide rate of economic growth.

GG schedule reduces the growth rates of both output and productivity in the long run.

As we have already noted, devaluation has complex effects. For purposes of the present discussion, it can be seen as a means of cutting costs for both export and IS industries in conjunction with macroeconomic repercussions that can be far-reaching. In Fig. 5*d*, devaluation is assumed to stimulate productivity growth while leaving the *GG* locus unchanged (the contractionary short-run impact often observed in developing economies may be offset by a neutral or expansionary long-run effect). Under these conditions, long run growth and productivity performances improve. The implication is that the effects of a package mixing liberalisation and devaluation (that is, combining Fig 5*c* and *d*) are indeterminate. The benefits of devaluation have to be weighed against the likely adverse effects on long-term growth of thoroughgoing deregulation. If the exchange rate appreciates for the reasons discussed previously, the situation becomes that much more perilous.

Four final considerations: First, different sorts of trade regimes may induce different patterns of technical change. Long-run liberal regimes may well promote static comparative advantage, with infant IS and export industries with their 'created' advantages being underrepresented. If created advantage is what matters at the global level, then a liberal strategy may encourage an output mix with adverse effects on productivity growth. Offsetting factors are the possibilities for product upgrading and downstream expansion from a natural resource base, and the costs of infant industry protection (especially for small countries in an advanced import substitution phase). Dynamic learning economies increase the benefits of import substitution, but also its costs if globally competitive industries do not emerge.

Second, the implication is that promoting IS industries can be a desirable strategy on growth grounds, if policy tools can be deployed to push import substitution into export promotion. Sectors which never mature in this sense may not even satisfy Mill–Bastable criteria for success.

Third, if the economy becomes overloaded with 'immature' producing units, their transformation into exporters becomes an urgent matter. Widescale import liberalisation is unlikely to be up to the task, even combined with devaluation. Incentives contingent on successful penetration of foreign markets may be needed to make 'infant export industries' reach maturity.

Finally, possibilities for faster productivity growth depend crucially on specific national and sectoral characteristics. Trade policy reforms in general and trade liberalisation in particular appear to have modest leverage on technological advance in developing economies. Productivity is likely to respond much more to accumulation of human capital and the development of public and private institutions to facilitate the transfer, adaptation, and diffusion of more productive technologies.

3 EMPIRICAL EVIDENCE

In this section, we briefly review the empirical evidence regarding several points raised above – the overall impacts of trade liberalisation, distributional changes, and productivity growth.

3.1 Overall impacts

Two historical accidents heavily influence discussion of the effects of trade liberalisation. The first is that when neoclassical economists turned their attention to the problems of development in the late 1960s they were led by trade specialists.[11] The analysis
of trade interventions has been central to the debate ever since, overwhelming discussion of the production-related factors just mentioned.

Not long after, the World Bank began to invest heavily in economic research, under
the leadership of Hollis Chenery. For better or for worse, the methodologies he in-
stalled relied on cross-country regression analysis and computable general equilibrium
(or CGE) models. Very little effort was devoted to historical and institutional studies of
specific countries, undertaken by people with enough local knowledge to know what
they were talking about. CGE models with causal structures or 'closures' predeter-
mined to favour liberalisation[12] and meaningless regressions do not shed a lot of light
on how trade policy really operates.

By now, there are scores if not hundreds of econometric studies of the impacts of
exports on economic growth (either directly or via creation of a higher capacity to
import), the relationships between 'openness' (defined in terms of trade shares or the
prevalence of protection) and growth, and (in the CGE models) the growth and output effects of specific policy changes.

The regression equations typically leave a substantial part of total variance unex-
plained, so that even if they point to 'modest' positive effects of liberalisation or openness on growth, such conclusions cannot possibly hold for all the countries included in
the sample. For this and similar reasons, surveys such as Edwards (1993), Rodrik (1995),
and Helleiner (1995a) broadly conclude that trade policy changes do not matter very
much. Helleiner, in particular, argues that a stable (and preferably weak) exchange
rate is the best single explanation of successful trade performance in the medium run.
He also observes on the basis of the country studies he organised that an overly complex set of incentives can frustrate even the most entrepreneurial of potential traders,
an Austrian point forcefully argued by Kaldor (1959) in a famous study of Chile long
ago.

Historically based country analyses like those undertaken by Amsden (1989), Wade
(1990), and the scholars collected in Helleiner (1994, 1995b) share this agnosticism,
but also single out the historical importance of certain trade, industrial, and macro
policy manoeuvres in specific institutional contexts. They emphasise the role of inter-

---

[11] The most important early contributions were the studies of trade and industrial policy organised by
Little et al. (1970). Significantly, they relied heavily on the (then) high tech analysis of effective
protection to show that trade distortions were rampant in a sample of a half-dozen semi-industrialised
economies.

[12] Much of the Bank's case for liberalisation is based on Say's Law models of the type sketched in
Section 2.1 e.g. user-friendly computer packages incorporating a specification illustrated by Devarajan,
et al. (1995) which are heavily used to flog trade deregulation throughout the developing world. The
models' reliance on the exchange rate to 'clear' the current account stands in curious contrast to
Bank/IMF efforts to decontrol capital accounts, causing exchange rate movements to reflect financial
forces.

ventions contingent on performance (Section 1.6 here) and the fact that in an environment unregulated by Say's Law there is ample room for protection of both IS and export activities by the same firm or industry – the symmetry theorems are not relevant (Section 2.1).[13] The details are messy and successful interventions may not replicate easily across national frontiers, but the evidence for their existence is clearly present.

3.2 Distributional shifts

Two questions arise: Can we characterise the overall directions of distributional changes under liberalisation? If so, what can be said about the channels via which they occur? With regard to the first query, UNCTAD (1997) demonstrates that globalisation has been associated with increasing income inequality in several countries, both developed and developing. Berry (ed., 1997) adds complemetary evidence for Latin America. More generally, Berry et al. (1997) conclude that in the wake of (not just trade) liberalisation, 'Countries with abundant labour, sufficiently educated (and with other necessary conditions present) to take advantage of international markets to expand labour-intensive manufactured exports, showed some tendency for improving income distribution.[14] In contrast, middle-income countries with comparative advantage in some skill-intensive products, and upper income countries, with comparative advantage in capital and skill-intensive areas, showed a definite tendency for worsening in income distribution. African economies whose comparative advantage lay in peasant production were expected to show an improvement . . . but there mostly appears to have been a worsening in income distribution . . .'

With regard to channels, debate is open. In one survey, Robbins (1996) finds evidence for a skill twist against low wage labour in developing economies. In another, Milberg (1997) stresses the breakdown of Stolper–Samuelson predictions outside the OECD, and the fact that they provide at best a partial explanation for distributional changes within. What do matter, he argues, are labour market institutions and employment growth. The latter responds to growth of aggregate demand, and feeds back into productivity increases along the lines of Figs. 2 and 5. Some final observations about this crucial linkage are an appropriate way to conclude the present discussion.

3.3 Sectoral shifts and productivity growth

Chenery et al. (1986) remain a fundamental source on the dynamics of productivity and strutural change. Using data through the early 1980s, they concluded that total factor

---

[13] Of course, symmetry (or, better, asymmetry) applies in the sense that not everyone can benefit from state intervention. In the short run in Korea, for example, both IS and export industrial activities were subsidised, while domestic food prices were kept high. The price system was clearly biased against urban consumers and some productive sectors, but the former still benefited over time from steady productivity increases. Draconian controls, however, made sure that they had a long wait before they got access to imported 'luxury' consumer items (Chang, 1997).
[14] But, it might be added, there are always exceptions, Berry et al. (1997) emphasise a visibly worsening income distribution in Thailand since the mid-1980s.

productivity (TFP) growth contributed more to overall output growth in developed than developing countries, with factor accumulation thereby contributing more to output expansion in the latter.[15] An outlier group of 'success stories' (Japan, Israel, Spain, and East Asian NICs) was characterised by high TFP growth *and* factor accumulation.

Havrylyshyn (1990) later observed that rapid TFP growth was characteristic of these countries prior to their adoption of export-oriented strategies. Moreover, Chenery et al. pointed out forcefully that at the sectoral level, export expansion was almost uniformly preceded by a phase of successful import substitution. As detailed by Ocampo (1997) subsequent studies have demonstrated that in several countries, industries began to export even though their import protection was maintained.

Has this picture changed after the mid-1980s, broadly the period of liberalisation all 'round the world'? On the basis of a 30-country sample of data at the nine-sector level for output and employment, Pieper (1997) shows that post-1985 only five Asian countries maintained growth rates of better than 3% per year in *both* overall employment and labour productivity.[16] Their productivity expansion was balanced across sectors, with the rate in agriculture remaining high.

Off this Asian 'high road', the typical Latin American pattern was rapid employment but slow productivity growth, while in Africa both rates were under 3%. In these regions, productivity performance dropped off sharply after 1985 in comparison to the previous period. Finally, in almost all countries aggregate productivity growth correlated closely with the evolution of the output/labour ratio in manufacturing, with other sectors presenting no clear pattern.

The links between this evidence and trade and other forms of liberalisation are not direct (especially since many countries were still struggling with the after-effects of massive external shocks in the late 1980s) but are still suggestive.

First, manufacturing has always been the main focus of protection and economists in the Verdoorn–Kaldor tradition argue that productivity growth in that sector drives changes in the rest of the economy. Insofar as this argument is correct, the deindustrialisation observed in much of the developing world due to liberalisation, exchange rate appreciation, and high interest rates and other symptoms of austere policy could have far-reaching adverse consequences.

Second, they could play out over an extended time period if a prior phase of import substitution is needed to lay the base for subsequent export success. Countries with exploitable natural resources and/or cheap labour are partial exceptions to such a generalisation, but such windfalls do not last forever.

Finally, the good productivity performance in the Asian economies has been associated with outward-oriented, but distinctly *not* liberal trade regimes. Indeed, they have practised the sorts of policies sketched in the model of section 1.2 with great diligence. Their histories show that trade and other interventions are not always harmful; indeed, at least in terms of economic performance, they can promote substantial good.

---

[15] This particular stylised fact was well known to Chenery-style development economists for years before its recent rediscovery by Young (1994) – a good example of Schumpeter's (1954) oft-repeated lament that 'Economists don't read.'

[16] They are Indonesia, Korea, Malaysia, Singapore, and Thailand, with India having rapid productivity growth but less robust job expansion.

Appendix

Following Ocampo (1997), the model underlying the analysis of section 1.2 at the firm level is quickly sketched here.

The demand function the firm faces is

$$Q = Q[P/(1 + t)] \tag{A1}$$

where P is the domestic price of its product, and t is the tariff rate on its closest foreign substitute (the foreign price is normalised at unity).

The firm's inherited technology allows it to produce a unit of its product with b_0 units of a unique input, purchased at price P_b. It can lower b_0 by investing on a flow basis in a cost-reducing technology T. Unit costs are thereby

$$C = P_b \, b_0 \, [1 - \tau \, (T_c, \, b_0)] \tag{A2}$$

where τ has a positive first and negative second partial derivative with respect to T_c, and may well increase with b_0 (there is more room for cost-cutting when initial input requirements are high).

The firm may also sell in the foreign market as a price-taker. It can undertake technological investments T to learn international quality and marketing standards, and to project its product's existence abroad,

$$X = g(T_x) \tag{A3}$$

where g has positive first and negative second derivatives.

The firm chooses P, T_c, and T_x to maximise profits Π,

$$\Pi = (P - C) \, Q + (1 - C) \, X - (T_c + T_x)$$

subject to non-negativity constraints on Q, X, T_c and T_x. After some manipulation the first order conditions can be written as

$$P = (1 + \mu) \, C \tag{A4}$$

where $\mu = 1/(\varepsilon - 1)$ and ε is the (negative of the) price elasticity of demand from (A1);

$$\frac{d\tau}{dT_c} = \frac{1}{P_0 b_0 \, (Q + X)} \quad \text{or } T_c = 0 \tag{A5}$$

and

$$\frac{dX}{dT_x} = \frac{1}{(1 - C)} \quad \text{or } T_x = 0 \tag{A6}$$

Equation (A4) is the usual price determination rule for a monopolist. In (A5), T_c will be higher insofar as technological outlays can be 'spread' over a bigger output volume $Q - X$. In (A6) the firm will only invest in export technology T_x if its domestic costs C are already below international prices.

In the graphical representation in Fig. 2, the TT schedule represents (A5). The QQ curve shows how higher investments reduce costs (A2), which bid down prices in the domestic market (A5) and thereby increase sales (A1). Second order conditions for a profit maximum are satisfied when the slope of TT is less than that of QQ.

References

Amsden, Alice H. (1989) *Asia's Next Giant*, New York: Oxford University Press.

Baran, Paul, and Sweezy, Paul (1966) *Monopoly Capital*, New York: Monthly Review Press.

Berry, Albert (ed., 1997) *Economic Reforms, Poverty, and Income Distribution in Latin America*, Department of Economics, University of Toronto.

Berry, Albert, Horton, Susan and Mazumdar, Dipak (1997) 'Globalisation, adjustment, inequality, and poverty,' Department of Economics, University of Toronto.

Branson, William H. and Henderson, Dale W. (1985) 'The specification and influence of asset markets,' in (Ronald W. Jones and Peter B. Kenen, eds), *Handbook of International Economics*, vol. 2, Amsterdam: North-Holland.

Chakravarty, Sukhamoy and Singh, Ajit (1988) 'The desirable forms of economic openness in the South,' World Institute for Development Economics Research, Helsinki.

Chang, Ha-Joon (1997) 'Luxury consumption control and economic development,' Faculty of Economics and Politics, University of Cambridge.

Chenery, Hollis B. and Bruno, Michael (1962) 'Development alternatives in an open economy; the case of Israel,' *Economic Journal*, vol. 72, pp. 79–103.

Chenery, Hollis B., Robinson, Sherman and Syrquin, Moshe (1986) *Industrialization and Growth*, New York: Oxford University Press.

deMelo, Jaime and Robinson, Sherman (1982) 'Trade adjustment policies and income distribution in three archetype developing countries,' *Journal of Development Economics*, vol. 10, pp. 67–92.

Devarajan, Shanta, Go, Deltim S., Lewis, Jeffrey D., Robinson, Sherman and Sinko, Pekka (1995) 'Policy lessons from a simple open economy model,' The World Bank, Washington DC.

Dixit, Avinash and Stiglitz, Joseph E. (1977) 'Monopolistic competition and optimal product diversity.' *American Economic Review*, vol. 67, pp. 297–308.

Dornbusch, Rudiger (1974) 'Tariffs and non-traded goods,' *Journal of International Economics*, vol. 4, pp. 177–86.

Edwards, Sebastian (1993) 'Open-ness, trade liberalisation, and growth in developing countries,' *Journal of Economic Literature*, vol. 31, pp. 1358–93.

Fanelli, Jose Maria, Frenkel, Roberto and Taylor, Lance (1992) 'The World Development Report 1991: A Critical Assessment' in United Nations Conference on Trade and Development, *International Monetary and Financial Issues for the 1990s*, vol. 1, New York: United Nations.

Frenkel, Roberto (1983) 'Mercado financiero, expectativas cambiales, y movimientos de capital,' *El Trimestre Economico*, vol. 50, pp. 2041–76.

Harberger, Arnold (1959) 'Using the resources at hand more effectively,' *American Economic Review (Papers and Proceedings)*, vol. 49, pp. 134–46.

Harris, Richard, and Cox, David (1984) *Trade, Industrial Policy, and Canadian Manufacturing*, Toronto: Ontario Economic Council.

Hayek, Friedrich von (1988) *The Fatal Conceit: The Errors of Socialism (Collected Works of F. A. Hayek, vol. 1)* London: Routledge.

Havrylyshvn, Oli (1990) 'Trade policy and productivity gains in developing countries: a survey of the literature,' *World Bank Research Observer*, vol. 5, pp. 1–24.

Hazeldine, Tim (1990) 'Why do free trade gain numbers differ so much? The role of industrial organisation in general equilibrium,' *Canadian Journal of Economics*, vol. 23, pp. 791–806.

Helleiner, G. K. (ed., 1994) *Trade Policy and Industrialisation in Turbulent Times*, London: Routledge.

Helleiner, G. K. (1995a) 'Trade, trade policy, and industrialization reconsidered,' World Institute for Development Economics Research, Helsinki.

Helleiner, G. K. (1995b) *Manufacturing for Export in the Developing World: Problems and Possibilities*, London: Routledge.

Hikino, Takashi and Amsden, Alice H. (1994) 'Staying behind, stumbling back, sneaking up, soaring ahead: late industrialization in historical perspective,' in (W. J. Baumol, R. R. Nelson and E. N. Wolff, eds) *Convergence of Productivity: Cross-National Studies and Historical Evidence*, New York: Oxford University Press.

Hirschman, Albert O. (1958) *The Strategy of Economic Development*, New Haven CT: Yale University Press.

Howell, David R., Duncan, Margaret and Harrison, Benneti (1998) 'Low wages in the US and high unemployment in Europe: a critical assessment of the conventional wisdom,' Center for Economic Policy Analysis, New School, New York.

Isard, Peter (1995) *Exchange Rate Economics*, Cambridge: Cambridge University Press.

Kaldor, Nicholas (1959) 'Problems economics de Chile,' *El Trimestre Economico*, vol. 26 (no. 2), pp. 170–221.

Kaldor, Nicholas (1978) *Further Essays on Economic Theory*. London: Duckworth.

Krueger, Anne O. (1974) 'The political economy of the rent-seeking society,' *American Economic Review*, vol. 64, pp. 291–323.

Krueger, Anne O. (1997) 'Trade policy and economic development: how we learn,' *American Economic Review*, vol. 87. pp. 1–21.

Krugman, Paul and Taylor, Lance (1978) 'Contractionary effects of devaluation,' Journal of International Economics, vol. 8, pp. 445–56.

Lerner, Abba P. (1936) 'The symmetry between import and export taxes,' *Economica*, vol. 3, pp. 306–13.

Little, I. M. D., Scitovsky, Tibor and Scott, M. FG. (1970) *Industry and Trade in Some Developing Countries*, Oxford: Oxford University Press.

Milberg, William S. (1997) 'The revival of trade and growth theories: implications for income inequality in developing countries,' Department of Economics, New School, New York.

Mohanty, Mritiunjoy (1996) '*Restructuring of an economy: the Mexican experience after the 1982 debt crisis*,' unpublished Ph.D. Dissertation, Centre for Economic Studies and Planning, Jawaharlal Nehru University, New Delhi.

Ocampo, Jose Antonio (1997) 'Trade policy and productivity,' Ministry of Finance, Bogota.

Okun, Arthur M. (1962) 'Potential GNP: its measurement and significance,' reprinted in (Joseph Pechman, ed.) *Economics for Policy-Making*, Cambridge MA: MIT Press, 1983.

Okun, Arthur M. (1981) *Prices and Quantities: A Macroeconomic Analysis*, Washington DC: Brookings Institution.

Orchard, Lionel, and Stretton, Hugh (1997) 'Public choice,' *Cambridge Journal of Economics*, vol. 21, pp. 409–30.

Pieper, Ute (1997) 'Openness and structural dynamics of productivity and employment in developing countries: a case of de-industrialization?' Department of Economics, New School, New York.

Robbins, Donald J. (1996) 'Evidence on trade and wages in the developing world,' OECD Development Centre, Paris.

Rodrik, Dani (1994) 'The rush to free trade in the developing world: why so late? Why now? Will it last?' in (Stephan Haggard and Steven B. Webb, eds) *Voting for Reform*, New York: Oxford University Press.

Rodrik, Dani (1995) 'Trade and industrial policy reform,' in (Jere R. Behrman and T. N. Srinivasan, eds.) *Handbook of Development Economics*, vol. 3B, Amsterdam: North-Holland.

Samuelson, Paul A. (1948) 'International trade and the equalization of factor prices,' *Economic Journal*, vol. 58, pp. 163–84.

Schumpeter, Joseph (1954) *History of Economic Analysis*, New York: Oxford University Press.

Scitovsky, Tibor (1954) 'Two concepts of external economics,' *Journal of Political Economy*, vol. 62, pp. 143–51.

Solimano, Andres (1996) 'The Chilean economy in the 1990s: on a golden age and beyond,' Department of Economics, New School, New York.

Stanford, Jim (1995) '*Social structures, labour costs, and North American economic intergration: a comparative modeling analysis*,' unpublished Ph.D. dissertation, Department of Economics, New School, New York.

Stewart, Frances and Berry, Albert (1997) 'Globalization, liberalization, and inequality: expectations and experience,' Queen Elizabeth House, Oxford University.

Stolper, Wolfgang F., and Samuelson, Paul A. (1941) 'Protection and real wages,' *Review of Economics and Statistics*, vol. 9. pp. 58–73.

Taylor, Lance (1991) *Income Distribution, Inflation, and Growth*, Cambridge MA: MIT Press.

Taylor, Lance (1994) 'Gap models,' *Journal of Development Economics*, vol. 45, pp. 17–34.

Taylor, Lance (1998) 'Wealth accounting in a two-country portfolio balance model,' Center for Economic Policy Analysis, New School, New York.

Tullock, Gordon (1967) 'The welfare costs of tariffs, monopoly, and theft,' *Western Economic Journal*, vol. 3, pp. 224–33.

UNCTAD (United Nations Conference on Trade and Development, 1997) *Trade and Development Report*, New York: United Nations.

Verdoorn, P. J. (1949) 'Fattore che regolano lo sviluppo della produttivita del lavoro,' *L'Industria*, vol. 1, pp. 3–10.

Wade, Robert (1990) *Governing the Market*, Princeton NJ: Princeton University Press.

Wood, Adrian (1994) *North-South Trade, Employment, and Inequality: Changing Fortunes in a Skill-Driven World*, Oxford: Clarendon Press.

Young, Allyn A. (1928) 'Increasing returns and economic progress,' *Economic Journal*, vol. 38, pp. 527–42.

Young, Alwyn (1994) 'Lessons from East Asian NICs: a contrarian view,' *European Economic Review*, vol. 38, pp. 964–73.

7

TRADE REFORM, ADJUSTMENT AND GROWTH: WHAT DOES THE EVIDENCE TELL US?*

David Greenaway, Wyn Morgan and Peter Wright

The contrast between the growth performance of East Asia at one extreme and sub-Saharan Africa at the other is a striking one. Much has been written about the contrast, especially in relation to the former. The reason for the interest is obvious: if there are elements of the East Asian experience which can be reproduced elsewhere then let us identify and replicate. One such common factor which a number of analysts believe they have identified is openness to international trade. More specifically, the growth of exports and the growth of GDP appear to be highly correlated (even if causality is sometimes in doubt) and on average, through time, countries with a more open trade orientation appear to do better.

This proposition has underpinned an extraordinary wave of unilateral trade reform in developing countries. In the last twenty years over 90 countries have initiated some kind of reform or another. Some have been voluntary. Most, however, have been initiated by both Bretton Woods institutions but especially the World Bank under its Structural Adjustment Programme (SAP). Since 1980 a substantial proportion of total Bank lending has come through this window. Typically, any such loans are conditional on policy reform and in general trade policy reform figures prominently.[1] Although there are political economy considerations which are relevant to the emphasis on trade policy reforms (such as the relative ease of monitoring change in that domain compared with others), the basic economic rationale is straightforward: if there appears to be a long term association between performance and openness and if an economy is presently relatively closed, then liberalisation is a necessary bridge to becoming more open. One can finesse the rationale in various ways but fundamentally that is what it comes down to. Has it worked? Has liberalisation of the World Bank inspired (or some might say required) variety proved to be a successful bridge? In other words has it led to growth?

* The authors are grateful to the Ford Foundation and to the Wincott Foundation for financial support. Helpful comments from participants in a seminar at the Chinese University of Hong Kong and the Annual Congress of the Economic Society of Australia 1997 are also acknowledged.
[1] A detailed account of the SAL process and its ingredients can be found in Greenaway and Milner (1993). For a fine review of the evolution of thinking on trade reform, see Krueger (1997).

The reasons why it should or will not have been carefully presented by Dornbusch (1992) and Rodrik (1992, 1998) as well as Krueger and Taylor in this *Controversy*. Our concern here is not about the theory but the evidence. Overall is the evidence supportive of liberalisation providing a growth enhancing stimulus or not? In section 1 we begin by setting out a series of methodological issues centred on the difficulties of clearly identifying a liberalisation episode and reviewing the strategies adopted by different analysts. In section 2 we review the current stock of evidence, both cross section and time series and focus on the factors which explain the variation in outcome and the controversy surrounding trade reforms. Section 3 then adds to the empirical literature by providing some new evidence. Here we do not simply report yet another set of results. Instead we use a very large data base and a panel framework together with a range of measures of liberalisation and a more rigorous exploration of the dynamics of trade reform than hitherto. Section 4 discusses the outcomes and concludes.

1 METHODOLOGICAL ISSUES IN MODELLING LIBERALISATION

To model the impact of liberalisation on growth one first has to identify liberalisation. Different analysts have done so in different ways. That in itself indicates that it is not straightforward in practice, nor is it wholly transparent in theory outside the confines of the basic $2 \times 2 \times 2$ trade model.

1.1 Alternative concepts of liberalisation

There are at least three (not unrelated) concepts of trade liberalisation, all of which can be explained by reference to Fig. 1. *PF* is some small country's production frontier.

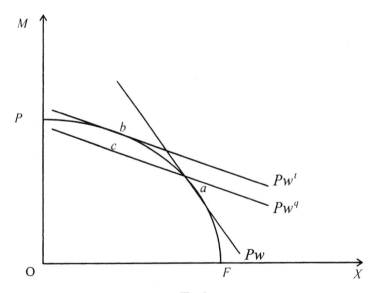

Fig. 1

World relative prices are depicted by *PW*. However, suppose that the economy is operating with an import tariff which sets domestic relative prices at PW^t, with an associated production equilibrium at *b*. The most obvious notion of liberalisation is removal of the tariff which restores the domestic price ratio to *PW* and shifts the production equilibrium to *a* where the economy is more specialised in production of exportables. This is unambiguously trade liberalisation and its practical analogue would be the reduction of import tariffs.

One way of thinking about the price ratio *PW* is as a neutral set of relative prices; neutral in the sense that aside from 'natural' comparative advantage drivers, there is no artificial incentive to produce importables (as with the import tariff) or exportables (as there would be with an export subsidy). One could of course secure neutrality in this sense by leaving the tariff in place and introducing an equivalent export subsidy. By the Lerner symmetry theorem, assuming appropriate lump sum transfers, this would have equivalent resource allocation effects to free trade. Thus a second notion of liberalisation is that associated with reducing anti-export bias.

The third concept of liberalisation, much used in practice, is that of 'second best' liberalisation. This results when one instrument of intervention is replaced by another, less distorting instrument. In Fig. 1, the relative price ratio PW^t could be achieved by a quota rather than a tariff. However, for a range of well known reasons, quotas are more costly forms of intervention than tariffs. Because they waste more resources, the resulting production equilibrium will be inside the production frontier at a point such as *c*. If the quota is converted into an equivalent tariff, the move from *c* to *b* is effected.

1.2 Measures of liberalisation

Clearly in order to evaluate empirically the impact of a particular liberalisation, one needs to identify an episode when it has occurred. As we have just seen, conceptually this is not straightforward; empirically it is even less so. As a consequence, practice has varied somewhat from study to study. Broadly speaking analysts have identified episodes using one or more of the following: policy accounts; relative price changes; output based measures; multiple criteria measures.

Policy accounts are an intuitively obvious starting point and refer to the practice of associating liberalisation with *perceived* changes in the policy environment. Many of the large cross-country studies make some use of this approach, most notably Papageorgiou, et al. (PMC) (1991) where some 36 episodes in 19 countries are identified and Whalley (1991) where 18 episodes in 10 countries are charted. This has the great advantage of being intuitively comprehensible and relatively straightforward to document. Its great disadvantage is that policymakers do not always do what they say they will do! Moreover, it is often the case that although the stated policy intent is followed (e.g. a reduction in import tariffs), there could be instrument substitution via the introduction of other measures (e.g. anti-dumping duties, luxury tariffs and so on). Thus although policy accounts are an obvious starting point, they must be complemented with more robust/more objective measures.

Since liberalisation has its effects through changing relative incentives, *relative price changes* are an obvious outcome measure to use. One option is an implicit tariff measure of the type:

$$Pm = Pm^* [e(1 + t)] \tag{1}$$

where *Pm* is the c.i.f. import price, *e* the exchange rate and *t* the implicit tariff rate. Its appeal is that it directly measures differences between world and domestic prices. As with all such summary measures one is faced with aggregation and weighting problems. Moreover, in using it (or to be more accurate, changes therein) to capture liberalisation one is characterising trade regime change by reference to the import side of the economy only. If there are interventions on the export side then, by analogy with equation (1):

$$Px = Px^* [e(1 + te)] \tag{2}$$

where *te* measures net export subsidies. The ratio of these two terms of trade indices then reduces to $(1 + te) / (1 + tm)$, which is the relative distortion of the price of exportables to importables. It is this which Krueger (1978) endeavoured to capture with her bias index,

$$B = \frac{\sum_{i=1}^{k} w_i \left[\frac{(Pm_i)}{(Qm_i)} \right]}{\sum_{j=1}^{n} w_j \left[\frac{(Px_j)}{(Qx_j)} \right]} \tag{3}$$

where *P*s and *Q*s refer to domestic and international prices respectively. Strictly speaking this is a measure of trade regime bias, with an index of unity representing neutrality, less than unity export orientation and greater than unity import orientation. Clearly, however, liberalisation can, and has been, proxied by changes in the index. Similar comments apply to the relative effective exchange rate for tradeables as used in the multi-country studies of Bhagwati (1978) and Balassa (1982):

$$ET = \frac{Em(1 + t + n)}{Ex(1 + s + r)} \tag{4}$$

where *Em* and *Ex* are the nominal exchange rates applied to imports and exports respectively, corrected by average effective import tariffs (*t*) and export subsidies (*s*) and any other import restraints (*n*) or export supports (*r*). Again, although one might use this as a measure of trade regime bias, changes in its value can proxy liberalisation.

Output based measures are less commonly used but might incorporate trade intensity measures, import counter-factuals or even macroeconomics indicators. The recent work of Easterly et al. (1997) essentially adopts this approach.

Clearly then there are no straightforward indicators of liberalisation. For these reasons a number of analysts have used *multiple criteria* to identify liberalisation episodes, some formulaically some judgmentally. The country studies in PMC (1991) adopt this approach using *inter alia* real effective exchange rates, effective tariffs, export subsidies, coverage of quotas and black market premia. Unfortunately from the standpoint of making cross-country comparisons, the criteria used vary from one study to another. By contrast Dean et al. (1994) use just four indicators: import tariffs; quantitative restrictions; export impediments/incentives; degree of exchange rate misalignments and they use all four for all 31 countries in their sample. Sachs and Warner (1995) use five criteria: the coverage of non-tariff barriers, average import tariffs, black market premia, existence or absence of state monopolies in the export sector and whether or not the economy in question is socialist. The great advantage of using multiple criteria is the additional richness it brings to the identification of what can in practice be a somewhat amorphous phenomenon. This richness comes at a price, however, because as the criteria are not straightforwardly additive an element of judgment is required in both the scaling of individual indicators and the relative weight to be attached to each.

2 EVIDENCE ON TRADE REFORMS, ADJUSTMENT AND GROWTH

There is considerable overlap across the empirical analysis of liberalisation and growth, exports and growth and trade orientation and growth. We confine our attention to the first of these only. (Reviews of the exports and growth and trade orientation and growth literature can be found in Greenaway and Sapsford (1994) and Edwards (1993) respectively.) In addition to the problems of defining liberalisation there are some rather important complications associated with conducting any evaluation of its effects. Three stand out. First what is the counterfactual? Should one just assume a continuation of pre-existing policies and performance in the country concerned? In practical terms this may be all one can do, although it has an important shortcoming; many liberalisations which are policy conditioned are initiated at a time of crisis when pre-existing policies are unlikely to be sustainable. Second, how does one disentangle the effects of trade reforms from other policy shifts and exogenous shocks? Third, supply responses and the process of adjustment will differ from economy to economy: how long should one wait before conducting an assessment?

Broadly speaking two approaches have been taken: cross-country and time-series. The literature on the former includes 'with–without' and 'before–after' and has recently been extended by panel methods. 'With-without' has been used by *inter alia* World Bank (1990) and Mosley et al. (1991*a, b*). It involves taking a sample of countries subject to trade reforms, matching them with comparators which were not subject to reforms and ascribing any differences in performance to the reform programme. 'Before–after' which is again used by *inter alia* World Bank (1990), Mosley et al. (1991*a, b*) and Greenaway, Morgan and Wright (1997) is similar in some respects but introduces a time dimension in that it compares the 'with–withouts' for a few years before and few years after. In some cases, like PMC (1991), it is only the 'withs' that are examined, in that case for three years before and three years after.

Time series analysis tends to be country specific and uses more or less sophisticated econometric methods. Examples include Harrigan and Mosley (1991), PMC (1991), Greenaway and Sapsford (1994), Greenaway, Leybourne and Sapsford (1997) and Onafowora et al. (1996). Harrigan and Mosley (1991) focus on Structural Adjustment

Loans (SALs) as one of a number of possible determinants of growth, export and investment performance. Greenaway and Sapsford (1994) use a structural break model to investigate whether or not specific liberalisation episodes appear to have a significant impact on growth. By contrast, Greenaway, Leybourne and Sapsford (1997) model growth as a smooth transition process then search for evidence of a coincidence of 'take off' and liberalisation. Onafowora et al. (1996) use VAR methods for a group of sub-Saharan African countries.

Despite the wide range of techniques used, the broad country coverage and the wide range of liberalisation experiences examined, some patterns regarding the effects of liberalisation can be picked out, with one notable exception, namely the PMC (1991) study. This is very supportive of the view that liberalisation is a panacea; it results in more rapid growth of exports, more rapid growth of real GDP. Equally importantly, it accomplishes this without serious transitional costs in unemployment and without significant effects on the government's fiscal position. These conclusions have been challenged by Greenaway (1993) and Collier (1993) primarily on methodological grounds. Using a smooth transitions framework Greenaway, Leybourne and Sapsford (1997) look specifically at the timing of the PMC episodes and can find no systematic evidence of a connection between trade reforms and growth acceleration. In some cases there is a positive correlation, in some negative, in others no apparent correlation whatsoever.

The remaining studies seem to suggest the following. First, liberalisations, and reform programmes more generally, tend to be associated with a fairly rapid improvement in the current account of the balance of payments and with an improvement in the growth rate of real exports. The degree of improvement in the former typically outstrips the latter indicating that some part of the change is operating through import compression. Second, the impact on growth is more ambiguous and/or more complicated. Both positive growth and negative growth impacts have been found. Thus in some cases growth performance does deteriorate following liberalisation. Of course it may not have deteriorated by as much as it would have done in the absence of reform and as we shall see later there are good grounds for believing that any short run reduction in growth may be purely temporary. Third, a proportion of countries which have undergone adjustment show a subsequent improvement in investment. However, many appear to have experienced an investment slump. Although Bleaney and Greenaway (1993) find other factors are more important in explaining investment slumps in the 1980s (terms of trade shocks, cost of capital) there are actually some plausible reasons for believing that adjustment programmes may be a contributory factor. In particular, deconfinement of the public sector may fail to crowd in private sector investment if there is a question mark against the credibility of the reforms.

How can one explain these results? Analysts have typically focused on three groups of explanations: programme design; programme implementation; weak supply response. Programme design can condemn an attempted liberalisation to failure at the outset if the reforms proposed are over ambitious. There are notable instances where this has been the case. Implementation too could be problematic. For instance, if a programme is multi-stage its sequencing might be inappropriate, or there may be instrument substitution. In the event that there is a weak supply response following liberalisation, there are no 'quick wins' from higher growth which may erode commitment to the reform programme resulting in slippage and perhaps ultimate programme collapse. A common explanation for weak supply response is programme credibility; because agents are not convinced that the new policy regime is permanent, the liberalisation fails to crowd in new investment. The other possibility is that export sectors might have low supply elasticities, which may be especially important where primary products are concerned.

These are all sensible factors in explaining variability of results across studies. There is one further explanation, namely that empirical analysis thus far is failing to model the dynamics of the adjustment process appropriately. It is likely that real output growth will respond to liberalisation with a lag, the length of which will depend upon the nature of the liberalisation, extent of pre-existing distortions, flexibility of markets and so on. Some countries will react quickly and others will react slowly. Unless one explicitly models the dynamics, results will depend very much on the sample. In general, time series work has not dealt with the problem since most liberalisations which have figured in the recent literature are themselves relatively recent. What we do in the next section is to provide a more extensive and exhaustive analysis of the growth impact of liberalisation, by working with a very large cross-section of countries to which we apply panel techniques.

3 A PANEL ANALYSIS OF LIBERALISATION AND GROWTH

A lack of consistency in results is perhaps inevitable when a range of measures/proxies for liberalisation are used, when the modelling framework varies from study to study and when the dynamics are not modelled, or modelled inadequately. To deal with some of these deficiencies, we have constructed a dataset of up to 73 countries.[2] For this sample we estimate a 'core' new growth theory model of the type which has now become fairly standard. We then introduce liberalisation. Rather than attempting to use a single liberalisation measure, we take those of Sachs and Warner (1995), Dean et al. (1994) and one based on World Bank (1993). For each we estimate a dynamic panel model to evaluate the short run impact and transitional effects of liberalisation on the growth of real per capita GDP.

3.1 Model specification

Following the empirical work of Levine and Renelt (1992) and others, which searched for a set of robust variables to model growth and the theoretical contributions to the new growth theory literature following Romer (1990), some convergence on empirical specification has occurred. Most empirical growth models include as explanatory variables investment, population growth, initial per capita GDP and initial human capital variables. We include all of these together with a terms of trade variable and various liberalisation proxies. The former is included because our samples include developing

---

[2] Details of dataset construction are available from the authors on request.

countries and terms of trade shocks can have a significant impact on growth.[3] Liberalisation is included for obvious reasons. Our base specification is one which is fundamentally a Levine-Renelt 'core variables' specification, with the addition of a terms of trade variable and a liberalisation indicator:

$$\Delta \ln y_{i,t} = \beta_1 \ln y_{i,65} + \beta_2 SCH_{i,65} + \beta_3 \Delta \ln TTI_{i,t} + \beta_4 \Delta \ln POP_{i,t}$$

$$+ \beta_5 \left(\frac{INV}{GDP}\right)_{i,t} + \beta_6 LIB_{i,t} + \Delta \varepsilon_{i,t} \tag{5}$$

where

$y_{i,t}$	= GDP per head
$y_{i,65}$	= GDP per head as at 1965
SCH 65	= level of secondary school enrolment as at 1965
TTI	= terms of trade index
POP	= population
INV/GDP	= the ratio of gross domestic investment to GDP
LIB	= dummy capturing liberalisation episode

Specifications of this type have been widely used, not to model movements from one steady state to another but rather the transitional effects of liberalisation/trade reform. Although they have been widely used, there are reasons for believing it to be dynamically mis-specified. We therefore specify a second estimating equation of the form:

$$\Delta \ln y_{i,t} = a\Delta \ln y_{i,t-1} + \beta_1 \ln y_{i,65} + \beta_2 SCH_{i,65} + \beta_3 \Delta \ln TTI_{i,t} + \beta_4 \Delta \ln POP_{i,t}$$

$$+ \beta_5 \left(\frac{INV}{GDP}\right)_{i,t} + \beta_6 LIB_{i,t} + \Delta \varepsilon_{i,t} \tag{6}$$

where y_{t-1} are lags of GDP per head. This has obvious intuitive appeal in that it models growth in a dynamic context and so liberalisation may have both short-run and longer-run impacts. However, since a correlation will exist between the error term and the lagged dependent variable this equation is estimated using the Generalised Method of Moments estimator of Arrelano and Bond (1991). This technique makes use of the fact that values of y lagged 2 periods or more are valid instruments for the lagged dependent variable. This will generate consistent and efficient estimates of the parameters of interest.[4]

   We work with three different definitions of liberalisation, those of Sachs and Warner (1995), Dean et al. (1994) and one based on World Bank (1993). The first is con-

---

[3] See the literature around the Bevan, Collier, Gunning project, for example Bevan et al. (1993).
[4] Consistency of the GMM estimator requires lack of second order serial correlation in the dynamic formulation, so tests for this are presented with the results. Overall instrumental validity is also examined using a Sargan test of over-identifying restrictions.

structed on the basis of measuring whether an economy is open or not. Their index of openness is based on five criteria relating to non-tariff barriers, average tariff levels, the black market exchange rate, whether state monopolies exist for major exports and whether the economy is socialist or not. This initially enters our model as an 'on-off' dummy where 'off' relates to a closed economy. By contrast Dean et al. (1994) is more qualitatively based. They use information on average nominal tariffs, QR coverage and average black market premia to identify when reform has taken place. This too enters initially as a dummy variable in an 'on-off' fashion. The liberalisation indicator based on World Bank (1993) is also 'on-off'. Here, however, we equate the first year of a SAL with a trade component as the beginning of the liberalisation episode. There are obvious qualifications to working with such an indicator; conditions vary from one SAL to another, they may take several years to be implemented and so on. Since, however, so many trade reforms are World Bank initiated, it is important to incorporate a proxy for such reforms.

3.2 Results

The results of estimating (5) and (6) are reported in Tables 1, 2 and 3. Refer first to Table 1. Here the model is estimated using the Sachs and Warner proxy. Column 1 refers to the base specification with the Sachs–Warner index included on the basis of a zero prior to reform and one after reform. In other words, liberalisation is picked up in the form of an intercept shift which measures average annual per capita growth changes following reform. All of the independent variables have the predicted sign. Thus, a low initial GDP and high initial level of schooling are associated with faster growth in GDP per capita as are a higher investment ratio and favourable terms of trade movement. Faster population growth is associated with slower GDP per capita growth and liberalisation appears to have on average a favourable and substantial (2.7%) impact on growth in years following liberalisation. All of the coefficient estimates are statistically significant at the 10% level at least. In order to look more closely at the timing of reform on growth, column 2 allows for the same base specification but the liberalisation proxy (Sachs2) switches on in the year of liberalisation only. This therefore indicates the growth impact of reform in the first year only rather than an average post reform effect. Lags pick up the impact of reform in subsequent years. The magnitude, signs and significance of the independent variables are robust to this change, with population growth increasing in significance. What is interesting about the results is the arrangement of signs: negative (but insignificant) in year 1; positive (but insignificant) in year 2 and positive, larger and significant in year 3; suggesting evidence of a J curve type effect of liberalisation on per capita GDP growth.

Equations like those in columns 1 and 2 are routinely used in studies of liberalisation, yet there are some obvious indications of mis-specification. Although first order serial correlation would be expected in differenced equations of this form, as the bottom panel reveals, there is evidence of second order serial correlation in column 2 which is commonly indicative of dynamic mis-specification. To correct for this an instrumental variables approach in a dynamic setting as per equation (6) above was estimated. The results are in column 3. First of all, note that the Sargan test for the

Table 1 Growth equations incorporating Sachs and Warner index

Variable	1 Coefficient	t-ratio	2 Coefficient	t-ratio	3 Coefficient	t-ratio
Constant	0.043255*	2.118412	0.042248*	1.941061	0.000962	0.21392
$\Delta \ln y_{t-1}$					0.500123*	9.507514
$\Delta \ln y_{t-2}$					0.075592	1.328895
$\Delta \ln y_{t-3}$					0.323692*	8.284271
$\ln y_{65}$	−0.01041*	−4.28583	−0.00815*	−2.8125	−0.00266*	−5.71723
SCH_{65}	0.007086*	2.868522	0.009449*	3.408015	0.002747*	3.722292
$\Delta \ln TTI$	0.029219*	2.630095	0.031058*	2.866638	0.031076*	5.140976
$\Delta \ln POP$	−0.68079*	−1.83952	−1.17128*	−3.22112	−0.4113*	6.13321
INV/GDP	0.114153*	3.25804	0.124893*	2.924524	0.005092	0.553742
Sachs1	0.027228*	6.457025				
Sachs2			−0.00826	−0.96252	0.009869*	2.00113
$Sachs2_{t-1}$			0.00752	0.925879	0.016802*	4.286088
$Sachs2_{t-2}$			0.015016*	1.9658	0.0199*	5.576351
1st Order serial correlation	3.786*		3.756*		−1.639*	
2nd Order serial correlation	1.439		2.073*		−0.986	
Sargan Test					0.63353	
No of countries	69		69		69	
Period	1975–1993		1975–1993		1975–1993	

Notes: Estimation is by generalised method of moments regression after first differencing. Heteroscedastic robust asymptotic t-ratios are in parentheses. The Sargan Test for the validity of the set of instruments is defined as Prob $(J > \chi_p^2)$, where p is the number of overidentifying instruments. Time dummies are not reported.
* Indicates coefficient significant at 10% level.

validity of instruments is satisfied and also note that the second order serial correlation problem has been dealt with. From the upper panel we see that all of the independent variables have the predicted sign and all apart from the investment ratio are statistically significant. The liberalisation effect is positive and significant in all three years, with a contemporaneous impact effect of just under 1%, with an additional 1.5% in year 2 and 2% in the subsequent year. Again, a lagged reaction to trade reform is suggested but without the initial decline in GDP per capita. Finally, because these increments persist, it is possible to estimate the long run contribution to GDP per capita growth as follows: $\Sigma\beta_i/(1 - \Sigma a_i)$ where β_i are the coefficients on the reform variables and a_i are the coefficients on the lagged dependent variables. This turns out to be 46%. At first blush this appears to be implausibly high for a 'liberalisation effect' and it most probably is. However, the Sachs–Warner measure is really a measure of openness rather than liberalisation. Thought of in this way one is essentially saying that in the long run, more open developing countries will be around half as rich again in GDP per capita terms as more closed developing countries, which is not quite so implausible.

Table 2 reports results using the Dean et al. (1994) measure. Columns 1, 2 and 3 have exactly the same interpretation as in Table 1. *Dean*1 and *Dean*2 proxies of liberalisation should be interpreted in the same way as *Sachs*1 and *Sachs*2: the first is an average year on year growth impact of reform and the second with persistence over three years. As with Table 1 coefficients have the expected sign in columns 1 and 2 and all, apart from the terms of trade variable, are statistically significant. From column 1 we see that liberalisation has a positive impact on growth though this is only significant at the 90% level and somewhat smaller magnitude than with the Sachs–Warner measure (0.9%). The arrangement of signs in column 2 is negative (and insignificant), positive (and insignificant) and positive and significant in year 3. Again, however, there are problems of serial correlation and so we estimate a dynamic equation with instruments on the lagged dependent variables, the results of which are reported in column 3. All the independent variables have the expected sign and are significant (apart, again, from the terms of trade), suggesting a robust specification and the diagnostics suggest an appropriately specified equation. The arrangement of signs and significance on the liberalisation variable is again suggestive of a J curve response, with the strongest effect (1.1%) coming through in the third year (with this coefficient estimate also being statistically significant). Again it is possible to estimate the long-run augmentation of GDP per capita which this implies. In this case it amounts to around

Table 2 Growth equations incorporating Dean et al. index

Variable	1 Coefficient	t-ratio	2 Coefficient	t-ratio	3 Coefficient	t-ratio
Constant	0.020181	1.026341	0.022776	1.146378	0.03366*	5.490992
$\Delta \ln y_{t-1}$					0.62393*	6.453612
$\Delta \ln y_{t-2}$					−0.13934*	−2.17327
$\ln y_{65}$	−0.00607*	−3.02276	−0.006655*	−3.329572	−0.0046*	−4.70817
SCH_{65}	0.007692*	2.663746	0.008179*	2.711165	0.003555*	2.454232
$\Delta \ln TTI$	0.026814*	1.654616	0.027876*	1.767175	0.003461	0.381875
$\Delta \ln POP$	−1.06805*	−4.43586	−1.034336*	−4.215407	−0.63361*	−4.69743
INV/GDP	0.213587*	6.417527	0.219872*	6.543907	0.101023*	3.287087
*Dean*1	0.008747*	1.777425				
*Dean*2			−0.001407	−0.131516	−0.00461	−0.92447
$Dean2_{t-1}$			0.002317	0.289284	0.003839	0.803088
$Dean2_{t-2}$			0.017674*	2.379555	0.011362*	2.614598
1st Order serial correlation	3.763*		3.814*		−2.470*	
2nd Order serial correlation	2.324*		2.620*		0.048	
Sargan Test					0.9157	
No of countries	73		73		73	
Period	1985–1993		1985–1993		1985–1993	

Notes: See Table 1.

2%. This is substantially different to the estimate implied using the Sachs–Warner index. It could be due to the fact that the estimates pertain to a somewhat shorter period and/or the Dean et al. measure is unambiguously a proxy for liberalisation rather than openness.

In Table 3, we turn to the results when using the SAL indicator where we take the commencement of a SAL as our marker for liberalisation. The pattern of results is qualitatively similar to those for the other two indicators. In the base equations (columns 1 and 2) all of the coefficients have the expected sign and, with the exception of the terms of trade proxy, all are statistically significant. In column 1, the liberalisation proxy suggests an improvement in GDP per capita growth of 0.6% but this is not statistically significant. In column 2 we report a negative/positive/positive arrangement of signs but again none are significant. In the dynamic equation (column 3) all coefficient estimates have the expected sign and, with the exception of TTI, all are significant. We again get a negative/positive/positive arrangement of signs on the liberalisation variable though on this occasion that in year 2 is significant and consistent with a 1% enhancement of per capita GDP growth. If we calculate the long run effects, the total augmentation to growth is less than 2%. Overall therefore the results we get here are qualitatively and quantitatively similar to those we get with the Dean index.

Table 3 Growth equations incorporating World Bank index

Variable	1 Coefficient	t-ratio	2 Coefficient	t-ratio	3 Coefficient	t-ratio
Constant	0.070784*	4.043276	0.072185*	4.346079	0.033771*	5.467871
$\Delta \ln y_{t-1}$					0.557319*	7.69089
$\Delta \ln y_{t-2}$					−0.08695*	−3.01735
$\ln y_{65}$	−0.009445*	−4.082292	−0.009232*	−4.242907	−0.00486*	−6.55075
SCH_{65}	0.00887*	3.020704	0.009513*	3.274106	0.003574*	3.45503
$\Delta \ln TTI$	0.004339	0.222145	0.005329	0.271436	0.001811	0.27496
$\Delta \ln POP$	−1.465261*	−5.002127	−1.482078*	−4.99262	−0.96574*	−7.63625
INV/GDP	0.15322*	3.289354	0.152784*	3.268246	0.088202*	5.242885
$WB1$	0.005682	1.328921				
$WB2$			−0.003241	−0.531683	−0.00609	−1.60429
$WB2_{t-1}$			0.004865	−0.541899	0.009973*	2.170767
$WB2_{t-2}$			0.002247	0.292728	0.001673	0.557066
1st Order serial correlation	3.193*		3.279*		−2.837*	
2nd Order serial correlation	0.585		0.568		−0.476	
Sargan Test					0.70170	
No of countries	73		73		73	
Period	1979–1991		1979–1991		1979–1991	

Notes: See Table 1.

3.3 Discussion

We have reported results for a base 'new growth' model similar to that used by a large number of analysts. Since we feel there are good reasons for believing this to be a mis-specified growth model, we have also estimated a dynamic version. Since the 'measurement' of liberalisation is controversial, rather than confine ourselves to a single measure or marker, we have included three measures on more or less the same sample size, albeit for different time periods. A number of findings come through quite clearly. First, our dynamic model is well specified and the results we obtain are robust: there is an encouraging degree of consistency as we move from one equation to another. Second, the outcomes for our core growth model are as expected: initial GDP, initial schooling, the investment ratio, population growth and (sometimes) terms of trade changes are all influential in determining cross-country patterns of growth. Third, we get similar patterns of results on the liberalisation effect across several measures of/ markers for liberalisation. This is especially interesting in part because we have explored the dynamics of liberalisation to good effect and in part because of the consistent story which seems to be revealed. This is that the growth enhancing effects of liberalisation are unlikely to be instantaneous: we have clear evidence of a J curve effect, evidence which is consistent across samples and measures of liberalisation. Moreover, orders of magnitude for impact effects (one year) and medium-run effects (three years) exhibit some consistency but also some differences. The growth effects appear to be strongest when the Sachs–Warner index is used and weakest with the SAL, indicator. This ordering is much as one would expect given that the Sachs–Warner indicator is effectively a measure of *ex post* openness, i.e. it only includes as 'liberalised' countries those which have actually opened. By contrast, the SAL indicator is an *ex ante* measure; in effect it is a statement of intent to liberalise. That being so, it includes trade reformers which are destined to failure as well as reformers destined for success. Moreover, it is often the case that SALs are introduced contemporaneously with IMF Stabilisation Loans and these invariably include an expenditure contraction component. Two of our models suggest a long-run enhancement of around 2% whereas a third points to a long-run pay-off of 46%. This is a huge difference which could be due to the fact that in the first two cases we are unequivocally using a liberalisation measure whilst in the third case it is equally unambiguously a measure of openness.

Given the inconsistency in the results currently extant in the literature, our results are surprising for their consistency but also revealing. They suggest that at least four factors may be at work in explaining why the previous literature is so inconsistent. First there is the obvious point that sample sizes and composition vary as do methodological approaches. Second, different analysts have used different measures; some are *ex ante* indicators of liberalisation, some are *ex post* and others are clearly indicators of openness. Third it is clear that many models which have been estimated are mis-specified. Fourth, it is important to model the dynamics in order to distinguish between short-run and longer-run effects.

4 CONCLUSIONS

We began this paper by explaining why liberalisation might impact favourably upon growth but also pointed to reasons why, at least in the short-run, it might not. Following a review of alternative measures of liberalisation we discussed the various strands of the literature which feed into the empirical analysis of trade policy and economic growth. As we saw, this is a genuinely controversial literature. We then proceeded to test a dynamic model of growth in the context of several samples and, more importantly, using several measures of liberalisation. We report a surprisingly consistent set of results both qualitatively and quantitatively. These suggest that liberalisation and openness do impact favourably on the growth of GDP per capita. In the case of the former, the impact may not necessarily be straightforward and as theory suggests, the response is in all probability lagged. Moreover, it is also relatively modest. That is not so surprising since liberalisations vary in their depth and intensity and rarely if ever amount to an immediate shift to free trade. The liberalisations which are picked up are often first steps rather than final steps. Through time of course economies become more open, partly as a consequence of incremental trade reforms but also of course as a consequence of other factors: reductions in transportation and communication costs, technological change and so on. The pay-off to this increased openness is likely to be far greater and that is what our results confirm. Perhaps therefore the most important lesson of our results is that in evaluating the impact of trade policy and changes in trade policy on growth it is vital not to equate liberalisation with openness and equally vital to remember that openness is a function of many factors not just liberalisation.

References

Arellano, M. and Bond, S. (1991). 'Some test of specification for panel data: Monte Carlo evidence and an application to employment equations'. *Review of Economic Studies*, vol. 58, pp. 277–92.

Balassa, B. (1982). *Development Strategies in Semi-Industrialized Countries*, Baltimore: Johns Hopkins University Press.

Bevan, Collier and Gunning (1993). 'Trade shocks in developing countries', *European Economic Review*, vol. 37, pp. 557–65.

Bhagwati, J. (1978). *Foreign Trade Regimes and Economic Development*, Cambridge MA: Ballinger Press.

Bleaney, M. F. and Greenaway, D. (1993). 'Adjustment to external imbalance and investment slumps in developing countries', *European Economic Review*, vol. 37, pp. 577–85.

Collier, P. (1993). 'Higgledy-piggledy liberalisation', *The World Economy*, vol. 16, pp. 503–12.

Dean, J., Desai, S. and Riedel, J. (1994). 'Trade policy reform in developing countries since 1985: a review of the evidence', World Bank Development Policy Group, mimeo.

Dornbusch, R. (1992). 'The case for trade liberalisation in developing countries', *Journal of Economic Perspectives*, vol. 6, pp. 69–85.

Easterley, W., Loayza, N. and Montiel, P. (1997). Has Latin America's post-reform growth been disappointing? *Journal of International Economics*, vol. 43(3–4), pp. 287–311.

Edwards, S. (1993). 'Openness, trade liberalisation and growth in developing countries', *Journal of Economic Literature*, vol. 31, pp. 1358–93.

Greenaway, D. (1993). 'Liberalising foreign trade through rose tinted glasses', *Economic Journal*, vol. 103, pp. 208–23.

Greenaway, D. and Milner, C. R. (1993). *Trade and Industrial Policy in Developing Countries*, London: Macmillan.

Greenaway, D. and Sapsford, D. (1994). 'What does liberalisation do for exports and growth', *Weltwirtschaftliches Archiv*, vol. 130, pp. 152–74.

Greenaway, D., Leybourne, S. J. and Sapsford, D. (1997). 'Modelling growth (and liberalisation) using smooth transitions analysis', *Economic Inquiry*, vol. 35, pp. 798–814.

Greenaway, D., Morgan C. W. and Wright, P. W. (1997). 'Trade orientation and economic performance', *World Development*, vol. 25, pp. 1885–92.

Harrigan, J. and Mosley, P. (1991). 'Evaluating the impact of world bank structural adjustment lending: 1980–87. *Journal of Development Studies*, vol. 27, pp. 63–94.

Krueger, A. O. (1978). *Foreign Trade Regimes and Economic Liberalisation*, Lexington, MA: Ballinger.

Krueger, A. O. (1997). 'Trade policy and economic development: how we learn', *American Economic Review*, vol. 87. pp. 1–22.

Levine, R. and Renelt, D. (1992). 'A sensitivity of cross country growth regressions', *American Economic Review*, vol. 82, pp. 946–63.

Mosley, P., Harrigan, J. and Toye, J. (eds) (1991*a*). *Aid and Power: The World Bank and Policy-based Lending. Volume 1: Analysis and Policy Proposals*, London: Routledge.

Mosley, P., Harrigan, J. and Toye, J. (eds) (1991*b*). *Aid and Power: The World Bank and Policy-based Lending. Volume 2: Case Studies*, London: Routledge.

Onafowora, O. A., Owoye, O. and Nyatepe-Coo, A. (1996). 'Trade policy, export performance and economic growth: evidence from Sub-Saharan Africa. *Journal of International Trade and Economic Development*, vol. 5, pp. 341–60.

Papageorgiou, D., Michaely, M. and Choksi, A. (eds) (1991). *Liberalising Foreign Trade*, Oxford: Basil Blackwell.

Rodrik, D. (1992). 'The limits of trade policy reform in developing countries'. *Journal of Economic Perspectives*, vol. 6, pp. 87–105.

Rodrik, D. (1998). 'Globalisation, social conflict and economic growth', *The World Economy*, vol. 21, pp. 143–58.

Romer (1990). 'Endogenous technological change', *Journal of Political Economy*, vol. 98, pp. 71–102.

Sachs, J. D. and Warner, A. (1995). 'Economic reform and the process of global integration', *Brookings Papers on Economic Activity*, vol. 1 pp. 1–118.

Whalley (1991). *The Uruguay Round and Beyond*, London: Macmillan.

World Bank (1990). 'Report on adjustment lending II: Policies for the recovery of growth', Document R90–99. Washington D.C., The World Bank.

World Bank (1993). *Report on Structural Adjustment Lending III*, Washington DC: World Bank.

Part 3

REGIONALISM VERSUS MULTILATERALISM

INTRODUCTION

Sajal Lahiri

Regionalism can broadly be defined as a tendency towards some form of preferential trading arrangements between a number of countries belonging possibly to a particular region. The word 'preferential' is the key word here and it necessarily implies that countries not belonging to a particular regional arrangement are discriminated against. The controversy regarding the desirability of regionalism is not a new one. The discriminatory aspect of regional agreements led Jacob Viner to question, in his famous 1950 book,[1] the then conventional wisdom that such agreements are necessarily welfare improving by drawing attention to the possibility of significant 'trade diversion'. Subsequent formation of the European Common Market gave fresh impetus to the controversy in the 1950s and the 1960s when many attempts were made at different parts of the world to form regional trading blocks. Most of these agreements, with the notable exceptions of the European Common Market, did not really get off the ground. Those attempted arrangements are sometimes called the 'old' or 'first' regionalism.

The controversy remained latent for nearly two decades and came back with a vengeance in recent years with the advent of 'new' or 'second' regionalism. In this second phase of regionalism, preferential trading agreements are being formed at unprecedented speed with the explicit blessings of influential political forces (the US administration, for example).[2] Some estimates suggest that currently there are nearly one hundred regional arrangements. This is the 'new' or 'second' regionalism.

The old issues such as trade diversion have not been forgotten in the debate on new regionalism, although influential economists such as Professor Summers have tried to 'laugh off' those issues. Recent works by some economists at the World Bank have found significant evidence of trade diversion in the case of the MERCOSUR in Latin America. Professors Bhagwati, Greenaway and Panagariya in their contribution to follow this introduction have made a very powerful case that trade diversion should be taken very seriously in assessing the welfare effects of preferential trading agreements.

---

[1] For the exact reference, see the contribution by Bhagwati et al. and Ethier in this *Controversy*.

[2] It should however be pointed out that the actual agreements vary very significantly from one another. For example, in the European Single Market agreement free mobility of workers between the member states is an important element, but in the North American Free Trade Agreement (NAFTA) no such provision is made. In fact, some people believe that one of the reasons for bringing Mexico into NAFTA was to stem the flow of (illegal) workers from Mexico to the United States.

However, the old and the new regionalism have many important differences and these differences may explain why new regionalism could prove to be more successful than the old one. Professor Ethier in his contribution has pointed to many of the fundamental differences.

In the time of the old regionalism, the multilateral trading system was at its infancy. In contrast, today the World Trade Organisation (WTO) has wide ranging powers with an explicit goal of multilateral free trade not only in commodities but also in services and capital. The simultaneous existence of regionalism and multilateralism has obviously led to a new controversy. Various questions are being asked. Will the spread of regionalism undermine the progress of multilateralism? Does the success with multilateralism necessarily lead to the spread of regionalism? Does regionalism affect the enforcement provisions built in the Articles of WTO? All these and many other questions are essentially dynamic in nature and their analyses require endogenising many of the issues that were treated as exogenous in the old controversy.

Clearly, economists differ in their analyses of the desirability of regionalism in the present context. The three articles to follow this introduction take very different standpoints in this controversy. I shall make no attempt to summarise the views expressed, and the results obtained, in the three articles. Instead, I shall conclude this introduction by raising an issue which has not received much attention in the literature so far.

It is true that during the current decade there has been a proliferation of regional agreements. However, in some sense the reverse has also happened in some regions. For example, the demise of the Soviet Union also saw the end of the East European economic block, namely the COMECON. Casual empiricism suggests that trade between many of the former members of COMECON has more or less collapsed. Presumably, they were trading 'too much' (compared to the 'ideal' situation) between themselves before the break up, and now it seems that they are trading 'too little'. One wonders if this significant diversion of trade in favour of the countries in the European Union (EU) is a strategic move on the part of the East and Central European countries to influence future decisions by the EU on new membership. Another example can be found in South Asia. In spite of the formation of the South Asian Association for Regional Cooperation (SAARC) in the mid-eighties, intra-regional trade between the member countries remain negligible even in absolute terms. Trade between India and Pakistan is restricted by numerous quantitative and administrative measures. This can be called inverse regionalism. The political process in the two countries have a lot to do with this inverse regionalism. Clearly such restrictions to trade can be reduced by regional agreements without necessarily imposing trade restrictions against countries outside South Asia. Such reversals of inverse regionalism could only reinforce the multilateral trading system.

8

TRADING PREFERENTIALLY: THEORY AND POLICY*

Jagdish Bhagwati, David Greenaway and Arvind Panagariya

The best kind of economic theory has almost always reflected policy concerns, while informing policy in turn. This is particularly so when it comes to the theory of international trade, going back to Adam Smith's discovery of the demerits of mercantilism and his invention of economic science, both in *The Wealth of Nations*. The theory of preferential trading is no exception.

The original burst of creative theorising about Preferential Trade Agreements (PTAs), associated with what Bhagwati (1991) has called the First Regionalism[1], is well known to have come from Jacob Viner's (1950) work on what he called the 'customs union issue' and was a result of his having been commissioned by the Carnegie Endowment to examine the appropriate design of the world trading system with the end of the Second World War. In turn, the impending formation of the Common Market, leading to the Treaty of Rome in 1957, played a role in the further development of the theory at the hands of James Meade (1955), Richard Lipsey (1958) and others.[2]

* Thanks are due to Kym Anderson, Kyle Bagwell, Robert Baldwin, Richard Baldwin, Claude Barfield, Christopher Bliss, Magnus Blomström, Max Corden. Clive Crook, Don Davis, Alan Deardorff, Vivek Dehejia, Elias Dinopoulos. Henry Flam, Robert Feenstra, Caroline Freund, Ross Garnaut, Earl Grinols, Gene Grossman, Elhanan Helpman, Gary Hufbauer, Douglas Irwin, Pravin Krishna, Paul Krugman, Anne Krueger, Patrick Lane, Phil Levy, Rachel McCulloch, Chris Milner, John Nash, Andre Sapir, Gary Saxonhouse, Alasadair Smith, Robert Staiger, Robert Stern, Sethaput SuthiwartNarueput, T. N. Srinivasan, Wendy Takacs, David Tarr, John Whalley, Alan Winters, Martin Wolf, Kar-yiu Wong, Ron and Paul Wonnacott, and Ian Wooton for conversations that have contributed to the development of our thinking over the last decade on the issues covered in this paper. Some of these economists have their own take on the rapidly expanding theory of PTAs; e.g. Winters (1996), and Baldwin and Venables (1996). A set of key contributions to the theory of PTAs, starting from Viner (1950), organised by major analytical approaches to the subject, is given in Bhagwati et al. (1998). Ajay Panagariya drew the figures skillfully for us.

[1] The late 1950s and early 1960s, which constitute the period of the First Regionalism, were witness to attempts at forming customs unions (CUs) and free trade areas (FTAs) in several developing countries, inspired partly by the Treaty of Rome but reflecting a different rationale which is discussed below in Section 1.4. It should be stated that the general usage of the word Regionalism interchangeably with PTAs or FTAs is not desirable since PTAs are occasionally formed with members who do not meet any reasonable definition of a 'region': e.g. United States and Israel. For a discussion of this relationship, or rather lack of it, see Bhagwati and Panagariya (1996a, pp. 4 and 31–5) and the spoof, 'The Watering of Trade' by Bhagwati (1996)

[2] Other non-Vinerian developments of the 'static' approach to the analysis of PTAs, pioneered by Viner, are discussed in the text below. These too have been interactive with policy questions, as we argue in the text.

The recent burst of theorising about PTAs is also a reflection of the new policy questions raised by the fact that the United States abandoned in the early 1980s its policy of avoiding PTAs, even though sanctioned by Article 24 of the GATT, and concentrating exclusively on multilateral trade negotiations (MTN) which lead to reductions of trade barriers characterised by MFN. The subsequent proliferation of PTAs has made this Second Regionalism a period of 'success' whereas the First Regionalism was generally marked by aborted efforts.

Whereas the Vinerian analysis of PTAs in the First Regionalism reflected 'static' questions concerning the welfare effects of unions with defined membership, the Second Regionalism has been preoccupied with what Bhagwati (1993) has described as the 'dynamic' time-path question: i.e., in broad terms (to be refined below), whether PTAs can provide an impetus to, or whether they will detract from, the worldwide nondiscriminatory freeing of trade. In other words, in the phrasing and conceptualisation of Bhagwati (1991), will PTAs be 'stumbling blocks' or 'building blocks' in the freeing of trade multilaterally?

The very success of the Second Regionalism, and the continuing proliferation of PTAs which we confront today even as their number is already in three digits (Bhagwati and Panagariya, 1996a, Chapter 1, Appendix), has led to a substantial shift away from the complacency among international economists that attended this proliferation. Not merely have the old concerns about trade diversion revived, with several studies now challenging the assertions that trade diversion is not an important issue in practice, but the *systemic* effects of having numerous PTAs present in the world trading system have also attracted analytical and policy attention.

In the following review of the present state of the theory of PTAs, we consider in section 1 the 'static' theories, in Viner's tradition and outside of it; in section 2 we address the 'systemic' issues which have been raised in the static framework: in section 3, the 'dynamic' time-path theories are reviewed; and in section 4, we consider briefly the state of the current policy debate.

1 'STATIC' THEORIES: VINER AND OTHERS

There are by now four alternative theoretical approaches to the 'static' implications of PTAs, with recent theoretical developments of interest in most of them.

1.1 Viner and extensions: trade diversion and the 'natural trading partners' issue

Two issues in particular can be highlighted in the modern extensions of Viner's analysis of the 'static' welfare implications of PTAs.

Is trade diversion a red herring?

Viner distinguished between trade creation and trade diversion. The notion that any move towards free trade, even if preferential, would necessarily be welfare-improving, appeared intuitive until Viner's seminal work. Today, these pre-Vinerian attitudes have reappeared, as in Lawrence Summers' (1991, page 299) remarkable statement: 'I find it surprising that this issue [of trade diversion] is taken so seriously – in most other situations, economists laugh off second best considerations and focus on direct impacts.'[3] But the pro-PTA implication is not sustainable for at least three reasons.

First, from an analytical viewpoint, Panagariya (1995; 1996) has shown that, if the effect of a PTA on a member country's welfare is to be examined, the transfer of revenue among the members following the abolition of tariffs within the PTA will generally lead to tariff revenue redistribution among the members. This 'Panagariya rectangle', measuring the loss of tariff revenue on inter-member trade, can outweigh any net gain on the Harberger–Johnson 'triangles' that trade creation and trade diversion imply. This point is of relevance when a high-tariff country like Mexico joins a low-tariff country like the United States in a PTA.[4]

Second, increasing numbers of empirical studies are now beginning to show that trade diversion is not necessarily a negligible phenomenon in current PTAs. Thus, Yeats' (1996) study of MERCOSUR (among Uruguay, Argentina, Paraguay and Brazil) turned up significant evidence of trade diversion: the diversion of textile trade to Mexico from the Caribbean, thanks to NAFTA which excludes the latter and includes the former, has been a source of discord; and Wei and Frankel (1997) have argued that the EU has led to trade diversion. We are sure that more evidence of trade diversion will mount as economists, no longer under political pressure to swim with the tide in favour of PTAs, return to their first economic principles and begin to distinguish à la Viner between preferential and nonpreferential trade liberalisation.

In fact, now that we have interesting analytical political-economy-theoretic papers by Grossman and Helpman (1995) and Krishna (1998) which show that trade diversion is an important motive (among others noted by us in Section 4) leading to PTAs, it is not surprising that the evidence of trade diversion occurring as a result of PTAs is not hard to find. It is not remarkable that those who indulge their preference for preferential trade arrangements are seen also to use the preferences.

Third, the complacency about PTAs not leading to trade diversion was aided by the notion that the external trade barriers were no longer very high and that, therefore, preferences could not lead to significant trade diversion. But this is not true for several reasons.

To begin with, even trade tariffs are still very high, both in developing and in developed countries. In the latter, the Uruguay Round has still left several peak tariffs in specific products whereas the tariffication of agricultural support has created truly substantial tariffs. In the former, countries in South Asia and in Latin America are also not free from high trade barriers, making PTAs particularly dangerous.

Besides, the external trade barriers are today only a part of the protectionist story. 'Administered protection', the term we owe to Michael Finger, consisting of instruments such as anti-dumping (AD) actions, has become the favoured policy of protectionists who cleverly use the appealing notion of 'fair trade' to unfairly gain protection

[3] The several analytical fallacies in this statement have been noted in Bhagwati and Panagariya (1996*a*, pp. 5–7). The fact that *empirically* trade diversion is not negligible and cannot be dismissed is yet another criticism.

[4] On the importance of analysing revenue effects in undertaking trade policy changes more generally, see Greenaway and Milner (1991). Greenaway (1993) considers other pertinent issues as well.

and advantage against successful foreign rivals. But then these instruments typically yield protection that is elastic and selective. Thus, AD duties, which bear little relationship to 'predation' in the economic sense and hence have in practice no economic justification[5], are often based on adjusted prices that are estimated in ways calculated to find dumping[6] or on essentially arbitrary 'reconstructed cost' when the AD methodology compares, not foreign and domestic prices, but foreign costs and domestic prices. Thus, within broad margins, it is arguable that AD calculations and actions will seek to accommodate the needs of the protectionist petitioners in the spirit of the story where the interviewing commissar asks candidates what the sum of 2 and 2 is, and the job goes to the candidate who answers: whatever you want, sir. In addition to their being therefore *elastic*, AD actions are *selective* in the sense that they are mounted against specific countries and even specific firms within those countries. Thus, it is possible to use them to zero in against your most potent foreign rivals.

It follows then that, unless such administered protection is severely regulated, the temptation on the part of PTA members will be to protect each other with such protection at the expense of nonmembers, when internal competition among members breaks out with the PTA formation. In short, protection against nonmembers then becomes *endogenous* to the PTA. The consequence is that, as trade creation occurs within a PTA, the endogenous raising of protection converts it into trade diversion instead. E.g. as Mexico starts crowding out inefficient US producers, the United States accommodates imports from Mexico by reducing imports from the most efficient nonmember supplier, Taiwan, using AD actions against Taiwan. This possibility, noted in Bhagwati (1993, pp. 36–7), has been formally demonstrated in Bhagwati and Panagariya (1996a, pp. 38–41), and Panagariya and Findlay (1996).

Such a phenomenon is not an idle theoretic speculation. Instances of such endogenous raising of protection against nonmembers have been observed. An example is the raising of (unbound) tariffs on over 500 non-NAFTA tariffs by Mexico during the 1995 peso crisis, while tariffs against NAFTA members were not. EU experience has been discussed by Hindley and Messerlin in their contribution to Anderson and Blackhurst (1993). Hence, Bhagwati (1993) and Serra et al. (1996) have argued that the reform of GATT Article 24 on PTAs is not enough; enhanced discipline on administered protection, especially AD actions, is equally necessary to reduce the damage from PTAs today.

The 'natural trading partners' issue

But if the issue of trade diversion has been a matter of controversy among trade theorists and policymakers, a related issue has also attracted attention, again with claims made by prominent economists and being rebutted by serious new analytical research. The claim has been that if PTAs are formed among 'natural trading partners', then they can be expected to be welfare-improving for the members. The phrase 'natural trading partners' comes from Wonnacott and Lutz (1989, page 69) who used it in

---

[5] An excellent review of the theoretical and policy literature on predatory dumping and the lack of its relationship to AD practice in trade law is to be found in Clarida (1996).

[6] See Hindley (1997) for current EC practice; he has been a longstanding critic of the intricate calculating methodology that stacks the cards against foreign suppliers.

several different senses, of which two have been put into circulation by their endorsement by Summers (1991) and Krugman (1991): that the initial volume of trade among the partners is high, and that the distance between them is low. But, as Bhagwati and Panagariya (1996a) and Panagariya (1997a,b) have demonstrated, each criterion is flawed and should be rejected.

The volume-of-trade criterion

Of course, this criterion is neither symmetric nor transitive. The United States is Mexico's largest trading partner, but the reverse is not true. Then, the United States is the largest trading partner of Canada and Mexico, but the latter have little trade with each other. But even waiving these objections, there are difficulties with the Summers–Krugman assertion.

The presumption that high initial volume of trade among members reduces the potential for trade diversion is presumably based on the view that if there is little trade with nonmembers, the *scope* for trade diversion is reduced. But what we need to know is the *likelihood* of trade diversion instead. The scope for trade diversion in an instance may be twice as high as in another; but the actual trade diversion that occurs may be only half as much.

The actual trade diversion will reflect the underlying fundamentals such as elasticities of substitution among products, not the average initial trade volumes! This was understood, of course, by the early theorists of PTAs; see the discussion of Meade (1955) and Lipsey (1958) in Bhagwati (1993), and Panagariya's (1997a) analysis of the classic Meade (1955) model.

In fact, as Bhagwati and Panagariya (1996a, pp. 22–7) show, analysing a model based on Meade (1955) with each member country specialised on a different product when all products are imperfect substitutes, the steady reduction of tariff preferentially by one country on another will first improve its welfare and then progressively reduce it at some stage, so that reaching a 100% reduction, implying an FTA, may reduce welfare even below the starting level. This is shown in Fig. 1 where the superscripts *b* and *c* refer to countries *B* and *C*; the reduction of *A*'s tariff on *B* preferentially, maintaining the tariff on nonmember *C* throughout, is plotted; and so is the welfare of home country *A*. In this diagram, as the tariff on partner country *B* reduces steadily to the left, the volume of trade by *A* with *B* also grows absolutely and relatively to trade with nonmember country *C*, turning *A* and *B* progressively into more and more 'natural trading partners'. But, any further such increase in 'naturalness' beyond the point at which welfare of *A* begins to fall makes any further preferential tariff reduction in favour of *B* harmful, not beneficial: so, the more natural trading partner you get to be, the more likely it is that you will be in the zone where preferential trading will reduce welfare.[7]

---

[7] That a 100% preferential tariff reduction à la Article 24 could be harmful whereas a lesser preference could be beneficial has been known to readers of Lipsey (1958) for over four decades. But it does not follow that we should therefore weaken Article 24 to allow all sorts of preferential reductions provided they are calculated to produce greater welfare. That question raises a number of other issues, such as the wisdom of having PTAs made admissible on the basis of such calculations. For a discussion of the economics and the political economy of Article 24 requirement that only 100% preferential reduction of inter-member trade barriers is to be allowed, see Bhagwati (1991, 1993).

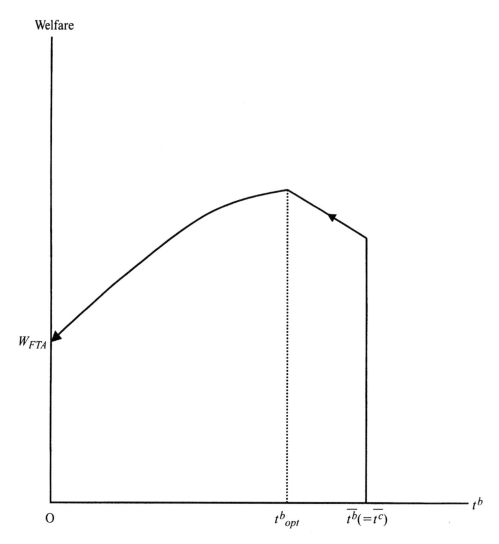

Fig. 1 Effect of preferential tariff reduction on welfare
Source: Bhagwati and Panagariya (1996)

Yet another implication of the demonstration in Fig. 1 is that there need be nothing 'natural' about initial high volumes of trade. These may reflect earlier preferences, leading the proponents of the natural trading partners argument in effect to advocate more preferences on the basis of existing preferences! This possibility is not a theoretical curiosum: the volume of trade between the United States and Mexico has certainly increased thanks to the Offshore Assembly Provision which has differentially assisted Mexican production and exports to the United States; similarly, the trade with Canada has profited considerably from the auto agreement which established free trade in the sector between the two countries but not for producers elsewhere.[8]

The transport-cost criterion

If the volume-of-trade criterion fails to work, so does the transport-cost criterion, whose appeal is intuitive to many but still rests on error. Of course, any freeing of trade can be frustrated if high transport costs – in the limit, physical inability to transport goods – prevent trade opportunities so opened up from being utilised. But this does not translate into the current prescription concerning desirable PTAs.

To see this, it is enough to see the counterexample constructed in Bhagwati and Panagariya (1996a, pp. 36–8).[9] Thus, consider Fig. 2 and three countries, A, B and C.

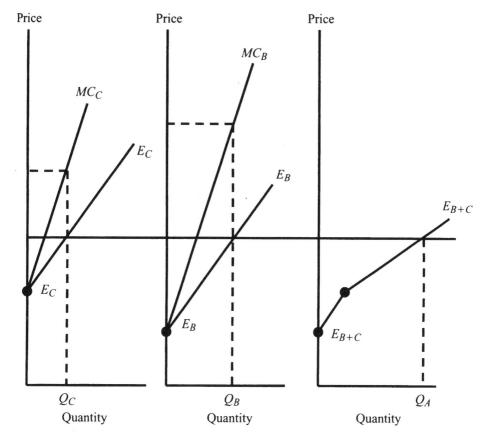

Fig. 2 A union with the distant country C is superior

[8] Among other criticisms, we must include also the 'Panagariya rectangle' concerning the transfer of revenue among member countries, which we noted in the text earlier. This adverse effect will be the larger, the larger is the volume of initial trade with the member country whose exports to oneself are freed from duties, turning the 'natural trading partners' presumption of no damage into just the opposite presumption of larger damage.

[9] In the following, we omit some of the more subtle points that these authors consider, such as what would happen if the supply curves were perfectly elastic.

Country *A* has the option to join a PTA with either *B* or *C*. Countries *B* and *C* are identical except for the fact that *B* is less distant. Three panels are drawn. The first two panels show the export supply curves of *C* and *B*, whereas the third panel shows the combined supply curve. Assuming a fixed transport cost per unit, country *C*'s supply curve (c.i.f.) is higher than country *B*'s since *B* is closer. The third panel shows the trade equilibrium when both *B* and *C* pay identical tariffs in *A*; *A*'s demand curve is not shown. Note that the initial volume of imports from the proximate country *B* is larger than from the distant country *C*.

Now, by drawing the marginal cost curves derived from the export supply curves, we see immediately the paradoxical conclusion: at the initial non-discriminatory equilibrium, the marginal cost of imports from the more distant country *C* is lower than that from *B* which is the proximate country and hence is the 'natural trading partner' by the transport-cost criterion. It follows, of course, that the efficient choice of the PTA partner would be the distant country *C*.

It is easy to see why. Country *A* is best seen as a discriminating monopsonist. So, for any quantity of total purchases, the supplier with the higher elasticity should be paid the higher price. Here, this translates into a lower duty on the supplier with the higher elasticity. Transport costs make the distant country *C*'s supply curve more elastic than that of the proximate country *B*, making the PTA with *C* more attractive for country *A*.[10]

It is fair then to say that these analyses have laid to rest the 'natural trading partners' hypotheses, whether of the volume-of-trade or of the transport-cost variety, that became fashionable when prominent economists such as Summers (1991) and Krugman (1991) embraced them, and they gained the attention of policymakers and were reported in influential magazines such as *The Economist*.[11]

1.2 The Kemp–Wan approach: Parting with Viner's formulation

The Vinerian attack on the presumption that preferential trade liberalisation is beneficial is clearly then of great importance. But there is an altogether different question that Kemp and Wan (1976) addressed and answered completely: suppose that any arbitrarily-specified subset of countries were to form a CU, and could choose their external tariff (so that the external tariff became endogenous whereas the Vinerian analysis took it as given), could they *always* devise a CU which left the welfare of the nonmembers where it was while it improved member country welfare?

Kemp and Wan showed that they could. The essence of their argument was beautifully concise.[12] If the external trade vector of the arbitrarily chosen members of a CU

---

[10] Since, in this example, the proximate country is also the one with the higher initial volume of imports, this example serves also as a demonstration of the unreliability of the volume-of-trade criterion as a guide to selecting PTA partners.

[11] *The Economist* ran an Economics Focus Column on the subject, as a report on the 1991 Jackson Hole Conference where the Summers and Krugman papers were presented.

[12] The Kemp–Wan paper was preceded by a fragment of an argument by Kemp earlier and more systematic attack on the problem by Ohyama (1972) in an obscure Japanese journal. Baldwin and Venables (1996) claim that Meade anticipated the Kemp–Wan argument; but this claim cannot be sustained, as shown in Panagariya (1997*a*). Yet another way of arriving at the Kemp–Wan existence solution is provided in Krishna and Bhagwati (1997).

was frozen, the nonmembers' welfare would be frozen too. If then the inter-member barriers were fully removed, the resulting competitive equilibrium would be Pareto-superior and hence, with lumpsum transfers, each member country could be made better off.[13] The difference between the domestic price vector that emerged in this CU equilibrium, when set against the frozen external price vector, would then yield the endogenously-determined trade tariff and subsidy vector that would support the necessarily welfare-enhancing Kemp–Wan CU.[14]

Kemp and Wan would appear to be restoring the preVinerian intuition about PTAs. In fact, however, the preVinerian intuition is, strictly speaking, not restored by Kemp and Wan, since that intuition was that all PTAs (and indeed all kinds of trade liberalisation short of free trade), were desirable because they all moved trade barriers down, i.e. that welfare of liberalising countries and world welfare would improve monotonically as trade barriers came down, no matter how they came down. Rather, Kemp and Wan show that a *particular PTA* which reduces trade barriers among member states, could *always* be *crafted* which would improve the welfare of member countries and of the world. In essence, therefore, the Kemp–Wan argument is an existence argument. In itself, it does not provide a clue to the structure of the endogenous tariff that would emerge in the Kemp–Wan welfare-improving CU.[15]

1.3 The Brecher-Bhagwati approach: Distributional effects within a Common Market

Suppose, however, that a Common Market (variety of PTA) exists, such as the European Union 'core', where there is also free mobility of factors of production within the PTA. In that case, the analyst can ask a variety of important policy questions: e.g. what happens to the welfare of each 'national' set of factors, defining a member country, as the common external tariff changes, or as capital accumulates in one country or technical change occurs in another, or as new members of varying sizes relative to the average size in the PTA are added? In essence, this is identical to the income distributional analysis within a single nation (wherein we conventionally assume factors to be mobile), where the focus is not on overall welfare of the nation but on the welfare of individual factors by class: e.g. by race, by gender, by ownership of assets etc., when fundamentals such as capital and technology are assumed to change and policies such as trade policy are changed.

Bhagwati and Tironi (1993), reacting to the policy concerns in South America that freeing of trade would benefit the foreign multinationals operating in South America while immiserising the host countries, had already opened up the analysis of the effect

---

[13] The internal barriers must be removed altogether, so that we can invoke without difficulty the welfare theorem that a competitive equilibrium is a Pareto-efficient equilibrium.

[14] Although the Kemp–Wan proof relates to the formation of a CU, with a common external tariff, we suspect that the proof can be extended to the formation of an FTA with each country having its external tariff: in that case, the proof must have as a building block the freezing, not just of the aggregate external trade of all members together, but of each country's external trade vector.

[15] On the other hand, the Kemp–Wan tariff structure has been explored by Grinols (1981), Bliss (1994) and Srinivasan (1997).

of change in trade policy on national welfare when foreign factors of production are present in the economy, so that 'national' welfare (defined over national factors of production, and hence not including the foreign-owned factors) must be distinguished from 'domestic' welfare (which does not do so). However, their analysis was limited to the freeing of trade and foreign investment issue and the broad implication regarding the analysis of PTAs in shape of Common Markets was also not seen.

Brecher and Bhagwati (1981) generalised the analysis to a formal treatment of the income distributional issue when welfare analysis must be disaggregated down to classes of factors, analysing the effects of parametric and policy changes on such groups of factors, while explicitly stating the applicability of the analysis to changes in national welfare in a Common Market of the EU variety. Indeed, the effect on individual member countries of liberalisation of the common EU tariff was precisely the problem that the Brecher–Bhagwati analysis equipped one to analyse. More recently, Casella (1996) has analysed a similar problem, differentiating among different member countries by their size, in the framework of the theory of imperfect competition with scale economies.

1.4 The Cooper–Massell–Johnson–Bhagwati approach: Forming a CU to minimise the cost of import substitution

The policy problem for developing countries in the 1960s, as they confronted the high cost of each country's import substitution strategy, was: *given* any level of import substitution vis-à-vis the developed countries, could the developing countries open up trade *preferentially among themselves* and reduce the cost of their individual import substitution? By invoking scale economies, Cooper and Massell (1965*a,b*), Johnson (1965) and Bhagwati (1968) argued that they could. In fact, attempts were made at forming such PTAs in East Africa and in Latin America. These attempts, part of the aborted First Regionalism, failed because these countries were wedded to planning at the time and saw trade as accommodating to a planned allocation of the import-substituting industries among the member countries, instead of letting trade decide which industry went where, thus putting the cart before the horse and killing the forward momentum.

But, while scale economies were invoked to advance the theoretical underpinning of such an approach to forming PTAs, recently Krishna and Bhagwati (1997) have shown that the Cooper–Massell–Johnson–Bhagwati argument can be formalised simply without them. In essence, they show that the solution involves, as is intuitive once you think of it, a Kemp–Wan CU along with production tax-cum-subsidies to achieve the import-substituting industrialisation objectives of member states as indicated by the theory of optimal intervention in the presence of noneconomic objectives.

This approach is now principally of a historical-explanatory value since nearly all developing countries are convinced today of the pitfalls associated with the import substitution strategy; they have also seen that export oriented strategies have led to far more rapid industrialisation in the Far East and elsewhere. The renewed preference for PTAs among several developing countries is now premised on quite different grounds, many political rather than economic (as argued in the final section below).

2 THE SYSTEMIC ISSUES RAISED BY PROLIFERATION OF PTAS: THE 'SPAGHETTI BOWL' PHENOMENON

The static welfare effects of PTAs would be seriously incomplete today if it were not extended to their 'systemic' implications because of the massive proliferation of PTAs, ridiculed in Bhagwati (1997), in the period of Second Regionalism.

These systemic implications arise because PTAs magnify the problems that arise in essence because we try to restrict or liberalise trade on the basis of which product comes from which country, or what Bhagwati (1995) has called the 'who is whose' problem (in Bhagwati and Krueger (1995)). Thus, for instance, as soon as the United States wishes to liberalise the imports from Israel preferentially, it must decide whether an import coming from Israel is Israeli. That is, it must establish a 'rule of origin' which usually takes the form of some sort of 'content' rule such that a product is considered to be Israeli only if its Israeli content exceeds an arbitrarily specified share in gross value.[16] The arbitrariness of this share *specification* is further compounded by the arbitrariness inherent in *computing* such content. Thus, consider the import of ingots of steel which, in conjunction with homogeneous domestically-produced ingots, go into producing scissors and forks. How is one to determine which of these two products got what share of the imported as against the domestic ingots?[17] Again, if forks need to be coated with plastics, we know that even if the plastics are immediately produced at home, their gross value (as in Leontief's analysis of direct and indirect requirements to support a vector of final demand) would generally include imported intermediates at several stages of manufacture, which are impossible for the same reasons to identify and quantify meaningfully. Again, even if we were to estimate such imported shares meaningfully, the imports are likely in turn to include, in today's globalised production, intermediates produced by us and used by the producers abroad. The difficulties are myriad, even endless.

All of these problems, which inherently lead to absurd arbitrariness in trying to identify the origin of products, are seriously present when an FTA inevitably requires that the origin be established for virtually all traded products. Since there are different external tariffs among members in an FTA, the problem is additionally acute since the fear of nonmember goods coming into one's territory at a lower tariff than one's own, simply by entering through another lower-tariff member country, is palpable. But the problem does not disappear in a CU despite the common external tariff. Thus, whether a Nissan produced in Britain is a Japanese car that must be allowed free entry into France as a British car or must pay the external tariff as a Japanese car, has been a source of discord: the problem arises since the EU would like to treat the tariff on Japanese cars differently from that on other cars. By wanting to treat Japanese cars at a preferential disadvantage, the CU (which is a PTA) also runs inherently into problems of arbitrary definitions of origin.

---

[16] An alternative rule is the 'substantial transformation' test.

[17] In development economics, this problem has long been known in the context of the impractical Hirschman recommendation that backward linkages be utilised to create the maximum inducement to invest. In the Leontief input-output framework, one cannot meaningfully break down the a_{ij} coefficients into d_{ij} (domestic) and m_{ij} (imported) coefficients for competitive imports.

In reality, FTAs have created yet further problems by having many different rules of origin, varying by products (as in NAFTA, for instance) and by FTAs (when, say, the EU has FTAs with different rules with several different non-EU countries). Indeed, by making possible the manipulation of rules of origin, PTA countries are open to protectionist capture.[18] The problems inherently posed by PTAs in regard to the rules of origin that they require are yet further compounded since FTAs are on different schedules of tariff cutting by sector and are not synchronised (having been negotiated at different points of time and with different schedules for reaching zero tariff outcomes), so that we typically find a large and chaotic set of applicable tariffs on the same good, depending on which source the good is assigned to.

The result is what Bhagwati (1995) has called the 'spaghetti bowl' phenomenon of numerous and crisscrossing PTAs and innumerable applicable tariff rates depending on arbitrarily-determined and often a multiplicity of sources of origin (see Fig. 3).[19] In short, the systemic effect is to generate a world of preferences, with all its well-known consequences, which increases transaction costs and facilitates protectionism. In the guise of freeing trade, PTAs have managed to recreate the preferences-ridden world of the 1930s as surely as protectionism did at the time. Irony, indeed!

3 'DYNAMIC' TIME-PATH ANALYSIS: BUILDING VERSUS STUMBLING BLOCKS

In contrast to the question whether the immediate (static) effect of a PTA is good, we may ask whether the (dynamic time-path) effect of the PTA is to accelerate or decelerate the continued reduction of trade barriers towards the goal of reducing them worldwide.[20] I.e. we have now, in the dynamic time-path case, the key concepts, introduced by Bhagwati, of PTAs acting as 'stumbling blocks' or 'building blocks' towards worldwide nondiscriminatory trade liberalisation, just as Viner introduced the key concepts of trade diversion and trade creation for the static analysis.

3.1 Defining the 'dynamic' time-path question

The time-path question needs to be properly specified. It can be formulated analytically in two ways:

Question 1: Assume that the time-path of MTN (multilateral trade negotiations) and the time-path of PTAs are separable and do not influence each other, so that

---

[18] The pioneering account of the protectionist outcomes resulting from rules of origin manipulation is by the lawyer David Palmeter (1993) whereas the analytics of such protectionist outcomes with rules of origin have been developed by Krishna and Krueger (1995).

[19] A beautiful example of how this spaghetti bowl phenomenon arises is provided by Richard Snape (1996), whose illustration of the phenomenon for the European Union is reproduced here as Fig. 3. Such illustrations were pioneered by Ron Wonnacott who has also focused the profession's attention on what is now known as the 'hub-and-spoke' problem.

[20] The following analysis draws heavily on Bhagwati and Panagariya (1996*b*).

neither hurts nor helps the other. Will then the PTA time-path be character-ised by stagnant or negligible expansion of membership; or will we have expanding membership, with this even turning eventually into worldwide membership as in the WTO, thus arriving at nondiscriminatory free trade for all? The analysis can be extended to a comparison of the two time-paths, ranking the efficacy of the two methods of reducing trade barriers to achieve the goal of worldwide free trade for all.

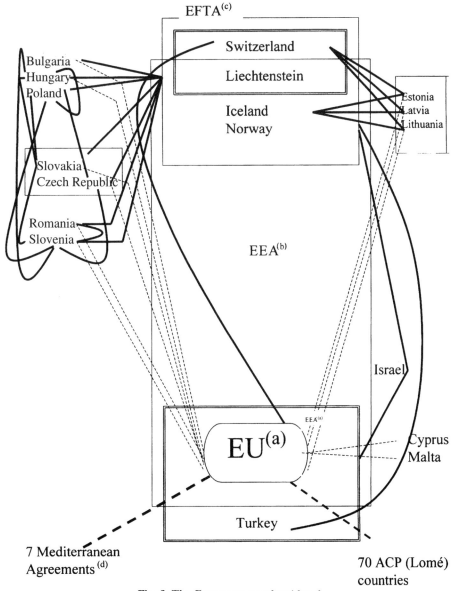

Fig. 3 The European spaghetti bowl

NB: Does not include countries of the former Soviet Union other then Baltic countries.

(a) European Union comprises Austria, Belgium, Denmark, Finland, France, Germany, Greece, Ireland, Italy, Luxembourg, Netherlands, Portugal, Spain, Sweden, and United Kingdom.

(b) European Economic Area

(c) European Free Trade Area

(d) Algeria, Egypt, Jordan, Lebanon, Morocco, Syria, Tunisia

    ⬭   EU Single Market

══════ Customs Union

▬▬▬▬ Free Trade Area

----------- EU Association Agreements

▬ ▬ ▬ ▬ Non-reciprocal agreements

Fig. 3 *Continued*

Question 2: Assume instead, as is plausible, that if both the MTN and the PTA time-paths are embraced simultaneously, they will interact. In particular, the policy of undertaking PTAs will have a malign or a benign impact on the progress along the MTN time-path.

Question 1 can be illustrated with the aid of Fig. 4 which portrays a sample of possibilities for the time-paths. World welfare is put on the vertical and time on the horizontal axis. For the PTA time-paths drawn, an upward movement along the path implies growing membership; for the MTN time-paths, it implies nondiscriminatory lowering of trade barriers among the nearly worldwide WTO membership instead. The PTA and MTN time-paths are assumed independent of each other, not allowing for the PTA time-path to either accelerate or decelerate the course of MTN (thus ruling out Question 2-type issues). The goal can be treated as reaching U^*, the worldwide freeing of trade barriers on a nondiscriminatory basis, at a specified time.

Then, Question 1 above can be illustrated by reference to the PTA paths I–IV. Thus, PTAs may improve welfare immediately, in the static sense or reduce it. In either case, the time-path could then be stagnant (as with time-paths II and III), implying a fragmentation of the world economy through no further expansion of the initial PTA. Else, it can lead (as in time-paths I and IV) to multilateral free trade for all at U^*

through continued expansion and coagulation of the PTAs. Under process multilateralism, i.e. MTN as a multilateral process of reducing trade barriers as distinct from multilateralism as the goal desired, the time-path may fail to reach U^* and instead fall short at U_m because of free-rider problems.

As indicated, if the PTA and MTN time-paths are interdependent, we can address Question 2. In that case, the MTN time-path becomes a function of whether the PTA time-path is travelled simultaneously.

The questions that we have distinguished above spring, as we noted at the outset, from a shift in US policy in favour of going Article 24 when the Europeans blocked the initiation of a new MTN Round at the GATT in 1981. In Bhagwati (1991; 1993), the challenge to international trade theorists to analyse these questions was first identified and a preliminary set of arguments offered. We now review the theoretical literature that has developed subsequently. At the outset, we consider recent theoretical approaches which, however interesting in themselves, are not helpful in thinking seriously about the time-path questions at hand. The more pertinent literature will be considered next.

3.2 Exogenously determined time-paths: Conventional approaches

Kemp–Wan

The approach of Kemp and Wan (1976) seems to be pertinent to our questions but is not. Evidently, the PTA time-path to U^* in Fig. 4 can be made monotonic provided the expanding membership of a PTA always satisfies the Kemp–Wan rule for forming a CU. But what this argument does not say, and indeed cannot say, is that the PTA will necessarily expand and, if so, in this Kemp–Wan fashion.

Krugman

The same argument applies to the theoretical approach introduced by Krugman (1993), where again the expansion of membership is treated as exogenously specified, as in Viner, and the world welfare consequences of the world mechanically dividing into a steadily increasing number of symmetric blocs are examined. Srinivasan (1993) has critiqued the specific conclusions as reversible when symmetry is dropped. Deardorff and Stern (1994) have also advanced a similar critique.

But the main problem is that the Krugman formulation is again in the conventional mould of taking the membership of a PTA and its expansion as exogenously specified and examining its consequences. Instead, what we need is a rigorous political-economy-theoretic incentive-structure analysis which endogenises the question of membership expansion and thus helps to address the time-path questions.

3.3 Endogenously determined time-paths: Recent theoretical analyses

The analysis of the time-path question has therefore moved into formal political-economy-theoretic modelling. We provide here a synoptic review of the few significant contributions to date, organising the literature analytically in light of the two questions distinguished above.

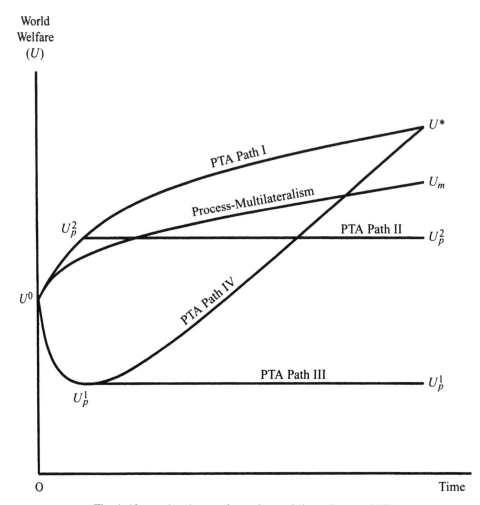

Fig. 4 Alternative time paths under multilateralism and PTA
Source: Adapted from Bhagwati (1993)

This figure illustrates the 'building blocks' and 'stumbling blocks' concepts in the context of the question whether the regionalism (that is, PTA) dynamic time-path will show increasing or stagnant membership. The PTA may improve welfare immediately, from U^0 to U_p^2 or (because trade diversion dominates) reduce it to U_p^1. The time-path with PTA, in either case, could then be stagnant (paths II and III), implying a fragmentation of the world economy through no further expansion of the initial trading bloc. Or, it could lead (paths I and IV) to multilateral free trade for all at U^* through continued expansion and coagulation of the PTA. Under 'process multilateralism', the time-path may fail to reach U^* and instead fall short at U_m because of free-rider problems. Or it may overcome them and reach U^*. This diagram assumes that the time-paths are independent: embarking on the PTA path does not affect the process-multilateralism path. This interdependence is discussed in the text.

Question 1

The single contribution that focuses on Question 1, i.e. the incentive to add members to a PTA, is by Baldwin (1993), who concentrates, in turn, on the incentive of non-members to join the PTA. He constructs a model to demonstrate that this incentive will be positive: the PTA will create a 'domino' effect, with outsiders wanting to become insiders on an escalator. The argument is basically driven by the fact that the PTA implies a loss of cost-competitiveness by imperfectly-competitive nonmember firms whose profits in the PTA markets decline because they must face the trade barriers that member countries' firms do not have to face. These firms then lobby for entry, tilting the political equilibrium at the margin towards entry demands in their countries. The countries closest to the margin will then enter the bloc, assuming that the members have open entry, thus enlarging the market and thereby increasing the cost of nonmembership and pulling in countries at the next margin. Given the assumptions, including continuity, this domino model can take the PTA time-path to U^* in Fig. 4.

Question 2

The rest of the theoretical contributions address Question 2, i.e. whether the PTA possibility and/or time-path helps or harms the MTN time-path. Here, the two major analyses to date, addressed directly and quite aptly to this question, by Krishna (1998) and Levy (1994), reach the 'malign-impact' conclusion.

Krishna models the political process in the fashion of the government acting in response to implicit lobbying by firms as a 'clearinghouse', showing in his oligopolistic-competition model that the PTA reduces the incentive of the two member countries to liberalise tariffs reciprocally with the nonmember world and that, with sufficient trade diversion, this incentive could be so reduced as to make impossible an initially feasible multilateral trade liberalisation.

Levy, who models the political process instead as in a median-voter model works with scale economies and product variety to demonstrate that bilateral FTAs can undermine political support for multilateral free trade. At the same time, a benign impact is impossible in this model: if a multilateral free trade proposal is not feasible under autarky, the same multilateral proposal cannot be rendered feasible under any bilateral FTA.

The Krishna and Levy models therefore throw light on the incentive-structure questions at hand when the agents are the lobbying groups and interests that are affected by different policy options.

4 POLICY TODAY

The policy debate on PTAs today finds economists arrayed on different sides. The main divisions appear to be among those who find them a mixed bag and would therefore content themselves with an effort at reducing their downside by reforming Article 24 and other disciplines (such as on AD actions) at the WTO so as to minimise the damage they can create, those who would reject them as a pox on the trading system and would like to see either a standstill or even a rollback, and those who would go along with them on a 'GATT plus' view of trade policy. It is fair to say that those who are sceptical or hostile have gained some ground on the intellectual side.

Their success is not commensurate on the policy level. However, there is definite progress. The US desire to turn APEC, the Pacific ocean trade grouping, into an FTA has been rejected so far by its Asian members who have embraced instead the notion that any trade liberalisation under APEC auspices should be on an MFN basis. Similarly, the proposal for TAFTA, floated initially by Foreign Minister Klaus Kinkel of Germany, covering the Atlantic ocean, has been transmuted into a non-FTA initiative. The Indian Ocean initiative, started by India, is also unlikely to become an FTA.

Meanwhile, the European Council of Ministers has recently resolved, in light of the concerns expressed by the anti-PTA economists, that the 'current architecture' of the EU's trading system will be frozen, implying a standstill on new PTAs, except when a strong case can be made, satisfying several criteria. Also, the WTO is addressing the problem of Article 24 reform through its Committee on Regional Trade Agreements. The media have also reported extensively on the 'new thinking' on the wisdom of PTAs and their proliferation.

The only substantial FTA project that is still making the headlines is the FTAA, the Free Trade Area of the Americas, backed by the Clinton administration which seeks to leave its own stamp on something big – the Uruguay Round and NAFTA were inherited by them. It is also an agenda that has endorsement from several South American nations, whose enthusiasm for PTAs reminds one of the earlier attachment of Latin policymakers to import substitution and to preferences for the developing nations.[21]

Meanwhile, the 'small' PTAs, usually without some big country providing the centre to them, continue to proliferate, chiefly (though not exclusively) among the developing countries.[22] The incentives to have these are often political. Each Trade Minister, and his Prime Minister, wish to leave their names behind on some trade grouping of their own; multilateralism produces no such rewards. Then there is the CNN theory of such PTAs: whereas multilateralism produces photo-op only for the big players such as Sir Leon Brittan and Ambassador Mickey Kantor, and nothing for the others, matters are more balanced at the regional trade meetings. Bureaucrats also get prestigious positions with each new PTA their nations sign up to. Then, of course, PTAs multiply by imitation: if MERCOSUR is going ahead, ASEAN follows suit, then SAPTA (among the South Asian nations) is started, and Gresham's Law takes over.[23] And finally, we must not forget that politicians, and much of the media, often do not understand the distinction between Free Trade and Free Trade Areas: they hold preVinerian 'all-trade-is-good' views for the simple reason that they have not been taught the distinction.

---

[21] The former was advanced by the Prebisch school, though it had its own intellectual origins elsewhere. Its costs have been fully analysed in numerous studies by now. The latter, embodied in the GSP schemes advanced at the UNCTAD, proved to be a fruitless distraction from MFN liberalisation, as argued by several economists who have studied it, among them Robert Baldwin. Richard Cooper and Andre Sapir.

[22] A complete list of preferential trade agreements under Article 24 terms, as also of partial ones under waivers and Enabling Clause exclusions, is included in the Appendix in Bhagwati and Panagariya (1996a):

[23] In fact, the expansion of PTAs just when MFN trade liberalisation has brought down trade barriers worldwide has made economists wonder whether there is also a deeper link between the two. See, for instance, the recent theoretical analysis by Freund (1997), in her Columbia University dissertation, which neatly produces PTAs as an outcome of reduced MFN barriers.

There is enough evidence therefore for continuing concern on the part of economists who oppose PTAs. A rollback, such as through a 'sunset clause' in Article 24 which would bring external tariffs down to the internal tariffs within a definite time period for existing and future PTAs, is improbable even though many economists have suggested it. More PTAs will doubtless be added meanwhile to the many already in existence or in conception, including the substantial FTAA.

The strategy of the anti-PTA economists has to be three-pronged: first, continue the education and the agitation to alert policymakers to the dangers posed by PTAs; second, join forces to accelerate reform of Article 24 and of other disciplines at the WTO such that PTAs can do less harm; and third, push for worldwide freeing of trade at the border, preferably through the embrace of a visionary terminal date and a corresponding practical agenda to get there, so that the preferences implied by the PTAs are rendered void because preferences relative to zero are zero.[24]

References

Anderson, Kym and Blackhurst, Richard (eds), (1993) *The Greening of World Trade Issues*. London: Harvester and Wheatsheaf.

Baldwin, Richard. (1993) 'A domino theory of regionalism.' CEPR Working Paper no. 857, November.

Baldwin, Richard and Venables, Anthony. (1996) 'Regional Economic Integration.' in (Gene Grossman and Kenneth Rogoff, eds). *Handbook of International Economics*, Vol. 3, Amsterdam: North Holland.

Bhagwati, Jagdish. (1968) 'Trade liberalization among LDCs, trade theory and GATT rules,' in (J. N. Wolf, ed.) *Value, Capital, and Growth*. Oxford: Oxford University Press.

Bhagwati, Jagdish. (1991) *The World Trading System at Risk*. Princeton: Princeton University Press.

Bhagwati, Jagdish. (1993) 'Regionalism and multilateralism: an overview,' in (Melo and Panagariya, eds.).

Bhagwati, Jagdish. (1995) 'U.S. trade policy: the infatuation with free trade areas.' In Bhagwati and Krueger (1995).

Bhagwati, Jagdish. (1996). *The Watering of Trade*. Mimeo. Columbia University.

Bhagwati, Jagdish. (1997) 'The watering of trade.' *Journal of International Economics*. February, vol. 42, pp. 239–12.

Bhagwati, Jagdish and Krueger, Anne. (1995) *The Dangerous Drift to Preferential Trade Agreements*. Washington D.C: AEI Press.

Bhagwati, Jagdish and Panagariya, Arvind. (1996a) 'Preferential trading areas and multilateralism: strangers, friends or foes.' in (Jagdish Bhagwati and Arvind Panagariya, eds.) *The Economics of Preferential Trade Agreements*. Washington, D.C.: AEI Press.

Bhagwati, Jagdish and Panagariya, Arvind. (1996b) 'The theory of preferential trade agreements: historical evolution and current trends.' *American Economic Review*, Vol. 86. pp. 82–7.

Bhagwati, Jagdish and Tironi, Ernesto. (1993) 'Tariff change, foreign capital, and immiserization: a theoretical analysis.' *Journal of Development Economics*. February. pp. 103–15.

Bhagwati, Jagdish, Krishna, Pravin and Panagariya, Arvind (eds). (1998) *Trading Blocs: Alternative Approaches to Analyzing Preferential Trade Agreements*. Cambridge, Mass.: MIT Press.

[24] Such a target was first proposed by Martin Wolf in *The Financial Times* and has been repeatedly endorsed by several economists.

Bliss, Christopher. (1994) *Economic Theory and Policy for Trading Blocs.* Manchester and New York: Manchester University Press.

Brecher, Richard and Bhagwati, Jagdish. (1981) 'Foreign ownership and the theory of trade and welfare.' *Journal of Political Economy*, (June), BI(3), pp. 497–511.

Casella, Alessandra. (1996) 'Large countries, small countries and the enlargement of trade blocs', *European Economic Review.* vol. 40. (June) pp. 391–405.

Clarida, Richard. (1996) 'Anti-dumping: theory and policy.' In (Jagdish Bhagwati and Robert Hudec (eds.) *Fair Trade and Harmonization: Prerequisites for Free Trade?*, vol. 1. Cambridge. Mass.: MIT Press.

Cooper, C. A. and Massell, B. F. (1965a) 'Towards a general theory of customs unions for developing countries.' *Journal of Political Economy*, vol. 73(5), pp. 461–76.

Cooper, C. A. and Massell, B. F. (1965b) 'A new look at customs union theory.' *Economic Journal*, vol. 75. pp. 742–7.

Deardorff, Alan and Stern, Robert. (1994) 'Multilateral trade negotiations and preferential trading arrangements.' In (Alan Deardorff and Robert Stern. eds). *Analytical and Negotiating Issues in the Global Trading System.* Ann Arbor: Michigan University Press.

Freund, Caroline. (1997) 'Multilateralism and the endogenous formation of preferential trade agreements.' (Mimeo.) Economics department, Columbia University. (March).

Greenaway, David. (1993) 'Liberalising foreign trade through rose tinted glasses.' *Economic Journal*, vol. 103, pp. 209–22.

Greenaway, David and Milner, Chris. (1991) 'Fiscal dependence on trade taxes and trade policy reform.' *Journal of Development Studies.* vol. 27, pp. 95–134.

Grinols, Earl. (1981) 'An extension of the Kemp-Wan theorem on the formation of customs unions.' *Journal of International Economics*, vol. 11, pp. 259–66.

Grossman, Gene and Helpman, Elhanan. (1995) 'The politics of free trade agreements.' *American Economic Review.* (September) pp. 667–90.

Hindley, Brian. (1997) 'EU anti-dumping: has the problem gone away?' *Trade Policy Review* 1996/97. Centre for Policy Studies: London.

Johnson, Harry. (1965) 'An economic theory of protectionis, tariff bargaining, and the formation of customs unions.' *Journal of Political Economy*, (June) vol. 73, pp. 256–83.

Kemp, Murray C. and Wan, Henry. (1976) 'An elementary proposition concerning the formation of customs unions.' *Journal of International Economics*, (February) vol. 6, pp. 95–8.

Krishna, Kala and Krueger, Anne. (1995) 'Implementing free trade areas: rules of origin and hidden protection'. National Bureau of Economic Research Working Paper no. 4983.

Krishna, Pravin. (1998) 'Regionalism and multilateralism: a political economy approach.' *Quarterly Journal of Economics*, vol. 113(1), pp. 227–51.

Krishna, Pravin and Bhagwati, Jagdish. (1997) 'Necessarily welfare-enhancing customs unions with industrialization constraints.' *Japan and the World Economy*, December, 441–6.

Krugman, Paul. (1991) 'The move to free trade zones.' Federal Reserve Bank of Kansas City, *Policy Implications of Trade and Currency Zones.*

Krugman, Paul. (1993) 'Regionalism versus multilateralism: analytical notes.' In de Melo and Panagariya (1993).

Levy, Philip. (1994) 'A political economic analysis of free trade agreements.' Discussion Paper no. 718, Economic Growth Center, Yale University, forthcoming in *American Economic Review*, 1997.

Lipsey, Richard. (1958) *The Theory of Customs Unions: A General Equilibrium Analysis.* Ph.D. Dissertation, published as LSE Research Monographs 7. London School of Economics: London. 1970.

Meade, James. (1955) *The Theory of Customs Unions.* Amsterdam: North Holland.

Melo, Jaime de and Panagariya, Arvind, eds (1993) *New Dimensions in Regional Integration.* Cambridge: Cambridge University Press.

Ohyama, Michihiro. (1972) 'Trade and welfare in general equilibrium', *Keio Economic Studies.* vol. 9. pp. 37–73.

Palmeter, David. (1993) 'Rules of origin in customs unions and free trade areas'. In Anderson and Blackhurst (1993).

Panagariya, Arvind. (1995) 'Rethinking the new regionalism.' Paper presented at the Trade Expansion Program Conference of the UN Development Programme and World Bank, January.

Panagariya, Arvind. (1996) 'The free trade of the Americas: good for Latin America?' *The World Economy,* vol. 19(5), pp. 485–515.

Panagariya, Arvind. (1997*a*) 'The Meade model of preferential trading: history, analytics and policy implications.' (mimeo), University of Maryland. In (Benjamin Cohen, ed.), *International Trade and Finance: New Frontiers for Research. Essays in Honour of Peter Kenen* Cambridge: Cambridge University Press.

Panagariya, Arvind. (1997*b*) 'Preferential trading and the myth of natural trading partners.' (mimeo) University of Maryland. (Forthcoming in *Japan and the World Economy*).

Panagariya, Arvind and Findlay, Ronald. (1996) 'A political economy analysis of free trade areas and customs unions,' in (Robert Feenstra: Gene Grossman and Douglas Irwin eds). *The Political Economy of Trade Policy: Essays in Honor of Jagdish Bhagwati,* Cambridge, Mass.: MIT Press.

Serra, Jaime Puche et al. (1996) *Regional Trade Agreements.* Report Issued by the Carnegie Endowment for International Peace. Washington D.C..

Snape, Richard. (1996) 'Trade discrimination – yesterday's problem?' *Economic Record.* vol. 72 (219), pp. 381–96 (December).

Srinivasan, T. N. (1993) 'Discussion', in de Melo and Panagariya (1993).

Srinivasan, T. N. (1997) 'The common external tariff of a customs union: Alternative approaches', *Japan and the World Economy,* 9(4), (December), pp. 447–65.

Summers, Lawrence. (1991) 'Regionalism and the world trading system.' Federal Reserve Bank of Kansas City, *Policy Implications of Trade and Currency Zones.*

Viner, Jacob. (1950) *The Customs Union Issue.* New York: Carnegie Endowment for International Peace.

Wei, Sheng-Jin and Frankel, Jeffrey. (1997) 'Open regionalism in a world of continental trade blocs.' Presented at the American Economic Association Meetings. January 3–6. (mimeo 1996).

Winters, Alan. (1996) 'Regionalism versus multilateralism.' *World Bank Policy Research Working Paper Series,* No. 1687. Washington D.C.

Wonnacott, Paul and Lutz, Mark. (1989) 'Is there a case for free trade areas?' in Jeffrey Schott *Free Trade Areas and U.S. Trade Policy.* Washington, D.C.: Institute for International Economics, pp. 59–84.

Yeats, Alexander. (1996) 'Does Mercosur's trade performance justify concerns about the effects of regional trade arrangements? Yes!' (mimeo) World Bank.

9

THE NEW REGIONALISM

Wilfred J. Ethier

Once again, regionalism is afoot. Twin late-1980s announcements, by the United States and Canada of negotiations for a free-trade area, and by the EU of an attempt to complete its internal market, ignited a conflagration of regional integration. Well over a hundred regional arrangements, involving most nations, now exist. *Deja vu*: the 1950s and 1960s had likewise witnessed many 'old regionalism' initiatives. Except for Western Europe, these in the end amounted to little, however, and efforts for preferential trade became quiescent, until the dramatic advent of the 'new regionalism'.

1 INTRODUCTION

Trade theorists have responded to the new regionalism by investigating two questions. Will the formation of regional trading blocs raise or lower welfare? Will regionalism help or hinder multilateral trade liberalisation? Answers have been mixed.[1] These investigations have adopted a Vinerian perspective on regional integration as a combination of trade creation and trade diversion[2] (developed in response to the old regionalism) augmented, in many cases, with a significant use of game theory (reflecting developments in economic thought since the days of the old regionalism). Notable by its absence is investigation of the more fundamental question of *why* the new regionalism has emerged – it has simply been treated as exogenous.

Also absent has been appreciation of the fact that the international environment greeting the new regionalism differs from that experienced by the old regionalism in three dramatic, fundamental, and critical ways.

- The multilateral liberalisation of trade in manufactured goods among the industrial countries is much more complete now than it was then.

  The GATT rounds of multilateral tariff reductions, still gathering steam in the days of the old regionalism, now constitute perhaps the most successful exercise of deliberate economic policy making in history. But the second distinguishing feature is even more important.
- Scores of economically less advanced countries have abandoned the basically

---

[1] See Bhagwati and Panagariya (1996), Krugman (1991), Bond and Syropoulous (1996) and Bagwell and Staiger (1996*a*, *b*, 1997).

[2] See Viner (1950), Lipsey (1960), Ethier and Horn (1984) and Panagariya (1996).

autarkic, anti-market, policies they followed during the days of the old regionalism and are now actively trying to join the multilateral trading system.

During the 1950s and 1960s the communist bloc was still communist and
import substitution ruled the Third World, with most less developed countries
highly suspicious of both trade and foreign direct investment. All this changed
just as the new regionalism appeared. The third distinction involves the changing role of direct investment.

- Direct investment is much more prominent now than in the days of the old
  regionalism, and it has been surging since the advent of the new regionalism.

Formerly, direct investment was largely a matter of U.S. manufacturing firms
expanding horizontally into other developed countries (aside from the traditional vertical integration by extractive firms). Since then, direct investment by
the developed countries has become increasingly two-way, is growing faster than
trade, and is increasingly likely to flow into developing and reforming countries.

Because of this radical change in environment one can make a *qualitative* distinction
between the old regionalism and the new. To appreciate what this might be, it is
necessary to investigate the causes of the new regionalism and not merely use the
traditional tools to try to deduce its consequences. The old regionalism was, to a large
extent, motivated by a desire to substitute for insufficient multilateral liberalisation
and/or to facilitate holding aloof from what multilateral liberalisation there was. The
Vinerian paradigm of trade creation versus trade diversion provided a natural frame of
reference from which to analyse such an environment. Thus the Vinerian perspective
was appropriately central to theoretical models motivated by the old regionalism. I
argue that the new regionalism, by contrast, is largely motivated by a desire to facilitate
entrance into a now much more developed multilateral trading system. The Vinerian
perspective, though not irrelevant, should be secondary in theoretical models appropriate to an analysis of the new regionalism.

This paper concerns appropriate models of the new regionalism, models in which
regionalism might emerge as a consequence of past multilateral success and extensive
current reform attempts. But first I must set out what I believe to be the important
characteristics of the new regionalism.

2 CHARACTERISTICS OF THE NEW REGIONALISM

The following six characteristics are neither exhaustive nor universal (current regional
initiatives are quite diverse), but do apply in varying degree to most of the more important regional arrangements.

*(a) The new regionalism typically involves one or more small countries
linking up with a large country*

In NAFTA, Mexico and Canada are each small, economically, relative to the United
States; the new members of the EU (Austria, Finland and Sweden) are tiny relative to
the EU itself; the same is true of the central European adherents to the Europe Agreements with the EU; Brazil will likely dominate Mercosur, etc.

(b) Typically, the small countries have recently made, or are making, significant unilateral reforms

This is dramatically true of the Europe Agreements' central European participants, who had abandoned communism, of the members of MERCOSUR, and of Mexico in NAFTA. But it also characterises, to a lesser degree, the small industrial country participants in regional initiatives. Canada had turned away from Trudean-style economic nationalism before negotiating a free trade agreement with the United States, and the Scandinavian applicants to the EU (except Norway, which, significantly, declined to join) had made important reforms in some sectors (e.g. agriculture). Note that, in Mercosur, the large country, Brazil, is also a reformer.

(c) Dramatic moves to free trade between members are not featured: the degree of liberalisation is typically modest. Thus the Vinerian paradigm is not a natural starting point

For example, NAFTA actually provides only modest liberalisation: United States tariffs were already low and NAFTA hedges sensitive sectors in all sorts of ways. Canada and Mexico have done somewhat more, but the most significant measures (largely Mexican) were unilateral and not part of NAFTA. The accession of new members to the EU is even more glaring: because of their membership in the EA, the trade relations of Austria, Finland and Sweden with the EU are virtually identical to what they would have been had they decided not to join! The Europe Agreements provide for little in the way of concrete liberalisation. Even with the admittedly more ambitious Mercosur the liberalisation involved is not large relative to the unilateral liberalisations of the members.

(d) The liberalisation achieved is primarily by the small countries, not by the large country: the agreements are one-sided

The liberalisation in NAFTA is due much more to 'concessions' by Mexico and Canada than by the United States. In negotiations over enlargement, the EU has been flexible on financial responsibilities and periods of adjustment, but has always maintained a take-it-or-leave-it attitude regarding the nature and structure of the EU itself. The Europe Agreements involve virtually no 'concessions' by the EU: Indeed the EU instituted antidumping measures against some of its new partners even as the initial agreements were coming into effect! In a sense this asymmetry is a direct reflection of how the world has changed since the days of the old regionalism: one reason the small countries get only small tariff advantages is simply that the large countries have small tariffs to begin with. Mercusor is an exception: Brazil has made concessions at least as large as those of the smaller members. But recall that Brazil is also a reformer.

(e) Regional arrangements often involve 'deep' integration: the partners seldom confine themselves to reducing or eliminating trade barriers, but also harmonise or adjust diverse assortments of other economic policies

The EU is a clear and dramatic example of this. The United States–Canada free-trade agreement and the subsequent NAFTA included a host of economic reform commitments by Canada and by Mexico. Sometimes partners in regional arrangements exempt each other from acts of administered protection (such as antidumping duties), but often they do not (e.g., NAFTA). Sometimes partners are in effect granted rights of appeal denied to nonpartners (NAFTA again). The three latest GATT rounds of multilateral negotiations tried, with significant success, to broaden the scope of multilateral arrangements. But a major attraction of the new regionalism is that negotiations with a small number of partners broadens the range of instruments over which negotiation is feasible.

(f) Regional arrangements are regional geographically: the participants are neighbours

Unlike the other five stylised facts, this characteristic was probably just as true of the old regionalism as it is of the new.

In summary, regional integration now usually involves reform-minded small countries 'purchasing', with moderate trade concessions, links with a large, neighbouring country that involve 'deep' integration but that confer relatively minor trade advantages.

3 REGIONALISATION

Next, I advance several hypotheses inspired by the stylised facts of the new regionalism and by the differences in environment alluded to above, and I introduce theory to consider the hypotheses further. For exposition, I split this into three parts, introducing one by one the three ways in which the international environment has changed between the days of the old regionalism and today. This section exploits the fact that multilateral liberalisation is much more extensive now.

3.1 Hypotheses

The first set of hypotheses relate to regionalisation (an increase in the amount of trade with geographic neighbours relative to total trade) and its relation to liberalisation.

Hypothesis 1: *Liberalisation promotes regionalisation*
The familiar gravity equation – predicting that the volume of trade between two countries is positively related to their GDPs and negatively related to the economic distance between them – has repeatedly been shown to describe actual trade patterns well.[3] Economic distance equals geographic distance (presumably proxying for transport costs and perhaps other things) plus trade barriers. A nondiscriminatory liberalisation, by making geographic distance more important relative to trade barriers, might be expected to cause a country's trade to become more regional. This is true both for multilateral liberalisation and for unilateral reform.

---

[3] The gravity equation can be thought of as a reduced form consistent with many trade models, so that its empirical success reveals little about the underlying causes of trade. See Deardorff (1995).

Hypothesis 2: *the fewer the number of participants in trade negotiations, the easier it is to reach agreement*

Fewer participants presumably mean fewer conflicts of interest and fewer areas of potential disagreement. Furthermore, a solution to a conflict between two participants is less likely to provoke a conflict with another participant the fewer the number of additional participants.

Hypothesis 3: *the fewer the number of participants in trade negotiations, the larger the number of issues on which it is possible to reach agreement*

That is, the deeper is the integration that can be negotiated.

3.2 Theory

I now discuss, in general terms,[4] theoretical considerations suggested by the above hypotheses. The discussion reflects the stylised facts (f), that regional arrangements are established by geographical neighbours, and (e), that they often involve 'deeper' integration. Consider the following model.

- Countries are identical, except that they are spatially separated. Assume, in particular, that countries are grouped into N continents of n countries each; the distance between any two countries in the same continent is less than the distance between any pair in different continents.
- The government of each country may negotiate a mutual reduction in trade barriers with other governments, but each government is constrained by negotiating costs. In subsequent periods there will be new rounds of negotiations, with the governments constrained by the same costs in negotiating further reductions in trade barriers.

  At the outset of each negotiating round, each government decides whether to negotiate *regionally* (only with other countries in the same continent) or *multilaterally* (with all other countries); because of the symmetry, all governments make the same choice. The negotiating costs relate to the government's political support, not modelled explicitly. Hypotheses 2 and 3 suggest representing these costs as follows:

$$c = l + \gamma\pi \tag{1}$$

  where c denotes the cost, l the degree of liberalisation that is achieved, and π the number of negotiating partners to whom that liberalisation applies. Thus π equals $n - 1$ if negotiations are regional and $nN - 1$ if they are multilateral. γ is a parameter reflecting the relative importance of the two determinants of c. I assume the total cost a government is willing to incur in a negotiating round is exogenously given.

- In its negotiations, each government strives to maximise, subject to the constraint on costs, an index of benefits. Benefits are greater the greater the reduc-

---

[4] See Garriga and Sanguinetti (1995, 1997); also see Ethier (1997).

tion in trade barriers and the greater the number of partners to which those reductions apply.

Represent the benefits by:

$$b = l - \delta\pi \tag{2}$$

- The parameter δ is a decreasing function of the ratio of aggregate trade with negotiating partners to aggregate trade with nonpartners.

  The government, for political reasons, wants to reduce the 'tax' on as much trade as possible, and existing trade matters more than trade that would exist if barriers were lower. Also, a higher partner-to-nonpartner trade ratio will likely imply a higher trade-creation-to-trade-diversion ratio.[5] Let δ_R denote the value δ would have if a country were initially to embark on regional negotiations, previous negotiations, if any, having all been multilateral. Hypothesis 1 suggests that the ratio of partner to nonpartner trade is a decreasing function of t, the existing trade barrier. So assume that δ_R is an increasing function of t, $\delta_R(t)$.

What will countries do? Maximising b subject to the constraint that c equal an exogenous value requires that π be minimised – that is, that negotiations be regional – if and only if $\gamma > \delta_R$. If initially $\gamma > \delta_R(t)$, countries will embark on regional negotiations which will reduce δ_R still more, so that multilateral negotiations cannot even start until regionalism has gone to the limit. The world looks Vinerian. If, on the other hand, $\delta_R(t) > \gamma$ initially, negotiations will be multilateral. But the outcomes of these negotiations will drive $\delta_R(t)$ down toward γ. If the free-trade value, $\delta_R(0)$, exceeds γ, regionalism will never become appealing, and countries will continue on the multilateral path toward free trade. But if $\delta_R(0) < \gamma$, sufficiently successful multilateral negotiations will eventually be replaced by regional negotiations.

The latter possibility is the especially interesting one. Here the *success* of multilateral liberalisation *induces* a switch to regionalism, and this switch sustains the pace of liberalisation above what multilateral negotiations could deliver.

4 COMMITMENT TO REFORM

The previous section exploited just one of the three basic changes in the international environment between the time of the old regionalism and that of the new: multilateral trade liberalisation. Now I add a second: efforts for fundamental reform by the former communist countries and throughout the third world.

4.1 Hypotheses

Bringing the economy into the multilateral trading system is central to all contemporary reform programmes. Presumably the benefits that can be expected by being part of this system help determine how tempting reform is.

---

[5] But see Bhagwati and Panagariya (1996) for a contrary view.

Hypothesis 4: *the greater the degree of multilateral integration, the greater the benefits to be expected from being part of the multilateral system*

A major concern of most economic reformers is that their reforms not be undone in the future. That is, they want to *bind* future regimes to the reforms. This is desirable not only for its own sake, but also because a faith in the permanence of the reform effort is crucial to its success. One way – sometimes the only way – to bind future regimes to the reforms is to establish an external commitment.

Hypothesis 5: *the more likely that backsliding from an external commitment will induce retaliation, the more likely such a commitment is to sustain reform*

If future regimes can walk away without cost from an external commitment to reform, that commitment will not accomplish much.

Hypothesis 6: *The more that specific reform measures are embodied in an external commitment, the likelier that commitment is to sustain reform*

A vague commitment can be gutted in substance while fully adhered to in form.

4.2 Theory

Implications of the hypotheses are immediate. Successful multilateral liberalisation by the industrial countries makes participation in the international economy more rewarding, and thereby contributes to the decision to reform. Multilateral negotiations also offer reforming countries a potential external commitment binding future governments to the reform measures.

Multilateral negotiations are, however, of little practical use for this purpose. They provide no enforcement mechanism should a country backslide, and large industrial countries can hardly be expected to put the multilateral system at risk merely to punish a single deviant reformer. Even if they wanted to punish they are likely to have little formal justification for doing so, since multilateral agreements would not embody detailed reform measures by individual countries.

But regional arrangements can address both problems. The fact that the agreement is with a big country (often the dominant trading partner) adds a credible enforcement mechanism. Because such arrangements allow for deeper integration, they can contain obligations to undertake specific measures central to the reform effort. This is clearly illustrated by the free trade agreement between Canada and the United States and by the subsequent NAFTA.

Thus the stylised facts important here are (a), (b), and (e): reform-minded small countries linking up with a larger country in an arrangement featuring deeper integration.

5 COMPETITION FOR FOREIGN DIRECT INVESTMENT

The previous sections have exploited two of the three basic changes in the international environment between the time of the old regionalism and that of the new. Now I bring in the third: foreign direct investment.

5.1 Hypotheses

This section,[6] like the previous, utilises the stylised facts that regionalism usually involves a big country linking up with one or more small ones making significant reforms. In addition, the stylised facts (c) and (d), that the degree of liberalisation is modest and asymmetrical, play a critical role. Thus all six stylised facts will have been brought in.

Hypothesis 7: *Reforming countries see the ability to attract foreign direct investment as the key to successful entry into the multilateral trading system*
Multinational firms are a prime means of technology transfer, and they can supply international contacts and modern commercial methods to countries which, because of their past policies, have precious little of either.[7]

Hypothesis 8: *Competition among reforming countries to attract foreign direct investment is likely to be keen*
Countries comprising a large part of the world are trying to reform at the same time, and most of them see direct investment as the key to success.

Hypothesis 9: *A small national advantage offers the hope of attracting a large amount of foreign direct investment*
There are three mutually reinforcing reasons to expect this. First, with similar countries competing, small advantages can prove decisive. Second, direct investment is lumpy: you have to put a factory in one place. Third, the basic advantages that reforming countries see in direct investment involve externalities, and these externalities render a site more attractive for additional direct investment.

5.2 Theory

Consider the following abstract framework. A large number of countries, hitherto aloof from the multilateral trading system, seek to undertake fundamental reform and become part of that system, at least in part because of the success of past multilateral liberalisation. These reforming countries do see direct investment as a key to successful reform (Hypothesis 7), and they will compete with each other to attract it (Hypothesis 8). Firms in the industrial countries are tempted to invest in the potential reformers, because of the latter's comparative advantages, but the former have substantial latitude in deciding where to invest, since there are many reformers with fairly similar economic characteristics.

A reform effort will presumably be more successful the more foreign direct investment the country can attract. To put this consideration into sharp relief, assume that a reform effort will succeed if and only if some direct investment is attracted. To focus on competition among reforming countries, assume that they are all alike so that,

---

[6] For a full account see Ethier (1996).
[7] Not 'of Ethier,' though that is true too.

other things equal, industrial-country firms are indifferent about where to locate their foreign subsidiaries. But they will tend to locate together, because of the lumpy nature of direct investment and because of positive externalities between foreign subsidiaries.

The previous section's discussion of the relation between regional integration and the ability of a reforming government to bind the country to the reforms is also relevant here. In practice, the credibility of the commitment of the government to its announced reform can be crucial in attracting direct investment and, in that way, ensuring the success of the reform. Even a regional arrangement with only modest big-country preferences for the small country establishes an external commitment to reform that (weakly) binds future governments, thereby making the future preservation of reform (slightly) more credible. What matters here is what the small reforming country *gives*, in terms of trade concessions, not what it *gets*, because it is the former which influences the likelihood of relation by the partner in the event of backsliding. The external commitment in turn makes the country more attractive for direct investment, relative to similar countries without such external commitments. Thus, Hypothesis 9 suggests, the ability of a regional arrangement to bind the government to reform can be important for the success of that reform even when it confers only modest direct benefits.

But the credibility of a country's commitment to reform is but one consideration pertinent to a multinational firm's decision of where to invest. To focus on other considerations, assume now that the commitment of each reforming country to the reform is not in doubt. Suppose, further, that the industrial countries are all alike, except that their final products are differentiated – the basis for trade between them. These products are produced in multiple stages, with the more labour-intensive stages presumably candidates for transfer to subsidiaries in the reforming countries.

Under these circumstances, successful reform by an individual country will be uncertain, but more probable the greater the aggregate amount of direct investment from the industrial countries relative to the number of countries attempting reform, that is, relative to the number of potential targets of that investment. So its prospects will be improved if a reforming country can somehow distinguish itself from its rivals.

Consider the role of regional arrangements in this regard. Define a regional agreement to be an agreement between one industrial country and one reforming country in which the reforming country commits –

- to the details of an attempted reform
- to give the goods of its partner preferential treatment

and the developed country commits – to make a *small* reduction in the duty applicable to goods imported from its partner country. Note that this definition reflects the stylised facts that regional arrangements tend to involve one or more small reforming countries linking up with a large country in an arrangement characterised by asymmetrical concessions and deep integration.

Suppose for simplicity that each potential reformer regards the products of all industrial countries as perfect substitutes. Together with the assumptions already made, this will expunge from the analysis the possibility of negative welfare effects due to trade diversion. This oversimplification will emphasise that the changed world and the distinctive features of the new regionalism have made the old Vinerian concerns less important, and it will also highlight the new concerns.

Consider first the effects of such an arrangement on a potential reformer. The arrangement would establish an external commitment to reform, as discussed earlier. Also, the trade preference implies that all imports will come from the partner country, since the reforming country regards the goods of all industrial countries as perfect substitutes. But this trade diversion is of no consequence in this model, with the concern of the old regionalism assumed away to focus on the concerns of the new.

But the preference granted by the industrial-country partner, though only marginal, is much more significant. From the point of view of firms considering direct investment to provide intermediate stage inputs for the industrial country partner's products, all reforming countries are equivalent, except for this marginal preference. Thus it attracts all such investment.[8] This ensures the reform will succeed because of the 'investment diversion' the regional arrangement implies.

This explains why reforming countries find regional arrangements attractive even though they typically receive only 'minor' concessions from their partners. The goal is to compete with other *similar* countries for direct investment, not to expand greatly exports to their partners or to attract from them direct investments that would otherwise not be made at all. Such 'investment creation' will be modest at best.

A regional arrangement will not be uniformly benign. Other countries desiring reform will suffer. Suppose one country that would undertake reform anyway enters into a regional arrangement. Then direct investment producing intermediate goods for that country's partner will all be diverted there, and the country still remains a potential host for other direct investment. Less direct investment remains for other reforming countries, reducing their prospects for success and perhaps deterring some of them from even embarking upon reform. Regionalism produces 'reform destruction', causing fewer countries to attempt reform and lowering the proportion of those who succeed. On the other hand, the country with the regional arrangement may not itself have attempted reform in its absence: 'reform creation'. Thus the number of countries attempting reform may either rise or fall, depending on the balance between reform creation and reform destruction.

Thus far I have considered the effects of an isolated regional arrangement. But in fact they are becoming ubiquitous. So consider next the general equilibrium that will emerge if all countries are allowed freely to negotiate regional arrangements of the kind I have hypothesized, including the possibility of a single country entering multiple relationships.[9]

If several reforming countries establish regional arrangements with a single industrial country, the value of the arrangements to the former will be eroded because direct investment may well tend to cluster mainly in some subset of them all. For this reason, the reforming countries will tend to spread themselves out in their choices of partners. If there are at least as many industrial countries as potential reformers, each

---

[8] But if the externalities between foreign subsidiaries – which induce them to locate together – are strong enough, more than 'small' concessions may be required by the industrial partner.
[9] These are sometimes called 'hub and spoke' arrangements. See Wonnacott (1996).

of the latter can find a partner that will guarantee the success of its reform effort. This may or may not be true if there are fewer industrial countries, depending upon the amount of direct investment that will be forthcoming. Nevertheless, the ability to enter freely into regional arrangements will maximise the extent and the probability of successful reform, and, by doing so, also maximise the number of countries that are induced to attempt reform.

In this framework, the global interest calls for successful reform to be as widespread as possible. This will maximise the extent of the multilateral trading system, accentuating both the benefits that it generates and the number of nations which receive those benefits. But this global externality will be ignored by multinational firms, who will be likely to cluster their foreign investments together. A single regional arrangement may be either good or bad in its results. But a *regional general equilibrium* as just described will in effect internalise the global externality and produce an outcome unambiguously superior to what can be achieved without regionalism.

The model of this and the preceding sections described the small-country participants as concerned with fundamental economic reform. But, although the small industrial countries entering into regional arrangements (e.g., Austria, Canada, Finland, Sweden) are also typically undertaking reforms, these reforms are hardly fundamental in the sense of what is happening in the third world or with the former communist countries.

For small industrialised nations, the model needs to be altered, but the basic analysis applies. For the small countries joining the EU, for example, the problem is not so much to attract new direct investment as to remain attractive sites, in an increasingly integrated world, for activities currently conducted there. The small advantages they obtain from regional arrangements are not additional preferences, but future participation in EU decision making.[10] Thus the basic story applies.

6 CONCLUDING REMARKS

This paper has argued for a non-Vinerian analytical approach to regional integration, capable of explaining why the new regionalism has come about, and motivated by the stylised facts of the new regionalism and by the dramatic differences in international environment between the days of the old regionalism and today. The approach suggests the following relation of regionalism to multilateralism.

- The new regionalism is, in good part, a direct result of the success of multilateral liberalisation.
- Regionalism is the means by which new countries trying to enter the multilateral system (and small countries already in it) compete among themselves for the direct investment necessary for their successful participation in that system.
- Regionalism – by internalising an important externality – plays a key role in expanding and preserving the liberal trade order.

[10] For more on this, see Baldwin and Flam (1994)

An individual regional arrangement may by itself do more harm than good. But widespread regionalism of the sort we are experiencing in effect internalises a critical global externality and produces an outcome superior to that obtainable by multilateralism alone.

My analytical framework has given a highly abstract picture of the world so that essentials stand out clearly. Additional detail of course adds ambiguity. Thus even someone who accepts with enthusiasm the basic arguments suggested above could well retain serious concerns about the new regionalism. I suggest four such grounds for concern.

- I have made assumptions that render trade diversion innocuous. In reality it remains a cause for concern, especially in some parts of the world.

    Still, this just is not nearly as important now as it was thirty years ago. Under present conditions, a huge *volume* of trade diversion could well imply little effect on *welfare*.
- Even if regional arrangements have come into existence for the reasons indicated above, and even if they are in fact promoting successful reform, they still might ultimately lead to a break-up of the world economy into hostile blocs.

    I see no signs that this is in fact about to happen, but things could change. The remaining two concerns, though, I regard as more significant than the first two.
- Protection-seeking, special-interest groups will always be with us, and the fact that regionalism is where the action is means that this is where the battles will be fought. Furthermore, the deeper integration characteristic of the new regionalism gives projectionists more avenues of attack. This is a powerful reason to maintain a healthy level of vigilance and suspicion toward new regional initiatives.
- In the above theory regionalism plays a transitory, though critical, role in the reform process, but the regional arrangements themselves are permanent, so 'what happens next' matters.

But make no mistake: The bottom line of this paper is that the new regionalism reflects the success of multilateralism – not its failure.

References

Bagwell, K. and Staiger, R. W. (1996*a*), 'Multilateral tariff cooperation during the formation of customs unions,' *Journal of International Economics*. (forthcoming).

Bagwell, K. and Staiger, R. W. (1996*b*), 'Regionalism and multilateral tariff cooperation,' unpublished manuscript.

Bagwell, K. and Staiger, R. W. (1997). 'Multilateral tariff cooperation during the formation of free trade areas.' *International Economic Review*, vol. 38 (2), pp. 291–320.

Baldwin, R. E. and Flam, H. (1994), 'Enlargement of the European Union: the economic consequences for the Scandinavian countries.' CEPR Occasional Paper No. 16.

Bhagwati. J. and Panagariya. A. (1996). 'Preferential trading areas and multilateralism: strangers, friends or foes? University of Maryland Center for International Economics Working Paper no. 22.

Bond, E. and Syropoulos, C. (1996), 'Trading blocs and the sustainability of inter-regional cooperation.' In (M. Canzoneri, W. J. Ethier and V. Grilli, eds), *The New Transatlantic Economy*, Cambridge: Cambridge University Press, pp. 118–41.

Deardorff, A. V. (1995), 'Determinants of bilateral trade: does gravity work in a neoclassical world?' Discussion Paper No. 382, Research Forum on International Economics, University of Michigan.

Ethier, W. J. (1996), 'Regionalism in a multilateral world.' Working paper, Department of Economics, University of Pennsylvania. Forthcoming: *Journal of Political Economy*.

Ethier, W. J. (1997), 'Regional regionalism.' Working paper, Department of Economics, University of Pennsylvania.

Ethier, W. J. and Horn, H. (1984), 'A new look at economic integration.' In (H. Kierzkowski, ed.). *Monopolistic Competition and International Trade*, Oxford: Oxford University Press, pp. 207–29. Reprinted in (A. Jacquemin and A. Sapir, eds) (1989), *The European Internal Market: Trade and Competition*, Oxford: Oxford University Press.

Garriga, M. and Sanguinetti, P. (1995). 'Es el Mercosur un bloque natural? Efectos de la política commercial y la geografía sobre el intercambio regional. *Estudios*, vol. 18 (73), pp. 59–68.

Garriga, M. and Sanguinetti, P. (1997). 'The determinants of regional trade in Mercosur: geography and commercial liberalisation.' Unpublished manuscript, Departamento de Economía, Universidad Torcuato Di Tella, Buenos Aires, Argentina.

Krugman, P. (1991). 'Is bilateralism bad? In (E. Helpman and A. Razin, eds), *International Trade and Trade Policy*, Cambridge MA: MIT Press.

Lipsey, R. G. (1960), 'The theory of customs unions: a general survey,' *Economic Journal*, vol. 70 (279), pp. 496–513. Reprinted in (R. E. Caves and H. G. Johnson) (1968), *Readings in International Economics*, Homewood: Richard D. Irwin.

Panagariya, A. (1996). 'The Meade model of preferential trading: history, analytics and policy implications.' University of Maryland Center for International Economics Working Paper No. 21.

Viner, J. (1950). *The Customs Union Issue*, New York: Carnegic Endowment for International Peace.

Wonnacott, R. J. (1996). 'Free-trade agreements: for better or worse?' *American Economic Review*, vol. 86 (2), pp. 62–6.

10

WILL PREFERENTIAL AGREEMENTS UNDERMINE THE MULTILATERAL TRADING SYSTEM?*

Kyle Bagwell and Robert W. Staiger

Is bilateralism bad? This question was the title of Paul Krugman's provocative paper on regionalism (Krugman, 1991a), and the pursuit of an answer has spawned the *regionalism versus multilateralism* debate. The answer to this question turns largely on how one answers the related question posed by Jagdish Bhagwati (Bhagwati, 1991): will regional agreements – or more accurately, *preferential* agreements – undermine the multilateral trading system? On one side of the debate are those who argue that preferential agreements can complement existing multilateral efforts to foster greater economic integration among countries, and should therefore be encouraged. On the other side are those who see such agreements as a threat to the multilateral system.

But what is 'the multilateral system' that may or may not be threatened by preferential agreements? Much of the literature treats it as a 'black box' synonymous with the goal of 'multilateral free trade', and proceeds to ask whether preferential agreements contribute to or interfere with the attainment of this goal. Introductory references are typically made to the GATT/WTO, but the analysis is often carried out with little or no reference to the structure of this multilateral institution. In this paper we argue that understanding GATT's structure is vital to the debate over regionalism versus multilateralism.

There are three components that together comprise the cornerstones of the GATT system: the principles of *reciprocity* and *non-discrimination*, which are regularly identified as the 'pillars' of the GATT architecture, and the *enforcement* mechanisms, which Dam (1970, p. 81) calls the 'heart' of the GATT system. Below we describe how preferential agreements may be expected to interact with the multilateral system in light of each of its three principle components.

We approach the question posed at the outset in two parts. We first ask, will preferential agreements undermine a multilateral trading system that is built on the pillars of reciprocity and non-discrimination? A remaining question is then, how do preferential agreements affect the enforcement provisions of the GATT? To lay the foundation for

* This paper was completed while Staiger was a Fellow at the Center for Advanced Study in the Behavioral Sciences, Staiger is also grateful for financial support provided by The National Science Foundation Grant #SBR–9022192.

an answer to the first question, we describe a framework within which the pillars of reciprocity and non-discrimination can themselves be interpreted and understood. From this perspective, we then offer support for the view that preferential agreements pose a threat to the multilateral system. An answer to the second question requires an understanding of how GATT agreements are enforced. Observing that these agreements must be *self-enforcing*, we describe circumstances under which preferential agreements can either enhance or detract from the performance of the GATT system through their impacts on enforcement at the multilateral level.

In order to establish these answers, we must first articulate a theory of the multilateral trading system within which the workings of reciprocity, non-discrimination and enforcement mechanisms can be understood. Any attempt to construct such a theory immediately confronts a most-basic question: Why have governments found reciprocal trade agreements to be appealing? One view is that these agreements provide governments with an escape from a terms-of-trade driven Prisoners' Dilemma. This view has a long history, originating with Torrens (1844), Mill (1844), Scitovsky (1942) and Johnson (1953–4), who posed their arguments in the context of national-income maximising governments that set 'optimal tariffs' to exploit monopoly power in world markets.

While the terms-of-trade view is logically correct, many economists are sceptical of its practical relevance: a common position is that these arguments become secondary in explaining the appeal of reciprocal trade agreements once more realistic government objectives that include political concerns are introduced. A popular view is then that governments are attracted to such agreements as a means to achieve political objectives.

To evaluate these two views, we therefore begin in the next section by constructing a general model in which governments are motivated by both political and terms-of-trade considerations. Our framework is sufficiently general to include all the major political economy models of trade policy formulation as special cases. Within this framework, we show that more general government objectives do not change the view that trade agreements provide an escape from a terms-of-trade driven Prisoners' Dilemma, and that this is *all* that trade agreements do. Political forces shape the trade objectives that governments seek to achieve, but political considerations play no role in explaining why governments seek reciprocal trade agreements. Rather, it is the terms-of-trade externality that creates an inefficiency when policies are set unilaterally and that therefore explains why governments need a reciprocal trade agreement in order to accomplish their objectives.[1]

As it turns out, this observation both clarifies the purpose of trade agreements in the leading models of trade policy and, as we will demonstrate, reveals a simple logic to GATT's principles of reciprocity and non-discrimination. Furthermore, with this theory of the multilateral trading system at hand, we are then able to offer our answers concerning the consequences of preferential trading agreements for the functioning of the multilateral trading system.

---

[1] Political considerations might provide a separate motivation for reciprocal trade agreements if governments seek such agreements to gain commitment relative to their private sectors, a possibility explored by Maggi and Rodriguez (1988) and Staiger (1995). It has not yet been demonstrated, however, whether this hypothesis could account for the principles of reciprocity and non-discrimination that form the pillars of GATT.

1 THE PURPOSE OF RECIPROCAL TRADE AGREEMENTS

We develop here a general model of the trade policy choices of politically motivated governments. Our initial goal is to understand the appeal of reciprocal trade agreements for such governments. We present a full treatment of the issues contained in this and the next section in Bagwell and Staiger (1997a).

1.1 The economic environment

We first describe the economic environment, which is a standard two-good two-country general equilibrium trade model. A home (no*) and foreign (*) country trade two goods, x and y, which are normal goods in consumption and produced in competitive markets under conditions of increasing opportunity costs. With x (y) the natural import good of the home (foreign) country, define $p = p_x/p_y$ to be the local relative price facing home producers and consumers, and similarly define $p^* = p_x^*/p_y^*$ to be the local relative price facing foreign producers and consumers. Letting τ denote one plus the (non-prohibitive) *ad valorem* import tariff imposed by the home country, and defining τ^* analogously for the foreign country, it then follows that $p = \tau\, p^W \equiv p(\tau, p^W)$ and $p^* = p^W/\tau^* \equiv p^*(\tau^*, p^W)$, where $p^W \equiv p_x^*/p_y$ is the 'world' (i.e., untaxed) relative price. The home country (foreign country) terms of trade is then given by $1/p^W$ (p^W).

Within each country, local relative prices determine competitive production decisions, which we represent by the domestic and foreign production functions $Q_i = Q_i(p)$ and $Q_i^* = Q_i^*(p^*)$ for $i = \{x, y\}$, respectively. National consumption is determined by the local relative price, which defines the tradeoff faced by consumers and implies the level and distribution of factor income in the economy, and by tariff revenue, which is distributed to consumers lump-sum. In the usual way, tariff revenue can be expressed as a function of local and world prices, so that we may represent national consumption in each country as $C_i(p, p^W)$ and $C_i^*(p^*, p^W)$. Finally, home country imports of x, denoted by $M_x(p(\tau, p^W), p^W)$, are given by the difference between home country consumption and production of x, while home country exports of y, denoted by $E_y(p(\tau, p^W), p^W)$, amount to the difference between home country production and consumption of y. Foreign country imports of y, $M_y^*(p^*(\tau^*, p^W), p^W)$, and exports of x, $E_x^*(p^*(\tau^*, p^W), p^W)$, are similarly defined.

We may now express the trade balance and equilibrium conditions. For any world price, home and foreign budget constraints imply that

$$p^W M_x(p(\tau, p^W), p^W) = E_y(p(\tau, p^W), p^W) \text{ and} \tag{1a}$$

$$M_y^*(p^*(\tau^*, p^W), p^W) = p^W E_x^*(p^*(\tau, p^W), p^W) \tag{1b}$$

The equilibrium world price, $\tilde{p}^W(\tau, \tau^*)$, is then required to clear the market for good y:

$$E_y(p(\tau, \tilde{p}^W), \tilde{p}^W) = M_y^*(p^*(\tau^*, \tilde{p}^W), \tilde{p}^W) \tag{2}$$

with market clearing for good x then implied by (1) and (2). Hence, given any pair of non-prohibitive tariffs, the equilibrium world price will be determined through (2), and the equilibrium world price and the given tariffs then determine in turn the local prices and thereby production, consumption, import, export and tariff revenue levels. Throughout we assume that the Metzler and Lerner paradoxes are ruled out, so that

$$\frac{dp}{d\tau} > 0 > \frac{dp^*}{d\tau^*} \text{ and } \frac{\partial \tilde{p}^W}{\partial \tau} < 0 < \frac{\partial \tilde{p}^W}{\partial \tau^*}$$

1.2 Government objectives

We adopt a representation of government objectives which is general enough to include as special cases national income maximisation as well as each of the major modelling approaches to the political economy of trade policy. The key observation is that politically motivated governments are sensitive to the distributional as well as the efficiency properties of the local price implications of their trade policy choices. We thus represent the objectives of home and foreign governments by the general functions $W(p(\tau, \tilde{p}^W), \tilde{p}^W)$ and $W^*(p^*(\tau, \tilde{p}^W), \tilde{p}^W)$, respectively. The only structure we place on these functions is that, holding local prices fixed, each government is assumed to achieve higher welfare when its terms-of-trade improve:

$$\frac{\partial W(p, \tilde{p}^W)}{\partial \tilde{p}^W} < 0 \text{ and } \frac{\partial W^* (p^*, \tilde{p}^W)}{\partial \tilde{p}^W} > 0 \tag{3}$$

For fixed local prices, an improvement in a country's terms of trade amounts to an income transfer from its trading partner (brought about by an increase in the country's tariff and a corresponding decrease in the tariff of its trading partner). Throughout, we also assume that the second-order conditions associated with the maximisation problems developed below are globally satisfied.

1.3 Unilateral trade policies

Consider first the unilateral trade policies that governments would choose in the absence of a trade agreement. Supposing that each government would set its trade policy to maximise its objective function taking as given the tariff choices of its trading partner, the associated home and foreign reaction functions are defined implicitly by:

Home: $W_p + \lambda W_{p^w} = 0$ \hspace{2cm} (4a)

Foreign: $W^*_{p^*} + \lambda^* \, W^*_{p^w} = 0$ \hspace{2cm} (4b)

where subscripts denote partial derivatives, and where

$$\lambda \equiv \frac{\left(\frac{\partial p^W}{\partial \tau}\right)}{\left(\frac{dp}{d\tau}\right)} < 0 \text{ and } \lambda^* \equiv \frac{\left(\frac{\partial p^W}{\partial \tau^*}\right)}{\left(\frac{dp^*}{d\tau^*}\right)} < 0$$

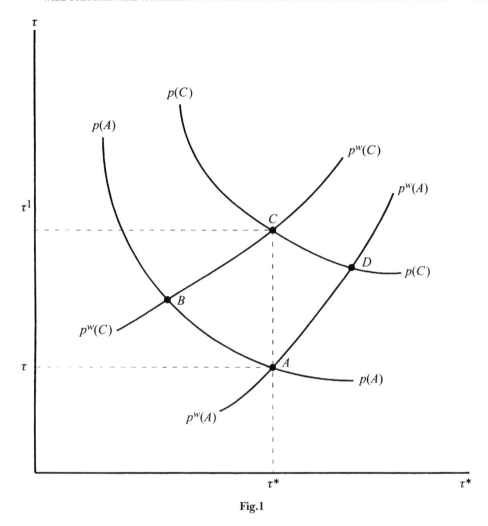

Fig.1

As (4) illustrates, the best-response tariff of each government is determined by the combined impact on welfare of the induced local and world price movements.

The best-response conditions can be further interpreted with the aid of Fig. 1. An initial tariff pair is given by point $A \equiv (\tau, \tau^*)$. Associated with the point A is an iso-local-price locus, denoted as $p(A) \rightarrow p(A)$, and an iso-world-price locus, labelled $p^W(A) \rightarrow p^W(A)$.[2] If the home government were to raise its tariff unilaterally to τ^1, then a new tariff pair would be induced, represented by the point $C \equiv (\tau^1, \tau^*)$ in Fig. 1, and this tariff pair rests on a new iso-local-price locus $p(C) \rightarrow p(C)$ and also a new iso-world-price locus $p^W(C) \rightarrow p^W(C)$. Hence, with a unilateral increase in its tariff, the home government induces a local price that is higher and a world price that is lower as compared to the prices associated with the original point A.

---

[2] Excluding the Metzler and Lerner paradoxes, the iso-local-price locus is negatively sloped while the iso-world-price locus has positive slope.

In analogy with $(4a)$, Fig. 1 can be used to disentangle the overall movement from A to C induced by a unilateral tariff increase by the domestic government into separate movements in the local and world prices, respectively. The movement from A to B isolates the induced reduction in the world price, and its welfare significance for the domestic government is captured in $(4a)$ by the term W_{pw}. Similarly, the movement from B to C isolates the local price change, and its welfare significance for the domestic government is captured in $(4a)$ by the term W_p. The welfare implications of the local-price change implied by the movement from B to C reflect a weighing of the costs of the associated domestic distortions in production and consumption against any domestic distributional benefits. The welfare implications of the change in the world-price implied by the movement from A to B, in contrast, reflect the benefits accruing to the domestic government as it shifts the costs of its policy onto the foreign government through a terms-of-trade improvement. It follows that, if the home government seeks to implement a local price corresponding with the iso-local-price locus $p(C) \rightarrow p(C)$, then a unilateral increase in the domestic import tariff will shift a portion of the costs of achieving this policy goal onto the foreign government. A similar interpretation holds for $(4b)$.

A tariff pair that simultaneously satisfies $(4a)$ and $(4b)$ constitutes a Nash equilibrium of the game that arises when both governments set tariffs unilaterally. We will assume that such a tariff pair, which we take to be unique, corresponds to the tariff choices that governments would make in the absence of a trade agreement, and we will denote this tariff pair by (τ^N, τ^{*N}). The next task is to determine whether these tariff choices are inefficient for the governments making them and, if they are, to identify the source of the inefficiency that a trade agreement can correct.

1.4 Why unilateral trade policy choices are inefficient

To determine whether the tariff choices made by governments in the absence of a trade agreement are efficient for the governments given their objectives, we need to characterise the set of tariff pairs that lie on the efficiency frontier and ask whether (τ^N, τ^{*N}) is an element of this set. The efficiency frontier can be given the general representation $(d\tau/d\tau^*)|_{dW=0} = (d\tau/d\tau^*)|_{dW^*=0}$, but it can also be represented more concretely as the set of tariffs that satisfy:

$$(1 - AW_p)(1 - A^* W^*_{p*}) = 1 \tag{5}$$

where $A \equiv (1 - \tau\lambda)/(W_p + \lambda W_{pw})$ and $A^* \equiv (1 - \lambda^*/\tau^*)/(W^*_{p*} + \lambda W^*_{pw})$ with $A \neq 0$ and $A^* \neq 0$ under the further assumption that the partial derivatives of the welfare functions are always finite.[3]

---

[3] If governments maximise national income, the efficiency locus reduces to the form $\tau = 1/\tau^*$, as Mayer (1981) demonstrates. In this case, tariffs are adjusted along the efficiency locus so as to maintain equality in relative local prices between the domestic and foreign countries, with different tariff pairs along the efficiency locus reflecting different world prices and therefore different distributions of income across trading partners. In the more general representation of government preferences considered here, the efficiency locus still determines a relationship between domestic and foreign tariffs, but it need no longer be the case that this relationship equates relative local prices across trading partners.

It is now immediate from a comparison of (4) and (5) that Nash tariffs are inefficient. This is not surprising since, as we have described above, when governments set their trade policies unilaterally they are motivated to shift costs onto one another through the world-price changes that their tariffs imply. It is perhaps also not surprising that these cost-shifting motives will lead governments to adopt trade policies that are unambiguously too restrictive relative to efficient choices given their objectives: it can be shown that both governments can achieve welfare gains relative to the Nash equilibrium only if each agrees to lower its tariff below the Nash level.[4]

What is perhaps more surprising is that this terms-of-trade externality is the *only* inefficiency that a trade agreement can remedy, despite the fact that we have allowed governments to have political motivations of a quite general nature. To establish this, we consider a hypothetical world in which governments are not motivated by the terms-of-trade consequences of their trade policies. To this end, we define *politically optimal tariffs* as any tariff pair (τ^{PO}, τ^{*PO}) satisfying the following two conditions:

$$\text{Home:} \quad W_p = 0 \quad\quad\quad (6a)$$

$$\text{Foreign:} \quad W^*_{p^*} = 0 \quad\quad\quad (6b)$$

We assume that a unique set of politically optimal tariffs exists and that the associated second-order conditions are globally satisfied.

When governments set politically optimal tariffs, it is as if they ignore any welfare gains attributable to changes in the world price that would be induced by their tariff choices. If both governments sought to maximise national income, politically optimal tariffs would correspond to reciprocal free trade. More generally, however, government objectives may reflect political considerations as well, and in this case there is no presumption that politically optimal tariffs will correspond to free trade.

It can now be seen that politically optimal tariffs are efficient, as tariffs that satisfy (6) will lie along the efficiency locus defined by (5). As a consequence, once the terms-of-trade motivations are eliminated from the trade-policy choices of governments, there is no further scope for Pareto improving changes in trade policy. To gain intuition for this finding, suppose that tariffs have been set at their politically optimal levels, so that the terms-of-trade motivations have been removed from trade-policy choices and each government has set its trade policy so as to achieve its preferred local prices. Consider now a small increase in the tariff of the domestic country. This change has three effects. First, it induces a small increase in the local price in the domestic economy, but this has no first-order effect on domestic government welfare as domestic local prices were already at their preferred level. Second, the domestic tariff increase induces a small reduction in the local price of the foreign country, but this has no first-order effect on the welfare of the foreign government since it too has already achieved its preferred local prices. Finally, the domestic tariff increase causes the world price to fall, but this cannot generate an efficiency gain as it represents a pure international transfer of tariff revenue.

---

[4] A reduction in tarrifs from the Nash level, however, is not sufficient to guarantee mutual welfare gains. For example, as Johnson (1953–4) and Kennan and Riezman (1988) demonstrate, a large country may be worse off under reciprocal free trade than in the Nash equilibrium if countries are asymmetric.

Hence, once the terms-of-trade motivations have been removed from trade-policy choices, there are no further Pareto gains for governments to achieve.

Fig. 1 illustrates the essential inefficiency that prevents governments from reaching the efficiency frontier with unilateral trade policy decisions. We suppose again that, beginning at point A, the home government considers a unilateral tariff increase to achieve the local price associated with point C. If the government allows the terms-of-trade consequences (i.e., the movement from D to C) of its tariff selection to influence its decision concerning whether to proceed with this tariff increase, then it will recognise that some of the costs of achieving the higher local price at C can be shifted onto its trading partner as a result of the reduced world price, and the tariff increase will look especially attractive. As a consequence, Nash tariffs are always inefficient, leading to tariffs (trade volumes) that are too high (low). Alternatively, if the government were not permitted to let the terms-of-trade consequences of its tariff selection influence its decision of whether or not to proceed with the tariff increase, then it would prefer choosing the higher tariff to induce point C if and only if it also prefers point D to point A. In this case, the potential appeal of point C to the home government is independent of any cost-shifting benefits that may arise with the consequent change in the world price, and so it has the 'right' incentives when deciding whether to proceed with a tariff increase.[5] If each government were to choose tariffs in this way, then a resulting set of consistent tariffs is politically optimal and efficient.

The findings described here can be summarised with the aid of Fig. 2, which depicts the locus of efficient tariff pairs by the curve $E \to E$, the politically optimal tariffs by the point on the efficiency locus labelled PO, and the Nash tariffs by the point labelled N positioned to the northeast of the efficiency locus.[6] Notice that the iso-welfare curves of the two governments are tangent at every point along the efficiency locus, including the political optimum. The novel feature of the politically optimal tariffs is that the iso-welfare curves at these tariffs are also tangent to the iso-world-price locus (the locus labelled p_{PO}^W. The bold portion of the efficiency locus corresponds to the contract curve.

Fig. 2 clarifies the central task that governments face when they design a trade agreement. Without cooperation, governments would set trade policy unilaterally, leading to the Nash outcome N. A trade agreement can then offer governments a means to co-operate and move from the inefficient. Nash point to some alternative tariff pair that rests on the contract curve. Among the points on the contract curve, the politically optimal tariffs are focal, as they remedy in a direct fashion the terms-of-trade inefficiency that keeps governments from reaching the contract curve with their unilateral choices. As Fig. 2 makes clear, when governments have political objectives the effi-

---

[5] The movement from point A to point D in Fig. 1 induces no externality through the terms-of-trade but it does alter the foreign local price. If the foreign government also selects tariffs that are politically optimal, however, then a small change in the foreign local price will have no first order effect on foreign government welfare.

[6] We draw this picture under the assumptions that a unique Nash equilibrium exists, a unique political optimum exists, and that the political optimum lies on the contract curve (i.e., it is on the efficiency locus and yields greater-than-Nash welfare for each government). The last assumption is new to our discussion and it will be satisfied if countries are sufficiently symmetric.

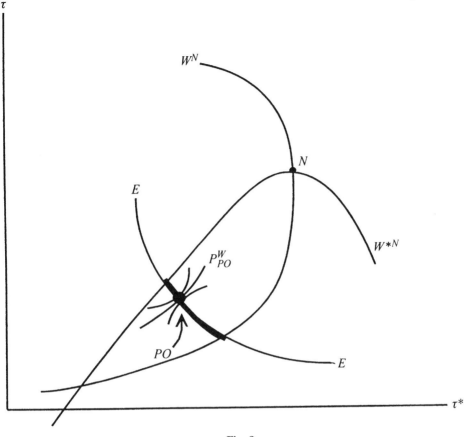

Fig. 2

ciency locus need not pass through the point of reciprocal free trade. But while political concerns will effect government preferences over tariffs (e.g., the location of the efficiency locus), it is the terms-of-trade externality that creates a 'problem' with unilateral tariff choices which an appropriately designed trade agreement can 'solve'.[7]

---

[7] The degree to which countries are able to affect their terms of trade significantly is an issue of some debate. We note the following points of support. First, at the level of theory, even ostensibly small countries have some power over their terms of trade, if the industry is monopolistically competitive (Gros, 1987). Second, our theory does not require that all countries have the ability to alter world prices, but it does imply that only those countries that can alter world prices will be actively involved in reciprocal tariff negotiations, an implication that is consistent with the 'principal supplier' rules of GATT negotiations (see Bagwell and Staiger, 1996). Third, with regard to empirical evidence, a large

continued overleaf

2 RECIPROCITY, NON-DISCRIMINATION AND PREFERENTIAL AGREEMENTS

With the basic framework now described, we are prepared to consider the principles of reciprocity and non-discrimination, and how preferential agreements will affect a multilateral trading system built on these two pillars.

2.1 The meaning of reciprocity

Within GATT, the term 'reciprocity' refers broadly to the ideal of mutual changes in trade policy that bring about equal changes in import volumes across trading partners.[8] Using the model presented above, we may define reciprocity more formally as follows: a set of tariff changes $\Delta\tau \equiv (\tau^1 - \tau^0)$ and $\Delta\tau^* \equiv (\tau^{*1} - \tau^{*0})$ conforms to *the principle of reciprocity* provided that

$$\tilde{p}^{W0} \left[M_x(p(\tau^1, \tilde{p}^{W1}), \tilde{p}^{W1}) - M_x(p(\tau^0, \tilde{p}^{W0}), \tilde{p}^{W0}) \right] =$$
$$[M_y^*(p^*(\tau^{*1}, \tilde{p}^{W1}), \tilde{p}^{W1}) - M_y^* (p^*(\tau^{*0}, \tilde{p}^{W0}), \tilde{p}^{W0})]$$

where $\tilde{p}^{W0} \equiv \tilde{p}^W (\tau^0, \tau^{*0})$, $\tilde{p}^{W1} \equiv \tilde{p}^{W1} (\tau^1, \tau^{*1})$, and where we have measured changes in import volumes at existing world prices. Using the trade balance condition (1) and the equilibrium condition (2), this expression may be rewritten as

$$[\tilde{p}^{W1} - \tilde{p}^{W0}] M_x (p(\tau^1, \tilde{p}^{W1}), \tilde{p}^{W1}) = 0 \tag{7}$$

Hence, as (7) makes clear, mutual tariff changes that conform to reciprocity leave world prices unchanged. The potential significance of this property can be appreciated when viewed from the perspective of the finding, reported above, that a government's tariff choice will be inefficient if and only if it is motivated by the *change* in the world price that its tariff choice implies.

2.2 The practice of reciprocity in GATT

Having now defined the general meaning of the principle of reciprocity, we turn to the application of this principle within GATT practice. To understand the importance of

---

literature documents imperfect 'pass-through' in the face of exchange rate shocks. If symmetric empirical patterns arise when the cost increase is associated with a tariff increase, then the finding of imperfect pass-through would offer evidence of a reduction in the world price, i.e., a terms-of-trade externality. Feenstra (1989) provides empirical support for the symmetric pass-through hypothesis. Finally, we note that empirical studies of trade policy confirm that the potential world-price implications of alternative trade policy choices can have important effects on the national desirability of intervention (see, for example, the discussion in Feenstra, 1995; p. 1579).

[8] The meaning of reciprocity in GATT, and the various ways in which reciprocity has been implemented in practice, is discussed in Dam (1970: pp. 58–61 and pp. 87–91) and WTO (1995a; p. 949).

the principle of reciprocity in GATT, it is useful to distinguish between two broad circumstances in which reciprocity applies. A first circumstance is when governments seek greater access to the markets of their trading partners, and engage in a 'round' of negotiations under GATT's Article XXVIII bis. In the context of these negotiations, opening one's own market is deemed a 'concession'. In this circumstance, the principle of reciprocity reflects the 'balance of concessions' that governments seek through a negotiated agreement. This practice is described by Dam (1970, p. 59), who explains that, under the language of Article XXVIII bis, negotiations are voluntary and are to be conducted in a 'reciprocal and mutually advantageous basis'. Dam (1970, p. 59) explains further that:

> This permissive approach to the content of tariff agreements is often referred to under the heading of *reciprocity*. From the legal principle that a country need make concessions only when other contracting parties offer reciprocal concessions considered to be 'mutually advantageous' has been derived the informal principle that exchanges of concessions must entail reciprocity.

The emphasis that governments place on reciprocity in this sense stands in contrast to standard economic logic, which holds that optimal unilateral policy for a country is free trade. From this perspective, it is perplexing that a government would require a 'concession' from its trading partner in order to do what is in any event best for its country. Appealing to this apparent violation of economic logic, it is tempting to interpret the observation that governments seek reciprocity in negotiated agreements as direct evidence that government negotiators adopt a mercantilist perspective that is incompatible with basic economic reasoning and that therefore derives from underlying political forces.[9]

Here we simply note that the mercantilist logic that drives actual trade negotiations admits a simple economic interpretation within the framework developed in the preceding section. In particular, the nature of the terms-of-trade externality described above ensures that, in the absence of a trade agreement (i.e., at the Nash point), each government would prefer to reduce its tariff and induce lower import-competing prices and greater imports *if the increased trade volume could be obtained without a deterioration in the terms of trade* (see (4)).[10] Acting unilaterally, a government cannot achieve this. But by balancing one country's 'concessions' against another's, this is precisely what liberalisation conforming to the principle of reciprocity will deliver.

While reciprocity in this circumstance reflects the broad manner in which governments appear to approach rounds of trade negotiations under Article XXVIII bis, there is in fact no requirement in GATT that negotiations proceed in this manner. There is, however, a second broad circumstance in which the principle of reciprocity applies in GATT practice, and in this case GATT rules do require reciprocity. Here we refer to the circumstance in which a government wishes to reduce foreign access to its

---

[9] Many have expressed this view, Krugman (1991*b*, 1997) provides an especially clear articulation of this position.

[10] This follows from (3) and (4*a*) which indicate that $W_p<0$ along the domestic government's reaction curve. A similar observation holds for the foreign government.

markets below a previously negotiated level. An important mechanism through which GATT provides for this possibility is contained in Article XXVIII.[11] Under this article, a country may at any time propose to modify or withdraw a concession agreed upon in a previous round of negotiation. In this circumstance, if the country and its trading partner cannot agree on a renegotiated tariff structure, then the country is free to carry out the proposed changes to its tariffs, and the notion of reciprocity is then invoked to moderate the allowable response of the country's trading partner, who is permitted to withdraw *substantially equivalent concessions* of its own.

This suggests that GATT negotiations may be understood as a multi-stage game, in which governments first agree to an initial set of tariffs, and then each government considers whether to propose a more restrictive tariff knowing that, under GATT's reciprocity rules, its trading partner can do no more than respond with reciprocal withdrawals of concessions which preserve the world price implied by the original agreement. Viewed from this perspective, it is clear that when governments evaluate the desirability of a proposed initial agreement, they must take account of any future incentives to renegotiate the agreement under GATT's reciprocity rules. But it should now also be clear that an initial agreement will be renegotiated if either government decides that the protection from imports provided under the agreement is inadequate at the existing world price. The implications of this observation can be illustrated with the help of a figure.

Consider then Fig. 3, which depicts three possible tariff pairs that might represent an initial agreement. We represent these tariff pairs by the points *A*, *B*, and *PO*. Each tariff pair is efficient (all three points lie on the efficiency locus), but the political optimum point PO is distinguished from the others by the fact that the iso-world-price locus running through *PO* is tangent to the iso-welfare contours of each government at this point.

Consider first an initial agreement that corresponds to point *A*. Observe that in this case the foreign government would request a renegotiation to raise its tariff and further restrict imports knowing that, under GATT's reciprocity rules, the domestic government would then withdraw a substantially equivalent concession that would preserve the world price and therefore deliver the tariff pair at point *A'*. Thus, while the tariff pair at point *A* is efficient, it is not robust to the type of renegotiation that GATT allows through Article XXVIII. A similar argument applies to the efficient tariff pair at point *B*, except that the roles of the foreign and domestic government are now switched. In fact, there is only one efficient tariff pair which, if agreed to originally, would not be lost in the renegotiation process. This tariff pair is the politically optimal tariff pair, since this is the only point on the efficiency locus at which each government achieves its preferred local prices given the associated world price.

This suggests that the principle of reciprocity can be viewed as a mechanism by which governments are guided in GATT negotiations to efficient politically optimal outcomes.[12] There is a certain appeal to this finding, since the politically optimal tariffs

---

[11] For further discussion of Article XXVIII and its importance in GATT practice, see Dam (1970, pp. 79–99), Jackson (1989, p. 119) and Enders (1997). Provisions for temporary suspension of GATT obligations are provided in Article XIX, where similar reciprocity rules apply.

[12] Actually, we establish in Bagwell and Staiger (1997a) that governments will indeed negotiate to politically optimal outcomes in this setting unless sufficient asymmetries are present.

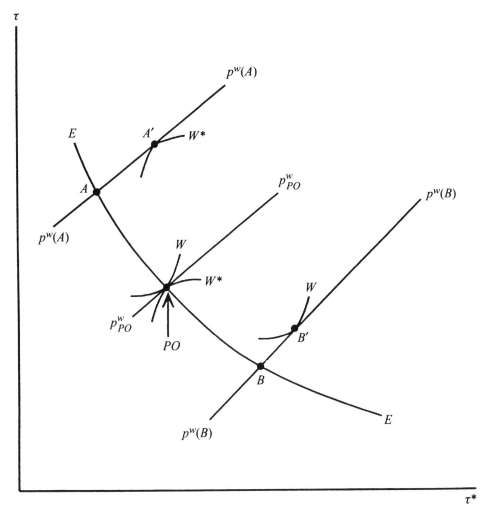

Fig. 3

are also those tariffs which arise when the source of the inefficiency – government's motivations to influence the terms of trade – is eliminated.

2.3 The importance of MFN

If the principle of reciprocity reveals a basic economic logic, can the importance of the principle of non-discrimination in GATT practice be similarly understood? Is there a *reason* for these two principles to coexist in the same multilateral institution? This is a crucial question for the debate over regionalism versus multilateralism, since preferential agreements amount to blatant violations of the principle of non-discrimination.

Hence we would like to know whether the ability of reciprocity to implement an efficient trade agreement depends in any fundamental way on the restriction that tariffs conform to MFN. We now confront this question and ask, Can reciprocity implement an efficient multilateral trade agreement that allows for discriminatory tariffs? To address this question, we must extend our two-country model to a many-country framework. This is done in Bagwell and Staiger (1997a), and here we simply provide an intuitive account of the results.

It is perhaps easiest to begin by imagining a multi-country world in which all tariffs conform to MFN, and consider whether reciprocity can still deliver an efficient agreement in this environment. The key observation is that, by requiring that a government levy the same tariff on imports of a good regardless of the identity of the source (i.e., exporting) country, the principle of non-discrimination preserves the simple pattern of externalities found in the two-country setting depicted above. That is, with all tariffs conforming to MFN, a common world price will prevail, and externalities continue to pass through this world price. As a consequence, reciprocity, by neutralising the world price implications of a government's tariff decisions, can guide governments to efficient politically optimal outcomes when their tariffs are non-discriminatory.

Now consider a world in which tariffs are discriminatory. If a country imports the same good from several sources and its government applies different tariff rates to imports from each source, then all else equal it would prefer to import relatively more of the good from the country to which it applies a higher tariff owing to the lower associated world (i.e., export) price and the greater associated tariff revenue. But this implies that the pattern of externalities is now more complicated, as the government's interest in the pattern of bilateral imports from its trading partners provides a reason for concern over both world prices *and* the local prices in the markets of its trading partners (since these determine the relative shares of the import good coming from each supplying country). As a consequence, reciprocity, which serves well to neutralise externalities which travel through the world price but which is ill-equipped to handle the local-price externalities that are created when tariffs are discriminatory, fails to deliver an efficient trade agreement in this environment.

These arguments suggest a fundamental efficiency link between the principles of reciprocity and non-discrimination. Reciprocity serves to neutralise the world-price effects of a country's trade policy decisions. Provided that the externalities associated with trade intervention travel through the world price, reciprocity therefore works well as a principle with which to undo the terms-of-trade driven restrictions in trade and achieve efficient trade volumes. The principle of non-discrimination thus complements reciprocity, since it ensures that all externalities indeed are channelled through the world price.

2.4 Why preferential agreements may undermine GATT

Having identified a basic economic logic to GATT's principle of reciprocity and an efficiency link between reciprocity and the principle of non-discrimination, we turn next to consider how preferential agreements will affect a multilateral trading system built on these two pillars. GATT's Article XXIV permits preferential agreements, provided that member countries eliminate tariffs on substantially all trade between them in a reasonable period of time. This exception to the principle of non-discrimination was controversial in its inception and has met with renewed controversy recently as many GATT members – but most especially the United States – have increasingly exercised their rights under this article to negotiate preferential trading agreements. These agreements may take either of two forms. When countries form a *free trade area*, they eliminate barriers to internal trade but maintain independent external trade policies. Under a *customs union*, member-countries also agree to harmonise their external trade policies and create a common external-tariff-setting authority.

We start with free trade areas. An immediate implication of the preceding discussion is that an efficient set of tariffs cannot be implemented under reciprocity when a free trade agreement is present. Intuitively, a free trade agreement violates MFN, and as a consequence externalities travel through both local and world prices in its presence. In this environment, as we have seen, reciprocity cannot serve to implement an efficient trade agreement. The broader implication is that the efficiency properties of a multilateral trading system founded on the principles of reciprocity and non-discrimination will be undermined when exceptions from MFN are granted for the formation of free trade areas.

Consider next the implications of customs unions for the multilateral trading system. We cannot immediately conclude from the above discussion that the introduction of a customs union is incompatible with the pursuit of an efficient set of multilateral tariffs through reciprocity. This is because the formation of a customs union creates a new environment in which, while there is now tariff discrimination, there are also fewer external-tariff-setting authorities operating, and thus it does not immediately follow from our earlier discussion that the presence of tariff discrimination will again undermine the efficiency properties of reciprocity. Nevertheless, the arguments above provide the essential intuition, once it is noted that a customs union will be analogous to a single country so long as the countries that form the union are similar in an appropriate sense. This would imply that the principle of reciprocity can then deliver an efficient agreement in the presence of a customs union between such countries so long as all *external* tariffs continue to conform to the principle of non-discrimination.

The required similarity among customs-union members that permits this result is that member-countries must share similar political goals so that the elimination of tariffs between them is internally efficient. When this relationship fails, customs unions will be like free trade areas, and it will be impossible to implement efficient tariffs under reciprocity when either type of preferential agreement is present.

More generally, we have identified a basic tension between a multilateral system built on the principle of reciprocity and the formation of preferential trading arrangements. We have shown that there is a logic to the principle of reciprocity when it is combined with the principle of non-discrimination, in the sense that the former principle serves well to deliver efficient tariffs provided that tariffs also satisfy MFN. When preferential agreements are introduced, tariffs no longer satisfy MFN, and the presumption that a multilateral system based on reciprocity will deliver an efficient outcome is severely undermined.

3 PREFERENTIAL AGREEMENTS AND ENFORCING MULTILATERAL COMMITMENTS

Up to this point we have compared non-cooperative outcomes with efficient trading arrangements, finding that the difference is entirely attributable to terms-of-trade externalities and that the principles of reciprocity and non-discrimination can serve to implement an efficient arrangement. We have abstracted, however, from the way in which such arrangements might be enforced. We now turn to issues of enforcement, and consider how preferential agreements can affect the ability to enforce trade commitments at the multilateral level.

3.1 The problem of enforcement

As there is no 'world jail', an international agreement must be self-enforcing if it is to be credible (see, for example, Dam, 1970), and an agreement to open markets is in turn self-enforcing only if it also specifies credible retaliatory measures against any country that places additional restraints on trade in a way that violates the agreement. In this light, GATT can be seen as an agreement that specifies co-operative trade policies and acceptable retaliatory measures, with the maintenance of the former resting on the strength of the latter. Starting from this vantage point, the task of enforcing a reciprocal trade agreement amounts to maintaining a balance between (i) the short-term temptation to deviate unilaterally from an agreed-upon trade policy and enjoy the corresponding terms-of-trade benefits, and (ii) the long-term penalty of a consequent future loss of co-operation (i.e., the cost of a future retaliatory 'trade war').[13] Viewed in this way, it is evident that any event that alters the current temptation to cheat or the value of maintaining co-operation into the future can upset this balance, and thus that the enforceable level of co-operation may fluctuate with underlying market conditions.

A preferential agreement introduces one possible source of 'imbalance', and raises the question of whether such agreements might affect the level of multilateral co-operation that can be enforced. Various implications of preferential agreements for the ability to enforce multilateral commitments have been explored in a number of papers, including Bagwell and Staiger (1997b, c, 1998), Bond and Syropoulos (1996), and Bond et al. (1996). Here we review a number of the themes from this literature.

---

[13] We draw a distinction between *unilateral deviations* from an agreed-upon trade policy and the lawful *withdrawal or modification of a previously negotiated concession* under Article XXVIII. The former may go undetected for some time but, once observed by trading partners, would trigger a retaliatory 'trade war'. The latter must be pre-announced to trading partners who are then free to simultaneously withdraw substantially equivalent concessions under the procedures of Article XXVIII described in Section 2.2 above.

3.2 Transition effects

Preferential agreements are typically formed over a lengthy *transition period* during which the trade policy changes associated with the agreement are being phased in, and so we begin by asking how emerging preferential agreements may affect the ability to enforce multilateral co-operation during this period of transition.[14] Our interest in this question is due in part to historical and current experiences with regard to preferential agreements and multilateral tariff co-operation. Beginning in 1957, the EC customs union was formed over a twelve year phase-in period, and it underwent a period of major expansion to include the United Kingdom, Denmark and Ireland beginning in 1972. These episodes of customs union formation and enlargement corresponded with periods of enhanced multilateral tariff co-operation and, as a recent WTO report concludes (WTO, 1995b, pp. 53–4), were factors behind the launching of the GATT Dillon Round (1960–2), Kennedy Round (1964–7) and Tokyo Round (1973–9) of multilateral negotiations. More recently, important preferential agreements include the 1988 U.S.-Canada free trade agreement and its expansion to include Mexico in the NAFTA. The implementation of these agreements, by contrast, appears to have taken place against a backdrop of strained multilateral relations in which preferential initiatives are viewed as a potential threat to the GATT system.[15]

In Bagwell and Staiger (1997b, c), we present formal models broadly consistent with these observations. To interpret the findings of these papers, we note that there are two principal effects of preferential agreements that are crucial in determining how they will affect enforcement at the multilateral level: a *trade diversion effect*, under which trade volumes among member countries increase at the expense of trade between member and non-member countries; and a *market power effect*, which occurs if the member countries form a customs union and adopt a common external tariff policy that enables them to impose higher tariffs on their multilateral trading partners should such punitive tariff action be desired.

Consider first the transition to a free trade area. The main ideas can be understood in terms of a three-country setting. Once countries *A* and *B* become firmly engaged in the lengthy transition process that will culminate in a free trade area, country *C* faces the prospect that it is currently trading more extensively with country *A* than it is likely

---

[14] GATT's Article XXIV acknowledges the practical need for 'interim agreements' to facilitate the process of preferential integration, and only requires that the transition to a completed free trade area or customs union be accomplished 'within a reasonable length of time'.

[15] According to the WTO report, existing preferential agreements were a less significant factor in the 1986 launching of the Uruguay Round of GATT negotiations, because '. . . at the time, regional integration was still confined mainly to Western Europe, with the United States maintaining its traditional multilateralism.' (WTO, 1995b, p. 54). Nevertheless, while the failure of these negotiations to conclude at the Brussels Ministerial in December 1990 reflected the strained multilateral relations of the time, this failure together with the subsequent increase in new preferential initiatives after 1990 were '. . . major factors in eliciting the concessions needed to conclude the Uruguay Round' in 1994 (WTO, 1995b, p. 54), as they raised the spectre that a failed Uruguay Round would lead to a world in which future trade and economic relations would be based primarily upon preferential agreements.

to in the future, since more of country A's future trade will be diverted to its free trade partner once the free trade agreement is fully implemented. Thus, while country C's current temptation to exploit its power over the terms of trade with country A is largely unaffected, owing to its as yet undiminished current trade volume with country A, country C is no longer as fearful of a future trade war with country A, since it expects that it will in any case trade less with country A in the future. Incentives are thus temporarily thrown out of balance as the transition to a free trade area between countries A and B begins, and as a result the trade policies that countries A and C can enforce will be less co-operative during the associated transition phase. It follows that the transition to a free trade area will bring about a period of temporarily heightened multilateral trade tensions in which trade disputes proliferate and further efforts to reduce multilateral tariffs become temporarily stalled. These predictions seem broadly compatible with recent experiences.

On the other hand, when countries A and B are in the lengthy transition process that will culminate in a customs union, country C is faced with the emergence of a new 'market power' effect. Intuitively, when a customs union is formed, its common external tariffs enable it to exert greater power over the terms of trade. As a consequence the union will find high import tariffs more tempting than do its individual member countries prior to uniting. This suggests that a trade war initiated in the transition phase might have heightened negative consequences for country C once the union is formed, as countries A and B will retaliate even more aggressively once they select a common tariff. Accordingly, country C's current temptation to cheat in the transition phase is now more than outweighed by its fear of the retaliation that a customs union could later mete out. Country C's incentives are again temporarily out of balance, but in this case it will tolerate even more liberal multilateral tariffs before the difficulty of enforcement again begins to bind. In this way, the transition to a customs union involves a period of improved multilateral tariff co-operation, much as historical experience suggests.

3.3 Steady state effects

Finally, in a more recent paper (Bagwell and Staiger, 1998), we ignore the transitional effects of preferential agreements and consider instead a three-country world in which two countries are better at co-operating than is the third. In particular, we assume that countries A and B are more patient, and are thus better able to enforce liberal trading policies, than is country C. Within this setting, we compare two trading regimes.

Consider first the case in which countries are constrained to adopt MFN tariffs. Countries A and B then co-operate best by acting as 'hegemons', extending tariff cuts to country C that exceed the cuts that country C offers in return. The impatient country is therefore 'pooled in' with the patient countries under MFN, and it gets to free ride on their liberalisation efforts.

Consider next a second regime, in which countries A and B form a preferential agreement, enabling them to offer a tariff to country C that differs from the zero tariff that they extend to one another. With the ability to discriminate, the patient countries need no longer co-operate multilaterally to co-operate bilaterally, and so the impatient country loses its free rider benefits.

The discriminatory tariff that is offered to country C in this second trading regime will often exceed the tariff it would face were the preferential agreement not allowed, and this leads to an overall deterioration in multilateral tariff co-operation once the preferential agreement is formed. However, the opposite can also occur, as it is possible that the discriminatory tariff offered to country C falls with the introduction of the preferential agreement between countries A and B. Which outcome occurs, and hence whether preferential agreements act as 'stumbling blocs' or 'building blocs' for multilateral tariff co-operation, depends in this setting on how close the multilateral system can get to an efficient trade agreement in the absence of tariff discrimination, which depends in turn on how patient the two 'hegemons' are. Weighing these factors, we find that preferential agreements can facilitate multilateral liberalisation, and that they have their most desirable effects on the multilateral system precisely when multilateral enforcement mechanisms are ineffective and the multilateral system is working poorly.

4 IS BILATERALISM BAD?

We have argued that the multilateral trading system can be understood as a co-operative arrangement among governments that is designed to eliminate the inefficient trade restrictions that are associated with governments' ability to manipulate the terms of trade. In the absence of enforcement difficulties, we find that GATT's principles of reciprocity and non-discrimination can work in tandem to implement an efficient outcome. As a corollary, we find that reciprocity cannot serve to implement an efficient agreement in the presence of free trade areas. An efficient agreement can be implemented under reciprocity in the presence of a customs union, but only if the union members have similar political preferences. These conditions are quite stringent, and so we offer little support for the hypothesis that reciprocity can deliver an efficient multilateral trade agreement in the presence of preferential trade agreements. Instead our results offer support for the view that preferential agreements pose a threat to the existing multilateral system.

Enforcement concerns, however, should not be ignored, as the threat of future retaliation may not be sufficient to deliver a fully efficient multilateral agreement. Consequently, significant changes in the trading environment, such as occur when major preferential integration initiatives are undertaken, can have an impact on the level of multilateral co-operation that can be enforced. This impact will depend critically on the period of analysis, i.e., transition or steady state, on the form that the preferential agreement takes, i.e., free trade agreement or customs union, and on the strength of the multilateral enforcement mechanism. Nevertheless, these results serve to qualify the more negative view of preferential agreements that obtains in the absence of serious limitations to the multilateral enforcement mechanisms, and the implied qualifications achieve their greatest force when multilateral enforcement mechanisms are at their weakest.

Finally, as to the question we posed at the outset, our results suggest that the efficiency of the multilateral trading system will be compromised by the creation of preferential agreements unless multilateral enforcement mechanisms are sufficiently weak. In this light, further strengthening of the enforcement mechanisms of the GATT/WTO will undercut the case for preferential agreements.

References

Bagwell, Kyle, and Staiger, Robert W. (1996). 'Reciprocal trade liberalization,' NBER Working Paper no. 5488, March.

Bagwell, Kyle, and Staiger, Robert W. (1997a). 'An economic theory of GATT,' NBER Working Paper no. 6049, May.

Bagwell, Kyle, and Staiger, Robert W. (1997b). 'Multilateral tariff cooperation during the formation of customs unions,' *Journal of International Economics*, February.

Bagwell, Kyle, and Staiger, Robert W. (1997c). 'Multilateral tariff cooperation during the formation of free trade areas,' *International Economic Review*, May.

Bagwell, Kyle, and Staiger, Robert W. (1998). 'Regionalism and multilateral tariff cooperation,' in (John Piggott and Alan Woodland, eds), *International Trade Policy and the Pacific Rim*, London: Macmillan, forthcoming.

Baldwin, Richard, (1987) 'Politically realistic objective functions and trade policy,' *Economic Letters*, vol. 24.

Bhagwati, Jagdish, (1991). *The World Trading System at Risk.* Princeton, New Jersey: Princeton University Press.

Bond, Eric W., and Syropoulos, Costas (1996). 'Trading blocs and the sustainability of interregional cooperation,' in M., Canzoneri, W., Ethier, and V. Grilli. (eds) *The New Transatlantic Economy*, Cambridge: Cambridge University Press.

Bond, Eric W., Syropoulos, Costas and Winters, Alan A., (1996). 'Deepening of regional integration and external trade relations,' CEPR Discussion Paper No. 1317.

Dam, Kenneth W., (1970). *The GATT: Law and International Economic Organization*, Chicago: University of Chicago Press.

Enders, Alice, (1997). 'The origin, nature and limitations of reciprocity in GATT 1947,' mimeo. Geneva: WTO, October.

Feenstra, Robert C., (1989). 'Symmetric pass-through of tariffs and exchange rates under imperfect competition: an empirical test,' *Journal of International Economics*, vol. 27, pp. 25–45.

Feenstra, Robert C., (1995). 'Estimating the effects of trade policy,' in (Gene M. Grossman and Kenneth Rogoff, eds) *The Handbook of International Economics*, vol. 3, North Holland.

Gros D., (1987) 'A note on the optimal tariff, retaliation and the welfare loss from tariff wars in a framework with intra-industry trade,' *Journal of International Economics*, vol. 23, pp. 357–67.

Jackson, John H., (1989). *The World Trading System*, Cambridge: The MIT Press.

Johnson, Harry G., (1953–4). 'Optimum tariffs and retaliation.' *Review of Economic Studies*, vol. 21, no. 2.

Kennan, John and Riezman, Raymond (1988). Do big countries win tariff wars?, *International Economic Review*, vol. 29, pp. 81–5.

Krugman, Paul R., (1991a). 'Is bilateralism bad?' in (Elhanan Helpman and Assaf Razin, eds.) *International Trade and Trade Policy*, Cambridge, MA and London, England. The MIT Press, pp. 9–23.

Krugman, Paul R., (1991b). 'The move toward free trade zones,' in *Policy Implications of Trade and Currency Zones*, A Symposium Sponsored by The Federal Reserve Bank of Kansas City, Jackson Hole, Wyoming, August 22–24.

Krugman, Paul R., (1997). 'What should trade negotiators negotiate about?,' *Journal of Economic Literature*, vol. 35, March 1997, pp. 113–20.

Maggi, Giovanni, and Rodriguez-Clare, Andres (1988). 'The value of trade agreements in the presence of political pressures,' *Journal of Political Economy*, forthcoming.

Mayer, Wolfgang, (1981). 'Theoretical considerations on negotiated tariff adjustments,' *Oxford Economic Papers*, vol. 33, pp. 135–53.

Mill, John Stewart, (1844). *Essays on Some Unsettled Questions of Political Economy*, London: Parker.

Scitovsky, Tibor, (1942). 'A reconsideration of the theory of tariffs,' *Review of Economic Studies*, vol. 9.

Staiger, Robert W., (1995). 'International rules and institutions for trade policy,' in (Gene M. Grossman and Kenneth Rogof, eds) *The Handbook of International Economics*, vol. 3, North Holland.'

Torrens, Robert, (1844). *The Budget: On Commercial and Colonial Policy*. London: Smith, Elder.

WTO, (1995a). *Analytical Index: Guide to GATT Law and Practice*, vol. 2. Geneva: WTO, April.

WTO, (1995b). *Regionalism and the World Trading System*. Geneva: WTO, April.

Part 4

Finance and Development

INTRODUCTION

Huw D. Dixon

In the early 1970s Ronald McKinnon and Edward Shaw attributed the poor performance of investment and growth in developing countries to financial repression. Interest rate ceilings, high reserve ratios and directed credit programmes were viewed as sources of financial repression, the main symptoms of which were low savings, credit rationing and low investment. Investment suffered not only in quantity but also in quality terms since bankers did not ration the available funds according to the marginal productivity of investment projects but according to their own discretion. Liberalisation of financial markets was thus suggested, so that with the real rate of interest adjusting to its equilibrium level saving and the total real supply of credit would expand and induce a higher volume of investment. Low-yielding investment projects would also be eliminated. Economic growth would, therefore, be stimulated not only through the increased investment but also due to an increase in the average productivity of capital.

Even though the McKinnon/Shaw thesis encountered increasing scepticism over the years, it nevertheless had a relatively early impact through the work of the IMF and the World Bank who, perhaps in their traditional role as promoters of free market conditions, were keen to encourage financial liberalisation in developing countries as part of more general 'liberalisation' reforms. It is now widely recognised that the experience of many countries from these experiments has been disappointing. In the Latin American experiments in particular, many banks collapsed. Moreover, econometric evidence on the McKinnon/Shaw thesis is at best mixed.

The reaction of advocates of financial liberalisation to the unfavourable evidence has been to argue that where liberalisation failed it was because of the existence of implicit or explicit deposit insurance coupled with inadequate banking supervision and macroeconomic instability. These conditions were conducive to excessive risk-taking by the banks, a form of moral hazard which can lead to 'too high' real interest rates, bankruptcies of firms and bank failures. This type of analysis has led to the introduction of new elements into the McKinnon/Shaw framework in the form of preconditions that have to be met at the outset of financial reforms. These are 'adequate banking supervision' – which aims to ensure that banks have a well diversified

loan portfolio – and 'macroeconomic stability' – which refers to low and stable inflation and a sustainable fiscal deficit. There have also been some very important changes
in emphasis, especially in relation to the channels through which interest rates affect
investment and growth. It is now conceded, even by the World Bank, that the effects of
higher interest rates on the total amount of saving are ambiguous because substitution
and income effects work in opposite directions. Nonetheless, it is claimed that financial savings are adversely affected by 'financial repression', which, in turn, influences
the productivity of investment, and, through this the rate of economic growth.

This 'controversy' section deals with three aspects of this debate. Maxwell Fry de-
fends the McKinnon/Shaw thesis. Fry concentrates on the 'second round' of the debate, which concerns itself with the necessary prerequisites for successful financial
liberalisation. These prerequisites were either ignored or insufficiently incorporated
and analysed by the 'first round' literature which promoted financial liberalisation. Fry
thus argues that the theoretical underpinnings of the 'first round' financial liberalisation were strengthened by the 'second round' financial liberalisation literature.

Ajit Singh marshalls the attack on the thesis. Concentrating on the stock market,
Singh highlights its importance to the whole debate, which has actually been neglected
by the McKinnon/Shaw proponents. For example, between 1982 and 1992 the total
market capitalisation of companies quoted on the stock exchanges in a number of
developing countries increased by a factor of twenty. Beyond their role in domestic
financial liberalisation, stock markets played a paramount role in external financial
liberalisation of developing countries. Singh examines closely the implications of these
developments to conclude that financial liberalisation, by making the financial system
more fragile, is not likely to enhance long-term growth in developing countries.

Philip Arestis and Panicos Demetriades explore the quantitative aspects of the controversy in an attempt to see what the evidence can tell us about the validity of the
thesis and its implications. They resort to two types of evidence. The first is on the
contribution of the financial system to the process of economic development. The
causality between the two becomes vital in this work. The second type is concerned
with financial liberalisation and its impact on investment and growth. Evidence is
reported from the experience of countries which practised financial reforms. New
evidence is also provided which concentrates on the relationship between stock market development and economic growth, and, also, on the direct effects of financial
repression.

11

IN FAVOUR OF FINANCIAL
LIBERALISATION*

Maxwell J. Fry

In practice, many developing country governments find it virtually impossible to satisfy their inter-temporal budget constraint with conventional tax revenue. Hence, they rely on revenue from the inflation tax and they reduce their interest costs through financial repression (Brock, 1989, p. 116; Giovannini and de Melo, 1993; Agénor and Montiel, 1996, p. 156; Fry, 1997). This paper suggests that financial repression is a particularly damaging quasi-tax from the perspective of economic growth.

A key stylised fact about financial systems in developing countries is that they are dominated by commercial banks (Fry, 1995, pp. 4–5; Rojas-Suárez and Weisbrod, 1995, pp. 4–11). Assets of insurance and pension companies are minuscule in most developing countries. Development financial institutions such as agricultural and development banks are also small compared with the commercial banks. Commercial bond markets are typically thin and government bond markets are often used only by captive buyers obliged to hold such bonds to satisfy liquidity ratio requirements or to bid for government contracts. Although equity markets are sizeable in several developing countries, their role in the process of financial intermediation between the household and business sectors remains small. Indeed, the relatively large Taiwanese equity market produces a transfer of resources from the business sector to the household sector in the form of dividends that exceeds the transfer from the household sector to the business sector in the form of new issue purchases. The net flow through stock exchanges is also relatively small in most Latin American countries (Rojas-Suárez and Weisbrod, 1995, p. 6). At best stock markets play a minor role; more often they resemble gambling casinos and may actually impede growth in developing countries (Singh, 1997). Hence, this paper focuses quite deliberately on commercial banks as the key institutions involved in the process of saving–investment intermediation that are affected by financial liberalisation.

1 THE FINANCIAL REPRESSION PARADIGM

In their analysis of financially repressed developing economies, McKinnon (1973) and Shaw (1973) argue that financial repression – indiscriminate 'distortions of financial

* This paper is based on research supported by the Economic and Social Research Council under its Research Programme on Pacific Asia, grant L 324253010. My thanks also go to Philip Arestis. Anthony Courakis, Keith Cuthbertson and Michael Summer for comments on an earlier draft.

prices including interest rates and foreign-exchange rates' – reduces 'the real rate of growth and the real size of the financial system relative to nonfinancial magnitudes. In all cases this strategy has stopped or gravely retarded the development process' (Shaw, 1973, pp. 3–4). The essential common elements of the McKinnon–Shaw model are: (*a*) a saving function that responds positively to both the real rate of interest on deposits and the real rate of growth in output; (*b*) an investment function that responds negatively to the effective real loan rate of interest and positively to the growth rate; (*c*) an administratively fixed nominal interest rate that holds the real rate below its equilibrium level (McKinnon, 1973, pp. 71–7; Shaw, 1973, pp. 81–7); and (*d*) inefficient non-price rationing of loanable funds.

In the McKinnon–Shaw model, banks allocate credit not according to expected productivity of the investment projects but according to transaction costs and perceived risks of default. Quality of collateral, political pressures, 'name', loan size, and covert benefits to loans officers may also influence allocation. Even if credit allocation is random, the average efficiency of investment is reduced as the loan rate ceiling is lowered because investments with lower returns now become profitable. Entrepreneurs who were previously deterred from requesting bank loans enter the market. Hence, adverse selection from the perspective of social welfare occurs when interest rates are set too low and so produce disequilibrium credit rationing of the type described here.[1]

Interest rate ceilings distort the economy in four ways. First, low interest rates produce a bias in favour of current consumption and against future consumption. Therefore, they may reduce saving below the socially optimum level. Second, potential lenders may engage in relatively low-yielding direct investment instead of lending by way of depositing money in a bank. Third, bank borrowers able to obtain all the funds they want at low loan rates will choose relatively capital-intensive projects. Fourth, the pool of potential borrowers contains entrepreneurs with low-yielding projects who would not want to borrow at the higher market-clearing interest rate. To the extent that banks' selection process contains an element of randomness, some investment projects that are financed will have yields below the threshold that would be self-imposed with market-clearing interest rates.[2]

Raising the interest rate ceiling towards its competitive free-market level increases both saving and investment. Changes in the real interest rate trace out the saving function in this disequilibrium situation. Raising the interest rate ceiling also deters entrepreneurs from undertaking all low-yielding investments that are no longer profitable at the higher real interest rate. Hence the average return to or efficiency of aggregate investment increases. The output growth rate rises in this process, so further increasing saving. Thus, the real rate of interest as the return to savers is the key to a higher level of investment, and as a rationing device to greater investment efficiency.

---

[1] As discussed below (section 3: adverse selection also occurs when interest rates rise too high because equilibrium credit rationing is not working properly.

[2] Chamley and Honohan (1993) pinpoint another drawback of loan rate ceilings in that they tend to deter bank spending on loan assessments. Since even in an unrepressed situation banks are likely to underspend on screening, this additional deterrence may be worse for social welfare than another form of repression that affects the financial system at a margin which is initially undistorted.

The increased quantity and quality of investment interact in their positive effects on the output growth rate. Growth in the financially repressed economy is constrained by saving; investment opportunities abound here (McKinnon, 1973, pp. 59–61; Shaw, 1973, p. 81). The policy prescription for the financially repressed economy examined by McKinnon and Shaw is to raise institutional interest rates or to reduce the rate of inflation. Abolishing interest rate ceilings altogether produces the optimal result of maximising investment and raising still further investment's average efficiency.

2 THEORETICAL ADVANCES

Over the past decade, a second generation of financial growth models incorporating both endogenous growth and endogenous financial institutions has emerged. Typically, financial intermediation is now modelled explicitly rather than taken for granted or treated in simple deterministic terms, as it is in the first-generation financial repression models. Various techniques, such as externalities and quality ladders, are used to model endogenous growth. However, the precise cause of endogenous growth does not affect the role of finance. Hence, it is possible to select alternative financial models for use with alternative endogenous or even non-endogenous growth models.

Finance and financial institutions become relevant in a world of positive information, transaction and monitoring costs. If monitoring costs are high, a simple debt instrument may dominate a more complicated state-contingent contract that resembles equity. By ignoring all contingencies, however, debt can lead to insolvency, a situation in which the borrower's net worth is no longer positive. The lender may reduce default risk by considering a potential borrower's balance sheet and taking collateral, rationing the borrower by providing less than requested or restricting the maturity of the loan.

One way of showing how financial intermediaries can offer higher expected returns is to construct a model in which individuals can choose between unproductive assets (consumer goods or commodity money) and an investment in a firm (Diamond and Dybvig, 1983). The investment in a firm is illiquid because it takes time to become productive. However, the expected return from a two-period investment in a firm is greater than the return from an inventory of consumer goods or currency. Uncertainty may force some individuals to liquidate or abandon their investments in firms after only one period. In such case, they would be worse off than had they held solely an inventory of consumer goods or currency (Bencivenga and Smith, 1991, 1992; Levine, 1993; Greenwood and Smith, 1997). Individuals may also be deterred from investing in a firm by productivity risk; some firms do better than others (King and Levine, 1993*b*).

Without banks, individuals must allocate their portfolios between capital and currency to maximise expected utility. Although they know the probability of the event which could make a productive investment worthless, their choice will also be affected by their degree of risk aversion. Those with greater risk aversion will choose a higher proportion of currency than those with less risk aversion. Any productive investment bears some risk of becoming worthless.

Bencivenga and Smith (1991, 1992), Greenwood and Smith (1997), and Levine (1993) embed the Diamond–Dybvig financial intermediation model in an overlapping-generations model with production and capital accumulation. With the introduction of banks, individuals can hold deposits which banks then invest in currency and capital. By exploiting the law of large numbers, banks ensure that they never have to liquidate capital prematurely. Banks also rely on the law of large numbers to estimate deposit withdrawals which are unpredictable individually but predictable for the economy as a whole. Hence, banks avoid the uncertainty which leads to resource misallocation by individuals. By ensuring that capital is never wasted, financial intermediation may produce higher capital/labour ratios and higher rates of economic growth. By engaging in maturity intermediation, financial institutions offer liquidity to savers and, at the same time, longer-term funds to investors. In so doing, they stimulate productive investment by persuading savers to switch from unproductive investment in tangible assets to productive investment in firms.

Those who do not use the Diamond–Dybvig model of financial intermediation posit other ways in which banks can stimulate endogenous growth. For example, Greenwood and Jovanovic (1990) stress the role of financial intermediaries in pooling funds and acquiring information that enables them to allocate capital to its highest valued use, so raising, the average return to capital. Specifically, Greenwood and Jovanovic (1990) allow capital to be invested in safe, low-yielding investments or risky, high-yielding investments. Risk is created by both aggregate and project-specific shocks. Individuals cannot differentiate between the two types of shock.

With large portfolio holdings, however, financial intermediaries can experiment with a small sample of high-yielding projects to determine the state of the world. With this expenditure on the collection and analysis of information, financial intermediaries determine their investment strategies in the knowledge of the current-period aggregate shock. Were a negative shock to make the high-risk investments less profitable than the low-risk investments, financial intermediaries would invest only in the low-risk projects. Provided the costs of information collection and analysis are sufficiently small, the ability to choose the appropriate set of projects in the knowledge of a given aggregate shock raises the expected return on the intermediaries' portfolios above that of individuals who must choose one or the other technology without any information about the aggregate shock.

King and Levine (1993*b*) suggest that financial institutions play a key role in evaluating prospective entrepreneurs and financing the most promising ones: 'Better financial systems improve the probability of successful innovation and thereby accelerate economic growth' (King and Levine, 1993*b*, p. 513). Following Schumpeter (1912), they stress that 'financial institutions play an active role in evaluating, managing, and funding the entrepreneurial activity that leads to productivity growth. Indeed, we believe that our mechanism is the channel by which finance must have its dominant effect, due to the central role of productivity growth in development' (King and Levine, 1993*b*, p. 515).

The main feature of endogenous growth models is that a broadly defined concept of the economy's capital stock does not suffer from diminishing returns; hence growth is a positive function of the investment ratio. For any endogenous growth model, growth rate comparisons can be made between economies with and without banks. 'Relative to the situation in the absence of banks (financial autarky), banks reduce liquid reserve holdings by the economy as a whole, and also reduce the liquidation of productive capital. Then, with an externality in production . . . higher equilibrium growth rates will be observed in economies with an active intermediary sector' (Bencivenga and Smith, 1991, p. 196).

Endogenous growth in all these models magnifies and prolongs the effects of financial conditions. In all these models, financial repression in the form of discriminatory taxes on financial intermediation reduces the growth rate. Financial sector taxes are equivalent to taxes on innovative activity, since they reduce the net returns that financial intermediaries gain from financing successful entrepreneurs. Whereas financial development improves overall productivity, discriminatory taxation of commercial banks, investment banks, mutual funds, and stock markets through high reserve requirements, interest and credit ceilings, directed credit programmes and inflation reduces the growth rate by impeding financial development. More generally, 'financial repression . . . reduces the services provided by the financial system to savers, entrepreneurs, and producers; it thereby impedes innovative activity and slows economic growth' (King and Levine, 1993*b*, p. 517). Indeed, the existence of externalities implies that welfare may be improved through some public subsidy of financial intermediation.

3 PREREQUISITES

Several interest-rate liberalisation experiments have failed to produce the results outlined above. The basic problem lies in the perverse reaction to higher interest rates by insolvent (or non-profit-motivated) economic agents – governments, firms or individuals. By definition, an insolvent agent (one whose liabilities exceed its assets) or 'distress borrower' is unable to repay its loans. Hence, it is not deterred from borrowing by a higher cost. It simply continues, if it can, to borrow whatever it needs to finance its losses. These inevitably increase with an increase in the interest rate which drives up the agent's cost of servicing its loans. Hence such agents exhibit loan demand functions that respond positively to the interest rate.

Pathologically high positive real interest rates, possibly triggered by fiscal instability, indicate a poorly functioning financial system. Inadequate prudential supervision and regulation enable distress borrowing to crowd out borrowing for investment purposes by solvent firms, so producing an epidemic effect (Stiglitz and Weiss, 1981; McKinnon, 1993, p. 38–41; Fry, 1995, pp. 305–6; Rojas-Suárez and Weisbrod, 1995). Funds continue to be supplied because of explicit or implicit deposit insurance. The end result is financial and economic paralysis.

This international experience over the past 20 years indicates that there are five prerequisites for successful financial liberalisation (Fry, 1995, pp. 454–60):

1 Adequate prudential regulation and supervision of commercial banks, implying some minimal levels of accounting and legal infrastructure.
2 A reasonable degree of price stability.
3 Fiscal discipline taking the form of a sustainable government borrowing requirement that avoids inflationary expansion of reserve money by the central bank either through direct domestic borrowing by the government or through the indirect effect of government borrowing that produces surges of capital inflows requiring large purchases of foreign exchange by the central bank to prevent

exchange rate appreciation.
4   Profit-maximising, competitive behaviour by the commercial banks.
5   A tax system that does not impose discriminatory explicit or implicit taxes on
    financial intermediation.

4 THE STIGLITZ CONTROVERSY

In a series of papers (e.g. Stiglitz, 1994), Stiglitz criticises financial liberalisation on the
grounds that financial markets are prone to market failures. He suggests that 'there
exist forms of government intervention that will not only make these markets function
better but will also improve the performance of the economy' (Stiglitz, 1994, p. 20).
Specifically, he advocates government intervention to keep interest rates below their
market-equilibrium levels.

An essential function of financial markets is collecting, processing and conveying
information for allocating funds and monitoring their use. Costly information creates
market failures. One market failure arising from costly information occurs because
monitoring is a public good. If one individual conducts research to determine the
solvency of a financial institution and then acts upon that information, others can
benefit from copying his actions. Because information about the management and
solvency of financial institutions is a public good, there is suboptimal expenditure on
monitoring them. When financial institutions know that they are not adequately mon-
itored by depositors, they have incentives to take greater risks with their deposits.

Costly information can also produce externalities. For example, when several banks
fail, depositors may assume that there is an increased probability that other banks will
fail. Their reaction in the form of deposit withdrawal may produce the predicted failures. Externalities can also be transmitted across markets. For example, the provision
of a bank loan makes it easier for a firm to raise equity capital. The bank loan provides
a signal that the firm is sound and prospective equity participants can also expect the
bank to monitor the firm in which they will be investing. Naturally, financial institutions are rarely concerned about these externality effects. Hence, private interest can
diverge from public interest.

Given information imperfections, Stiglitz (1994, pp. 39–42) argues that financial
repression can improve the efficiency with which capital is allocated. First, lowering
interest rates improves the average quality of the pool of loan applicants. Second,
financial repression increases firm equity because it lowers the cost of capital. Third,
financial repression could be used in conjunction with an alternative allocative mechanism such as export performance to accelerate economic growth. Fourth, directed
credit programmes can encourage lending to sectors with high technological spillovers.

The importance of information imperfections and the role of government intervention in the area of prudential regulation and supervision can be accepted without
accepting Stiglitz's case for financial repression. First, lowering interest rates does not
necessarily increase the average efficiency of investment because lower interest rates
can encourage entrepreneurs with lower-yielding projects to bid for funds (Fry, 1995,
Ch. 2). Second, financial repression may not lower the marginal cost of capital if
rationing forces borrowers into the curb market. Third, using past performance as a

criterion for allocating credit discriminates against new entrants and perpetuates monopoly power. Finally, directed credit programmes have invariably raised delinquency and default rates, so increasing the fragility of the financial system by forcing financial institutions to increase their risk exposure with no compensating return.

The overwhelming problem in implementing financial repression advocated by Stiglitz is that there is such a small range of real interest rates over which financial repression could be appropriate, if it is appropriate at all. Stiglitz claims that it should not reduce real deposit rates below zero. As an upper bound, real loan rates over 10 per cent are likely to indicate distress borrowing and pathological behaviour by banks. With bank operating cost ratios in developing countries typically at least twice the level of operating cost ratios in the OECD countries (Fry, 1995, pp. 325–7), this implies a maximum real deposit rate of only 4–5 per cent if banks are to remain solvent.

Real deposit rates in 85 developing countries for which any data exist ranged from −458 to +234 per cent over the period 1971–95.[3] The standard deviation of these 1,329 annual observations is 32 per cent. Hence, discussion over the desirability of manipulating real interest rates by 1 or 2 percentage points is akin to the debate over the number of angels that can stand on a pinhead. Establishing and maintaining an environment under which real deposit rates are likely to fall in the 0–5 per cent range is as much as one can realistically hope to achieve.

Stiglitz has amazing faith in government. The government in his papers is exemplary: disciplined, knowledgeable, long-sighted, objective. It pursues economic objectives without deviating into the many side alleys of patronage and sleaze. My main doubt about actual governments pursuing his policy is that, once they have an intellectual justification for intervention, they will use it for purposes that would horrify him.[4] I agree entirely with Arestis and Demetriades (1997, p. 796): 'market failure does not necessarily imply government success.'

Korea is often cited as an example of a country that has prospered without full-blown financial liberalisation. Any economist who has visited Korea and a sizeable sample of other developing countries over the past 25 years must concede that economic policy-making in Korea approximates Stiglitz's idealised world. Unfortunately, one also has to agree that there are extremely few other developing countries for which the same claim could be upheld. Indeed, the Korean government is particularly noteworthy in both its voracious appetite for economic knowledge and its ability to admit mistakes, e.g. over its encouragement of heavy petro-chemical industries in the late 1970s.

5 EMPIRICAL EVIDENCE

According to economists of almost all persuasions, financial conditions may affect the rate of economic growth in both the short and medium runs. Tobin's (1965) monetary growth model posits a negative impact of a higher real return on money holdings in the medium run but has nothing to say about the short run. The McKinnon–Shaw school expects financial liberalisation (institutional interest rates rising towards their

---

[3] For symmetry, I use continuously compounded rates throughout this paper.
[4] I have exactly the same concern about the misuse of strategic trade theory.

competitive free-market equilibrium levels) to exert a positive effect on the rate of economic growth in both the short and medium runs. The neostructuralists predict a stagflationary (accelerating inflation and lower growth) outcome from financial liberalisation in the short run. In the medium run, there is the possibility that the saving ratio will increase by enough to outweigh the negative influence of portfolio adjustments. In practice, neostructuralists, with the possible exception of Buffie (1984), view a dominant saving effect as unlikely.

A simple way of discriminating between the McKinnon–Shaw school and others would be to examine episodes of financial liberalisation and see whether or not these were accompanied by higher or lower rates of economic growth. In practice, however, most clear-cut cases of financial liberalisation were accompanied by other economic reforms (such as fiscal, international trade and foreign exchange reforms). In such cases, it is virtually impossible to isolate the effects of financial components of the reform package. This is unfortunate, since causality can be inferred when financial conditions have been deliberately and substantially changed, as in the case of a discrete financial liberalisation. Examining the association between financial conditions and economic growth over time provides in itself no evidence of causality. With this caveat, I now examine the empirical evidence on the association between financial conditions and rates of economic growth.

In one of the earlier studies of the effect of financial repression, Lanyi and Saracoglu (1983, appendix III) implicitly address the causality issue by dividing 21 developing countries into three groups. Lanyi and Saracoglu give a value of 1 to countries with positive real interest rates, 0 to countries with moderately negative but 'not punitively negative' real interest rates, and −1 to countries with severely negative real interest rates. Given the fact that deposit rates were fixed by administrative fiat in all the countries posting negative deposit rates, one can argue that these rates are exogenous to the growth process. The cross-section regression reported by Lanyi and Saracoglu (1983, table 4, p. 29) indicates a positive and significant relationship between the average rates of growth in real gross domestic product (GDP) and the interest rate dummy variable for the period 1971–80.

The World Bank (1989, pp. 30–2) uses the same methodology as Lanyi and Saracoglu for a sample of 34 developing countries. First, it shows in tabular form that economic growth in countries with strongly negative real deposit rates (lower than – 10 per cent on average over the period 1974–85) was substantially lower than growth in countries with positive real interest rates. Although the investment ratio was only 17 per cent higher in the countries with positive real interest rates, the average productivity of investment, as measured by the incremental output/capital ratio, was almost four times higher. As confirmed by others, financial repression exerts its main impact on the quality rather than the quantity of investment. It has very little, if any, direct effect on saving. Second, the World Bank also reports a regression showing a positive and significant cross-section relationship between average growth and average real interest rates over the period 1965–85.[5]

---

[5] In this regression, two observations, one for 1965–73 and the other for 1974–85, are included for each country, as well as a dummy variable for the 1974–85 period.

Several other studies present pooled time-series regression estimates showing positive and significant relationships between the rate of economic growth and the real deposit rate of interest. The empirical results reported in Fry (1978, p. 470; 1979, pp. 132–4; 1980, p. 324; 1981, pp. 87–8) suggest that on average a 1 percentage point increase in the real deposit rate of interest towards its competitive free-market equilibrium level is associated with a rise in the rate of economic growth of about half a percentage point in Asia, i.e. the coefficient of the real deposit rate of interest averages 0.5. The World Bank (1989, p. 32) estimates a coefficient of 0.2, Gelb (1989, p. 20) estimates coefficients of 0.2–0.26 for his sample of 34 countries, while Polak (1989, p. 67) estimates coefficients of 0.18–0.27 when regressing the average annual rate of growth in real GDP on the median real interest rate for 40 developing countries. For 53 countries over the period 1960–85, Roubini and Sala-i-Martin (1992, p. 22) also find that countries with real interest rates less than −5 per cent in the 1970s experienced growth rates that averaged 1.4 percentage points less than growth rates in countries with positive real interest rates. If the difference is approximately 10 percentage points, the implied interest rate coefficient is 0.14.[6] The global evidence suggests that Asian developing countries may be more sensitive to real interest rate changes than other groups of developing countries.

Recent empirical work has tended to resort to far larger data sets than were used in studies before 1990. For example, Ghani (1992) estimates growth equations for a sample of 50 developing countries following an approach used by Barro (1991). The initial levels of human capital (as measured by years of schooling) and financial development (as measured by the ratio of total assets of the financial system to GDP or the ratio of private sector credit to GDP) in 1965 yield significantly positive coefficients, while the initial level of *per capita* real GDP produces a negative coefficient in an equation explaining average growth rates over the period 1965–89 (Ghani, 1992, p. 17). De Gregorio and Guidotti (1995, p. 440) produce similar results for middle and low-income countries using Barro's data set.

King and Levine (1993*a, b, c*) examine links between finance and growth in a cross-section of 77 developing countries over the period 1960–89. They construct four financial indicators: (*a*) liquid liabilities divided by GDP (usually M_2 divided by GDP);[7] (*b*) domestic assets in deposit money banks divided by domestic assets of both deposit money banks and the central bank; (*c*) domestic credit to the private sector divided by aggregate domestic credit; and (*d*) domestic credit to the private sector divided by GDP. King and Levine also construct four growth indicators: (*a*) average rate of growth in *per capita* real GDP; (*b*) average rate of growth in the capital stock; (*c*) the residual between (*a*) and 0.3 of (*b*) as a proxy for productivity improvements; and (*d*) gross domestic investment divided by GDP.

King and Levine (1993*a*, pp. 725–7, *b*, p. 530) show that each financial indicator is positively and significantly correlated with each growth indicator at the 99 per cent confidence level. The same positive relationship is illustrated by dividing the 77 coun-

[6] See also Asian Development Bank (1985). Easterly (1993), and Fry (1991).
[7] To obtain mid-year estimates, beginning-of-year and end-of-year values of all financial variables are averaged.

tries into four groups with respect to the growth indicators; countries are divided into those with average *per capita* income growth above 3 per cent, greater than 2 but less than 3, greater than 0.5 but less than 2 and less than 0.5 per cent. There are about 20 countries in each group. In each case, the average value of the financial indicator declines with a move from a higher to a lower growth group. Multivariate analysis produces much the same picture (King and Levine, 1993c, pp. 180–1).

De Gregorio and Guidotti (1995, pp. 436–7) claim that real interest rates are not a good indicator of financial repression or distortion. They suggest that the relationship between real interest rates and economic growth might resemble an inverted U curve: 'Very low (and negative) real interest rates tend to cause financial disintermediation and hence tend to reduce growth, as implied by the McKinnon Shaw hypothesis. . . . On the other hand, very high real interest rates that do not reflect improved efficiency of investment, but rather a lack of credibility of economic policy or various forms of country risk, are likely to result in a lower level of investment as well as a concentration in excessively risky projects' (De Gregorio and Guidotti, 1995, p. 437).[8]

In fact, the point made by De Gregorio and Guidotti holds up well with data from 85 developing countries for the period 1971–95 prepared for this paper.[9] First I estimated the relationship between the annual rate of economic growth YG and the real rate of interest RR in equations of the basic form $YG = \beta_0 + \beta_1\,(RR + \beta_2)\,(RR + \beta_2)$. Since the parameter β_2 was not significantly different from zero, although its negative value implies that growth is maximised at some positive real interest rate, I drop it from the estimate reported here. A pooled time-series fixed-effect estimate including both the squared real interest rate and the absolute value of the cubed real interest rate gives the following result (1,296 observations, t statistics in parentheses):

$$YG = -\,0.033\;RR^2 + 0.008|RR|^3$$
$$(-3.949) \qquad\quad (3.598) \qquad\qquad\qquad\qquad (1)$$
$$\bar{R}^2 = 0.163$$

No intercept is reported because the fixed-effect model estimates separate constants for each country; this equation estimates 85 intercepts. The effect of a rising real interest rate on growth produced by (1) is illustrated in Fig. 1.

Evidently, growth is maximised when the real interest rate lies within the normal or non-pathological range of, say, −5 to +15 per cent.

Finally, I extend the empirical work on financial repression by estimating a simultaneous-equation system in which saving and investment ratios as well as export and output growth rates are affected by financial conditions. I also examine the effects of the excessively high real interest rates that have been experienced after several financial liberalisation experiments. These distorted financial conditions appear to be just as debilitating as financial repression. Following Shaw (1973, p. 3), I use both the real

---

[8] This criticism is based on work by Calvo and Coricelli (1992).
[9] Not all countries report data for the entire period. For the interest rate series, I use the geometric average of commercial bank deposit and loan rates, since these are the most prevalent interest rate data reported in the March 1996 *International Financial Statistics* CD-ROM. The continuously compounded inflation rate is then subtracted from the continuously compounded nominal interest rate.

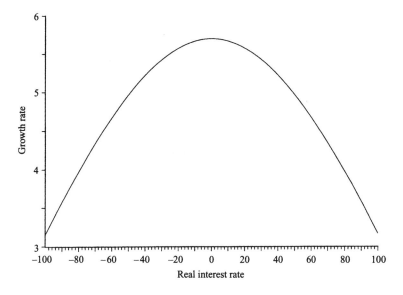

Fig. 1 Annual growth and real interest rates, 1971–95

deposit rate of interest *RR* and the black market exchange rate premium *BLACK* as proxies for financial distortions. Negative real interest rates generally reflect some government-imposed distortion in domestic financial markets (Giovannini and de Melo, 1993; Fry, 1995). Since governments using financial repression as a source of revenue attempt to prevent capital outflows that would erode their tax base, black market exchange rate premia also provide an indicator of financial repression.

The De Gregorio–Guidotti effect discussed earlier could also apply to saving behaviour. Increased risk and uncertainty leading to very high real interest rates can reduce measured national saving, particularly if the increased domestic risk encourages savers to remove their savings abroad through under-and overinvoicing. Again, I resolve the problem that both very low and very high real interest rates could deter saving not by abandoning real interest rates but rather by using the square of the real deposit rate. This ensures that large positive and negative values exert the same, presumably negative, effect on the saving ratio.[10]

For the empirical work reported here, I use data from a sample of 16 developing countries – Argentina, Brazil, Chile, Egypt, India, Indonesia, Korea, Malaysia, Mexico, Nigeria, Pakistan, Philippines, Sri Lanka, Thailand, Turkey and Venezuela – for the period 1970–88.[11] I use iterative three-stage least squares which is, asymptotically, full-

[10] I tested various alternative functional forms for the real interest rate in all the estimates reported here. None produced noticeably better or different results.
[11] The ending date was determined by the availability of black market exchange rates taken from the World Bank's *World Development Report 1991: Supplementary Data* diskette. All other data come from *International Financial Statistics* CD-ROM and the World Bank's *Socio-economic Time-series Access and Retrieval System: World Tables* diskette.

information maximum likelihood (Johnston, 1984, pp. 486–92). I estimate the 16 individual country equations for saving, investment, export growth, and output growth as systems of equations with cross-equation equality restrictions on all coefficients except the intercept. Hence, the estimates apply to a representative member of this sample of developing countries. The estimation technique corrects for hetero-scedasticity across country equations and exploits contemporaneously correlated disturbances.

The equations presented in Table 1 are derived in Fry (1998). The estimates indicate that financial distortions as measured by the real interest rate squared and the

Table 1 A simultaneous-equation system of financial distortions

$$SNY = 0.289 \ \widehat{YG} - 0.038 \ BLACK - 0.006 \ RR^2 - 0.198; \ (\widehat{YG} \ BLACK)$$
$$(123.359) \ (-39.816) \qquad (-3.981) \quad (-12.487)$$
$$-0.205(\widehat{YG} \ RR^2) + 0.812 \ SNY_{t-1} \tag{2}$$
$$(-5.696) \qquad (748.272)$$
$$R^2 = 0.861$$

$$IY = 0.251 \ \widehat{YG} - 1.628 \ RR^2 - 0.692 \ IY_{t-1}$$
$$(32.671) \ (-11.661) \quad (43.998) \tag{3}$$
$$R^2 = 0.794$$

$$NKG = 0.364 + \widehat{YG} + 0.179 \ \widehat{IY} + 0.496 \ \widehat{SIY} - 0.224 \ BLACK^2$$
$$(5.797) \qquad (3.756) \quad (11.941) \quad (-2.846) \tag{4}$$
$$R^2 = 0.153$$

$$YG = 0.226 \ \widehat{IKY} - 0.999 \ \widehat{IKY} \ BLACK) - 0.354 \ (\widehat{IKY} \ RR^2) + 0.098 \ \widehat{XKG}$$
$$(16.850) \quad (-9.786) \qquad (-11.389) \qquad (19.691) \tag{5}$$
$$R^2 = 0.202$$

Endogenous Variables

SNY	National saving/GNP (current prices).
IY	Domestic investment/GNP (current prices).
SIY	SNY − IY.
YG	Rate of growth in GNP (constant prices, continuously compounded).
IKY	Domestic investment/GNP (constant prices).
XKG	Rate of growth in exports (constant prices, continuously compounded).

Exogenous Variables

RR	Real deposit rate of interest (interest minus inflation rate, continuously compounded).
BLACK	Black market foreign exchange rate premium.

black market exchange rate premium reduce investment ratios and export growth. In turn, lower investment ratios and export growth reduce output growth rates. Output growth is also reduced directly by financial distortions, possibly through an impact on investment efficiency. Because a major determinant of saving ratios is the output growth rate, saving ratios are influenced substantially, albeit indirectly, by financial distortions through their effects on investment ratios, export growth, and output growth.

I now use the four equations in Table 1 to examine both the direct short-run and overall long-run effects of financial distortions on saving and output growth by comparing the estimated variations in the saving ratio and output growth rate caused by changes in the financial distortion variables in (2) and (5) with the estimated variations caused by changes in the financial distortion variables in the system of equations consisting of (2), (3), (4), and (5). The simulated changes in the financial distortion variables are confined to the observed range recorded for this country sample.

Fig. 2 illustrates both the direct effect from (2) and the overall effect from the joint simulation of (2), (3), (4), and (5) of a rising real interest rate on the national saving ratio. The simultaneous-equation model used to estimate the overall effect also contains identities defining the saving–investment gap and the equivalence of the nominal and real investment ratio. Fig. 2 is produced using the mean values of all the explanatory variables with the exception of the real deposit rate of interest. The mean value of the real deposit rate for the entire country sample is zero with a standard deviation of 23 per cent. Its minimum value is −83 per cent and its maximum value 221 per cent. Fig. 2 shows that the relationship between the real interest rate and the national saving ratio resembles an inverted U. Both very low and very high real interest rates reduce national saving mainly through the effects of these interest rates on output growth.

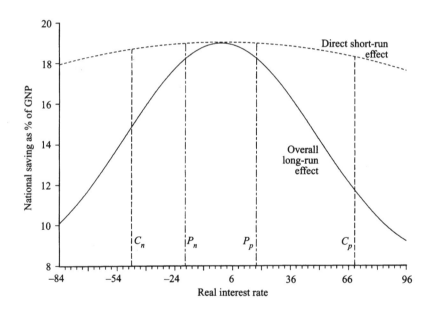

Fig. 2 Effects of real interest rates on national saving ratios

The line P_n denotes two standard deviations below the mean of all negative interest rates in the five Pacific Asian economics (Indonesia, Korea, Malaysia, Philippines and Thailand), C_n denotes two standard deviations below the mean of all negative interest rates in the remaining 11 countries (the control group), P_p denotes two standard deviations above the mean of all zero or positive interest rates in the Pacific Asian economics, while C_p denotes two standard deviations above the mean of all zero or positive interest rates in the control group countries. Evidently, real interest rates deviated from their saving-maximising level far more in the control group countries than they did in the Pacific Asian economies. Similar findings emerge when direct and overall effects of both real interest rates on output growth and black market exchange rate premia on saving and growth rates are simulated.

Over the period 1970–88, the national saving ratio in the five Pacific Asian countries averaged 23.8 per cent compared with 16.0 per cent in the 11 countries of the control group, while the continuously compounded output growth rate in the Pacific Asian countries averaged 6.2 per cent compared with 3.9 per cent in the control group. Over the same period, the black market exchange rate premium averaged 6.2 per cent in the Pacific Asian countries compared with 42.6 per cent in the control group, while the square of the real interest rate was 10 times greater in the control group than it was in Pacific Asia.

The overall effects of both financial distortion variables are estimated by simulating the model consisting of (2), (3), (4), and (5), together with identities defining the saving–investment gap and the equivalence of the nominal and real investment ratio. These simulations indicate that differences in the average values of the financial distortion variables in each country group account for 3.7 of the 7.8 percentage point difference in the national saving ratios between the Pacific Asian and control group countries and for 1.7 of the 2.3 percentage point difference in their output growth rates. In other words, these two financial distortions explain approximately 50 per cent of the difference in saving ratios and 75 per cent of the difference in output growth rates between these two country groups.

A large part of the above-average economic performance of the Pacific Asian developing market economies can be explained by their economic policies that ensured negligible levels of financial distortions, as measured both by the real rate of interest and the black market exchange rate premium. The macroeconomic policies that prevented seriously distorted financial and foreign exchange markets stimulated investment and export growth. High investment and rapid export growth accelerated output growth. Higher output growth rates and undistorted financial and foreign exchange markets raised both saving and investment ratios. The evidence suggests that conducive financial conditions fostered by government policies played an important role in producing the virtuous circles of high saving, investment, output growth, and export growth found in Pacific Asia.

6 CONCLUSION

Financial repression reduces economic growth. But abandoning financial repression as a cost-reducing device for the government deficit may result in extraordinarily high real interest rates that can be just as damaging. Experience indicates that, to be successful, financial liberalisation must be accompanied by fiscal reform aimed at ensuring that government debt will not explode in the aftermath of the liberalisation, as well as sound prudential supervision and regulation of the banking system.

In practice, financial repression appears to have yielded government revenue in the order of 2 per cent of GDP on average in samples of developing countries (Giovannini and de Melo, 1993; Fry et al. 1996, p. 36). If government finances are stable with this revenue from financial repression, the loss of such revenue requires higher revenue from alternative sources or expenditure cuts of a similar magnitude. Unless the government is committed to fiscal reform in conjunction with financial liberalisation, financial repression may be the lesser of two evils. 'Goodbye financial repression, hello financial crash' is the verdict of Diaz-Alejandro (1985) on the Latin American experiments with financial liberalisation since the mid-1970s. If government expenditure cannot be reduced or traditional tax revenue increased, abandoning financial repression may lead to an explosion in government debt, economic instability, and lower economic growth.

Since there is no question that financial repression inhibits growth, the debate should concentrate on the tricky problems of moving from the state of financial repression to a state of financial liberalisation. So far, the economics profession has failed to produce adequate blueprints for this crucial transition.

References

Agénor, P.-R. and Montiel, P. (1996). *Development Macroeconomics*. Princeton: Princeton University Press.

Arestis, P. and Demetriades, P. (1997). 'Financial development and economic growth: assessing the evidence.' *Economic Journal*, vol. 107 (May), pp. 783–99.

Asian Development Bank (1985). *Improving Domestic Resource Mobilization through Financial Development*. Manila: Asian Development Bank. Economics Office.

Barro, R. J. (1991). 'Economic growth in a cross section of countries.' *Quarterly Journal of Economics*, vol. 106 (May), pp. 407–43.

Bencivenga, V. R. and Smith, B. D. (1991). 'Financial intermediation and endogenous growth.' *Review of Economic Studies*, vol. 58 (April), pp. 195–209.

Bencivenga, V. R. and Smith, B. D. (1992). 'Deficits, inflation, and the banking system in developing countries: the optimal degree of financial repression.' *Oxford Economic Papers*, vol. 44 (October), pp. 767–90.

Brock, P. L. (1989). 'Reserve requirements and the inflation tax.' *Journal of Money, Credit and Banking*, vol. 21 (February), pp. 106–21.

Buffie, E. F. (1984). 'Financial repression, the new structuralists, and stabilization policy in semi-industrialized economies.' *Journal of Development Economics*, vol. 14 (April), pp. 305–22.

Calvo, G. A. and Coricelli, F. (1992). 'Stagflationary effects of stabilization programs in reforming socialist countries: enterprise-side vs. household-side factors.' *World Bank Economic Review*, vol. 6 (January), pp. 71–90.

Chamley, C. and Honohan, P. (1993). 'Financial repression and banking intermediation.' *Savings and Development*, vol. 17, pp. 301–8.

De Gregorio, J. and Guidotti, P. E. (1995). 'Financial development and economic growth.' *World Development*, vol. 23 (March), pp. 433–48.

Diamond, D. W. and Dyhvig, P. H. (1983). 'Bank runs, deposit insurance, and liquidity.' *Journal of Political Economy*, vol. 91 (June), pp. 401–19.

Diaz-Alejandro, C. (1985). 'Good-bye financial repression, hello financial crash.' *Journal of Development Economics*, vol. 19 (September–October), pp. 1–24.

Easterly, W. R. (1993). 'How much do distortions affect growth?' *Journal of Monetary Economics*, vol. 32 (November), pp. 187–212.

Fry, M. J. (1978). 'Money and capital or financial deepening in economic development?' *Journal of Money, Credit and Banking*, vol. 10 (November), pp. 464–75.

Fry, M. J. (1991). 'Domestic resource mobilization in developing Asia: four policy issues.' *Asian Development Review*, vol. 9, pp. 15–39.

Fry, M. J. (1995). *Money, Interest, and Banking in Economic Development*, 2nd ed. Baltimore: Johns Hopkins University Press.

Fry, M. J. (1997). *Emancipating the Banking System and Developing Markets for Government Debt.* London: Routledge.

Fry, M. J. (1998). 'Saving, investment, growth, and financial distortions in Pacific Asia and other developing areas.' *International Economic Journal*, vol. 12 (Spring). forthcoming.

Fry, M. J., Goodhart, C. A. E. and Almeida, A. (1996). *Central Banking in Developing Countries: Objectives, Activities and Independence.* London: Routledge.

Gelb, A. H. (1989). 'Financial policies, growth and efficiency.' PPR working paper WPS 202, World Bank, Country Economics Department (June).

Ghani, E. (1992). 'How financial markets affect long-run growth: a cross-country study.' PR working paper WPS 843, World Bank, Country Operations (January).

Giovannini, A. and de Melo, M. (1993). 'Government revenue from financial repression.' *American Economic Review*, vol. 83 (September), pp. 953–63.

Greenwood, J. and Jovanovic, B. (1990). 'Financial development, growth, and the distribution of income.' *Journal of Political Economy*, vol. 98. (October), pp. 1076–107.

Greenwood, J. and Smith, B. D. (1997). 'Financial markets in development, and the development of financial markets.' *Journal of Economic Dynamics and Control*, forthcoming.

Johnston, J. (1984). *Econometric Methods*, 3rd ed. New York: McGraw-Hill.

King, R. G. and Levine, R. (1993*a*). 'Finance and growth: Schumpeter might be right.' *Quarterly Journal of Economics*, vol. 108 (August), pp. 717–37.

King, R. G. and Levine, R. (1993*b*). 'Finance, entrepreneurship, and growth: theory and evidence.' *Journal of Monetary Economics*, vol. 32 (December), pp. 513–42.

King, R. G. and Levine, R. (1993*c*). 'Financial intermediation and economic growth.' In *Capital Markets and Financial Intermediation* (eds C. Mayer and X. Vives), pp. 156–89. Cambridge: Cambridge University Press for the Centre for Economic Policy Research.

Lanyi, A. and Saracoglu, R. (1983). 'Interest rate policies in developing countries.' Occasional paper 22, International Monetary Fund (October).

Levine, R. (1993). 'Financial structures and economic development.' *Revista de Análisis Económico*, vol. 8 (Junio), pp. 113–29.

McKinnon, R. I. (1973). *Money and Capital in Economic Development.* Washington, D. C.: Brookings Institution.

McKinnon, R. I. (1993). *The Order of Economic Liberalization: Financial Control in the Transition to a Market Economy*, 2nd ed. Baltimore: Johns Hopkins University Press.

Polak, Jacques, J. (1989). *Financial Policies and Development.* Paris: Development Centre of the Organisation for Economic Co-operation and Development.

Rojas-Suárez, L. and Weisbrod, S. R. (1995). 'Financial fragilities in Latin America: the 1980s and 1990s.' Occasional paper 132, International Monetary Fund (October).

Roubini, N. and Sala-i-Martin, X. (1992). 'Financial repression and economic growth.' *Journal of Development Economics*, vol. 39 (July), pp. 5–30.

Schumpeter, J. A. (1912). *Theorie der wirtschafthichen Entricklung.* Leipzig: Duncker & Humblot, 1912. [*The Theory of Economic Development: An Inquiry into Profits, Capital, Credit, Interest, and the Business Cycle.* Cambridge, MA: Harvard University Press, 1934 (translated by R. Opie).]

Shaw, E. S. (1973). *Financial Deepening in Economic Development.* New York: Oxford University Press.

Singh, A. (1997). 'Financial liberalisation and economic development.' *Economic Journal*, vol. 107 (May), pp. 771–82.

Stiglitz, J. E. (1994). 'The role of the state in financial markets.' In *Proceedings of the World Bank*

Annual Bank Conference on Development Economics 1993 (eds M. Bruno and B. Pleskovic), pp. 19–52. Washington, D.C.: World Bank.

Stiglitz, J. E. and Weiss, A. (1981). 'Credit rationing in markets with imperfect information.' *American Economic Review*, vol. 71 (June), pp. 393–410.

Tobin, J. (1965). 'Money and economic growth.' *Econometrica*, vol. 33 (October), pp. 671–84.

World Bank (1989). *World Development Report 1989*. New York: Oxford University Press for the World Bank.

12

FINANCIAL LIBERALISATION, STOCKMARKETS AND ECONOMIC DEVELOPMENT*

Ajit Singh

During the 1980s and 1990s, many developing countries (DCs) have been engaged in far-reaching reforms of their financial systems, liberalising them and making them more market-oriented. This liberalisation, involving *inter alia* 'financial de-repression' has been inspired partly by the work of the McKinnon (1973) and Shaw (1973) (M–S) school.

This paper suggests that, in addition to financial de-repression, there has been a major new element in the development of DC financial systems in recent years the establishment and fast expansion of stockmarkets. These markets have played a key role in the internal as well as external financial liberalisation processes in leading DCs. Further, the paper finds that the actual behaviour of these markets in many countries has led to outcomes which undermine the effects of the higher real interest rates arising from 'financial de-repression'. These important empirical phenomena have received scant attention from M–S economists, who need to incorporate them into their analysis of financial liberalisation. However, for DCs, the essential question is: what will be the impact of these developments on industrialisation and long-term economic growth? This paper argues that in general financial liberalisation and the associated expansion of stockmarkets in DCs is likely to hinder rather than assist their development.

The paper concentrates on the role of the stockmarkets in the liberalisation process in DCs in the 1980s and 1990s, and explores, among other things, their effects on the financing of corporate growth. The observed financing patterns will be seen to contradict the predictions of most economic models, and are therefore surprising not just for the M–S, but also for other economists. At the macroeconomic level, the paper considers foreign portfolio flows, the interactions between the stock and the currency markets, and their implications for the stability of the real economy and its long-term growth.

1 FINANCIAL LIBERALISATION AND STOCKMARKET EXPANSION IN DCS

Financial reforms in semi-industrial countries in the last decade have been characterised by an enormous growth of stockmarkets. Between 1983 and 1993, the combined capital-

* Helpful comments from Bruce Weisse and Rudy Mathias are gratefully acknowledged; the usual caveat applies.

isation of companies quoted on the 38 emerging markets in *The Economist*'s list rose from less than $100 bn to nearly $1,000 bn (Feldman and Kumar, 1994); the corresponding growth of industrial country markets was a little over three-fold – from three to ten trillion dollars. Several leading individual emerging markets (e.g. Mexico, Korea and Thailand) recorded a twenty-fold increase in market capitalisation, during this period which made them larger than the average medium-sized European stockmarket.

Relative to GDP, market capitalisation rose at an unprecedented rate in leading DCs during the 1980s. Mullins (1993) notes that it probably took 85 years (1810–95) for the US capitalisation ratio to rise from 7% to 71%, whilst the Taiwanese ratio rose from 11% to 74% in just ten years (1981–91). Feldman and Kumar's data show that the corresponding ratio for Chile increased from 13.2% in 1983 to 78% in 1993; for Mexico from 2% to 43%; for Thailand from 3.8% to 55.8%, etc. Other development indicators for emerging stockmarkets reveal similar growth. For example, the total value of shares traded on DC markets rose over twenty-fold between 1983 and 1992, from 2% to 10% of the global total (IFC, 1993).

However, despite their recent rapid development, even the most advanced emerging markets are not yet mature. Typically most trading occurs in a few stocks which account for a considerable part of the total market capitalisation. Leaving aside these actively-traded blue-chip shares, there are serious informational and disclosure deficiencies for other stocks. There are similar weaknesses in the transparency of transactions on these markets. The less developed of the stockmarkets suffer from a far wider range of such deficits.[1]

Apart from their role in domestic financial liberalisation, the stockmarkets have also been very important in recent years in external financial liberalisation of DCs. In the 1990s, these markets have emerged as a major channel for foreign capital flows to DCs. International equity flows to *The Economist*'s 38 emerging markets increased from $3.3 bn in 1986 to $61.2 bn in 1993.[2] Indeed, as the IMF economists El-Erian and Kumar (1995) note 'when compared to other episodes of large private capital flows to developing countries in the last 20 years, the [present] phenomenon differs in one basic respect: the dominant role of foreign portfolio flows as opposed to bank financing'. These portfolio flows have taken place through several channels as external liberalisation has progressed: country or regional funds; direct purchase of DC stocks by industrial country investors; the placement of DC equities on industrial country markets. Both 'push' (e.g. lower US interest rates in the early 1990s) and 'pull' factors (e.g. external liberalisation in DCs) have contributed to these huge portfolio flows to emerging markets. (Fernandez-Arias and Montiel, 1996; Smith and Walter, 1996).

2 THE STOCKMARKET AND THE MCKINNON–SHAW ANALYSIS

Despite their substantial present and growing practical significance for DCs outlined above, stockmarkets have received little empirical attention from M–S eco-

---

[1] Feldman and Kumar (1994) divide emerging markets into four groups according to their stage of development.
[2] El-Erian and Kumar (1995) table 3.

nomists.[3] This is puzzling since at the theoretical level, stockmarket development is acknowledged to be of critical importance to M–S analyses (Cho, 1986; McKinnon, 1988). In their seminal paper, Stiglitz and Weiss (1981) showed that under imperfect information, because of the 'adverse selection' and 'incentive' effects, credit-rationing may not just be due to financial repression but could also arise from the normal com-petitive operations of the credit markets. Accepting this criticism, M–S economists there-fore suggest that credit-rationing reduces economic growth only if the 'financially repressed' interest rate is below the competitive equilibrium credit-rationing rate; they, however, provide no guidance on how to distinguish in practice between the two rates.

Be that as it may, Cho (1986) showed analytically that to achieve efficient resource allocation, credit markets need to be supplemented by a well-functioning equity mar-ket. This is because, unlike bank borrowings, equity finance is not subject to adverse selection and moral hazard effects under the conditions assumed. Cho, therefore, concluded that substantial development of equity markets is essential for successful financial liberalisation[4] and in the absence of such markets there is a case for govern-ment intervention. However, there are difficulties with Cho's theoretical formulation. It overlooks (a) the fact that even with well-functioning stockmarkets there is an agency problem with respect to management-controlled large corporations; and (b) the prob-lems arising from asymmetric information between corporate management and inves-tors about project returns. As Myers and Majluf (1984) showed, in these circumstances, rational managers will adopt the 'pecking order' pattern of finance – preferring re-tained earnings to debt and only as a last resort tapping the equity market to raise finance for their investment needs. Thus, firms under asymmetric information can effectively be equity-rationed. If they are also credit-rationed and have insufficient retained profits to finance worthwhile projects, such projects will not be undertaken, resulting in socially sub-optimal investment.

As for the actual operation of DC stockmarkets, section 5 will show that in the 1980s these markets did not complement the effects of credit market reforms but rather in important respects subverted them. During that decade many DCs implemented credit market liberalisation and raised real interest rates. However, this increased only the price of debt capital, but not all capital. For the reasons presented in section 4, there

---

[3] An apparent justification provided for this neglect is that in the DCs there is only a small or negative flow of net resources from the household to the business sector via the stockmarket. It is further suggested that the stockmarket affects only the largest firms. However, following this logic, the stockmarket would not be regarded as important in the world's leading stockmarket economies, i.e. the United States and the United Kingdom. Corbett and Jenkinson (1994) suggest that over the period 1970–89, the stockmarket made a net negative contribution to the financing of corporate investment in the United Kingdom, and a small positive one overall in the United States. Moreover, in both countries, only a relatively small number of large firms tend to be listed. Nevertheless, these listed companies account for a considerable proportion of industrial production, as indeed such firms do in leading DCs.

More importantly, stockmarkets can influence the economy through a variety of other channels, some direct (e.g. takeovers) and some indirect (e.g. macroeconomic signalling, interactions between the foreign exchange and the stockmarkets). Such channels have become increasingly important for DCs in the recent period as discussed in the text.

[4] See also McKinnon (1988).

was a share price boom in many of these economies. The consequent sharp fall in the price of equity capital seriously undermined and indeed allowed large private corporations to bypass altogether the main channel of high real interest rates through which the M–S effects are supposed to operate.

Fry (1997) argues that the new work on finance and economic growth based on endogenous growth models strengthens the theoretical foundations of M-S analysis.[5] This work suggests *inter alia* that stockmarkets lead to faster economic growth – a thesis contested below.

3 WELL-FUNCTIONING STOCKMARKETS AND ECONOMIC DEVELOPMENT

In principle, a well-functioning stockmarket should affect economic development through channels similar to those by which the equilibrium interest rate is expected to influence it in M–S models,[6] i.e. through raising (a) the savings rate, (b) the quantity and (c) the quality of investments. However, unlike the interest rate, the stockmarket can in addition ensure through the takeover mechanism that past investments are (d) also most profitably utilised.

In the recent endogenous models of finance and development, King and Levine (1993) emphasise the merits of financial intermediation with respect to the promotion of technical progress and entrepreneurship. Others have stressed the risk-sharing, monitoring and screening functions which the stockmarket may perform with respect to new investment projects (Allen, 1993). Levine and Zervos (1995) suggest that the two main channels of financial intermediation – banks and the stockmarket – complement each other. Atje and Jovanovic (1993), however, conclude that whilst stockmarkets positively effect growth, raising it by a huge 2.5% p.a., banks have little influence.

The empirical work in the above contributions is mostly based on Barro-type inter-country cross-section analysis. Arestis and Demetriades (1997) note its important methodological limitations with respect to establishing causality. The limitations are particularly serious in the present context since these empirical exercises represent reduced form analyses, and do not consider the precise channels through which the stockmarket performs its tasks (a)–(d). The relevant channels are (1) the pricing process and (2) the takeover mechanism.

The stockmarket critics contend that contrary to the theory, these two mechanisms in practice operate imperfectly so that even well-functioning stockmarkets (such as those in the United States and the United Kingdom) do not perform the monitoring, screening and disciplinary function at all well. For example, both analytical work and

---

[5] There is an important difference of emphasis between the M-S economists and the new endogenous financial models. Some of the latter propose a fast and deliberate development of stock markets in developing countries in contrast to the traditional view of slow evolutionary growth favoured by Fry and others.

[6] The precise mechanisms are different in the two cases; on interest rates see Fry (1995); on the stockmarket see Singh (1993).

evidence suggest that the actual stockmarket prices, although they may be reasonably efficient in Tobin's (1984) 'information arbitrage sense', are subject to whims and fads, are often dominated by the 'noise traders' and are therefore not necessarily efficient in the critical sense of reflecting fundamental values.[7] Similarly, on the take-over mechanism, empirical evidence suggests that competitive selection in the market for corporate control takes place much more on the basis of size than performance. Due to various capital market imperfections, a large unprofitable firm has a greater survival probability than a small efficient firm. Indeed, the former may increase its chances of survival by further increasing its size through the takeover process itself.[8]

The critical school further contends that the actual operation of the pricing and takeover mechanisms in the well-functioning US and UK stockmarkets lead to short-termism and lower rates of long-term investment particularly in firm-specific human capital.[9] It also generates perverse incentives, rewarding managers for their success in financial engineering rather than creating new wealth through organic growth. These deficiencies are thought to put the Anglo-Saxon economies at a competitive disad-vantage with respect to Japan and Germany which operate without hostile takeovers and where historically various other institutional structures (e.g. group-banking rela-tionships) have insulated industrial firms from the vagaries of the stockmarket.[10]

4 STOCKMARKETS AND DCS: RECENT EXPERIENCE

There are important implications of the above analysis for DCs which require examina-tion.

4.1 Stockmarkets and economic development

If even well-organised stockmarkets do not perform their disciplinary, allocative and other tasks satisfactorily, and may impair international competitiveness, DC markets are likely to do worse in these respects. This is because even leading emerging markets (e.g. Taiwan or India) do not possess the regulatory infrastructure for well-functioning markets,[11] or adequate information-gathering and disseminating private firms. More-over, the young listed firms on these markets will not have long enough records for their reputations to be accurately assessed. All this will lead to a noisy stockmarket environment, with arbitrary pricing and considerable volatility (Tirole, 1991). In such circumstances, the monitoring, screening and disciplining functions of the stockmarkets

---

[7] For a review of the issues and evidence see JEP (1990).

[8] For a recent review of corporate takeovers, see Singh (1992).

[9] For a review of the issues see Singh (1995*b*), Porter (1992): for an opposite perspective, see Marsh (1992).

[10] Porter (1992); Dore (1985).

[11] With respect to Taipei, *The Economist* 9 September, 1989) noted. 'Taiwan's stockmarket is a rigged casino with a phenomenal turnover . . . Its family-controlled firms equate accountancy with tax-evad-ing creativity. Its courts react . . . to the nudges of the influential . . . it is as free-wheeling and corrupt as the Philippines, but . . . is a free-wheel that works.' (p. 20).

may be more efficiently performed by certain kinds of financial intermediaries, e.g. the group-banking system traditionally found in Germany and Japan (Mayer, 1989).

A central weakness of a stockmarket system with respect to finance-industry relationships is that it provides investors with almost instant liquidity. Although seen as a virtue by orthodox economists, this liquidity also means that the investors need have no long-term commitment to the firm (Bhide, 1994).[12] By contrast, the group-banking dominated financial systems can ensure such commitment. Further, because of the close bank-corporation relationships in these systems, group-banks can cope much better with asymmetric information, agency costs and transaction costs than the Anglo-Saxon stockmarket system (Hoshi et al. 1991; Allen and Gale, 1995).

4.2 Stockmarket volatility, corporate finance, savings and investment

For the reasons outlined above, share prices in emerging markets may be expected to fluctuate more than those in well-developed markets. However, a high degree of volatility is a negative feature of a stockmarket for several reasons: (a) it can undermine the financial system as a whole; (b) it makes share prices much less useful as a guide to resource allocation; (c) to the extent that it discourages risk-averse savers and investors, it raises the cost of capital to corporations; (d) it may also stop risk-averse firms from raising funds, or (e) even from seeking a listing on the stockmarket (Pagano, 1993).

Evidence supports the prediction of much higher share price volatility in DCs compared with industrial countries (Davis, 1995). In extreme cases El-Erian and Kumar (1995) report that between 1983 and 1993 stockmarket volatility in Mexico was nearly fifteen times and in Turkey more than twenty times as large as that in the United States or Japan. There is also evidence of information-arbitrage inefficiency in DC share prices (Claessens, 1995). More significantly, share prices in many emerging markets would appear to have deviated considerably from fundamentals in the share price booms of the last decade (see below).

However, some of the implications of stockmarket volatility itself are not supported by the DC experience during the last 15 years. During this period, not only has there

---

[12] Levine and Zervos (1995) and Atje and Jovanovie (1993) find in their econometric work a positive relationship between stockmarket liquidity (proxied by turnover) and economic development. However, as noted earlier, the question of causality there is problematical. For example, in some high-growth countries such as Taiwan it may be perverse to ascribe causality to stockmarket liquidity even if there is perfect co-movement between the two variables. This is because the *Economist's* description of the Taiwanese stockmarket as a 'rigged casino with a phenomenal turnover' in footnote 1 is an apt one. In 1989 the average value of shares traded for each three-hour trading day on the Taipei stockmarket was nearly three billion dollars. That was one billion dollars a day more than in London, and more than half of New York's trading. On 28 August 1989. Taipei recorded a trading volume of 7.6 billion dollars. The world's biggest stockmarket, Tokyo, traded just 4.2 billion dollars worth of shares on the same day. Share prices on the Taiwanese market in the relevant period were subject to huge medium-term swings which were not justified by changes in economic prospects (Singh, 1993). This kind of high turnover of shares and share price volatility may be generated by a public taste for speculation and gambling. It is likely to diminish rather than promote economic growth as it undermines the capitalistic ethic by destroying the link between effort and reward.

been a big increase in emerging market activity and listings, but DC firms have been raising considerable capital on stockmarkets.

In the first large-scale empirical studies of corporate finance for DCs, Singh and Hamid (1992) and Singh (1995a) examined the financing of corporate growth of net assets (i.e. the long term capital employed in the firm) in the 1980s in several countries – India, Turkey, Brazil, Malaysia, Thailand, Zimbabwe, Korea, Jordan, Pakistan and Mexico. Singh's (1995a) sample normally consisted of the top 100 listed corporations in each country. This research showed that large DC corporations rely heavily in general on (a) external funds, and (b) new share issues to finance their growth of net assets. In five of the ten sample countries, over 70% of corporate growth during the past decade was financed from external funds. In another two, the external financing proportion was more than half. Similarly, the importance of equity finance for DC corporations is indicated by the fact that in five of the nine sample countries with the relevant data, over 40% of the growth of net assets in the 1980s was financed by new share issues. In another two countries, equity finance accounted for over 25% of corporate growth during the relevant period.

These results are surprising for several reasons, including some suggested earlier. The DC financing pattern is not only different from that observed in advanced countries, it is also counter-intuitive and contrary to the predictions of most economic models. Advanced country corporations are normally thought to follow the 'pecking order' and issue very little equity, being funded largely by retained profits.[13] In view of the serious capital market imperfections and high share price volatility, DC corporations may be expected to rely much more on internal rather than external funds, and resort far less to equity finance than industrial country firms. Further, since the former are more likely to be family-controlled than the latter, this should also discourage corporate equity issuance for fear of losing control.

How then are the anomalous phenomena of the fast expansion of stockmarket listings in DCs and the heavy reliance on equity finance by the big DC corporations in the recent period to be explained? Singh (1995a) provides a set of interlinked hypotheses to account for these observations. Briefly, the stage of development theory of equity financing is rejected. It is argued that unlike the United States and the United Kingdom in the 19th century, stockmarket development in DCs today is not simply an evolutionary response to market forces. Rather, for various reasons (e.g. privatisation programmes), many DC governments have played a major proactive role in the expansion of these markets.

Further, Singh (1995a) suggests that an essential reason why DC corporations resorted so much to equity financing in the 1980s was that the relative cost of equity capital fell significantly during these years. This was due to a large rise in share prices which was in turn brought about by both internal and external financial liberalisation.[14] At the same time, the relative cost of debt financing increased because of the

[13] Mayer (1990): see however Meeks and Whittington (1975) and Singh (1995a).

[14] Prior to liberalisation, most DC savers had limited returns and avenues for savings due to financial repression. With internal liberalisation and easier access to the stockmarket, share ownership and stockmarket participation greatly increased in many countries in the 1980s. Further, a significant additional source of demand for DC corporate equities came from advanced country institutional investors seeking to achieve portfolio diversification (Singh, 1995a).

steep rise in international interest rates as well as financial de-repression measures which several countries embarked on during this period. Thus, the cost of equity capital relative to that of debt became much more favourable to equities during the course of the 1980s. To illustrate, Amsden and Euh (1990) note that in 1980 the average price/earnings ratio on the Korean stockmarket was about 3, and therefore roughly, the cost of capital through share issues was 33%. By 1989, the average price/earnings ratio had risen to 14 reducing the cost of equity capital to 7.1%. Euh and Barker (1990) estimate that in terms of cash flow, taking into account the tax element, the latter cost to the Korean corporations in 1989 was only 3%. This compares with a figure of 12.5% for preferential commercial bank loans.

Thus, contrary both to M–S and other economists' expectations, DC stockmarkets have contributed significantly to corporate growth in the 1980s and 1990s. However, important questions from the perspective of long-term economic growth are: has this led to increased aggregate savings and investments, or raised the productivity of investments? These issues have not been systematically investigated for most DCs. Some useful evidence for India, however, is provided by Nagaraj (1996). This shows that financial liberalisation and capital market growth in the 1980s in that country led simply to portfolio substitution from bank deposits to tradeable securities rather than greater aggregate national or *financial* savings.[15] Nagaraj notes that despite the stockmarket boom of that decade and the substantial resources raised there by Indian corporations, corporate investment in fixed assets declined. Nor does he find evidence of increased output growth in the private corporate sector. Both Singh (1995*a*) and Nagaraj (1996) report a secular fall in corporate profitability in India during the 1980s, which could in principle be due to product market liberalisation. However, it then becomes difficult to explain the stockmarket boom except in terms of market psychology and speculation (see also below).

4.3 External liberalisation, the stockmarket and the real economy

Foreign portfolio investment, following external financial liberalisation in DCs, has been particularly important for the foreign exchange-constrained Latin American economies in the recent period. The enormous portfolio flows to these countries in the 1990s helped to alleviate the constraint and enabled a modest economic growth (about 3.5% p.a. during 1990–4) after the 'lost decade' of the 1980s. At the microeconomic level, the portfolio inflows helped generate the stockmarket boom, lowering the cost of capital to Latin American corporations. In Mexico, considerable inflow went into the stockmarket and leaving aside the question of fluctuations, the share price index rose from 250 in 1989 to around 2,500 in 1994.

However, as Rodrik (1994) and Krugman (1995) point out these portfolio flows to Latin America were not responding to fundamentals but represented a misplaced euphoria and a 'herd' instinct. The market was not rewarding virtue, frugality and restraint, but in many countries subsidising consumption at the expense of investment. Despite evidence that countries like Mexico were running huge current account defi-

---

[15] For scattered evidence on these issues for other countries, see Singh (1993, 1995*a*).

cits and using inflows largely for current consumption, such flows continued. The Mexican trade balance shifted from a small surplus in 1988 to a deficit of US $20 billion in 1993; the current account deficit was about 6% of GDP in 1993 and 9% in 1994. Financial and trade liberalisation policies led to a fall in private savings from roughly 15% to 5% of GDP despite high interest rates (Taylor, 1996). Notwithstanding huge capital inflows in the 1990s, Mexico's rate of economic growth during 1990–4 was only 2.5% p.a. – barely equal to the rate of population growth.

The speculative bubble burst in December 1994 when portfolio flows to Mexico suddenly stopped. Share prices fell sharply not only in Mexico but also, through the 'contagion' effect, in most emerging markets.[16] The impact on the real economy was devastating – real GDP fell by 7% in 1995 in Mexico and by 5% in Argentina. Thus, even when financial markets have been expansionary,[17] their bandwagon and herd characteristics generate considerable instability for the real economy.

Portfolio capital was recommended to DCs for being less vulnerable to external interest rate shocks than debt (WIDER, 1990). However, in practice these inflows have proved to be just as destabilising. As Akyuz (1993) points out, external liberalisation through opening stockmarkets to non-residents leads to close links between two inherently unstable markets even when the capital account is not fully open – the stock and currency markets. Faced with an economic shock the two markets may interact with each other in a negative feed-back loop to produce even greater instability for the markets and the whole financial system. Moreover, the gyrations in these markets may discourage aggregate investment through various channels, e.g. depressing business expectations because of greater uncertainty; greater instability in aggregate consumption because of wealth effects caused by large fluctuations in stockmarket prices. These factors contribute to the instability of the real economy and may also reduce long-term economic growth.

Such negative feedback effects will be particularly pronounced if external financial liberalisation is carried out in 'dis-equilibrium' conditions of high and unpredictable inflation and fluctuating exchange rates. However, because of the structural characteristics of DCs which makes them subject to more external and internal shocks than advanced economies, many of these unfavourable outcomes are likely to prevail even under 'normal' conditions, and even if there were a correct 'sequencing' of financial reforms.

5 CONCLUSION

Stockmarket development has been an important part of both internal and external financial liberalisation in DCs in the 1980s and 1990s. The process is continuing with the encouragement of the Bretton Woods institutions – several more stockmarkets are

[16] The Mexican financial crisis . . . resulted in a linked collapse of stockmarket values in almost all developing countries, *regardless of economic policies and performance.* The 'contagion effect was clear . . .' Smith and Walter, 1996; emphasis added).

[17] In advanced countries, financial markets have generally worked in a 'deflationary' way, penalising governments which follow expansionary policies, Singh (1997).

being currently established in Africa and in transition economies.

This paper concludes that these developments are unlikely to help in achieving quicker industrialisation and faster long-term economic growth in most DCs. This is for several reasons. First, the inherent volatility and arbitrariness of the stockmarket pricing process under DC conditions make it a poor guide to efficient investment allocation. Secondly, the interactions between the stock and currency markets in the wake of unfavourable economic shocks may exacerbate macroeconomic instability and reduce long-term growth. Thirdly, stockmarket development is likely to undermine the existing group-banking systems in DCs, which, despite their many difficulties, have not been without merit in several countries, not least in the highly successful East Asian economies.[18]

This is not to overlook the problems with such systems in other DCs (e.g. monopolistic abuses; inadequate government regulations (Singh, 1993)). However, even these countries would have been better off reforming and expanding their extant group-banking systems rather than establishing stockmarkets.[19] Reforming the existing system would not only have absorbed less resources directly, it would also have been an easier option in terms of institutional capacity for the concerned DCs,[20] compared with the infrastructure required for well-functioning stockmarkets.

Stockmarkets are potent symbols of capitalism but paradoxically capitalism often flourishes better without their hegemony. Contrary to World Bank (1989), stockmarket expansion is not a necessary natural progression of a country's financial development. Historically, such progression has not occurred in leading continental European economies. In the more recent post-World War II period countries like Germany and Italy have been able to achieve their economic miracles with little assistance from the stockmarket (de Cecco, 1993; Pagano, 1993). Stockmarkets have also played little role in the post-war industrialisation of Japan, Korea and Taiwan (World Bank, 1993). There is evidence that Japan deliberately encouraged the development of the banking system rather than the stockmarket after World War II (Somel, 1992). Developing countries simply cannot afford the luxury of stockmarkets. As Keynes (1936, p. 159) noted, 'when the capital development of a country becomes the by-product of the activities of a casino, the job is likely to be ill-done'.[21]

---

[18] On the relationships between banks and industry in East Asian economics, see for example Cho (1989). Amsden (1989), Wade (1990), Kojima (1995), Singh (1996).

[19] See further Akyuz (1993).

[20] If a DC is not capable of running an above-board banking system, the establishment of a stockmarket is unlikely to help and may compound the problem. The recent history of both DCs and advanced countries is rife with stockmarket scandals, e.g. the huge 1992 stockmarket scam in India and regular scandals in Taiwan and Japan.

[21] This paper is concerned with analytical rather than policy issues. However, in the post-cold-war international economic order, since realistically, whatever their merits, DC stockmarkets are now here to stay, Singh (1993, 1994) has suggested two areas of immediate concern. The first involves the control of portfolio capital flows. Many countries, including notably Chile and South Korea, restrict such flows to their economic advantage (Akyuz and Cornford, 1994). In the wake of the Mexican crisis, now even the IMF and the BIS accept the wisdom of such controls (BIS, 1993). The important analytical point here is to throw sand into the interactions between the foreign exchange and the stockmarkets,

Continued on next page

References

Akyuz, Y. (1993). 'Financial liberalisation: the key issues.' In *Finance and the Real Economy* (eds Yilmay Akyuz and Gunther Held). Santiago: United Nations University.

Akyuz, Y. and Cornford, A. (1994). 'Regimes for international capital movements and some proposals for reform.' UNCTAD Discussion Papers, No. 83, Geneva.

Allen, F. (1993). 'Stock markets and resource allocation.' In *Capital Markets and Financial Intermediation* (eds C. Mayer and X. Vives). Cambridge: Cambridge University Press.

Allen, F. and Gale, D. (1995). 'A welfare comparison of intermediaries and financial markets in Germany and the US.' *European Economic Review*, vol. 39, pp. 179–209.

Amsden, A. (1989). *Asia's Next Giant*. New York: Oxford University Press.

Amsden, A. H. and Euh, Yoon-Dae, (1990). 'South Korea's 1980s financial reforms: good-bye financial repression maybe, hello new institutional restraints.' *World Development*, vol. 21, no. 3, pp. 379–90.

Arestis, P. and Demetriades, P. (1997). 'Financial development and economic growth: assessing the evidence.' *Economic Journal*, this issue.

Atje, R. and Jovanovic, B. (1993). 'Stock markets and development.' *European Economic Review*, vol. 37, pp. 632–40.

Bhide, A. (1994). 'The hidden cost of stock market liquidity.' *Journal of Financial Economics*, vol. 34, pp. 31–51.

BIS Bank of International Settlements (1995). *65th Annual Report*, Basle.

Cho, Y. J. (1986). 'Inefficiencies from financial liberalisation in the absence of well-functioning equity markets.' *Journal of Money. Credit and Banking*, vol. 18, no. 2, May, pp. 191–200.

Cho, Y. J. (1989). 'Finance and development: the Korean approach.' *Oxford Review of Economic Policy*, vol. 5, no. 4. Winter, pp. 88–102.

Claessens, S. (1995). 'The emergence of equity investment in developing countries: Overview.' *The World Bank Economic Review*, vol. 9. no. 1, January, pp. 1–18.

Corbett, J. and Jenkinson, T. (1994). 'The financing of industry, 1970–89: an international comparison'. Discussion Paper No. 948. London: Centre for Economic Policy Research.

Davis, E. P. (1995). *Pension Funds: Retirement-Income Security and Capital Markets: An International Perspective*. Oxford: Clarendon Press.

de Cecco, M. (1993). 'New forms of financial regulation and the evolution of financial firms.' In *New Challenges to International Cooperation. Adjustment of Firms. Policies and Organisations to Global Competition* (eds P. Gourevitch and P. Guerrieri). San Diego: University of California.

Dore, R. (1985). 'Financial structure and the longterm view.' *Policy Studies*, July, pp. 10–29.

Fernandez-Arias, Eduardo and Montiel, P. J. (1996). 'The surge in capital inflows to developing countries: an analytical overview.' *The World Bank Economic Review*, vol. 10, no. 1, January, pp. 51–80.

El-Erian, M. A. and Kumar. M. S. (1995). 'Emerging equity markets in middle eastern countries.' Paper presented at the World Bank Conference on 'Stock Markets, Corporate Finance and Economic Growth.' Washington, DC. February 16/7.

---

even if it may be infeasible and/or undesirable to sever the connection altogether. The second area concerns the market for corporate control which can compound the negative effects of stockmarkets. Singh (1994) suggests there are structural factors which make the 'spontaneous' emergence of such a market imminent in many DCs. He argues on efficiency grounds that such an evolution should be curbed. The cross of the stockmarket is heavy enough for the DCs to bear without being landed also with an Anglo-Saxon-type market for corporate control.

Euh, Yoon-Dae and Barker, J. (1990). *The Korean Banking System and Foreign Influence*. London: Routledge.

Feldman, R. A. and Kumar, M. S. (1994). 'Emerging equity markets: growth, benefits and policy concerns.' *IMF paper on Policy Analysis and Assessment*. PPAA/94/7, March.

Fry, M. J. (1995). *Money. Interest and Banking in Economic Development*. Baltimore: Johns Hopkins University Press.

Fry, M. J. (1997). 'In defence of financial liberalisation.' *Economic Journal*, vol. 107 (May), pp. 754–70.

Hoshi, Takeo, Kashyap, Anil and Sharfstein, David (1991). 'Corporate structure, liquidity and investment: evidence from Japanese industrial groups.' *Quarterly Journal of Economics*, vol. 106, February, pp. 33–60.

IFC (1993). *Emerging Stockmarket Factbook 1993*. Washington, D.C.: The World Bank.

JEP (1990). 'Symposium on bubbles.' *Journal of Economic Perspectives*, vol. 4. no. 2, (Spring).

Keynes, J. M. (1936). *The General Theory of Employment, Interest and Money*. New York: Harcourt Brace.

King, R. G. and Levine, R. (1993). 'Financial intermediation and economic development.' In *Capital Markets and Financial Intermediation* (eds Colin Mayer and Xavier Vives). Cambridge: Cambridge University Press.

Kojima, K. (1995). 'An international perspective on Japanese corporate finance.' RIEB Kobe University Discussion Paper. no. 45 (March).

Krugman, P. (1995). 'Dutch tulips and emerging markets.' *Foreign Affairs*, vol. 74, no. 4. July/August, pp. 28–44.

Levine, R. and Zervos, S. (1995). 'Policy, stock market development and economic growth.' Paper presented at the World Bank Conference on Stock Markets, Corporate Finance and Economic Growth, Washington, DC, February 16/7.

Marsh, P. (1992). 'Short termism.' In *The New Palgrave Dictionary of Money and Finance* (eds J. Eatwell, M. Milgate and P. Newman). London: Macmillan, pp. 446–52.

Mayer, C. (1989). 'Myths of the West: lessons from developed countries for development finance.' World Bank Working Paper, WPS301. Washington, DC.: World Bank.

Mayer, C. (1990). 'Financial systems, corporate finance and economic development', in *Asynonetric Information. Corporate Finance and Investment* (ed. R. Glen Hubbard), Chicago and London, University of Chicago Press.

McKinnon, R. I. (1973). *Money and Capital in Economic Development*. Washington, DC: Brookings Institution.

McKinnon, R. (1988). 'Financial liberalisation in retrospect: interest rate policies in LDCs.' In *The State of Development Economics* (eds G. Ranis and T. P. Stultz). Oxford: Basil Blackwell. pp. 386–415.

Meeks, G. and Whittington, G. (1975). 'Giant companies in the United Kingdom 1948–69.' *Economic Journal*, vol. 85, pp. 824–43.

Mullins, J. (1993). 'Emerging equity markets in the global economy.' *FRBNY Quarterly Review* (Summer), pp. 54–83.

Myers, S. C. and Majluf, N. S. (1984). 'Corporate financing and investment decisions when firms have information that investors do not have.' *Journal of Financial Economics*. vol. 13, pp. 187–221.

Nagaraj, R. (1996). 'India's capital market growth: trends, explanations and evidence.' Mimeo, New Delhi: Indira Gandhi Institute of Development Research.

Pagano, M. (1993). 'The flotation of companies on the stock market.' *European Economic Review*, vol. 37, pp. 1101–25.

Porter, M. E. (1992). 'Capital disadvantage: America's failing capital investment system.' *Harvard Business Review* (September–October), pp. 65–82.

Rodrik, D. (1994). 'The rush to free trade in the developing world: Why so late? Why now? Will it last?' In *Voting for Reform: The Politics of Adjustment in New Democracies* (eds S. Haggard and S. B. Webb). New York: Oxford University Press.

Shaw, E. S. (1973). 'Financial deepening in economic development.' The Hebrew University of Jerusalem. Working Paper no. 223.

Singh, A. (1992). 'Corporate takeovers.' In *The New Palgrave Dictionary of Money and Finance* (eds J. Eatwell, M. Milgate and P. Newman). London: Macmillan, pp. 480–6.

Singh, A. (1993). 'The stock market and economic development: should developing countries encourage stock markets?'. *UNCTAD Review*, no. 4, pp. 1–28.

Singh, A. (1994). 'How do large corporations in developing countries finance their growth?' In *The AMEX Bank Prize Essays: Finance and the International Economy*. no. 8 (ed. Richard O'Brien). New York: Oxford University Press, pp. 121–35.

Singh, A. (1995*a*): *Corporate Financial Patterns in Industrialising Economies: a Comparative International Study*. IFC Technical Paper No. 2. Washington, DC: World Bank.

Singh, A. (1995*b*). 'The anglo-saxon market for corporate control, the financial system and international competitiveness.' University of Cambridge. Department of Applied Economics Working Paper, no. AF16, March.

Singh, A. (1996). 'Savings, investment and the corporation in the East Asian miracle', *UNCTAD Discussion Paper on East Asian Development: Lessons for a New Global Environment*. Study no. 9, Geneva.

Singh, A. (1997). 'Liberalisation and globalisation: an unhealthy euphoria.' In *Full Employment without Inflation*: (eds J. Michie and J. Grieve Smith). Oxford: Oxford University Press. (Forthcoming).

Singh, A. and Hamid, J. (1992). *Corporate Financial Structures in Developing Countries*, IFC Technical Paper No. 1. Washington. DC: The World Bank.

Smith, R. C. and Walter, I. (1996). 'Rethinking emerging market equities.' Paper presented at the Conference on the Future of Emerging Market Capital Flows. New York University, May 23–4.

Somel, C. (1992). 'Finance for growth: lessons from Japan.' UNCTAD Discussion Paper, no. 44.

Stiglitz, J. E. and Weiss, A. (1981). 'Credit rationing in markets with imperfect information.' *American Economic Review*, vol. 71, no. 3, June, pp. 393–410.

Taylor, L. (1996). 'Globalisation, the Bretton Woods institutions and economic policy in the developing world.' New School of Social Research, NY, (April).

Tirole, J. (1991). 'Privatisation in Eastern Europe: incentives and the economics of transition.' In *NBER Macroeconomics Annual 1991* (eds O. J. Blanchard and S. S. Fischer), Cambridge, MA: MIT Press.

Tobin, J. (1984). 'On the efficiency of the financial system.' *Lloyds Bank Review*. July, pp. 1–15.

Wade, R. (1990). *Governing the Market*. Princeton: Princeton University Press.

WIDER (1990). *Foreign Portfolio Investment in Emerging Equity Markets*. Study Group Series no. 5. Helsinki: World Institute For Development Economics Research of the United Nations University.

World Bank (1989). *World Development Report 1989*. New York: Oxford University Press.

World Bank (1993). *The East Asian Miracle*. New York: Oxford University Press.

13

FINANCIAL DEVELOPMENT AND ECONOMIC GROWTH: ASSESSING THE EVIDENCE*

Philip Arestis and Panicos Demetriades

In this paper we take a fresh look at the empirical evidence on the relationship between financial development and economic growth with a view to identifying outstanding issues and offering some suggestions about how these may be addressed in the future. To illustrate our suggestions we also present some new evidence utilising the proposed approaches.

We examine the empirical literature from two angles. The first is the issue of whether, how and to what extent the financial system can contribute to the process of economic growth. Questions about the association amongst financial deepening, investment, and the efficiency of capital fall in this category. The question of causality between finance and growth can also be considered from this perspective. The second angle relates to the question of whether financial liberalisation can stimulate investment and growth. Evidence on this question has been adduced from countries where financial reforms took place. There is, also, a voluminous econometric evidence purporting to address this question by examining interest rate elasticities in saving, investment and growth equations.

The new evidence we offer relates to both aspects of the debate. In connection with the relationship between financial development and growth we examine the relationship between the latter and stock market development. This is an area which only recently began to attract attention in the literature (see also Singh (1997)). In relation to financial liberalisation, we offer new evidence on the direct effects of financial repression, using the example of South Korea, a country which has been something of a puzzle to empirical investigators.

The paper is structured as follows. Section 1 reviews the recent evidence on financial development and growth and argues that a time series approach is more fruitful than the cross-section approach which has been quite popular in recent studies. Section 2 examines the relationship between stock market development and economic growth, offering some new evidence. Section 3 surveys the evidence from financial reforms and

* We are grateful to Stephen Hall and Ajit Singh for their constructive comments. We would also like to thank Lisa Cassidy for excellent research assistance. Naturally, all remaining errors are our own. We acknowledge financial support from the ESRC (Grant No. Roo0236463).

discusses the issues of sequencing and pre-conditions which allegedly are at the root of successful reforms. Section 4 examines the econometric evidence on financial liberalisation and presents new results relating to the direct effects of financial repression in South Korea. Finally, we summarise and conclude in section 5.

1 FINANCIAL DEVELOPMENT AND GROWTH: CROSS-SECTION VERSUS TIME-SERIES EVIDENCE

The empirical literature on this issue utilises two different econometric methodologies: cross-country regressions, of the type popularised by Barro (1991), and time-series regressions.[1] In this section we will present evidence from both approaches, arguing that the time series approach is more fruitful in analysing the issues on hand.

Cross-country regressions have been used to examine a variety of macroeconomic relationships, including the one between financial development and long-run growth. This approach involves averaging out variables over long time periods (typically three decades) and using them in cross-section regressions aiming at explaining cross-country variations of growth rates. Thus, in principle the investigator is able to estimate the average influence of the determinants of economic growth. A number of studies have dealt with this issue; for example, Gelb (1989), World Bank (1989), Roubini and Sala-i-Martin (1992), Fry (1995) and, probably the most well-known, King and Levine (1993). This latter study epitomises both the merits and limitations associated with the cross-country regressions approach. King and Levine (1993) find that 'higher levels of financial development are significantly and robustly correlated with faster current and future rates of economic growth, physical capital accumulation and economic efficiency improvements' (pp. 717–8). From these results the authors conclude that the relationship between growth and financial development is not just a contemporaneous correlation and that 'finance seems importantly to lead economic growth' (p. 730).

A great deal of scepticism in relation to cross-country regressions is shared by many investigators. The sensitivity of the results to the set of conditioning variables is acknowledged by the users of the technique themselves (e.g. Levine and Zervos, 1996; Levine and Renelt, 1992). Evans (1995) discusses econometric problems which stem from heterogeneity of slope coefficients across countries. Lee et al. (1996) show that convergence tests obtained from cross-country regressions are likely to be misleading because the estimated coefficient on the convergence term contains asymptotic bias. Quah (1993) points out that the technique is predicated on the existence of stable growth paths and shows, using data from 118 countries, that long-run growth patterns are unstable. Thus, under these circumstances the cross-country variations in results are difficult to interpret.

In relation to King and Levine (1993), we argue elsewhere (Arestis and Demetriades,

---

[1] One might also add the approach adopted by Fry (1997) which employs a system of simultaneous equations. However, since this system is estimated by pooling data across countries it suffers from problems similar to those experienced by cross-country regressions. Additionally, it might suffer from the problem of dynamic heterogeneity which leads to inconsistent parameter estimates (Pesaran and Smith, 1995).

1996) that their causal interpretation is based on a fragile statistical basis. Using their data we show that the contemporaneous correlation between the main financial indicator and economic growth is much stronger than the correlation between lagged financial development and growth. In fact conditioning on contemporaneous financial development destroys the association between lagged financial development and economic growth completely. Thus, whilst we do not disagree with King and Levine that financial development and growth are robustly correlated, we do not think that the question of causality can satisfactorily be addressed in a cross-section framework. The cross-country regressions approach has one further limitation. It can only refer to the 'average effect' of a variable across countries. In the context of causality testing this limitation is particularly severe as the possibility of differences in causality patterns across countries is likely. Such differences are, in fact, detected by time-series studies. For example, Arestis and Demetriades (1996), which utilises data for 12 countries,[2] provides evidence which suggests that the causal link between finance and growth is crucially determined by the nature and operation of the financial institutions and policies pursued in each country. The related study by Demetriades and Hussein (1996), where causality tests are carried out for 16 developing countries, suggests that causality between financial development and growth varies across countries. In about half the countries examined Demetriades and Hussein detect a feedback relationship but in several countries the relationship runs from growth to finance, suggesting that it is by no means universal that financial development can contribute to economic growth.

2 FINANCIAL DEVELOPMENT AND GROWTH: THE ROLE OF THE STOCK MARKET

Much of the evidence on the relationship between finance and growth utilises bank-based measures of financial development such as the ratio of bank deposits to nominal GDP. More recently the emphasis has increasingly shifted to stock market indicators. World stock market capitalisation grew from $4.7 to $15.2 trillion between the mid-1980s and mid-1990s (Demirgüç-Kunt and Levine, 1996, p. 223). The total value of shares traded on developing countries' stock markets rose over twenty-five fold between 1983 and 1992 (Singh, 1997) and that on emerging markets jumped from less than 3% of the $1.6 trillion world total in 1985 to 17% of the $9.6 trillion world total in 1994 (Demirgüç-Kunt and Levine, 1996, p. 223). Contrary to Fry's (1997) claim, these figures clearly suggest that the role of stock markets could potentially be substantial.

Levine and Zervos (1996) argue that well-developed stock markets may be able to offer different kinds of financial services than banking systems and may, therefore, provide a different kind of impetus to investment and growth than the development of the banking system. Specifically, increased stock market capitalisation, measured either by the ratio of the stock market value to GDP or by the number of listed companies, may improve an economy's ability to mobilise capital and diversify risk. Liquidity

---

[2] The 12 countries mentioned in the text are: France, Germany, United Kingdom, Japan, United States, Korea, India, Greece, Spain. Turkey, Mexico and Chile.

is another important indicator of stock market development in that it may be inversely related to transactions costs, which impede the efficient functioning of stock markets. Liquidity may be measured by the total value of shares traded relative to either GDP or total market capitalisation. The latter is known as the turnover ratio and may be an indicator of the level of transactions costs. Finally, other aspects of stock market performance may be captured by the presence or absence of excess volatility of market returns, excessive concentration and asset pricing efficiency. Measures of the latter are inversely related to the degree of risk mis-pricing between domestic and world capital market stocks and may, therefore, indicate the degree of integration of national stock markets into world capital markets.

Levine and Zervos (1996) demonstrate that various measures of equity market activity are positively correlated with measures of real activity, across different countries, and that the association is particularly strong for developing countries. Using cross-country regressions and data for 41 countries covering the period 1976–93, Levine and Zervos (1996) evaluate the extent to which these measures are robustly correlated with current and future rates of economic growth, capital accumulation and productivity improvement. They also examine whether these effects are additional to those of banking system development by including both stock market and bank-based financial indicators in the same regressions. They conclude that after controlling for initial conditions and various economic and political factors, the measures of banking and stock market development are robustly correlated with current and future rates of economic growth, capital accumulation and productivity improvements. They, therefore, conclude that stock markets provide different financial services from banks. Atje and Jovanovic (1993), using a similar approach, also find a significant correlation between economic growth and the value of stock market trading relative to GDP for 40 countries over the period 1980–8.

A further aspect of the rapid growth of stock markets which warrants attention relates to the possible speculative pressures that may be generated (see also Singh, 1997). These pressures may emanate from transactions induced by the euphoria created by financial liberalisation which rewards speculators with short-term horizons and punishes those with a long-term view (Keynes, 1936, ch. 12). They may also emanate from non-financial corporations which enter financial markets in view of the higher returns induced by financial liberalisation, by borrowing to finance short-term financial speculation. Lenders in their turn may feel compelled to provide this type of finance, essentially because of fear of loss of market share (Minsky, 1986). An undesirable implication of these types of pressures is that economies may be forced to bear a greater degree of 'ambient' risk with financial liberalisation than without it (Grabel, 1995). This may reduce the total volume of real-sector investment while exerting upward pressures on interest rates in view of the higher risk (Federer, 1993).

By contrast, Levine (1996) argues that stock markets may affect growth through liquidity, which makes investment less risky. Companies enjoy permanent access to capital through liquid equity issues. This argument, based on the statistical work reported in Levine and Zervos (1996), leads to the conclusion that 'stock market development explains future economic growth' (Levine, 1996, p. 8). However, as this result is based on cross-country growth regressions it is subject to the criticisms outlined in the previous section. Thus, it is instructive to examine whether results of this type exhibit variation across countries, using a time-series analysis approach. As an illustration we provide an analysis of financial development and growth in Germany and the United States. We choose to focus on these two countries in view of the well known differences between their financial systems (Dimsdale and Prevezer, 1994; Arestis and Demetriades, 1996).

Our analysis extends the results in Arestis and Demetriades (1996) in one important direction. Specifically, we augment the relationship between economic growth and financial development by including indicators of stock market development and volatility. Thus, we utilise four variables for each country, employing quarterly data for the period 1979 (1)–91 (4).[3] Three of these variables are identical for both countries. They are the logarithms of real GDP per capita (LY), the stock market capitalisation ratio (LMC), measured by the ratio of stock market value to GDP, and an index of stock market volatility ($LSMV$). Stock market volatility is measured by the sixteen quarter moving standard deviation of the end-of-quarter change of stock market prices.[4] The fourth variable for Germany is the logarithm of the ratio of M2 to nominal GDP ($LM2Y$). In the case of the United States the fourth variable is the logarithm of the ratio of domestic bank credit to nominal GDP (LBC). The last two variables are, of course, indicators of the development of the banking system. The reason why we use different indicators of the two countries is that we were unable to detect cointegration in the United States using the $LM2Y$ variable. Furthermore, in the case of Germany the LBC indicator, whilst generating the same number of cointegrating vectors, produced implausibly high parameter values. In itself this finding may indicate another important difference in the two financial systems which, clearly, would be undetected by cross-country regressions.

We begin by carrying out unit root tests which suggest that the four variables are l(1).[5] We then estimate the VAR and test for cointegration using the trace statistic. The results, reported in Tables 1 and 2, detect two cointegrating vectors. A cointegrating rank of two is then imposed and further tests are carried out to reduce the system to economically interpretable relationships (see Pesaran and Shin, 1995). The first step is to test for the weak exogeneity of each of the variables to the system. The tests, which are distributed as χ^2 (2), show some similarities between the two countries but also reveal some important differences. In both countries the stock market volatility indicator is weakly exogenous. This restriction is, therefore, imposed in further estimation. In Germany market capitalisation is also weakly exogenous to the system and this restriction is, therefore, maintained. In the United States none of the three remaining variables appears to be weakly exogenous to the system. The next step is to test zero

---

[3] Stock market data (end-of-quarter price index and market value) were obtained from the online information system Datastream International. GDP, domestic bank credit and M2 data were obtained from *International Financial Statistics*. IMF, 1993).

[4] We first calculated the logarithmic first differences of the end-of-quarter stock market price index. The 16-term moving standard deviations were then computed from these quarter price changes, using as the mean the average rate of price change over a centred 4-year period. See, however, Pagan (1986) for a discussion of the limitations of volatility measures.

[5] The complete set of results for this paper (reported in Tables 1, 2 and 3), including unit root tests for all variables, can be obtained from the authors upon request.

Table 1 Financial development and economic growth in Germany (Johansen cointegration analysis)

Variables entered
    LY   = Logarithm of real GDP *per capita*
    LM2Y = Logarithm of M2/nominal GDP
    LMC   = Logarithm of stock market capitalisation
    LSMV = Logarithm of stock market volatility (moving standard deviation)
Lag length of VAR = 4
Sample period: 1979 Q2–1991 Q4

Ho:rank = p	Trace statistic
$p = 0$	106.90†
$p \leqslant 1$	42.08†
$p \leqslant 2$	16.6

System exogeneity tests: χ^2 (2)	LR test	p-value
LY weakly exogenous to system	48.18	0.00
LMC weakly exogenous to system	1.54	0.46
LM2Y weakly exogenous to system	11.64	0.00
LSMV weakly exogenous to system	2.12	0.35

Restricted cointegration analysis
Vector 1: $LY = -3.60 + 9.67\ LM2\ Y - 0.36\ LSMV$
Vector 2: $LM2\ Y = -1.00 + 0.20\ LMC$
Vector autocorrelation test (4th order): F(64.57) = 0.95 [0.58]
Joint test on all restrictions: χ^2 (5) = 5.62 [0.34]

Weak exogeneity tests on restricted system: χ^2 (6)	LR test	p-value
LY weakly exogenous to first vector	58.45	0.00
LY weakly exogenous to second vector	11.48	0.07
LM2Y weakly exogenous to first vector	6.32	0.39
LM2Y weakly exogenous to second vector	15.22	0.02

* Statistical significance at the 5% level.
† Statistical significance at the 1% level.

restrictions on the parameters of the cointegrating vectors. These tests are carried out sequentially and in cases where the tests do not reject the null the corresponding variable is dropped from the system. We are thus able to report the most parsimonious specification not rejected by the data in Tables 1 and 2 alongside the corresponding test of all joint restrictions. Each of the vectors is normalised on the variable for which we could find clear evidence of error correction. Thus, in the case of Germany the first vector is normalised on real GDP *per capita* and the second vector on the banking system development indicator. In the United States, the first vector is normalised on stock market capitalisation and the second on the banking sector indicator.

    The interpretation of the two cointegrating vectors for each country, even though not straightforward, does nevertheless manage to throw some light on the economic

Table 2 Financial development and economic growth in the United States (Johansen cointegration analysis)

Variables entered
LY   = Logarithm of real GDP *per capita*
LBC   = Logarithm of (bank credit/nominal GDP)
LMC   = Logarithm of stock market capitalisation
LSMV   = Index of stock market volatility (moving variance)
Lag length of VAR = 6
Sample period: 1979 Q4–1991 Q4
Ho:rank = p Trace
            statistic
$p = 0$ 84.47†
$p \leqslant 1$ 35.04*
$p \leqslant 2$ 11.1

System exogeneity tests: χ^2 (2)	LR test	p-value
LY weakly exogenous to system	6.28	0.04
LMC weakly exogenous to system	12.38	0.00
LBC weakly exogenous to system	28.03	0.00
LSMV weakly exogenous to system	3.29	0.19

Restricted cointegration analysis
Vector 1: $LMC = -44.30 + 4.26\ LY - 1.30\ LBC$
Vector 2: $LBC = -4.43 + 0.425\ LY + 0.05\ LSMV$
Vector autocorrelation test (6th order): $F(64.21) = 1.73\ [0.08]$
Joint test on all restrictions: χ^2 (3) = 5.67 [0.13]

Weak exogeneity tests on restricted system: χ^2 (4)	LR test	p-value
LY weakly exogenous to first vector	7.45	0.06
LY weakly exogenous to second vector	5.67	0.13
LBC weakly exogenous to first vector	7.35	0.06
LBC weakly exogenous to second vector	22.47	0.00
LMC weakly exogenous to first vector	15.89	0.00
LMC weakly exogenous to second vector	3.80	0.28

* Statistical significance at the 5% level.
† Statistical significance at the 1% level.

relationship in hand. In the case of Germany the first vector shows a positive relationship between real GDP *per capita* and banking system development. It also shows that stock market volatility, a variable exogenous to the system, is negatively related to real GDP. Given that the bank development indicator is weakly exogenous to the first vector and that real GDP *per capita* shows strong evidence of error correction to the first vector, the interpretation that the first vector explains long-run GDP is not an implausible one. Using the same logic, the second vector appears to be an equation which explains long-run banking sector development in terms of stock market capitalisation. What is rather surprising in this vector is the insignificance of real GDP. The lack of any long-run impact of real GDP on banking sector development is further exemplified by the weak exogeneity of $LM2Y$ to the restricted output equation. On the other hand, at the 5% level of significance, real GDP is weakly exogenous to the second vector. To conclude, in Germany there appears to be uni-directional causality from financial development to real GDP. Stock market capitalisation affects real GDP only through the banking system and stock market volatility has a clear negative effect on output.

In the case of the United States the picture is rather more complex. In large part, this is due to the endogeneity of stock market capitalisation. According to the first cointegrating vector, the latter is positively related to real GDP and negatively related to banking sector development. The second vector shows a positive relationship between banking sector development and real GDP. In the same vector, stock market volatility appears to be positively related to banking sector development (and negatively to real GDP). Again, this may reflect the inverse relationship between the banking system and the capital market. Interestingly, real GDP, which is not exogenous to the system, appears weakly exogenous with respect to each of these restricted vectors. Thus, there is insufficient evidence to suggest that in the United States financial development causes real GDP. On the other hand, there is abundant evidence of reverse causality, i.e. real GDP positively contributing to both banking system and capital market development.

In conclusion, whilst our results are only meant to be illustrative, they do, nevertheless, serve to highlight the possibility of important differences between countries. Not only is it possible that the long-run causality may vary across countries but it is also possible, indeed likely, that the long-run relationships themselves exhibit substantial variation. Thus, once again, we find evidence which suggests that a time series analysis may yield deeper insights into the relationship between financial development and real output than cross-country regressions.

3 FINANCIAL LIBERALISATION: EVIDENCE FROM REFORMS

A number of countries have implemented financial reforms since the early 1970s (for a recent review, see Caprio et al. 1994). These reforms began with the privatisation of commercial banks and with interest rates left free to be determined by the market. The Latin American experiences were particularly painful, manifested in excessively high real interest rates and undue risk-taking by banks. Real interest rates in many cases exceeded 20%, a number of 'bad' debts and waves of bank failures and other bankruptcies ensued along with extreme asset volatility, and the whole financial system reached a near collapse stage (see Corbo and de Melo, 1985; Diaz-Alejandro, 1985; Dornbusch and Revnoso, 1989; Burkett and Dutt, 1991). As a result the real sectors of these economies entered severe and prolonged recessions. On the whole, financial liberalisation in these, and other, countries had a destabilising effect on the economy and was abandoned. Financial liberalisation unleashed a massive demand for credit by households and firms that was not offset by a comparable increase in the saving rate. Loan rates rose as households demanded more credit to finance purchases of consumer durables, and firms plunged into speculative activities in the knowledge that government bailouts would prevent bank failures. In terms of bank behaviour, banks increased deposit and lending rates to compensate for losses attributable to loan defaults. High real interest rates completely failed to increase savings or boost investment – both actually fell as a proportion of GNP over the period. The only type of savings that *did* increase was foreign savings, i.e. external debt. This, however, made the 'liberalised' economics more vulnerable to oscillations in the international economy, increasing the debt/asset ratio and thus service obligations and promoting the debt crises experienced in the recent past.

On the other hand, the Korean experience, which is widely acknowledged to be one of the most successful cases of financial reform, was one in which the government maintained tight and effective control over most interest rates (see, for example, Fry and Nuti, 1992; Amsden and Euh, 1993) with interest rate policy aimed at maintaining positive, albeit low real interest rates. The first bout of 'financial liberalisation' in the 1960s was associated with higher real interest rates and a rapid growth of bank deposits which emanated from the 'curb' markets (Harris, 1988). The increased deposits allowed the government to finance a new industrial policy which promoted export-driven industrial growth. The involvement of the government in that way meant that risks associated with investment were shared so that commercial banks were involved in long-term planning rather than merely short-term activities (Cho, 1989). Whilst this description fits more with the first spurt of liberalisation in the mid-1960s, it is also applicable to the case of reforms in the 1980s. In this latter case, although government involvement was reduced, it was still substantial in that many interest rates and credit allocation continued to be either directly regulated or heavily influenced by the government (Amsden and Euh, 1993). The experience of Japan in the 1950s and 1960s should also be mentioned in that the government actively and successfully intervened in the pricing and allocation of credit (see World Bank, 1993). World Bank (1993) also contended that 'Our judgement is that in a few economies, mainly in North East Asia, in some instances, government interventions resulted in higher and more equal growth than otherwise would have occurred' (p. 6).

Clearly, therefore, events following the implementation of financial reforms did not provide much support to the theoretical premises of the liberalisation thesis. As a result, a revision of the main tenets of the thesis took place in Lakatosian fashion. Two types were initiated. The first was concerned with what has come to be labelled as 'the sequencing of financial liberalisation', and the second called attention to the broader macroeconomic environment within which financial reforms were to be undertaken. These *post hoc* theoretical revisions were thought of as sufficient to defend the original thesis of a disappointing empirical record (Fry, 1997). The sequencing argument was justified on two grounds: the first was based on the notion that there are different speeds of adjustment in the financial and goods markets, whereby the latter are sluggish. Thus, financial markets could not be reformed in the same manner and in the same instance as other markets, without creating awkward problems. Recognition of these problems has led the advocates of the liberalisation thesis to suggest the desirability of sequencing in financial reforms (Edwards, 1989; McKinnon, 1991). Successful reform of the real sector came to be seen as a prerequisite to financial reform. Thus, financial repression would have to be maintained during the first stage of economic liberalisation. The second was what Sachs (1988) labelled as competition of instruments. This relates to the possibility that different aspects of reform programmes may work at cross-purposes, disrupting the real sector in the process. Such conflict can occur when abrupt increases in interest rates cause the exchange rate to appreciate rapidly thus damaging the real sector. Sequencing becomes important again. It is thus suggested that liberalisation of the 'foreign' markets should take place after liberalisation of domestic financial markets. In this context, proponents suggest caution in 'sequencing' in the sense of gradual financial liberalisation emphasising the achievement of macroeconomic stability and adequate bank supervision as preconditions for successful financial reform. In a recent in-depth review of the financial reforms in six developing countries Caprio et al. (1994) argue that managing the reform process rather than adopting a *laissez-faire* stance is important, and that sequencing along with the initial conditions in finance and macroeconomic stability are critical elements in implementing successfully financial reforms.

4 FINANCIAL LIBERALISATION: ECONOMETRIC EVIDENCE

Much of the econometric evidence on the relationship between financial liberalisation and growth focuses on interest rate elasticities in saving, investment and productivity equation. These are the key links between financial liberalisation and growth in the financial liberalisation thesis. We review this type of evidence in the first part of this section. We then go on to present what seems to us to be a more promising line of research. This type of work examines the direct effects emanating from regime shifts and demonstrates that these may be much larger than those emanating from interest rate changes. We illustrate the advantages of this approach by presenting some new results on South Korea.

4.1 Key links of the financial liberalisation thesis

Three links have been particularly emphasised: the relationship between real interest rates and saving, that of credit availability and investment, and the relationship between real interest rates and the productivity of investment. Modigliani (1986) argues that 'despite a hot debate, no convincing general evidence either way has been produced, *which leads me to the provisional view that s* [the saving ratio] *is largely independent of the interest rate*' (p. 304). Dornbusch and Reynoso (1989) in their summary of the relevant evidence from the United States and other industrialised countries conclude on a sceptical note, in that 'virtually no study has demonstrated a discernible net effect (of real deposit rates on saving ratios)' (p. 205). By contrast, Olson and Bailey (1981) suggest that 'the case for positive time preference is absolutely compelling, unless there is an infinite time horizon with the expectation of unending technological advance combined with what we call 'drastically diminishing marginal utility.' This finding holds both in the positive and normative senses. *A corollary is that savings are interest elastic*' (p. I; emphasis added). Boskin (1978) in the case of a US saving function and Fry (1978, 1980) in a sample of fourteen Asian developing countries and Turkey, reveal significant positive interest rate effects on savings ratios. This evidence, however, is questioned by Giovannini (1983), whilst Gupta (1987), finds that the results exhibit substantial regional variations. Fry (1995) concedes that 'What is agreed, however, is that if an effect exists at all it is relatively small' (p. 157), and that 'positive interest rate effects are easier to find in Asia than in other parts of the developing world, but even in Asia the effects appear to have diminished over the past two decades, possibly because of financial liberalisation' (p. 158).

Fry (1980, 1995) finds supportive evidence on the second and third links but the results of Greene and Villanueva (1991) using different econometric techniques and a larger sample (twenty-three LDCs over 1975–87) reveal a negative and significant effect of real interest rates on investment. Moreover, work by Demetriades and Devereux (1992) on an even bigger sample (63 LDCs with data spanning over 1961–90) finds that the effect of higher domestic interest rates on the cost of capital outweighs the effect of an enhanced supply of investible funds on investment. Thus, interest rate liberalisation has, on balance, a negative effect on investment.

4.2 Direct effects of financial repression

Work in this area attempts to measure the direct effects of financial repression by incorporating measures of the latter in growth and/or financial development equations. Roubini and Sala-i-Martin (1992), utilising cross-country regressions on a sample of sixty countries for the period 1960–85, find various indicators of financial distortions to have negative effects. Demetriades and Luintel (1996a, b, 1997), employing time series techniques, demonstrate that the direct effects of financial repression can be more pronounced than the interest rate effects emphasised by previous literature. However, they also argue that these effects need not be negative. From a theoretical view point it is possible that market failure in the financial system, emanating either from imperfect competition or asymmetric information, reverses the conclusions of the financial liberalisation thesis. For example, Stiglitz (1994) has put forward seven types of market failure in the financial system which provide scope for government intervention. Under conditions of imperfect information some forms of financial repression, including interest rate ceilings, may contribute to lessening problems of moral hazard and adverse selection. In so doing, they may enhance the soundness of the financial system which may, in turn, encourage financial development. In sharp contrast, the high real interest rates which are associated with financial liberalisation may make the financial system vulnerable to crises by worsening the problems of adverse selection and moral hazard. Demetriades and Luintel also emphasise that the structure of the financial system may have important implications for the way in which interest rate deregulation affects the financial system. Under a cartelised banking system lending rate ceilings may encourage banks to manage their deposit liabilities more actively. In the presence of price controls banks might find that the only way to increase profit is to increase the volume of credit and deposits. Thus, financial repression might encourage banks to become more active in attracting depositors' money, either through opening new branches, more advertising or even providing a better quality of service.

In the rest of this section we offer some new evidence pertaining to the direct effects of financial repression in South Korea. Employing the same procedures as in Section

2, we set the VAR length to two years and incorporate the following five variables in the analysis: the logarithm of the ratio of bank deposits to nominal GDP (LF), which proxies financial depth, the logarithm of real GDP *per capita* (LY), the ex-ante real deposit rate of interest (R), assuming static inflation expectations, the logarithm of capital stock *per head* (LK) and a summary measure of financial repression (FR).[6] The latter is a weighted index of the principal components of five banking sector controls as follows: a ceiling on the deposit rate; a ceiling on the lending rate; the approximate percentage of total credit covered by the directed credit programme; the minimum reserve requirement on demand and time deposits. The policy data were collected from annual reports of the Bank of Korea (see Demetriades and Luintel (1996*b*) for further details). The constructed index is positively correlated with all the underlying controls. It exhibits correlation coefficients of 84 and 68% with the lending and de-posit rate ceilings respectively, 85 and 86% with the two reserve ratios and 12% with the directed credit variable.

The results from Johansen's cointegration analysis are summarised in Table 3. The trace statistic suggests the existence of two cointegrating vectors. Various tests allow us to impose weak exogeneity of the financial repression measure to the system and to drop the logarithm of the capital stock from the first vector, the restricted form of which can now be interpreted as a financial development equation. As far as the sec-ond vector is concerned, we are able to drop the financial repression index and the financial development indicator. The remaining variables represent a production func-tion type of relationship. The final restriction which is acceptable by the data is homo-geneity between the logarithms of output and capital in the second vector. Thus, the second cointegrating vector takes the simple interpretation of an AK production func-tion.[7]

Turning now to the economic interpretation of these results it may first be noted that the financial repression index has a positive effect on financial development, independently of the real interest rate which had a small positive effect. This finding is consistent with the monopoly banking model. Under monopolistic conditions, it is straightforward to show that the profit-maximising volume of deposits will increase with an appropriately selected lending-rate ceiling (see Courakis, 1984; Arestis and Demetriades, 1995; Demetriades and Luintel, 1996*a*). This may not be very far from the truth in the South Korean case. One indication of the cartelised nature of the South Korean banking system is provided by the following statement from the 1979 report of the Bank of Korea:

---

[6] The data on the capital stock are constructed using the perpetual inventory method, assuming a depreciation rate of 8% per annum. The data on real GDP, population, bank deposits and gross domestic fixed capital formation and other macroeconomic data (e.g. Retail Price Index) were ex-tracted from *International Financial Statistics* (IMF, 1993).

[7] The suggested normalisations receive support from the data. The weak exogeneity tests show that the hypothesis that financial depth is weakly exogenous with respect to the parameters of the first cointegrating vector can be rejected at the 3% level. Unfortunately, the same test could not be carried out in the case of the second cointegrating vector due to lack of convergence. However, the loading coefficient associated with the logarithm of real GDP's adjustment to the second vector was statistically significant and correctly signed.

Table 3 The direct effects of financial repression in South Korea (Johansen cointegration analysis)

Variables entered
- LF = Logarithm of the ratio of bank deposits to nominal GDP
- LY = Logarithm of real GDP *per capita*
- LK = Logarithm of capital stock *per head*
- R = ex-ante real deposit rate of interest
- FR = summary measure of financial repression

Lag length of VAR = 2
Sample period: 1956–94

Ho:rank = p	Trace statistic
$p = 0$	100.90†
$p \leqslant 1$	61.56†
$p \leqslant 2$	34.49

System exogeneity tests: χ^2 (2)	LR test	p-value
LF weakly exogenous to system	7.88	0.02
LY weakly exogenous to system	3.60	0.16
R weakly exogenous to system	18.12	0.00
FR weakly exogenous to system	2.24	0.33
LK weakly exogenous to system	1.62	0.45

Restricted cointegration analysis
Vector 1: $LF = -14.55 + 0.899 \, LY + 0.024 \, R + 0.360 \, FR$
Vector 2: $LY = 0.3720 - 0.097 \, R + 1.0000 \, LK$

Vector autocorrelation test: F (50, 58) = 1.33 [0.15]
LR test on joint restrictions‡: χ: (4) = 4.08 [0.40]

Weak exogeneity tests on restricted system: χ^2 (5)	LR test	p-value
LF weakly exogenous to first vector	12.03	0.03
LF weakly exogenous to second vector	4.18	0.52
LY weakly exogenous to first vector	10.29	0.07
LY weakly exogenous to second vector	N/A§	N/A§
R weakly exogenous to first vector	9.88	0.08
R weakly exogenous to second vector	5.25	0.39
LK weakly exogenous to first vector	4.72	0.45
LK weakly exogenous to second vector	4.50	0.48

* Statistical significance at the 5% level.
† Statistical significance at the 1% level.
‡ The joint restrictions include weak exogeneity of FR to the system.
§ Convergence failed.

'. . . the Bankers Association of Korea, considering that banks themselves are not used to determining interest rates decided to link the interest rates on loans to the central bank's rediscount rate.' (Bank of Korea Annual Report, 1979, p. 18).

The second cointegrating vector demonstrates the importance of the capital stock for long-run output growth, and provides support for a constant returns technology, as required by the endogenous growth literature. Moreover, it also shows that the real rate of interest had a negative effect on output, over and above that of the capital stock. This finding contradicts the liberalisation thesis which predicts a positive association between output growth and real interest rates (e.g. World Bank, 1989). It does, however, justify the Korean authorities preoccupation with low real interest rates, which was founded in the belief that keeping down the cost of capital is good for the economy (Amsden and Euh, 1993). It also seems to be in line with World Bank (1993) which states:

> A policy of moderate financial repression at positive interest rates may have boosted aggregate investment and growth in the HPAE's [High Performing Asian Economies] by transferring income from depositors, primarily households, to borrowers, primarily firms (World Bank, 1993, p. 238–9).

Finally, a word of caution is in order. Even though in South Korea financial repression seems to have worked positively on financial development and growth, this need not always be the case. This cautionary attitude is, in fact, supported by previous work on India by Demetriades and Luintel (1996a, 1997) which shows that the same kind of policies as those employed by the Korean authorities had negative effects. This may reflect differences in the effectiveness of government institutions as indeed is suggested by World Bank (1993) in relation to the 'East Asian Miracle'. The spirit of our conclusions may be encapsulated by the statement that market failure does not necessarily imply government success. Consequently, the effects of financial liberalisation depend upon the institutional context of the economy in question and, particularly, the existence or otherwise of good governance. Clearly under conditions of market failure and effective governmental institutions, government intervention may be able to improve matters; thus, in those circumstances liberalisation, by reducing the scope for government action, may prove detrimental.

5 SUMMARY AND CONCLUSIONS

In this paper we have reviewed empirical evidence relating to the relationship between financial development and economic growth. We have warned against the over-simplified nature of results obtained from cross-country regressions in that they may not accurately reflect individual country circumstances such as the institutional structure of the financial system, the policy regime and the degree of effective governance. The econometric evidence we have reviewed using time-series estimations on individual countries suggests that the results exhibit substantial variation across countries, even when the same variables and estimation methods are used. Thus, the 'average' country for which cross-country regressions must, presumably, relate to may well not exist. We have illustrated our concerns by offering some new evidence on Germany and the United States which reveals important differences in the links between finance and growth.

In view of our limited faith in the results obtained from cross-country regressions, we would suggest that there is still a great deal of work to be done in this area. Such work is likely to prove more fertile if it utilises time-series methods and takes into account individual country circumstances, including the institutional and policy considerations. In this context, we would suggest that there may be some merit in examining the direct effects of changes in the regime of financial policy. 'Regression' and 'liberalisation' may then be seen as the extreme bounds within which financial policy operates. More often than not, financial policy in LDCs moves slowly between these two bounds. Capturing its influence is undoubtedly not a straightforward empirical exercise but may well prove to be more fruitful than the one that looks for interest rate elasticities in saving and investment functions.

Finally, we would suggest that the empirical links between stock market development and economic growth warrant further investigation. Specifically, examining the impact of financial liberalisation on stock market volatility and the effects of the latter on investment and growth seem to us to be a promising avenue for future research.

References

Amsden, A. H. and Euh, Y. D. (1993). 'South Korea's 1980s financial reforms: good-bye financial repression (may be), hello new institutional restraints?' *World Development*, vol. 21, no. 3, pp. 379–90.

Arestis, P. and Demetraides, P. (1995). 'The ethies of interest rate liberalisation in developing economies.' In *Financial Decision-Making and Moral Responsibility* (eds S. F. Frowen and F. P. McHugh). Basingstoke: Macmillan.

Arestis, P. and Demetriades, P. (1996). 'Finance and growth: institutional considerations and causality.' Paper presented at the Royal Economic Society Annual Conference, Swansea University, April.

Atje, R. and Jovanovic, B. (1993). 'Stocks markets and development.' *European Economic Review*, vol. 37. no 2/3. pp. 634–40.

Barro, R. J. (1991). 'Economic growth in a cross-section of countries.' *Quarterly Journal of Economics*, vol. 36, pp. 407–43.

Boskin, M. J. (1978). 'Taxation, saving and the rate of interest.' *Journal of Political Economy*, vol. 86. no. 2ii, pp. S3–27.

Burkett, P. and Dutt, A. K. (1991). 'Interest rate policy, effective demand, and growth in LDCs.' *International Review of Applied Economics*, vol. 5, no. 2, pp. 127–53.

Caprio, G. Jr., Atiyas, I. and Hanson, J. A. (eds.) (1994). *Financial Reform: Theory and Experience.* Cambridge:. Cambridge University Press.

Cho, Y. J. (1989). 'Finance and development: the Korean approach.' *Oxford Review of Economic Policy*, vol. 5, no. 4. pp. 88–102.

Corbo, V. and de Melo, J. (1985). 'Liberalisation with stabilisation in the southern cone of Latin America.' *World Development*, Special Issue, vol. 13, no. 8, pp. 863–6.

Courakis. A. (1984). 'Constraints on bank choices and financial repression in less developed countries.' *Oxford Bulletin of Economics and Statistics.* vol. 46, no. 4, pp. 341–370.

Demetriades, P. and Devereux, M. P. (1992). 'Investment and "financial repression", theory and evidence from 63 LDCs.' Keele University. Working Paper in Economics 92/16 (December).

Demetriades, P. and Hussein, K. (1996). 'Financial development and economic growth: cointegration and causality tests for 16 countries.' *Journal of Development Economics*, vol. 51. December, pp. 387–411.

Demetriades, P. and Luintel, K. (1996*a*). 'Financial development, economic growth and banking sector controls: evidence from India.' *Economic Journal*, vol. 106, pp. 359–74.

Demetriades, P. and Luintel, K. (1996*b*). 'Financial repression in the South Korean miracle.' Keele University Working Paper in Economics, 96/13 (June).

Demetriades, P. and Luintel, K. (1997). 'The direct costs of financial repression: evidence from India.' *Review of Economics and Statistics* (forthcoming).

Demirgüç-Kunt. A. and Levine, R. (1996). 'Stock markets, corporate finance and economic growth: an overview.' *World Bank Economic Review*, vol. 10, no. 2, pp. 223–39.

Diaz-Alejandro. C. (1985). 'Good-bye financial repression, hello financial crash.' *Journal of Development Economics*, vol. 19, no. 1, pp. 1–24.

Dimsdale, N. H. and Prevezer, M. (eds) (1994). *Capital Markets and Corporate Governance*. Oxford: Claredon Press.

Dornbusch, R. and Reynoso, A. (1989). 'Financial factors in economic development.' *American Economic Review*, vol. 79, no. 2, pp. 204–9.

Edwards, S. (1989). 'On the sequencing of structural reforms.' Working Paper, no. 70. OECD Department of Economics and Statistics.

Evans, P. (1995). 'How to estimate growth equations consistently.' Mimeo, Ohio State University, presented at the 7th World Congress of the Econometric Society (Tokyo).

Federer, P. (1993). 'The impact of uncertainty on aggregate investment spending.' *Journal of Money, Credit and Banking*, vol. 25, no. 1, pp. 30–45.

Fry, M. J. (1978). 'Money and capital or financial deepening in economic development?' *Journal of Money, Credit and Banking*, vol. 10, no. 4, pp. 464–75.

Fry, M. J. (1980). 'Saving, investment, growth and the cost of financial repression.' *World Development*, vol. 8, no. 4, pp. 317–27.

Fry, M. J. (1995). *Money, Interest and Banking in Economic Development*, 2nd edn. Baltimore: Johns Hopkins University Press.

Fry, M. J. (1997). 'In favour of financial liberalisation.' *Economic Journal*, vol. 107 (May), pp. 754–70.

Fry, M. J. and Nuti, D. M. (1992). 'Monetary and exchange rate policies during Eastern Europe's transition: some lessons from further east.' *Oxford Review of Economic Policy*, vol. 8, no. 1, pp. 27–43.

Gelb, A. H. (1989). 'Financial policies, growth and efficiency.' Policy Planning and Research, Working Papers, no. 202, World Bank.

Giovannini, A. (1983). 'The interest rate elasticity of savings in developing countries: the existing evidence.' *World Development*, vol. 11, no. 7, pp. 601–7.

Grabel, I. (1995). 'Speculation-led economic development: a post-Keynesian interpretation of financial liberalization programs.' *International Review of Applied Economics*, vol. 9, no. 2, pp. 127–49.

Greene, J. and Villanueva, D. (1991). 'Private investment in developing countries: an empirical analysis.' *IMF Staff Papers*, vol. 38, no. 1, pp. 33–58.

Gupta, K. L. (1987). 'Aggregate savings, financial intermediation and interest rates.' *Review of Economics and Statistics*, vol. 69, no. 2, pp. 303–11.

Hall, S. G. and Milne, A. (1994). 'The relevance of p-star analysis to UK monetary policy.' *Economic Journal*, vol. 104, pp. 597–604.

Harris, L. (1988). 'Financial reform and economic growth: a new interpretation of South Korea's experience.' In *New Perspectives on the Financial System* (eds L. Harris, J. Coakley, M. Croasdale and T. Evans). London: Croom Helm.

IMF (1993). *International Financial Statistics,* Washington: International Monetary Fund.

Johansen, S. (1988). 'Statistical analysis of co-integrating vectors.' *Journal of Economic Dynamics and Control,* vol. 12, pp. 231–54.

Johansen, S. (1992). 'Testing weak exogeneity and the order of cointegration in UK money demand data.' *Journal of Policy Modelling,* vol. 14, pp. 313–34.

Keynes, J. M. (1936). *The General Theory of Employment, Interest and Money.* London: Macmillan.

King, R. G. and Levine, R. (1993). 'Finance and growth: Schumpeter might be "right".' *Quarterly Journal of Economics,* vol. 108, pp. 717–37.

Lee, K., Pesaran, M. H. and Smith, R. P. (1996). 'Growth and convergence: a multi-country empirical analysis of the Solow growth model.' Department of Applied Economics Working Papers, Amalgamated Series no. 9531, University of Cambridge.

Levine, R. (1996). 'Stock markets: a spur to economic growth.' *Finance and Development,* vol. 33, no. 1, pp. 7–10.

Levine, R. and Renelt, D. (1992). 'A sensitivity analysis of cross-country growth regressions.' *American Economic Review,* vol. 82, no. 4, pp. 942–63.

Levine, R. and Zervos, S. (1996). 'Stock market development and long-run growth.' *World Bank Economic Review,* vol. 10, no. 2, pp. 323–39.

McKinnon, R. (1991). *The Order of Economic Liberalization: Financial Control in the Transition to a Market Economy.* Baltimore: Johns Hopkins University Press.

Minsky, H. P. (1986). *Stabilizing an Unstable Economy.* New Haven, CT: Yale University Press.

Modigliani, F. (1986). 'Life cycle, individual thrift and the wealth of nations.' *American Economic Review.* vol. 76, no. 3, pp. 297–313.

Olson, M. and Bailey, M. J. (1981). 'Positive time preference.' *Journal of Political Economy,* vol. 89, no. 1, pp. 1–25.

Pagan, A. (1986). 'Two stage and related estimators and their applications.' *Review of Economic Studies,* vol. 53, no. 4, pp. 517–38.

Park, Y. C. and Kim, D. W. (1994). 'Korea: development and structural change of the banking system.' In *The Financial Development of Japan, Korea and Taiwan: Growth, Repression and Liberalization* (eds H. T. Patrick and Y. C. Park). Oxford: Oxford University Press.

Pesaran, M. H. and Shin, Y. (1995). 'Long-run structural modelling.' Mimeo, University of Cambridge.

Pesaran, M. H. and Smith, R. P. (1995). 'Estimating long-run relationships from dynamic heterogeneous panels.' *Journal of Econometrics,* vol. 68, pp. 79–113.

Quah, D. (1993). 'Empirical cross-section dynamics in economic growth.' *European Economic Review,* vol. 37, pp. 426–34.

Roubini, N. and Sala-i-Martin, X. (1992). 'Financial repression and economic growth.' *Journal of Development Economics,* vol. 39, no. 1, pp. 5–30.

Sachs, J. (1988). 'Conditionality, debt relief and the developing countries' debt crisis.' In *Developing Country Debt and Economic Performance* (ed. J. Sachs). Chicago: University of Chicago Press.

Singh, A. (1997). 'Stock markets, financial liberalisation and economic development.' *Economic Journal,* vol. 107, (May), pp. 771–82.

Stiglitz, J. E. (1994). 'The role of the state in financial markets.' In *Proceedings of the World Bank Annual Conference on Development Economics, 1993* (eds M. Bruno and B. Pleskovic), pp. 19–52. Washington: World Bank.

Villanueva, D. and Mirakhor, A. (1990). 'Strategies for financial reforms: interest rate polices, stabilisation, and bank supervision in developing countries.' *IMF Staff Papers,* vol. 37, no. 3, pp. 509–36.

World Bank (1989). *World Development Report.* Oxford: Oxford University Press.

World Bank (1993). *The East Asian Miracle: Economic Growth and Public Policy.* Oxford: Oxford University Press.

Part 5

ECONOMICS AND THE MEASUREMENT OF HAPPINESS

INTRODUCTION*

Huw D. Dixon

In 1749, Ludovico Antonio Muratori, published a book titled *Della Pubblica Felicita* that introduced the use of the term 'public happiness'. He saw public policy as seeking to find the best economic means to achieve the 'public happiness'. Other contemporary Italian economists[1] developed the link between the theory of value (based on the individual's calculus between pleasure and pain) and the theory of public policy based on 'public happiness'. The historical foundations of the modern economic model of individual choice were largely utilitarian. Many neoclassical economists in the late nineteenth and early twentieth century would have considered themselves to be utilitarians: Edgeworth, Jevons and Wicksteed to name a few. For such economists, 'utility' was a word that referred to something substantial, a mental state which might someday be measured. Edgeworth named the as yet uninvented machine to measure utility the 'hedonometer'. This view was by no means universal: Marshall was one of the most notable critics of the utilitarian viewpoint in his *Principles*, at least in its more extreme hedonist version.

However, since World War II, the conventional view has been that there is no place for utility in this substantial sense. 'Utility' is just a number given to possible outcomes that can, in some sense, explain or predict choices. The reasons for this switch seemed quite compelling at the time. First, the rejection of the notion that utility was in principle measurable. Since satisfaction/pleasure and happiness are purely subjective, the idea of an objective scientific measure of utility is put into question[2]. Second, the development of ordinal utility theory showed that cardinal utility was unnecessary for economics, even for much of welfare economics. Since it was both suspect and unnec-

* I would like to thank Andrew Clark for helping me to set up this *Controversy* and Massimo Paradiso for informing me about the early Italian Utilitarians.

[1] The most notable examples being the Neapolitans Antonio Genovesi and Giuseppe Palmieri writing in the 1760s.

[2] However, it is not precluded. Hot and cold were for most of human history purely subjective sensations, subject to many ambiguities and seeming paradoxes. That has not meant that we have been unable to develop an objective measure of temperature that is closely related to the subjective.

essary, the utilitarian foundations of choice theory were rejected, although the vocabulary lived on. Together, these arguments have proven persuasive to most of the economics profession for the last half century.

Things may, however, be changing. This controversy brings together three economists from different backgrounds who all believe that happiness should take a more central role in economics once again[3]. They all share the view that it makes some sense to talk of 'measuring' utility. This is done not by placing electrodes on the heads of people (although that may come), but by asking people questions. While this may well not be an exact way of measuring an individual's well-being, the answers to such questions from a large number of people can be used as a guide to what factors, in general, make people feel happier. In particular, we can certainly use this type of data to explore some of the basic maintained hypotheses of economics: for example, the notion that utility is an increasing function of income at the individual and aggregate level.

Andrew Oswald opens the controversy with a paper that focuses on the empirical side of what we can find from existing data on happiness and its relation to economic performance. He presents several broad findings that he has drawn from the data. One of the first economists to take a look at this data was Richard Easterlin in 1974. He formulated the hypothesis that well-being depends on relative income, not absolute income: this arose from the consideration of cross-country comparisons, and within-country time-series. Oswald argues that, using US data, there is a very small tendency for happiness to be increasing over the post-war period: the results are similar but much more mixed in Europe. For Oswald, the evidence is quite clear that while money might buy a little happiness, it does not buy very much. On the other hand, there are certain factors which do seem to influence overall well-being: for example, happiness is U-shaped in age with a minimum in the early thirties, unemployment makes people very unhappy and so on. There is clearly plenty of data available on well-being, and it should (Oswald argues) be used by economists.

Bob Frank explores, in some detail, the policy implications of the Easterlin hypothesis. He draws the conclusion from the data that relative consumption determines well-being (this was an idea also put forward earlier by Fred Hirsch and Tibor Scitivsky in the mid-1970s). If everyone in a society seeks to maximize their own welfare, then there is an externality present: an increase in my own consumption makes me better off relative to you, and hence my consumption decreases your utility. The end result is that the equilibrium in society is inefficient: we all end up consuming more than is socially optimal. Since consumption uses up resources, we can all gain if we consume less: with lower average consumption across the population, utility would not be reduced. However, the real resources released from the production of consumer goods (including durables and housing) would be released for other uses (education, health and leisure), which could make everyone better off. This is a very simple argument, but it has powerful and clear policy implications. Frank himself argues strongly for a consumption tax as a practical implication of his analysis.

---

[3] Of course, one might accept that one can measure well-being to some degree of accuracy, yet still reject the notion of a utilitarian social welfare function or moral system. The arguments for and against utilitarianism as a moral system are perhaps as extensive as they are inconclusive.

Yew Kwang Ng approaches the problem from the perspective of a traditional welfare economist. He argues very strongly against the orthodox view that cardinal notions of utility should be rejected. While he accepts that there are measurement problems, he believes that it makes sense to talk about cardinal utility, and that it is certainly more in tune with common sense than the pure ordinalist's view. If we accept this, then the whole focus of welfare economics (and indeed economics as a whole) should shift towards a science of promoting well-being and happiness. Conventional measures of welfare such as per-capita GDP are highly misleading if this is our objective. Like Frank, he argues that great increases in well-being can be achieved if we take happiness seriously.

Bill Nordhaus' paper examines a rather different angle: one of measurement. If we accept the conventional view of economics and welfare, we can use a price-index to track changes in real income or well-being over time. However, the nature of products changes over time, with the services provided by products improving. Nordhaus argues that conventional measures of the cost of living fail to take this into account properly, with the result that the degree of inflation is overestimated. This has been the subject of the Boskin Committee report in the USA, which suggests that real income growth has been underestimated: over the period 1959–1995, Nordhaus estimates that the growth in real wage income was 70% rather than the conventional figure of 10%.

Perhaps more than 200 years after Muratori argued for founding public policy on the notions of private and public happiness, it is time for economists to re-evaluate the foundations of their prejudices. Perhaps by excluding notions of well-being and happiness from economics, we have created an artificial limitation which precludes economics from answering some of the most important questions. While the hedonometer may take some years to be invented, you can reach your own conclusion after reading these persuasive papers. Even if you are unmoved by these arguments and stick to the conventional view, then Nordhaus's paper should make you worry about how we conventionally measure the cost of living.

14
HAPPINESS AND ECONOMIC PERFORMANCE*

Andrew J. Oswald

Those who say that money can't buy happiness don't know where to shop.

Anon

Do you think your children's lives will be better than your own? Probably not; nobody does these days . . . In all countries there is doom and gloom, a universal sense of decay.

Norman Stone, historian

What we call happiness in the strictest sense of the word comes from the (preferably sudden) satisfaction of needs which have been dammed up to a high degree.

Sigmund Freud, psychologist

Happiness is the sublime moment when you get out of your corsets at night.

Joyce Grenfell, actress

Economic performance is not intrinsically interesting. No-one is concerned in a genuine sense about the level of gross national product last year or about next year's exchange rate. People have no innate interest in the money supply, inflation, growth, inequality, unemployment, and the rest. The stolid greyness of the business pages of our newspapers seems to mirror the fact that economic numbers matter only indirectly.

The relevance of economic performance is that it may be a means to an end. That end is not the consumption of beefburgers, nor the accumulation of television sets, nor the vanquishing of some high level of interest rates, but rather the enrichment of mankind's feeling of well-being. Economic things matter only in so far as they make people happier.

This paper is concerned with the economics of happiness. Unlike gross domestic product and inflation, happiness is not something that governments try to record from

* For helpful advice, and for allowing me to draw upon joint research, I am grateful to Kamal Birdi, Danny Blanchflower, Andrew Clark, Rafael Di Tella, Robert MacCulloch, and Peter Warr. For research assistance. I thank Ed Butchart, Antonia Sachtleben and Francesca Silverton. For valuable discussions, I thank Michael Argyle, Nick Crafts, Mark Harrison, Daniel Kahneman, Mozaffar Qizilbash, Richard Layard, and Robert Skidelsky. Helpful comments were also received during presentations at Durham University and the London School of Economics. This work was financed by the Economic and Social Research Council UK and the Leverhulme Trust.

year to year. This essay will show that they could and, for the issues of *Economic Trends* in the next century, possibly should.[1]

Most politicians who pronounce about the economic matters of the day do so under a set of assumptions about human enjoyment that are usually not articulated to the listener. The chief of these, perhaps, is the belief that by raising its output and productivity a society truly betters itself. Real income has been rising in the Western countries for a long time. Like most other industrialized nations, Britain is approximately twice as rich as it was as recently as 1960, and almost three times richer than after the War. Has this new real income – an enormous improvement by the standards of the last few centuries – bought extra happiness? If so, how much, and what should governments now be trying to do? If not, why not, and what should governments now be trying to do?

Deciding how much authentic well-being is bought by economic progress is a difficult task. It seems logically necessary, however, if economic and social policy is to be designed in a rational way. If taxpayers' pound notes can be thought of as seed-corn, they could be scattered upon ground devoted to raising innovation and economic growth, or, for example, upon that aimed at combating social problems, or upon something different. Society has to pick those places to throw the seed-corn especially thickly. It is not easy to know how such choices can be made in a systematic way. However, a social scientist might help those who mould policy if he or she could point to unnoticed patterns in data on happiness and satisfaction. This paper takes a small step along that path.

1 HAPPINESS AND REAL INCOME IN THE UNITED STATES

Later pages use the answers that people give when asked questions about how happy they feel with life or how satisfied they feel with their job and work. There are limitations to such statistics, but, if the aim is to learn about what makes people tick, listening to what they say seems likely to be a natural first step. Sources of information exist that have for many years recorded individuals' survey responses to questions about subjective well-being. These responses have been studied intensively by psychologists,[2]

---

[1] Should economists study happiness, one might ask? There are some natural answers. First, presumably this subject really matters. Second, psychologists have for many years worked with data on self-reported happiness. They ought to know more about human psychology than we do. Third, there are grounds – laid out later – to believe that subjective well-being can be studied in a systematic way. Well-being regression equations have the same structure all over the world. Fourth, subjective wellbeing measures are correlated with observable phenomena. For example, people who report high happiness scores tend to laugh and smile more, and to be rated by others as happier (Pavot, 1991; Diener, 1984; Watson and Clark, 1991). Fifth, we might be able to use happiness data to test old ideas in new ways. For example, if one wished to know whether inflation is bad, one might ask whether, in inflationary periods, people *en masse* unknowingly tick lower down their happiness score sheets (Di Tella et al, 1996).

[2] Recent work includes Argyle (1989), Douthitt et al. (1992), Fox and Kahneman (1992), Larsen et al. (1984) and Mullis (1992). Comparatively little research seems to have addressed the issue of how well-being changes through the years.

studied a little by sociologists, and ignored by economists.[3] Some economists may wish to defend this neglect by emphasising the unreliability of such data. Most, however, are probably unaware that data of this sort are available, and have not thought of how such empirical measures might be used in their discipline.

Richard Easterlin (1974, 1995) was one of the first economists to study statistics over time on the reported level of happiness. His data came from the United States. Easterlin's 1974 paper's main objectives were, first, to suggest that individual happiness appears to be the same across poor countries and rich countries, and, second, to argue that economic growth does not raise well-being. Easterlin suggested that we should think of people as getting utility from a comparison of themselves with others close to them: happiness is relative. The modern stress on the benefits of higher total national income is then misplaced, because individuals all move up together. A similar theme is taken up in Hirsch (1976) and Scitovsky (1976), and still more recently in Frank (1985).[4]

Easterlin (1974) suggested a test for whether greater riches had made Americans happier. He looked at whether reported happiness rose as national income did. His paper concludes: '... in the one time series studied, that for the United States since 1946, higher income was not systematically accompanied by greater happiness' (p. 118). This result would mean that economic growth does not buy well-being.

Unfortunately, it is not obvious that Easterlin's data entirely support his conclusion. For example, his longest *consistent* set of happiness levels for the percentages of Americans saying they were 'very happy' and 'not very happy' (the highest and lowest of three bands into which they could place themselves) are shown in Table 1. Other data – using statistics with breaks and changes in definitions – given by Easterlin differ. But the above is the longest consistent series and might be thought to command the most weight. According to these data, well-being did rise through time in the United States.[5]

A more modern calculation can be done with the General Social Surveys of the United States, which have for many years been interviewing people annually about

Table 1 Happiness in the United States 1940s–1950s

Date	% Very happy	% Not very happy	N
1946	39	10	3,151
1947	42	10	1,434
1948	43	11	1,596
1952	47	9	3,003
1956	53	5	1,979
1957	53	3	1,627

Source: Table 8 of Easterlin (1974) using US AIPO poll data.

[3] Andrew Clark's recent work (for example, 1992, 1996*a, b*) is an exception.
[4] The late Fred Hirsch was a Warwick professor in the 1970s.
[5] The new paper by Easterlin (1995) presents modern US data showing that the % of people 'very happy' did not rise between 1972 and 1991. This appears a touch misleading, because the % unhappy fell quite markedly.

their levels of happiness. These surveys are of randomly selected samples of Americans, so the information they provide can be treated as representative of the nation as a whole. GSS data are available for almost all of the years from 1972 to the 1990s (there are no data for 1979 or 1981). The size of sample averages approximately fifteen hundred individuals per annum. Different people are interviewed each year: the GSS does not follow the same individuals.

Is America getting happier as it gets richer? Table 2 tabulates for three years the raw answers to the question:

> Taken all together, how would you say things are these days – would you say that you are very happy, pretty happy, or not too happy? (GSS Ques. 154–6)

The first thing that is noticeable is that 'pretty happy' is the typical answer, and that 'not too happy', which is the lowest score people can assign themselves, is given by slightly more than a tenth of the population.

First indications from Table 2 are not encouraging to the idea that growth leads to

Table 2 Happiness in the United States: 1972–90

	1972	1980	1990
Very happy %	30.3	33.9	33.4
Pretty happy %	53.2	52.7	57.6
Not too happy %	16.5	13.3	9.0
Number in sample	1,606	1,462	1,361

Source: Blanchflower et al. (1993) from US General Social Surveys. That paper gives data for each year. Weighted to control for oversampling of blacks in certain years.

more well-being. There is little sign of a time trend in the answer 'very happy'. The proportion of American respondents saying this was around one third both early in the 1970s and late in the 1980s. Over the period, however, a declining number of people seem to say that they are not too happy, and more state that they are pretty happy.

The raw data are consistent with the view that the category 'pretty happy' is expanding while 'not too happy' is shrinking. Nevertheless, the effect is not dramatic, and these are only raw data that may be being moulded predominantly by a population that is changing its composition. Blanchflower et al. (1993) explore the matter more systematically. They examine whether there is an upward trend in well-being after controlling for demographic and other compositional changes in the American economy. Their conclusion is that there is a positive time trend, but that it is very slight. Intriguingly, there seems to be evidence of a cycle in happiness (especially for men). Blanchflower et al. show that the rise in happiness has not been spread evenly. It seems that American men have got happier while American women have experienced little growth in subjective well-being. Blanchflower and Oswald (1996) find some evidence that the young are growing relatively happier.

These results are not consistent with the conclusion of Easterlin (1974) that, perhaps because of ever-increasing aspirations and concern for relativities, the human lot does not improve over time. They are more like the arguments of Andrews (1991) and Veenhoven (1991). Nevertheless, Easterlin was on the right track. It may be correct to suggest that little national happiness is bought by rising national income.

Finding 1. *Happiness with life appears to be increasing in the United States. The rise is so small, however, that it seems extra income is not contributing dramatically to the quality of people's lives.*

2 SATISFACTION WITH LIFE: EUROPE SINCE 1973

There is similar information for European countries. Although few economists seem to have used the data, the Eurobarometer Survey Series asks:

> On the whole, are you very satisfied, fairly satisfied, not very satisfied, or not at all satisfied with the life you lead?

Answers are available for random samples, from 1973 to the present, of approximately 1000 people per year per country. The nations are Belgium, Denmark, West Germany, Greece, Spain, France, Ireland, Italy, Luxembourg, The Netherlands, Portugal and Great Britain. Surveys have been held twice a year in each European Community country. Because of their late entry to the EC, there is no full run of data for Spain, Portugal and Greece. A valuable source of information about the Eurobarometer surveys is the comprehensive study by Inglehart (1990), who uses them to study changing cultural values.

Table 3 reports some of the data on life satisfaction for these countries. The first thing that is obvious is the large differences across nations. In Denmark, for example, more than half the population say they are 'very satisfied', while in Italy the figure is around one in ten. These divergent numbers are likely to reflect cultural and linguistic differences. This is partly the difficulty of translation (words like happiness, contentment and

Table 3 Life satisfaction in nine European countries from one decade to the next

Country	Average % 1973–81	Average % 1982–90	Well-being increased?
Proportion of the sample who reported themselves as 'very satisfied' with their lives			
Belgium	39.5	24.7	No
Denmark	51.7	62.8	Yes
France	12.4	13.7	Yes
West Germany	18.8	23.4	Yes
Ireland	38.8	31.1	No
Italy	9.0	13.2	Yes
Luxembourg	34.6	39.1	Yes
Netherlands	41.3	41.8	Yes
UK	31.7	30.9	No

Source: Own calculations using Eurobarometer Survey numbers provided by Ronald Inglehart of the University of Michigan. Sample size is approximately 1,000 people per year per country.

satisfaction have subtle distinctions in English, and in other languages). But it is not all variation in language. As Inglehart (1990) points out, Switzerland makes an ideal laboratory to test this. German-speaking Swiss, French-speaking Swiss, and Italian-speaking Swiss all express higher satisfaction levels than do native Germans, French and Italians.

The second thing that is noticeable is that well-being is not moving uniformly upwards. Table 3 calculates from country to country the mean level, for each of the two halves of the period, of those answering 'very satisfied'. This smooths out some of the (fairly large) fluctuations in people's year-to-year answers. Thus in the period 1973–81 in Belgium, for example, on average 39.5% of the people interviewed said that they were very satisfied with their lives. Over the ensuing decade, this figure dropped dramatically. For 1982–90, the proportion of respondents saying very satisfied was 24.7%. This evidence shows no gain over time of the sort to be expected if real income growth raises well-being. However, as the rest of Table 3 reveals, Belgium is not typical. Denmark, France, West Germany, Italy, Luxembourg and Netherlands all record increases in the numbers of individuals saying they feel very satisfied with life. Ireland posts a large drop. The United Kingdom experiences a small fall.

There is only slight evidence here that greater economic prosperity leads to more well-being in a nation:

Finding 2. *Since the early 1970s, reported levels of satisfaction with life in the European countries have on average risen very slightly.*

There is another way to measure well-being, and that is to study psychiatric measures of mental distress. The new British Household Panel Study gives mental well-being scores from a form of psychiatric evaluation known as the General Health Questionnaire. The first sweep of the British Household Panel Study provides information, for the year 1991, about a random sample of approximately six thousand working Britons. One way to assess these people's feelings of subjective well-being is to use their scores from the General Health Questionnaire (GHQ) section of the survey. Argyle (1989) argues that a GHQ assessment is one of the most reliable indicators of psychological distress or 'disutility'. In its simplest form this assessment weights the answers to the following set of questions.

Have you recently:

    *1.   been able to concentrate on whatever you are doing?
     2.   lost much sleep over worry?
    *3.   felt that you are playing a useful part in things?
    *4.   felt capable of making decisions about things?
     5.   felt constantly under strain?
     6.   felt you couldn't overcome your difficulties?
    *7.   been able to enjoy your normal day-to-day activities?
    *8.   been able to face up to your problems?
     9.   been feeling unhappy and depressed?
    10.   been losing confidence in yourself?
    11.   been thinking of yourself as a worthless person?
   *12.   been feeling reasonably happy all things considered?

People's answers to these questions are coded on a four-point scale running from 'disagree strongly' to 'agree strongly'. Starred items are coded in reverse, so that, for example, zero then corresponds to 'agree strongly'. These twelve are then combined into a total GHQ level of mental distress in which high numbers correspond to low feelings of well-being. The data provide a mental stress or, much less accurately, un-happiness level for each individual in the sample.

There are various ways to work with GHQ responses. One is to calculate so-called Caseness scores. These are produced by taking people's answers to the twelve questions that are listed above and summing the number of times the person places himself or herself in either the fairly stressed or highly stressed category. With this method, the lowest possible level of well-being corresponds to a caseness level of 12 (meaning that the individual felt stressed on every one of the twelve questions). The highest level of well-being corresponds to 0 (meaning that the individual felt stressed on none of the twelve questions). Individuals with high caseness levels are viewed by psychologists as people who would benefit from psychiatric treatment.

The British Household Panel Survey data show that income has no strong role to play, but that joblessness does. Clark and Oswald (1994) fail to find any statistically significant effect from income. The sharp impact of unemployment, however, is illus-trated by Tables 4 and 5. These use data on 6,000 British workers in 1991. Mental distress is twice as high among the unemployed as among those who have work.

Table 4 Measuring the distress levels of people in the labour force in Britain in 1991

Labour market status	Number in sample	Average mental distress*
Unemployed	522	2.98
Employee	4,893	1.45
Self-employed	736	1.54

* These numbers are on a scale where the minimum is 0 and the maximum is 12. Calculating means in this way imposes an implicit assumption of cardinality.
Source: Clark and Oswald (1994) using BHPS data on GHQ scores.

Table 5 Distress levels in Britain by educational attainment

	Number in sample	Mental distress
High education (HNC up to degree)		
In work	1,612	1.48
Unemployed	86	3.44
Medium education (GCSE up to A level)		
In work	2,157	1.43
Unemployed	161	3.15
Low education (less or no qualifications)		
In work	1,848	1.43
Unemployed	2.73	2.70

Source: Clark and Oswald (1994) using BHPS data on GHQ scores.

Interestingly, research suggests that the worst thing about losing one's job is not the drop in take-home income. It is the non-pecuniary distress. To put this differently, most regression results imply that an enormous amount of extra income would be required to compensate people for having no work.

Eurobarometer data, in Table 6 and Fig. 1, also show that the unemployed feel

Table 6 The microeconomics of happiness in Europe: 1975–86

	All	*Unemployed*
Very happy (%)	23.4	15.9
Pretty happy (%)	57.9	51.1
Not too happy (%)	18.6	33.0

	Lowest-income quartile people	*Highest-income quartile people*
Very happy (%)	18.8	28.4
Pretty happy (%)	54.5	58.5
Not too happy (%)	26.7	13.1

Source: Di Tella et al. (1996) using Eurobarometer data. Total sample 108,802 observations.

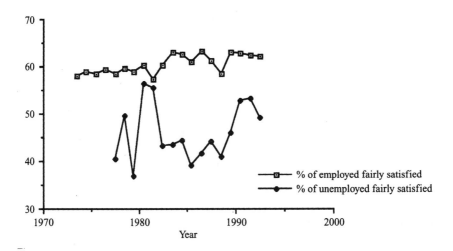

Fig. 1 Life-satisfaction levels of the employed and the unemployed: the European countries 1970s–1990s.

Notes: The vertical axis measures the proportion of people saying they were 'fairly satisfied with life' as a whole. The data source is the Eurobarometer Surveys, which provide a random sample here of approximately 120,000 European men. Running a trend line through each series produces almost exactly the same gradient, namely, just over 0.2.

much less satisfied with life[6], and indicate that the relative distress from unemployment does not appear to be trending downwards through the years (the 'unhappiness gap' is not secularly shrinking). In passing, this might be thought to raise doubts about the oft-expressed view that an increasingly generous welfare state is somehow at the root of Europe's economic problems. A review of psychologists' earlier work is available in Warr et al. (1988).[7] The upshot of all this evidence is:

Finding 3. *Unemployed people are very unhappy.*

More generally, it is now well known that there are systematic patterns in micro data on people's subjective well-being. In other words, if one takes a random sample of people, and estimates a well-being regression equation of form 'reported well-being = f(personal characteristics)', the results tend to be the same across different periods, different countries, and even different measures of well-being. Summarising:

Finding 4. *Reported happiness is high among those who are married, on high income, women, whites, the well-educated, the self-employed, the retired, and those looking after the home. Happiness is apparently U-shaped in age (minimising around the 30s).*

These stem from coefficients in cross-section equations, but some have been verified in panel data.

3 EXTREME UNHAPPINESS: SUICIDE AND ATTEMPTED SUICIDE

Getting information on high levels of happiness is likely to be difficult, because there is no need for such statistics to be recorded. There is, however, a method of studying the other extreme.

Suicide is a significant cause of death across the world. In Denmark it accounts for approximately 1 in every 3,000 deaths; in Britain the figure is approximately 1 in every 12,000 deaths; in the United States of America around 1 in every 7,000 deaths are the result of suicide. Large numbers of people, therefore, take the decision that life is not worth living. Moreover, the numbers just given understate what is really happening. First, most writings on the subject express the view that, for understandable reasons, suicide statistics are probably under-reported versions of the truth. Second, the number of individuals attempting suicide is much larger than of those who do kill themselves.

The medical term for attempted suicide is para-suicide. Data in Smith (1985) record the probably little-appreciated fact that in Britain a fifth of all emergency admissions to hospital are due to para-suicide. Dooley et al. (1989) report that para-suicide is between 8 and 20 times more common than successful suicide. Five million Americans, they estimate, have attempted suicide at some time in their lives. The data that Platt and

---

[6] Longitudinal studies by psychologists have demonstrated that this is not merely because unhappy people have trouble finding jobs.

[7] New work by Kammerling and O'Connor (1993) shows that around Bristol the local area unemployment rates are strong predictors of the rate of psychiatric admission by area.

Kreitman (1985) gather on Edinburgh males suggest that, among unemployed men in the lowest social class (Class V), one in twenty try to kill themselves in a given year.

Is this topic best left to doctors? Although analysis has a long history (Durkheim, 1897, being a landmark), most social scientists are not used to working with suicide statistics. Economists, especially, are likely to see this area as far from their usual concerns, and of little relevance to them.

This attitude may not be the right one. As writer Wilfred Sheen remarked: suicide is about life, being in fact the sincerest criticism that life gets. If the aim is to understand human well-being and the value of life, suicide data offer rich – though upsetting – information that would be impossible to glean in any other way. The reason is that suicides represent choices in response to (un)happiness that are intrinsically more compelling than replies made to happiness survey questions, and data that, by their nature, cannot be generated in a laboratory experiment. It might, of course, be argued by a social scientist that suicide decisions are not rational. Perhaps they are simply a sign of mental illness, and therefore do not contain reliable information. Medical opinion has debated this view and not accepted it in a wholehearted way. There is evidence that suicides occur more frequently both among those who in an objective sense have the least to live for, and after unpleasant events in a person's life. The latter include unpleasant economic events. Humphry (1992) and Richman (1992) discuss the notion of, and evidence for, rational suicide.

For the post-war period, suicide is dropping through time. By such a benchmark, life looks like it is improving. There is little reason to impute causality, but the data do not contradict the natural idea that greater real income might make fewer people so miserable that they want to kill themselves. Data for the whole century, in so far as they are reliable, suggest the same. In 1911, 2,600 men committed suicide in England and Wales. In 1990, 2,800 did so. The population over that period nearly doubled. In this sense, extreme unhappiness might be said to be dropping. Historical statistics also reveal that total suicide deaths reached their maximum in the Great Depression, which is consistent with the idea that economics may have some role to play in this area.

Figure 2 provides data on a dozen rich countries. Although it would probably be unwise to read too much into the plot, high real income is positively, not negatively, correlated with the suicide rate.

To explore the idea that money buys happiness, it might be natural to look at data on suicide and low income. This can be done in an indirect way. Charlton et al. (1992) show that the suicide death rate is largely independent of social class. Thus, roughly speaking, economically prosperous people do not take their own lives less than the poor. There is one type of exception to this: those men unemployed and seeking work at census were at 2–3-fold greater risk of suicide death than the average, Charlton et al. (1992). The study by Platt and Kreitman (1985) produces Table 7, on para-suicide by length of joblessness. It shows that being without work is associated with a twelve times greater-than-average chance of attempted suicide, and that the long-term unemployed are especially at risk.

There is a little evidence that time-series movements in unemployment are accompanied by movements in suicide. *Population Trends* of Spring 1994 recorded the fact that, among men, suicide has been rising in almost all Western countries since the early 1970s. This period coincides with the mushrooming of unemployment.

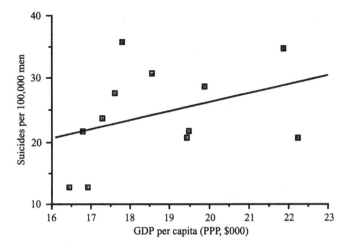

Fig. 2 Suicides and GDP in the rich industrial nations
Notes: This figure depicts the suicide rates and purchasing power parity GDP per capita figures of
the dozen nations with the highest HDI (human development index) scores as calculated by the
UN. The twelve countries are Canada, Switzerland, Japan, Sweden, Norway, France, Australia,
United States, Netherlands, UK, Germany, and Austria. The data are for the early 1990s.
Source: of the data: Tables 28 and 30 of *Human Development Report.* United Nations, Oxford
University Press, 1994.

Divorce and being single are apparently also significant triggers of suicidal behaviour. In the words of Charlton et al, there may be a protective effect from marriage.
Married men commit suicide – holding age constant – only one third as often as others.

Finding 5. *Consistent with the patterns in happiness data, suicidal behaviour is more prevalent
among men, the unemployed, and those with marital problems. Over the long run, as Britain has got
richer, the suicide rate has declined (though this is not true for men since the 1970s). Rich countries
apparently have more suicides.*

Finding 6. *High unemployment may swell the numbers of people taking their own lives. Suicide data
suggest that joblessness is a major source of distress.*

Table 7 Parasuicide rates by duration of unemployment: Edinburgh city males, 1982

Duration of unemployment	Para-suicide rate/100,000	Relative risk
Less than 4 weeks	1,012	8.8
5–26 weeks	615	5.4
27–52 weeks	1,193	10.4
Over 52 weeks	2,164	18.9
All unemployed	1,345	11.8
All employed	114	1.0

Source: Platt and Kreitman (1985).

4 JOB SATISFACTION IN BRITAIN AND THE UNITED STATES

On the grounds that work is a big part of life, this section examines information about job satisfaction. Following Blanchflower et al. (1993), data are available for Great Britain and the United States. The *General Social Surveys* of 1972–90 are again the source of US information. The relevant question, asked of approximately 13,000 workers, is:

> On the whole, how satisfied or dissatisfied are you with the work you do – would you say you are very satisfied, moderately satisfied, a little dissatisfied, or very dissatisfied? (GSS Ques.)

For Britain, the *General Household Surveys* of 1973–83 can be used. These offer a sample of approximately 126,000 employed individuals. The question asked is:

> How satisfied are you with your job as a whole – very satisfied, fairly satisfied, neither satisfied nor dissatisfied, rather dissatisfied, or very dissatisfied? (GHS Ques.)

The wordings thus differ slightly between countries, but seem sufficiently similar to allow rough comparison. In both countries the samples for the paper's analysis are restricted to current employees. Although an interesting special case, the self-employed are omitted. There is a small literature suggesting that they have intrinsically greater job satisfaction than employees.

Tables 8 and 9 give the raw numbers on job satisfaction for each country. Table 8

Table 8 Job satisfaction in the United States: 1972–90

	1972	*1980*	*1990*
Very satisfied %	46.2	44.4	46.0
Moderately satisfied %	38.0	37.7	40.1
A little dissatisfied %	12.2	13.8	9.9
Very dissatisfied %	3.6	4.2	4.0
Number in sample	777	698	734

Source: Blanchflower et al. (1993) from US *General Social Surveys*. That paper gives data for each year. Weighted to control for oversampling of blacks in certain years.

Table 9 Job satisfaction in the United Kingdom: 1973–83

	1973	*1978*	*1983*
Very satisfied %	42.7	44.5	39.3
Fairly satisfied %	42.8	39.4	43.5
Neither sat. nor dissat. %	7.7	4.6	5.3
Rather dissatisfied %	4.4	7.9	8.0
Very dissatisfied %	2.4	3.5	4.3
Number in sample	13,845	11,814	8,417

Source: Blanchflower et al. (1993) from the *General Household Surveys*.

reports the statistics for the overall US sample. The raw numbers reveal fairly large fluctuations – the number jumped to almost 56% in 1975 and was as low as 43% in 1987 – so it is especially difficult to find a time trend in the statistics.

British data are given in Table 9. The proportion stating 'very satisfied' with their job is on average 43% over the period, which is similar to the numbers for the United States. In 1973, the proportion of British adults calling themselves very satisfied at work was 42.7%. In 1983, at the end of the period for which GHS data are available, the number was 39.3%. There is thus if anything some sign of a slight fall in the level of job satisfaction in Britain.

This finding of fairly flat job satisfaction levels through time mirrors Weaver (1980) on earlier US data. One interpretation, supported by the evidence in Clark and Oswald (1994), is that satisfaction is somehow inherently relativistic, and based on comparisons with others.

Finding 7. *In Britain and America, the level of job satisfaction is not rising over time.*

5 CONCLUSIONS

Every day, in every industrialised country of the world, journalists and politicians give out a conscious and unconscious message. It is that better economic performance means more happiness for a nation. This idea is rarely questioned. We feel we would be more cheery if our boss raised our pay, and assume that countries must be roughly the same.

The results in this paper suggest that, in a developed nation, economic progress buys only a small amount of extra happiness. Four main pieces of evidence have been offered for this claim.

1 Reported happiness in the United States has gone up only fractionally over the post-war period.
2 Reported levels of 'satisfaction with life' in Europe are only slightly higher than they were twenty years ago. Some countries show falls.
3 Although the rate of suicide in Britain has fallen by approximately one third over the last hundred years, the number for men has risen, in almost all Western nations, from the 1970s to the present. Rich countries seem to have high suicide rates.
4 Job satisfaction has not increased, over those parts of the last quarter of a century for which data are available, in the United States and the United Kingdom.

These gains in national well-being appear to be so slight that a case could be made, as by Richard Easterlin (1974), that economic growth is worthless. This paper argues that Easterlin is wrong – but only just.

Because the task of measuring well-being is a difficult and relatively unconventional one, the paper's results cannot be accepted uncritically. First, it might be argued that interview responses to happiness and satisfaction questions do not mean anything reliable. Second, it might be argued that the use of suicide data as an indicator of a society's happiness is too strange to be taken seriously, or that such data are unhelpful because they are a reflection of mental illness and not of any objectively low quality of life. There is no wholly convincing way to dispose of such objections. As in any area of social science, it is prudent to view the paper's punchlines cautiously. Nevertheless, a simple reply to critics is that these kinds of statistics are probably the only ones available to us if we wish to measure well-being, and that, at the very least, they raise doubts about routine beliefs. Moreover, counter-arguments to the methodological criticisms have been produced many times. It is known in the psychological and medical literatures that objective economic events are correlated with happiness scores and with suicide (and para-suicide).

Another possible line of attack on the paper's conclusions is to appeal to common-sense observation. How can it be, one might ask, that money buys little well-being and yet we see individuals around us constantly striving to make more of it? The answer may be that what matters to someone who lives in a rich country is his or her relative income. A spectator who leaps up at a football match gets at first a much better view of the game; by the time his neighbours are up it is no better than before. If there is something to this, it would explain why intuition is capable of misleading us about the national benefits of economic performance. Such intuition has been built up by observing how each of us feels as our income rises. Yet, implicitly, that holds others' incomes constant. Hence common sense may not be a good guide to what happens when a whole society gets richer.

The conclusions of the paper do not mean that economic forces have little impact on people's lives. A consistent theme through the paper's different forms of evidence has been the vulnerability of human beings to joblessness. Unemployment appears to be the primary economic source of unhappiness. If so, economic growth should not be a government's primary concern.

6 BACKGROUND NOTES

The main sources of information used in the paper are the *Eurobarometer Surveys* of 1973 onwards, the British *General Household Surveys* of 1973 onwards, the first 1991 sweep of the *British Household Panel Study*, and the US *General Social Surveys* of 1972 onwards. These are face-to-face surveys of randomly sampled individuals. Suicide data come from the Office of Population Censuses and Surveys. All the paper's sources of data are publicly available. This paper has not attempted to document its literature sources in the way a normal academic paper would. The paper's general conclusions in some cases agree or overlap with those in Andrews (1991), Smith (1979), Shin (1980), Thomas and Hughes (1986), Veenhoven (1991, 1993) and Weaver (1980). Although little-read by economists, the pioneering work on the statistical study of well-being includes Andrews and Withey (1976), Andrews and Inglehart (1978), Campbell et al. (1976), Campbell (1981), Cantril (1965), Diener (1984), and Larsen et al. (1984). A good introduction is Argyle (1989). Economists interested in dipping into a huge recent literature might also look at Andrews (1991), Warr (1987, 1990*a*, *b*) and Ng (1996). Blanchflower and Oswald (1996) conclude that the young are getting systematically happier. Birdi et al. (1995), Clark et al. (1996) and Warr (1992) argue that job satisfaction is U-shaped in age, and give other results. Blanchflower and Oswald (1997) find the self-employed are happier.

Hirsch (1976) is a well-known critique of the value of increased real national income. Scitovsky (1976) makes similar arguments. My attention has been drawn to an early happiness study in this *Journal*, Morawetz (1977). Many of the British results on the distress caused by unemployment are due to Jahoda (1982), Warr (1978 onwards) and Jackson et al. (1983). New work includes Whelan (1992) and Gallie and Russell (1995). The unemployment findings are now conventional in the psychology literature but probably still not well-known among economists. Innovative early work by economists includes Bjorklund (1985) and Edin (1988), who fail to find marked effects for Sweden. More recent research has uncovered large negative effects of joblessness upon well-being. The findings of Gerlach and Stephan (1996), Korpi (1997) and Winkelmann and Winkelmann (1997) seem particularly important. They control for person-specific fixed effects. The coefficient on unemployment in a panel well-being equation turns out to be fairly similar to that in a pure cross-section equation.

There are potential links between the happiness literature and the literatures on the quality of life and the Human Development Index, but they have yet to be forged. Nussbaum and Sen (1993) contains a set of essays on the border between philosophy and economics. Smith (1993) is a critical inquiry into HDI. Crafts (1997) is a recent application of HDI methods.

If well-being depends upon relative income, most of economists' optimal tax theory is incomplete or worse. The standard literature assumes that in setting taxes a government should pay no attention to people's feelings of how they compare with others: little or no role is assigned to personal notions of justice or relative deprivation. Some of the few attempts to change this are Boskin and Sheshinski (1978), Layard (1980) and Oswald (1983).

International comparisons using the multi-national *International Social Survey Programme* are given in Birdi et al. (1995), Blanchflower and Freeman (1997) and Curtice (1993). This paper focuses on well-being in developed countries. It seems likely that real income growth does buy a lot of happiness in a developing nation. Veenhoven (1991) presents evidence consistent with that.

References

Andrews, F. M. (1991). 'Stability and change in levels and structure of subjective well-being: USA 1972 and 1988.' *Social Indicators Research*, vol. 25, pp. 1–30.

Andrews, F. M. and Inglehart, R. F. (1978). 'The structure of subjective well-being in nine western societies.' *Social Indicators Research*, vol. 6, pp. 73–90.

Andrews, F. M. and Withey, S. B. (1976). *Social Indicators of Well Being*, New York: Plenum Press.

Argyle, M. (1989). *The Psychology of Happiness*. London: Routledge.

Birdi, K. M., Warr, P. B. and Oswald, A. J. (1995). 'Age differences in three components of employee well-being.' *Applied Psychology: An International Review*, vol. 44, pp. 345–73.

Bjorklund, A. (1985). 'Unemployment and mental health: some evidence from panel data.' *Journal of Human Resources*, vol. 20, pp. 169–83.

Blanchflower, D. G. and Freeman, R. B. (1997). 'The legacy of communist labor relations,' *Industrial and Labor Relations Review*, forthcoming.

Blanchflower, D. G. and Oswald, A. J. (1996). 'The rising well-being of the young.' Paper presented at an NBER Conference on Disadvantaged Youth, North Carolina, December.

Blanchflower, D. G. and Oswald, A. J. (1997). 'What makes an entrepreneur?' *Journal of Labor Economics*, forthcoming.

Blanchflower, D. G., Oswald, A. J. and Warr, P. B. (1993). 'Well-being over time in Britain and the USA.' Paper presented at an Economics of Happiness Conference, London School of Economics.

Boskin, M. and Sheshinski, E. (1978). 'Optimal redistributive taxation when individual welfare depends upon relative income.' *Quarterly Journal of Economics*, vol. 92, pp. 589–601.

Campbell, A. (1981). *The Sense of Well-Being in America*, New York: McGraw Hill.

Campbell, A., Converse, P. E. and Rodgers, W. L. (1976). *The Quality of American Life*, New York: Russell Sage Foundation.

Cantril, H. (1965). *The Pattern of Human Concerns*, New Brunswick: Rutgers University Press.

Charlton, J., Kelly, S., Dunnell, K., Evans, B., Jenkins, R., Wallis, R. (1992). 'Trends in suicide deaths in England and Wales'. *Population Trends*, vol. 69, Autumn, Parts I and II.

Clark, A. E. (1992). 'Job satisfaction and gender: why are women so happy at work?' University of Essex, Economics Department Working Paper 415.

Clark. A. E. (1996*a*). 'Job satisfaction in Britain', *British Journal of Industrial Relations*, vol. 34, pp. 189–217.

Clark, A. E. (1996*b*). 'Working and well-being: some international evidence', mimeo, OECD, Paris.

Clark, A. E. and Oswald, A. J. (1994). 'Unhappiness and unemployment.' *Economic Journal.*, vol. 104, 648–59.

Clark, A. E. and Oswald, A. J. (1996). 'Satisfaction and comparison income.' *Journal of Public Economics*, vol. 61, pp. 359–81.

Clark, A. E., Oswald, A. J. and Warr, P. B. (1996). 'Is job satisfaction U-shaped in age?' *Journal of Occupational and Organizational Psychology*, vol. 69, pp. 57–81.

Crafts. N. F. R. (1997). 'Some dimensions of the "quality of life" during the British industrial revolution', mimeo, London School of Economics.

Curtice, J. (1993). 'Satisfying work if you can get it.' In *International Social Attitudes and the Tenth BSA Report* (ed. R. Jowell et al.). London: Dartmouth.

Diener, E. (1984). 'Subjective well-being.' *Psychological Bulletin*, vol. 95, pp. 542–75.

Di Tella, R., MacCulloch, R. and Oswald, A. J. (1996). 'The macroeconomics of happiness', mimeo, Oxford and Warwick.

Dooley, D., Catalano, R., Rook, K. and Serxner, S. (1989). 'Economic stress and suicide: multi-level analysis', Parts 1 and 2, *Suicide and Life-Threatening Behaviour*, vol. 19, pp. 321–36 and 337–51.

Douthitt, R. A., MacDonald, M. and Mullis, R. (1992). 'The relationship between measures of subjective and economic well-being: a new look.' *Social Indicators Research*, vol. 26, pp. 407–22.

Durkheim, E. (1897). *Suicide: A Study in Sociology*, 1992 reprinting, London: Routledge.

Easterlin, R. (1974). 'Does economic growth improve the human lot? Some empirical evidence.' In *Nations and Households in Economic Growth: Essays in Honour of Moses Abramowitz* (eds P. A. David and M. W. Reder). New York and London: Academic Press.

Easterlin, R. (1995). 'Will raising the incomes of all increase the happiness of all?' *Journal of Economic Behaviour and Organization*, vol. 27, pp. 35–48.

Edin, P.-A. (1988). 'Individual consequences of plant closures, Uppsala University, doctoral dissertation.

Fox, C. R. and Kahneman, D. (1992). 'Correlations, causes and heuristics in surveys of life satisfaction.' *Social Indicators Research*, vol. 27. pp. 221–34.

Frank, R. H. (1985). *Choosing the Right Pond*. New York and Oxford: Oxford University Press.

Gallie, D. and Russell, H. (1995). 'Unemployment, gender and life satisfaction', mimeo, Nuffield College.

Gerlach, K. and Stephan, G. (1996). 'A paper on unhappiness and unemployment in Germany', *Economics Letters*, vol. 32, pp. 325–30.

Hirsch, F. (1976). *The Social Limits of Growth*, Cambridge, Mass: Harvard University Press.

Humphry, D. (1992). 'Rational suicide among the elderly.' *Suicide and Life-Threatening Behaviour*, vol. 22, pp. 125–9.

Inglehart, R. (1990). *Culture Shift in Advanced Industrial Society.* Princeton: Princeton University Press.

Jackson, P. R., Stafford, E. M., Banks, M. H. and Warr, P. B. (1983). 'Unemployement and psychological distress in young people: the moderating role of employment commitment.' *Journal of Applied Psychology*, vol. 68, pp. 525–35.

Jahoda, M. (1982). *Employment and Unemployment: A Social Psychological Approach.* Cambridge: Cambridge University Press.

Kammerling, R. M. and O'Connor, S. (1993). 'Unemployment rate as predictor of rate of psychiatric admission.' *British Medical Journal*, vol. 307, pp. 1536–9.

Korpi, T. (1997). 'Is utility related to employment status?', *Labour Economics*, vol. 4, pp. 125–48.

Larsen, R. J., Diener, E. and Emmons, R. A. (1984). 'An evaluation of subjective well-being measures.' *Social Indicators Research*, vol. 17, pp. 1–18.

Layard, R. (1980). 'Human satisfactions and public policy.' *Economic Journal.* vol. 90, pp. 737–50.

Morawetz, D. (1977). 'Income distribution and self-rated happiness: some empirical evidence.' *Economic Journal*, vol. 87, pp. 511–22.

Mullis, R. J. (1992). 'Measures of economic well-being as predictors of psychological well-being.' *Social Indicators Research*, vol. 26, pp. 119–35.

Ng, Y.-K. (1996). 'Happiness surveys: some comparability issues and an exploratory survey based on just perceivable increments.' *Social Indicators Research*, vol. 38, pp. 1–27.

Nussbaum, M. C. and Sen, A. (1993), eds *The Quality of Life.* Oxford: Oxford University Press.

Oswald, A. J. (1983). 'Altruism, jealousy and the theory of optimal non-linear taxation.' *Journal of Public Economics*, vol. 20, pp. 77–87.

Pavot, W. (1991). 'Further validation of the satisfaction with life scale: evidence for the cross-method convergence of well-being measures.' *Journal of Personality Assessment*, vol. 57, pp. 149–61.

Platt, S. and Kreitman, N. (1985). 'Para-suicide and unemployment among men in Edinburgh 1968–82.' *Psychological Medicine*, vol. 291, pp. 1563–6.

Richman, J. (1992). 'A rational approach to rational suicide.' *Suicide and Life-Threatening Behaviour*, vol. 22, pp. 130–41.

Scitovsky, T. 1976:. *The Joyless Economy.* Oxford: Oxford University Press.

Shin, D. C. (1980). 'Does rapid economic growth improve the human lot? Some empirical evidence.' *Social Indicators Research*, vol. 8, pp. 199–221.

Smith, P. (1993). 'Measuring human development.' *Asian Economic Journal*, pp. 89–104.

Smith, R. (1985). 'I can't stand it any more: suicide and unemployment.' *British Medical Journal*, vol. 291, pp. 1563–6.

Smith, T. W. (1979). 'Happiness: time trends, seasonal variation, inter-survey differences and other mysteries.' *Social Psychology Quarterly*, vol. 42, pp. 18–30.

Thomas, M. E. and Hughes, M. (1986). 'The continuing significance of race: a study of race, class, and quality of life in America. 1972–1985, *American Sociological Review*, vol. 5, pp. 830–41.

Veenhoven, R. (1991). 'Is happiness relative?' *Social Indicators Research*, vol. 24, pp. 1–34.

Veenhoven, R. (1993). *Happiness in Nations: Subjective Appreciation of Life in 56 Nations 1946–1992.* Rotterdam: Erasmus University Risho.

Warr, P. B. (1978). 'A study of psychological well-being.' *British Journal of Psychology*, vol. 69, pp. 111–21.

Warr, P. B. (1987). *Work, Unemployment, and Mental Health*. Oxford: Oxford University Press.

Warr, P. B. (1990*a*). 'The measurement of well-being and other aspects of mental health.' *Journal of Occupational Psychology*, vol. 63, pp. 193–210.

Warr, P. B. (1990*b*). 'Decision latitude, job demands, and employee well-being.' *Work and Stress*, vol. 4, pp. 285–94.

Warr, P. B. (1992). 'Age and occupational well-being.' *Psychology and Aging*, vol. 7, pp. 37–45.

Warr, P. B., Jackson, P. and Banks, M. (1988). 'Unemployment and mental health: some British studies.' *Journal of Social Issues*, vol. 44, pp. 47–68.

Watson, D. and Clark, L. (1991). 'Self versus peer ratings of specific emotional traits: evidence of convergent and discriminant validity.' *Journal of Personality and Social Psychology*, vol. 60, pp. 927–40.

Weaver, C. N. (1980). 'Job satisfaction in the United States in the 1970s.' *Journal of Applied Psychology*, vol. 65, pp. 364–7.

Whelan, C. T. (1992). 'The role of income, life-style deprivation and financial strain in mediating the impact of unemployment on psychological distress: evidence from the Republic of Ireland.' *Journal of Occupational and Organizational Psychology*, vol. 65, pp. 331–44.

Winkelmann, L. and Winkelmann, R. (1997). 'Why are the unemployed so unhappy? Evidence from panel data.' *Economica*, forthcoming.

15

THE FRAME OF REFERENCE AS A PUBLIC GOOD*

Robert H. Frank

Does consuming more goods make people happier? For a broad spectrum of goods, available evidence suggests that beyond some point the answer is essentially no. Much of this evidence is from the large and growing scientific literature on the determinants of life-satisfaction and psychological well-being.[1] Evidence from this literature also suggests, however, that there are ways of spending time and money that do have the potential to increase people's satisfaction with their lives, and herein lies a message of considerable importance for policy-makers.

The psychologist's conception of human well-being is somewhat different from the economist's. Economists speak of an individual's utility, which in traditional economic models is assumed to be an increasing function of present and future consumption of goods, leisure, and other amenities that people typically view as desirable. Faced with a limited income, the individual is assumed to choose among alternatives so as to maximise her utility. The analogous construct in the psychological literature is 'subjective well-being', a composite measure of life-satisfaction, positive affect, and negative affect.

Operational measures of subjective well-being take one of several forms. By far the most popular approach in the psychological literature has been simply to ask people how happy or satisfied they are.[2] For example, people may be asked to respond, on a numerical scale, to a question like, 'All things considered, how satisfied are you with your life as a whole these days?' Or, 'Thinking of your life as a whole, would you consider yourself (*a*) very happy; (*b*) fairly happy; or (*c*) not happy?' Another approach measures the frequency and intensity of positive affect by asking people the extent to which they agree with such statements as: 'When good things happen to me, it strongly affects me.'

More recently, neuroscientists have also used brainwave data to assess positive and negative affect. Subjects with relatively greater electrical activity in the left prefrontal region of the brain are likely to indicate strong agreement with statements like the ones above, while those with relatively greater electrical activity in the right prefrontal region are much more likely to disagree with these statements.[3] The left prefrontal

* I thank Jeremy Chua, Rajib Das, Nadja Marinova, Rupal Patel, Lisa Shenouda, and Andrea Wasserman for their able research assistance.
[1] For an excellent and accessible survey of this literature, see Myers (1993).
[2] See Easterlin (1974).
[3] Davidson (1992).

region of the brain is rich in receptors for the neurotransmitter dopamine, higher concentrations of which been shown independently to be correlated with positive affect.[4]

Satisfaction as identified by any of these measures is predictive of a variety of observable behaviours that most of us take to be indicative of well-being. For example, people who call themselves happy, or who have relatively high levels of electrical activity in the left prefrontal region, are more likely to be rated as happy by friends; more likely to initiate social contacts with friends; more likely to respond to requests for help; less likely to suffer from psychosomatic illnesses; less likely to be absent from work; less likely to be involved in disputes at work; less likely to die prematurely; less likely to attempt suicide; less likely to seek psychological counselling.[5] In short, it seems that what the psychologists call subjective well-being is a real phenomenon. Empirical measures of it have high consistency, reliability, and validity.[6] In what follows, it is not my claim that the only goal of a person or a society should be to achieve the highest possible levels of subjective well-being. (Would you prefer to be Socrates dissatisfied or a pig satisfied?) For the purposes of this discussion, I need assume only that an increase in subjective well-being counts as a good thing if it is achieved without having to compromise other important values.

My claim is that available evidence on the determinants of subjective well-being suggests a variety of ways this could be achieved. The basic idea is simple – namely, that, whereas across-the-board increases in many forms of material consumption goods have little discernible effect on subjective well-being in the long run, the same resources can be used in alternative ways that do give rise to lasting increases in subjective well-being.

1 THE DETERMINANTS OF SUBJECTIVE WELL-BEING

Richard Easterlin was the first to call economists' attention to survey data that illuminate the relationship between material living standards and subjective well-being.[7] Easterlin saw three significant patterns in the self-reported satisfaction data. First, he noted that satisfaction levels across individuals within a given country vary directly with income – richer people, on the average, are more satisfied than their poorer countrymen. This relationship is illustrated in Fig. 1, which plots average satisfaction against annual income for a US sample of 4,942 persons surveyed between 1981 and 1984.

Second, Easterlin noted that the average satisfaction levels within a given country tend to be highly stable over time, even in the face of significant economic growth. Fig. 2, for example, plots the percentage of Americans surveyed who respond 'very happy' when asked, 'Taken all together, how would you say things are these days – would you say that you are very happy, pretty happy, or not too happy?' Veenhoven (1993) found

---

[4] Reported by Goleman (1996).
[5] For surveys of this evidence see Frank (1985*b*, chapter 2) and Clark and Oswald (1996).
[6] Diener and Lucas (1997).
[7] Easterlin (1974).

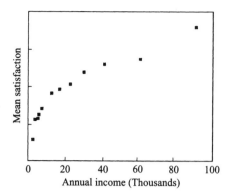

Fig. 1 Income *vs.* satisfaction in the United States, 1981–4
Source: Diener et al. (1993).

mean subjective well-being over time for Japan to be almost completely stable over the period 1958–87, a particularly striking result in view of the fact that *per-capita* income in that country grew more than fivefold during that period.

A third and final pattern noted by Easterlin is that although average reported satisfaction levels exhibit substantial variation across countries, they are not strongly correlated with average levels of national income. Easterlin argued that these patterns are consistent with the hypothesis that relative income is far more important than absolute income as a determinant of individual satisfaction levels. His pessimistic conclusion was that economic growth does not improve the human condition, since no matter how prosperous a society becomes in absolute terms, the frequency with which people experience relative deprivation will not be much affected.

Subsequent work has suggested the need to qualify Easterlin's claims in several ways. For example, most careful studies find a clear time-series relationship between subjective well-being and absolute income at extremely low levels of absolute income. Thus,

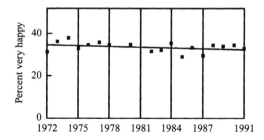

Fig. 2 Percent very happy, United States, 1972–91
Source: National Opinion Research Center (1991).

in a country in which most people lack minimally adequate shelter and nutrition, across-the-board increases in income appear, not surprisingly, to yield significant and lasting improvements in subjective well-being.[8] In the same vein, it now appears that average satisfaction levels are in fact significantly lower in extremely poor countries than in rich ones.[9] Subsequent work has also shown that even within countries, the positive link between income and reported satisfaction is significant primarily at the lowest levels of relative income.[10] For individuals in the middle and upper portions of the income distribution within such countries, variations in income explain less than 2% of variations in reported satisfaction levels.[11] But it still does appear that average satisfaction levels within a country are not significantly correlated over time with income.

2 BEHAVIOURAL EVIDENCE FROM THE ECONOMICS LITERATURE

Unlike psychologists, who often rely on survey evidence, economists prefer behavioural evidence when attempting to make inferences about sources of human satisfaction. The relevant literature is not extensive, but there are several studies that shed light on the strength of concerns about relative consumption. In one recent paper, for example, Neumark and Postlewaite (1996) investigate how individual labour supply decisions depend on the incomes of important reference group members. The difficulty in such efforts has always been that it is hard to know which others a person includes in her reference group. Neumark and Postlewaite solve this problem by examining the behaviour of sisters. Does a woman's decision about whether to work outside the home depend on her sister's economic circumstances? In conventional models it would not, but Neumark and Postlewaite find differently for a sample of women whose sisters are not employed. Specifically, they find that sister A is 16–25% more likely to work outside the home if sister B's husband earns more than sister A's husband.[12]

Sheryl Ball and her co-authors have shown that even simple laboratory manipulations of status can have profound implications for the terms of market exchange.[13] In one experiment, for example, they awarded half of their subjects 'stars' on the basis of their performance on a transparently meaningless quiz. These subjects consistently received better terms when they exchanged goods with subjects who did not receive stars.

In *Choosing the Right Pond*, I described additional behavioural evidence consistent with the view that status concerns have significant weight in economic decisions. There I showed that the wage distributions within firms are typically much more compressed than we would expect if workers did not care about relative income.[14] Likewise, the incidence of piece-rate pay schemes is much lower, and the frequency with which

---

[8] Diener and Diener (1995).
[9] Ibid.
[10] Ibid.
[11] Ibid.
[12] Their Table 3.
[13] Ball et al. (1996).
[14] Frank (1985*b*, chapter 4). See also Frank (1984).

workers go on strike is much higher, than we would expect if relative income did not matter. In addition, the observed structural differences between the compensation packages of unionised firms and non-unionised firms – for example, the fact that unionised workers tend to receive a much larger share of total compensation in the form of non-monetary fringe benefits – are difficult to explain without reference to collective action problems that arise from concerns about status.[15] The fact that the rich save significantly higher proportions of their permanent incomes than do the poor[16] is inconsistent with traditional economics models,[17] but this pattern is predicted by models in which utility depends on relative consumption.[18]

In a recent paper I have attempted to estimate the significance of occupational status in career choices using earnings and occupation data from a survey of recent graduates of Cornell University.[19] I found a strong negative correlation between annual earnings and the degree to which an employee's occupation was viewed by outsiders as being socially responsible. I found the same pattern by examining the fees paid to expert witnesses who testify on behalf of the tobacco industry and their counterparts who testify for the American Heart Association and other public interest groups; and the same pattern shows up in pay differences between public interest lawyers and those employed in other segments of the legal profession. I also described survey evidence from a sample of graduating seniors who reported that they would require very large premiums before being willing to switch to a less socially responsible employer.

In sum, the claim that satisfaction depends heavily on relative position is supported by considerable evidence from both the psychological literature on subjective well-being and by at least fragmentary evidence from the behavioural economics literature. I am aware of no empirical or theoretical evidence against this claim.

3 DOES *ANYTHING* MATTER?

Once people escape the physical deprivations associated with abject poverty, do absolute living standards matter at all? It is easy to see how Richard Easterlin could have interpreted patterns in the data on subjective well-being to suggest that they do not. After all, the struggle to get ahead seems to play out with much the same psychological effects in rich societies as in those with more modest levels of wealth. In each case, people who are doing well relative to others, or whose conditions are improving over time, appear more satisfied than those who are doing poorly relative to others or whose conditions are deteriorating over time.

Perhaps the clearest message of the psychological literature is that, beyond some point, across-the-board increases in spending on many types of material goods do not produce any lasting increment in subjective well-being. Imagine people from two soci-

---

[15] Frank (1985*b*, chapter 8).
[16] Dynan et al. (1996).
[17] In particular it is inconsistent with the permanent income hypothesis (Friedman, 1957) and the life-cycle hypothesis (Modigliani and Brumberg, 1955).
[18] See Duesenberry (1949), Kosicki (1987).
[19] Frank (1996).

eties that are identical in every respect save one: In society A, everyone lives in a house with 5,000 square feet of floor space, whereas in society B each house has only 3,000 square feet. Provided people from the two societies do not come into frequent contact with one another, psychologists and neuroscientists are unlikely to be able to discern any significant differences in their respective average levels of subjective well-being. Each society will have its own local norm for what constitutes adequate housing, and people in each society will therefore be equally likely to be satisfied with their houses and other aspects of their lives.

Of course, it takes more real resources to build 5,000 square-foot houses instead of 3,000 square-foot houses. Is there some alternative way of spending these resources that could have produced a lasting increment in subjective well-being? If the answer to this question is no, then policy-makers face an empty agenda. In fact, however, the scientific literature has identified a number of ways in which additional resources can be used to create large and enduring increases in subjective well-being.

Consider the following sequence of thought experiments in which we compare people from two societies with equal wealth levels but different spending patterns. In each case, let us again suppose that residents of one society live in 5,000 square-foot houses while those in the other live in 3,000 square-foot houses. And in each case, let us suppose that the residents of the society with the smaller houses use the resources thus saved to bring about some other change in the conditions of their lives. For example:

Who is more satisfied, residents of Society A, who have 5,000-square-foot houses and a one-hour automobile commute to work through heavy traffic, or residents of Society B, who have 3,000-square foot houses and a 15-minute commute by rapid transit? The only difference between these societies is that they have allocated their resources differently between housing and transportation. The residents of society B have used the same resources they could have employed to build larger housing to transform the nature of their commute to work. The evidence, as noted, suggests that their smaller houses predict no persistent difference in their subjective well-being. Of course, someone who moved from society B to society A would be pleased at first to experience the additional living space, but in time would adapt and consider the larger house the norm. Someone who moved from society B to society A would also initially experience stress from the extended commute through heavy traffic. Over time, his consciousness of this stress would diminish. But there is an important distinction: unlike his adaptation to the larger house, which will be essentially complete, his adaptation to his new commuting pattern will be only partial. Even after long periods of adjustment, most people experience the task of navigating through heavy commuter traffic as stressful. In this respect, the effect of exposure to heavy traffic is similar to the effect of exposure to noise and other irritants. For example, even though a large increase in background noise at a constant, steady level is experienced as less intrusive as time passes, prolonged exposure nonetheless produces lasting elevations in blood pressure. If the noise is not only loud but sporadic, people remain conscious of their heightened irritability even after extended periods of adaptation, and their symptoms of central nervous system distress become more pronounced. Commuting through heavy traffic is in many ways more like exposure to loud sporadic noise than to constant background noise. Delays are difficult to predict, and one never quite gets used to being cut off by others who think their time is more valuable than anyone else's.

Neurophysiologists would find higher levels of cortisol, norepinephrine, and other stress hormones in the cerebro-spinal fluid of residents of the society with the lengthy commute. The prolonged experience of such stress is also known to suppress immune function and shorten longevity.[20] Urban bus drivers, for example, experience an unusually high number of stress-related illnesses.[21] Among people who commute to work, the incidence of such illness rises with the length of commute,[22] and is significantly lower among those who commute by bus or rail.[23] No one has done the experiment to discover whether people from Society *A* would report lower levels of life satisfaction than people from Society *B*. But even in the absence of such survey evidence, we may suspect that most people would prefer to see their children live in society *B*.

Who is more satisfied, residents of Society A, *who have* 5,000-*square-foot houses and no time to exercise each day, or residents of Society* B, *who have* 3,000-*square-foot houses and exercise for* 45 *minutes each day?* Again we have two societies that have different bundles from the same menu of opportunities. Residents of society *B* could have built larger houses, but instead they spent less time at work each day and devoted the time saved to exercise. Numerous studies have documented the positive physiological and psychological effects of regular aerobic exercise.[24] Exercisers report more frequent and intense positive feelings and tend to have better functioning immune systems.[25] Exercisers have higher life expectancy and are less likely to suffer from heart disease, stroke, diabetes, hypertension, and a variety of other ailments.[26] Evidence for the causal nature of these relationships is seen in the fact that subjects randomly assigned to exercise programmes experience improved physical and psychological well-being.[27] And although many people report that exercise is an unpleasant experience at first, most adapt to it quickly and come to think of it as pleasurable. Here again, the evidence weighs heavily in favour of the residents of society *B*.

Who is more satisfied, residents of society A, *who have* 5,000-*square-foot houses and one evening each month to get together with friends, or residents of Society* B, *who have* 3,000-*square-foot houses and get together with friends four evenings a month?* The question is again whether one use of time produces a larger impact on subjective well-being than another. Because the residents of society *A* work longer hours, they can build larger houses but have less time to socialise with friends. Here again, the evidence suggests that whereas the payoff when all have larger houses is small and fleeting, the pleasures that result from deeper social relationships are both profound and enduring. People with rich networks of active social relationships are much more likely to call themselves happy, and are much more likely to be described as happy by friends.[28] People who lack such networks tend to be less physically healthy, and confront a higher risk of dying at every

---

[20] DeLongis et al. (1988) and Stokols et al. (1978)
[21] Evans (1994)
[22] Koslowsky et al. (1995)
[23] Taylor and Pocock (1972)
[24] For a survey, see Plante and Rodin (1990)
[25] Fontane (1996)
[26] Blair (1989)
[27] Palmer (1995)
[28] Argyle (1997)

age.[29] In this case, too, the neurophysiologists would have no difficulty discerning which people came from society *B*.

4 IF SPENDING DIFFERENTLY WOULD MAKE US HAPPIER, WHY DON'T WE DO IT?

There are at least two plausible explanations for our failure to allocate available resources in the best possible way. Our spending patterns are in part a result of incomplete information about the extent to which we will adapt to different goods and experiences; and in part they are a result of the fact that many forms of consumption appear much more attractive to individuals than they are to society as a whole. On the first point, consider a person whose wage is such that he could purchase a 30% more expensive car by working an additional Saturday each month, which in his case would mean not spending that Saturday with friends. Standard economic theory suggests that he will work the extra Saturday if the satisfaction afforded by the nicer car outweighs the satisfaction provided by the company of his friends. Since the individual will typically not know how each alternative will alter his subjective well-being, he is forced to construct rough estimates.

Introspection may provide reasonably good estimates of how changes in consumption will affect subjective well-being in the short run. But because adaptation is inherently difficult to anticipate, the long-run effects of such changes will be harder to forecast. In the choice at hand, this may create a strong bias in favour of choosing the more expensive car over the extra day with friends. Thus, if the new car is substantially faster than the individual's current car, its acquisition will provide an initial thrill. Over time, however, he will grow accustomed to the car's capabilities and its capacity to stimulate will decay.

The contribution to subjective well-being of additional time spent with friends will have a markedly different time profile. As relationships continue over time, the satisfaction they provide tends to increase rather than diminish. In the long run, extra time spent with friends might well prove the better choice. Yet the short-run increment in satisfaction might easily be higher with the new car. And to the extent that these short-run effects are the most available source of information to the individual at the moment of decision, they bias choice in favour of the nicer car.

A second, more important, source of bias in our spending patterns would exist even in a world of fully informed consumers. It stems from the fact that when payoffs depend on relative position, the individual payoff from many types of spending is different from the collective payoff. Military arms races provide perhaps the clearest illustration. From each individual nation's point of view, the worst outcome is not to buy armaments while its rivals do. Yet when *all* spend more on weapons, no one is more secure than before. Most nations recognise the importance of maintaining military parity, and the result all too often has been a wasteful escalation of expenditures on arms. Nations would spend much less on weapons if they could make their military

---

[29] Berkman and Syme (1979), House et al. (1982).

spending decisions collectively. And with the money thus saved, each side could then spend more on things that promote, rather than threaten, human well-being.

Similar forces affect each family's decision about how much to save. Parents want to save for retirement, but they also have other important goals. For instance, they want to make sure that their children receive an education that qualifies them for the best jobs. For the typical American family, that means buying a home in the best school district it can afford. Most of us thus confront an almost irresistible opportunity to do more for our children: by saving a little less for retirement, we can purchase homes in better school districts.

From the collective vantage point, however, such moves are futile in the same way that military arms races are futile. When each family saves less in order to buy a house in a better school district, the net effect is merely to bid up the prices of those houses. Students end up at the same schools they would have attended if all families had spent less. In the process, an important goal – being able to maintain an adequate living standard in retirement – is sacrificed for essentially no gain. Yet no family, acting alone, can solve this problem, just as no nation can unilaterally stop a military arms race.

Housing is of course not the only expenditure that is driven by forces similar to those that govern military arms races. Spending on cars fits the same pattern, as does spending on clothing, furniture, wine, jewelry, sports equipment, and a host of other goods. The things we feel we 'need' depend on the kinds of things that others have, and our needs thus grow when we find ourselves in the presence of others who have more than we do. Yet when all of us spend more, the new, higher spending level simply becomes the norm.

There is yet another difficulty, one that is independent of the mechanics of the human psychological reward system. It lies in the fact that promotion decisions on the job often depend heavily on the relative number of hours someone works. Thus, an associate in a law firm who goes home at 5 p.m. each day instead of 8 p.m. not only earns less in relative terms, she is also less likely to be promoted to partner. If all the associates left the office a little earlier, of course, no one's promotion prospects would be affected. But each individual has control over only the hours that she herself works. She cannot unilaterally decree that everyone scale back. Landers et al. (1996) report that associates in large law firms voice a strong preference for having all work fewer hours, even if that means lower pay, and yet few dare take that step unilaterally.

To the extent that misallocations result from our failure to anticipate different patterns of adaptation in different domains, there is the possibility for unilateral action to improve matters. By becoming better informed and more disciplined, we can make decisions that will better promote our long-term interests. The brisk sales of books urging the adoption of simplified styles of living suggest that many people are at least receptive to this possibility.

To the extent, however, that misallocations are the result of the fact that certain forms of consumption are more attractive to individuals than to society as a whole, the potential for improvement through unilateral action may be sharply limited. Thus, as we have seen, the problem confronting individuals who must decide how to spend their time and money is in many ways like the one confronting nations that must decide how much to spend on armaments. Just as nations end up spending too much on weapons and too little on other things, ordinary people end up spending too much time earning money to buy private goods, and too little time doing other things.

When nations attempt to curtail military arms races, they try to negotiate agreements that specify precisely what kinds and quantities of weapons are permissible. The idea of private citizens conducting similar negotiations about how to allocate their time and money seems wildly impractical. Fortunately, however, the underlying problem can be attacked without trying to micro-manage people's spending decisions at all.

5 ONE SOLUTION: A PROGRESSIVE CONSUMPTION TAX

If our problem is that certain forms of private consumption currently seem more attractive to individuals than to society as a whole, the simplest solution is to make those forms less attractive by taxing them. Without raising our overall tax bill at all, a progressive consumption tax would change our incentives in precisely the desired ways.

Proposals to tax consumption raise the spectre of forbidding complexity – of citizens having to save receipts for each purchase, of politicians and producers bickering over which products are to be exempt, and so on. Yet a system of progressive consumption taxation could be achieved by a simple one-line amendment to the federal tax code – namely, by making savings exempt from tax. This is so because the amount a family consumes each year is simply the difference between the amount it earns and the amount it saves. Administratively, a progressive consumption tax is thus essentially the same as our current progressive income tax. An example is provided in the appendix.

The progressive consumption tax illustrated in the appendix is different from other consumption taxes like the value added tax or the national sales tax. Those taxes are levied at the same rate no matter how much a family consumes, and have therefore been criticised as regressive on the grounds that wealthy families typically save much higher proportions of their incomes than poor families. But the consumption tax proposed is not a regressive tax. Its escalating marginal tax rates on consumption, coupled with its large standard deduction, assure that total tax as a proportion of income rises steadily with income, even though the assumed savings rate is sharply higher for high-income families.

Consumption taxation has been proposed before.[30] Its proponents have stressed that it will encourage savings, and hence stimulate economic growth. This is indeed an important benefit – more important, by far, than even the proponents of consumption taxation have realised. Yet the most significant gains from progressive consumption taxation lie elsewhere. Properly designed and implemented, such a tax can eliminate trillions of dollars of waste from the American economy.

The key to understanding how this would work is the observation that when the price of a good rises, we buy less of it. It follows that if consumption were taxed at a progressive rate, we would save more, buy less expensive houses and cars, and feel less pressure to work excessively long hours. And this, on the best available evidence, would improve the quality of our lives.

---

[30] See Hall and Rabushka (1995) for a discussion of the so-called flat tax, a form of consumption tax. The flat tax, value-added tax and national sales tax are discussed extensively in Aaron and Gale (1996).

It might seem natural to worry that a tax that limits consumption might lead to recession and unemployment. This is not a serious concern, however, because money that is not spent on consumption is saved and invested. The result is that some of the people who are now employed to produce consumption goods will instead be employed to produce capital goods – which, in the long run, increase the economy's productive capacity. The government knows how to stimulate the economy when recession threatens. Indeed, a central problem of recent decades has been to contain the inflationary pressures that result when demand grows more rapidly than the economy's capacity to produce goods and services. By stimulating savings and investment, the progressive consumption tax will increase the rate at which the economy's productive capacity grows, and thus reduce the threat of inflation.

The extraordinary beauty of the progressive consumption tax is its ability to generate extra resources almost literally out of thin air. It is a win-win move, even for the people on whom the tax falls most heavily. Transition problems could be minimised by phasing the programme in gradually – with phased increases in the amount of savings a family could exempt and phased increases in the highest marginal tax rates.

6 EFFECTS ON SAVINGS AND GROWTH

The case for the progressive consumption tax is strong even if we ignore its effects on growth in our national income. But once we take these effects into account, it becomes compelling. Proponents of consumption taxation have long stressed that it will increase savings, and they are right. These same proponents go on to predict that the increase will be small, and that the resulting increase in growth and well-being, though steady, will be small as well.[31] The latter predictions, however, are significantly off the mark.

Switching to a consumption tax from an income tax would affect savings through several channels. Past advocates of consumption taxation have focused on two. First, the tax would put more resources in the hands of those whose savings rates were highest to begin with. (The less someone consumes, the less tax she pays, and hence the more she is able to save.) And second, a consumption tax would increase the monetary reward for saving. But, as past advocates of consumption taxes have realised, both effects are relatively small.[32]

Where past predictions have gone away is in having ignored the effect of community consumption standards on savings rates. This is by far the most important channel through which a progressive consumption tax would stimulate savings. Even though the direct effect of the tax might be to reduce our consumption only slightly, this would initiate a self-reinforcing sequence of indirect effects. Thus, when others consume less, the amount that we consume would decline still further, and our responses would then influence others, and so on. Once these multiplier effects are taken into account, the effect on savings rates turns out to be substantial.

Higher savings rates, in turn, are the surest path to more rapid economic growth.

---

[31] See Auerbach and Slemrod (1997), Hubbard and Skinner (1996), Poterba et al. (1996) and Slemrod (1990).
[32] See especially Engen et al. (1996).

Some might wonder whether achieving higher growth rates would be such a good thing in the end since, after all, people do tend to adjust quickly to changes in material living standards. One might also worry that more consumption means more garbage and more greenhouse gases. On the first point, the evidence suggests that although we adjust rather quickly to any stable standard of living, we seem to derive continuing satisfaction from an ongoing increase in our standard of living.[33] The faster the economy is growing, the more satisfied people seem to be. Opportunities are greater in a rich society than in a poor one. The former Soviet Union generated more pollution than any nation on earth not because of its high rate of economic growth, but because its productivity lagged so far behind that of its rivals. A richer society has more resources for medical research, more resources for rapid transit, more time for family and friends, more time for study and exercise – and more resources for better insulated houses and cleaner, more fuel-efficient cars.

7 ARE POSITIONAL EXTERNALITIES A LEGITIMATE CONCERN OF TAX POLICY?

Most economists accept the proposition that market allocations may be suboptimal when production is accompanied by the discharge of environmental pollutants. Most tend also to be enthusiastic in their embrace of effluent taxes as a solution to the problem of environmental pollution. The dependence of utility on relative consumption gives rise to what I have elsewhere called positional externalities.[34] Analytically, these externalities are no different from ordinary environmental pollutants. My proposal to tax consumption is thus precisely analogous to an effluent tax.[35] Most economists accept the existence of positional externalities as a purely descriptive matter.[36] Yet many of these same economists may question whether such externalities are proper targets for public policy intervention. On the face of it, this is a curious position for the profession that has always insisted that 'a taste for poetry is no better than a taste for pushpins'.

Of course, it is one thing to say that a person's tastes are her own business, and quite another to say that A's discomfort from B's consumption constitutes grounds for restricting B's consumption. As parents most of us try to teach our children not to worry about what others consume, and perhaps this is the best posture for the state to assume as well. And yet many forms of consumption cause not only injured feelings in others but also more tangible economic losses.[37] The job seeker gains a leg up on his rivals,

[33] See Shin (1980) and Frank and Hutchens (1993).

[34] Frank (1991)

[35] Many others have suggested taxes to mitigate the externalities that arise from the dependence of utility on relative income or relative consumption. See, for example, Bagwell and Bernheim (1996), Boskin and Sheshinski (1978), Layard (1980), Ng (1987), Oswald (1983) Kosicki (1987), Ireland (1994, 1997).

[36] There is indeed an extensive literature in which economists have discussed the dependence of satisfaction on relative living standards. In addition to the authors previously cited see Kapteyn and van Herwaarden (1980), van Praag (1993), Easterlin (1974, 1995), Sen (1983, 1987), Hirsch (1976) and Scitovsky (1976).

[37] Sen (1987) emphasises this point.

for example, by showing up for his interview in a custom-tailored suit. The best response for others may be to show up in custom-tailored suits as well. Yet all job seekers might prefer the alternative in which all spent less on their professional wardrobes. Likewise when *A* sends his child to an expensive private school, he may not intend to reduce the likelihood that the children of others will be accepted to top universities, but that is a consequence of his action nevertheless, and it may be the best response of others to follow suit. And yet all might find that outcome less attractive than when all send their children to the public schools.

To acknowledge that our utility from consumption depends on context is simply to note an obvious fact of the human condition. Because each individual's consumption affects the frame of reference within which others evaluate their own consumption, this frame of reference becomes, in effect, a public good. The uncoordinated consumption decisions of individuals are not more likely to result in the optimal level of this public good than the uncoordinated actions of individuals are likely to result in an optimal level of military preparedness. The progressive consumption tax is a simple policy measure that can help mould the frame of reference in mutually beneficial ways.

But not even a steeply progressive consumption tax can fully neutralise the externalities that arise from competition for spots atop various local hierarchies. At best, it can reduce some of their costs. Even with such a tax, it will still prove useful to ameliorate consumption externalities through a variety of less formal means – adoption of social norms, choice of personal reference groups, introspection, and so on. As policy interventions go, a consumption tax is not especially intrusive. After all, we have to tax something anyway. And available evidence suggests that across-the-board consumption reductions will not entail significant utility losses for middle- and upper-income citizens, the only people who might experience a heavier tax burden under a progressive consumption tax.

8 CASH ON THE TABLE

'Cash on the table' is the familiar economist's metaphor for situations in which people seem to be passing up opportunities for gain. Each year, Americans leave literally trillions of dollars on the table as a result of wasteful consumption arms races. This waste can be curbed by a disarmingly simple policy change – in essence, a one-line amendment that exempts savings from the federal income tax. Adoption of a progressive consumption tax would greatly enhance every citizen's opportunity to pursue his or her vision of the good life.

The only intelligible reason for having stuck with our current tax system for so long is that we have not understood clearly how much better the alternative would be. But we now have all the evidence we could reasonably demand on this point. In the face of this evidence, the progressive consumption tax emerges as by far the most exciting economic opportunity of the modern era.

References

Aaron, Henry J. and Gale, William G. (1996). *Economic Effects of Fundamental Tax Reform.* Washington, DC: Brookings Institution.

Argyle, Michael (1997). 'Causes and correlates of happiness.' In *Understanding Well-Being: Scientific Perspectives on Enjoyment and Suffering,* (eds Daniel Kahneman, Ed Diener and Norbert Schwartz) New York: Russell Sage.

Auerbach, Alan and Slemrod, Joel (1997). 'The economic effects of the tax reform act of 1987.' *Journal of Economic Perspectives,* forthcoming.

Bagwell, Laurie Simon and Bernheim, B. Douglas. (1996). 'Veblen effects in a theory of conspicuous consumption.' *American Economic Review,* vol. 86, (June), pp. 349–73.

Ball, Sheryl, Eckel, Catherine, Grossman Philip and Zame, William (1996). 'Status in markets.' Department of Economics Working Paper. Virginia Polytechnic Institute, (January).

Berkman, L. F. and Syme, S. L. (1979). 'Social networks, host resistance, and mortality: a nine-year followup of Alameda county residents.' *American Journal of Epidemiology,* vol. 109, pp. 186–204.

Blair, S. N. (1989). 'Physical fitness and all-cause mortality: a prospective study of healthy men and women.' *Journal of the American Medical Association,* vol. 262, pp. 2396–401.

Boskin, Michael and Sheshinski, E. (1978). 'Optimal redistributive taxation when individual welfare depends on relative income.' *Quarterly Journal of Economics,* vol. 92, pp. 589–601.

Clark, Andrew and Oswald, Andrew (1996). 'Satisfaction and comparison income.' *Journal of Public Economics,* vol. 61, pp. 359–81.

Davidson, Richard J. (1992). 'Emotion and affective style: hemispheric substrates.' *Psychological Science,* vol. 3. pp. 39–43.

DeLongis, Anita, Folkman, Susan and Lazarus, Richard S. (1988). 'The impact of daily stress on health and mood: psychological and social resources as mediators.' *Journal of Personality and Social Psychology,* vol. 54, pp. 486–95.

Diener, Ed and Diener, Carol (1995). 'The wealth of nations revisited: income and the quality of life.' *Social Indicators Research,* vol. 36, pp. 275–86.

Diener, Ed and Lucas, Richard E. (1997). 'Personality and subjective well-being.' In *Understanding Well-Being: Scientific Perspectives on Enjoyment and Suffering* (ed. Daniel Kahneman, Ed Diener and Norbert Schwartz), New York: Russell Sage.

Diener, Ed, Sandvik, Ed, Seidlitz, Larry and Diener, Marissa (1993). 'The relationship between income and subjective well-being: relative or absolute?' *Social Indicators Research,* vol. 28, pp. 195–223.

Duesenberry, James (1949). *Income, Saving, and the Theory of Consumer Behavior.* Cambridge, Mass.: Harvard University Press.

Dynan, Karen E., Skinner, Jonathan and Zeldes, Stephen P. (1996). 'Do the rich save more?' Federal Reserve Board mimeo (November).

Easterlin, Richard (1974). 'Does economic growth improve the human lot?' In *Nations and Households in Economic Growth: Essays in Honor of Moses Abramovitz* (ed. Paul David and Melvin Reder), New York: Academic Press.

Easterlin, Richard (1995). 'Will raising the incomes of all increase the happiness of all?' *Journal of Economic Behavior and Organization,* vol. 27, pp. 35–47.

Engen, Eric, Gale, William and Scholz, John Karl (1996). 'The illusory effects of saving incentives on savings.' *Journal of Economic Perspectives,* vol. 10. pp. 113–38.

Evans, Gary W. (1994), 'Working on the hot seat: urban bus drivers.' *Accident Analysis and Prevention,* vol. 26, pp. 181–93.

Fontane, Patrick E. (1996). 'Exercise, fitness, and feeling well.' *American Behavioral Scientist,* vol. 39, January, pp. 288–305.

Frank, Robert H. (1984). 'Are workers paid their marginal products?' *American Economic Review,* vol. 74, September, pp. 549–71.

Frank, Robert H. (1985a). 'The demand for unobservable and other nonpositional goods.' *American Economic Review*, vol. 75, March, pp. 101–16.

Frank, Robert H. (1985b). *Choosing the Right Pond*. New York: Oxford University Press.

Frank, Robert H. (1991). 'Positional externalities.' In *Strategy and Choice: Essays in Honor of Thomas C. Schelling* (ed. Richard Zeckhauser), pp. 25–47. Cambridge, MA: MIT Press.

Frank, Robert H. (1996). 'What price the moral high ground?' *Southern Economic Journal*, vol. 63(1), July, pp. 1–17.

Frank, Robert H. and Hutchens, Robert (1993). 'Wages, seniority, and the demand for rising consumption profiles.' *Journal of Economic Behavior and Organization*. vol. 21, pp. 251–76.

Friedman, Milton (1957). *A Theory of the Consumption Function*. Princeton, NJ: Princeton University Press.

Goleman, Daniel (1996). 'Forget money; nothing can buy happiness, some researchers say.' *New York Times*, 16 July, pp. C1, C3.

Hall, Robert E. and Rabushka, Alvin (1995). *The Flat Tax*, 2nd Ed., Stanford, CA: The Hoover Institution Press.

Hirsch, Fred (1976). *Social Limits to Growth*. Cambridge. MA: Harvard University Press.

House, James S., Robbins, C. and Metzner, H. M. (1982). 'The association of social relationships and activities with mortality: prospective evidence from the Tecumsah community health study.' *American Journal of Epidemiology*, vol. 116, pp. 123–40.

Hubbard, R. Glenn, and Skinner, Jonathan (1996). 'Assessing the effectiveness of savings incentives.' *Journal of Economic Perspectives*, vol. 10, pp. 73–90.

Ireland. Norman (1994). 'On limiting the market for status signals.' *Journal of Public Economics*, vol. 53, pp. 91–110.

Ireland. Norman (1997). 'Status-seeking, income taxation and efficiency.' *Journal of Public Economics* (forthcoming).

Kapteyn, Arie and van Herwaarden, F. G. (1980). 'Interdependent welfare functions and optimal income distribution.' *Journal of Public Economics*, vol. 14, pp. 375–97.

Kosicki, George (1987). 'Savings as a nonpositional good.' *Southern Economic Journal*, vol. 54, October, pp. 422–34.

Koslowsky, Meni, Kluger, Avraham N. and Reich, Mordechai (1995). *Commuting Stress*. New York: Plenum.

Landers, Renee M., Rebitzer, James B. and Taylor, Lowell J. (1996). 'Rate race redux: adverse selection in the determination of work hours in law firms.' *American Economic Review*, vol. 86, June, pp. 329–48.

Layard, Richard (1980). 'Human satisfactions and public policy.' *Economic Journal*, vol. 90, pp. 737–50.

Modigliani, Franco and Brumberg, R. (1955). 'Utility analysis and the consumption function: an interpretation of cross-section data.' In *Post-Keynesian Economics* (ed. K. Kurihara). London: Allen and Unwin.

Myers, David G. (1993). *The Pursuit of Happiness: Who is Happy and Why?* New York: Avon.

National Opinion Research Center (1991).

Neumark, David and Postlewaite, Andrew (1996). 'Relative income concerns and the rise in married women's employment,' University of Pennsylvania Department of Economics mimeo.

Ng, Yew-Kwang. (1987). 'Diamonds are a government's best friend: burden-free taxes on goods valued for their values.' *American Economic Review*, vol. 77, pp. 186–91.

Oswald, Andrew J. (1983). 'Altruism, jealousy, and the theory of optimal nonlinear income taxation.' *Journal of Public Economics*, vol. 20, pp. 77–87.

Oswald, Andrew J. (1996). 'Happiness and economic performance.' University of Warwick Department of Economics Mimeo (September).

Palmer, Linda K. (1995). 'Effects of a walking program on attributional style, depression, and self-esteem in women.' *Perceptual and Motor Skills*, vol. 81, pp. 891–8.

Plante, Thomas G. and Rodin, Judith (1990). 'Physical fitness and enhanced psychological health.' *Current Psychology: Research and Reviews*, vol. 9, Spring, pp. 3–24.

Poterba, James, Venti, Steven and Wise, David (1996). 'How retirement saving programs increase savings.' *Journal of Economic Perspectives*, vol. 10. Fall, pp. 91–112.

Scitovsky, Tibor (1976). *The Joyless Economy*. New York: Oxford University Press.

Sen, Amartya (1983). 'Poor, relatively speaking.' *Oxford Economics Papers*, vol. 35, July, pp. 153–67.

Sen, Amartya (1987). *The Standard of Living*. Cambridge: Cambridge University Press.

Shin, D. C. (1980). 'Does rapid economic growth improve the human lot?' *Social Indicators Research*, vol. 8, pp. 199–221.

Slemrod, Joel (1990). 'The economic impact of the tax reform act of 1986.' In *Do Taxes Matter? The Impact of the Tax Reform Act of 1986* (ed. Joel Slemrod), pp. 1–12. Cambridge, MA: MIT Press.

Stokols, Daniel, Novaco, Raymond W., Stokols Jeannette and Campbell, Joan (1978). 'Traffic congestion, type A behavior, and stress.' *Journal of Applied Psychology*, vol. 63, pp. 467–80.

Taylor, P. and Pocock, C. (1972). 'Commuter travel and sickness: absence of London office workers.' *British Journal of Preventive and Social Medicine*, vol. 26, pp. 165–72.

van Praag, Bernard, M. S. (1993). 'The relativity of the welfare concept.' In *The Quality of Life* (ed. Martha Nussbaum and Amartya Sen). Oxford: Clarendon, pp. 363–92.

Veenhoven, Ruut (1993). *Happiness in Nations: Subjective Appreciation of Life in 56 Nations*. Rotterdam: Erasmus University.

Appendix – The progressive consumption tax: An Example

The following example illustrates how a progressive consumption would work for a family of four if the standard deduction were $7,500 per person. With a total standard deduction of $30,000 minus its savings minus its tax. A family whose income was no more than $30,000 plus the amount it saved would thus owe no tax at all under this plan. Suppose the tax rate on families with positive taxable consumption began at 20% and then gradually escalated as taxable consumption increased, as shown in Table A1.

Given this rate schedule, Table A2 shows how much tax families with different income and savings levels would pay.

Table A1 Tax rates on taxable consumption

Taxable consumption($)	Marginal tax rate (%)
0–39,999	20
40,000–49,999	22
50,000–59,999	24
60,000–69,999	26
70,000–79,999	28
80,000–89,999	30
90,000–99,999	32
100,000–129,999	34
130,000–159.999	38
160,000–189.999	42
190,000–219.999	46
220,000–249.999	50

Table A2 Illustrative income, savings, and tax values under a progressive consumption tax ($)

Income	Savings	Taxable consumption	Tax
30,000	1500	0	0
50,000	3000	14,167	2833
100,000	10,000	49,844	10,156
150,000	20,000	81,538	18,462
200,000	40,000	104,265	23,735
500,000	120,000	257,800	92,200
1,000,000	300,000	471,000	199,000

16
A CASE FOR HAPPINESS, CARDINALISM, AND INTERPERSONAL COMPARABILITY

Yew-Kwang Ng

Modern economists are strongly biased in favour of preference (in contrast to happiness), ordinalism, and against interpersonal comparison. I wish to argue for the opposite. The proposed change in perspective has important conceptual and policy significance, as also evidenced in the papers by Frank and Oswald in this issue that I strongly endorse.

1 ECONOMISTS' PREFERENCE FOR PREFERENCE AND ORDINALISM

Neoclassical economists used more subjective terms like satisfaction, marginal utility, and even happiness, pleasure, and pain. After the indifference-curve or ordinalism revolution in the 1930s, modern economists are very adverse to the more subjective concepts and very hostile to cardinal utility and interpersonal comparisons of utility. They prefer to use the more objective concepts like preference and choice. In a very important sense, these changes represent an important methodological advance, making economic analysis based on more objective grounds. However, the change or correction has been carried to an excess, making economics unable to tackle many important problems, divorced from fundamental concepts, and even misleading. In my view, while we should prefer using just the more objective concepts when they are sufficient, we should not shy from the more subjective concepts and even their interpersonal comparison when they are needed.

Similar changes happened in psychology. Classical psychologists spoke of mind, consciousness, and used introspection in their analysis. Then came the Watson–Skinner behaviourist revolution which prohibits the analysis of anything subjective: only actual behaviours are the proper subject matter of psychology. This achieved a huge advance in making psychology more scientific but also some felt it had 'gone out of its mind . . . and lost all consciousness' (Chomsky, 1959, p. 229). The reaction against the excesses of behaviourism resulted in the cognitive revolution which has been many decades old and has made much headway. It is time economists make a reassessment of their position, if not staging a subjectivist counter-revolution.

2 WHY IS HAPPINESS MORE IMPORTANT?

Happiness is more important than the more objective concepts of choice, preference and income (especially if narrowly interpreted and eschewing cardinal utility and interpersonal comparison, as is the usual practice in modern economics) for at least two reasons. First, happiness is the ultimate objective of most, if not all people. (See Veenhoven (1984) and Ng (1996*a*), pp. 13–14 for empirical evidence.) We want money (or anything else) only as a means to increase our happiness. If having more money does not substantially increase our happiness, then money is not very important, but happiness is.

Secondly, for economically advanced countries (the number of which is increasing) there is evidence suggesting that, for the whole society and in the long run (in real purchasing power terms) money does not buy happiness, or at least not much (Easterlin, 1974; Veenhoven, 1984; Argyle and Martin, 1991, p. 80; Oswald, 1997). The reasons are not difficult to see. Once the basic necessities and comforts of life are adequate, further consumption can actually make us worse off due to problems like excessive fat and cholesterol and stress. Our ways to increase happiness further then take on the largely competitive forms like attempting to keep up with or surpass the Joneses. From a social viewpoint, such competition is a pure waste (Frank, 1997). On top of this, production and consumption to sustain the competition continue to impose substantial environmental costs, making economic growth quite possibly happiness-decreasing (Ng and Wang, 1993). To avoid this sad outcome, a case can be made for *increasing* public expenditures (contrary to the currently popular view against public expenditures among economists) to safeguard the environment and to engage in research and development that will increase welfare (Ng, 1995*a*). This is especially so since relative-income effects makes the traditional estimate of optimal public expenditure sub-optimal (Ng, 1987). As the schoolmates of one's child all receive expensive birthday gifts, one feels the need to give as expensive gifts. Thus, the perceived importance of private expenditures is inflated relative to that for public spending.

There is a particular line of research that will lead to quantum leaps in our happiness which is yet largely disregarded. This is the stimulation of the pleasure centres in our brain. This was discovered nearly half a century ago by Olds and Milner (1954). Electrical, chemical, and magnetic stimulation of certain parts of our brain induces intense pleasure and obliterates emotional and physical pain without diminishing marginal utility, as the stimulation bypasses the peripheral nervous system. The genetic device to prevent excessive (from the viewpoint of survival) activities programmed our peripheral nervous system to ensure diminishing marginal utility. Since no animal was clever enough to stimulate its own brain directly without passing through the peripheral nervous system, evolution found it unnecessary to impose diminishing marginal utility on the pleasure centres themselves. Since we have time and resources in excess of simply ensuring survival, we may engage in welfare (i.e. happiness) maximisation. (This differs from the evolutionary process which maximises survival and propagation; see Ng (1995*b*) which raises and attempts to provide a partial answer to three basic questions in welfare biology.) The possibility of intense pleasure without diminishing marginal utility opens up a tremendous avenue for increasing our welfare by a quantum leap. (The only potentially more welfare-improving method is genetic engineering in the far future when it could be used safely to enhance our capacity for happiness.) Why is there no substantial research to ensure its feasibility for widespread application? (See Ng (1996b) for a case in favour of the widespread use of brain stimulation after sufficient research and certain safeguards.)

Some economists may argue that my point about the importance of happiness is valid only against the narrow concepts of income but not against the wider concepts of choice and preference. It is true that 'preference' could and should take account of such relevant factors as pollution and relative income. However, there are still a number of reasons making economists miss the important factors. First, individual choices are directly effective in affecting variables under her direct control. She can choose to work harder and consume more private goods but cannot on her own choose to have less pollution with less consumption for every person. Economists observe that people still engage in the rat race for earning more money despite affluence and incorrectly infer the importance of higher income to be greater than it really is. Secondly, people do not have perfect foresight and are typically myopic. For example, most people believe that a big windfall will spectacularly increase their happiness (witness the amount of money spent in buying lotteries) and that being crippled in an accident is worse than being killed. However, there is evidence that lottery winners are no happier than non-winner controls, and quadriplegics are only slightly less happy than healthy people (Brickman et al. 1978). After an initial period of adjustment, maimed victims can still enjoy life and are glad that they were not killed. Also, people typically underestimate the negative/positive effects of current enjoyment/suffering on future ability for enjoyment. (See Headley and Wearing, 1991.)

It is true that some economists have emphasised the importance of relative-income effects, environmental protection, public goods, etc. However, the majority have not taken into account the implications of these factors in their analysis. For example, after an otherwise competent cost–benefit analysis, Portney (1990) concludes that 'Congress and the President are about to shake hands on a landmark piece of environmental law [The Clean Air Act] for which costs may exceed benefits by a considerable margin. Why is this so?' (p. 179). The analysis of costs and benefits was based on ignoring the existence of relative-income effects, the full consideration of which may change the cost–benefit ratio rather dramatically (Ng and Wang, 1993). Moreover, by eschewing cardinal utility and interpersonal comparison, economists ensured that they cannot solve the paradox of social choice. (See Mueller 1989, ch. 19.)

3 CARDINAL UTILITY

Most modern economists use utility as only an indicator of choice or (ordinal) preference in the sense that the utility of a situation is larger than that of another if and only if the first situation is preferred to the second. In this sense, utility is only ordinal. Any positive monotonic transformation of a preference-representing utility function is also a suitable function. Moreover, for the positive theory of demand, this is sufficient. Different cardinal-utility numberings of the same set of indifference curves will give the same demand functions. Occam's razor requires shaving off the unnecessary assumption of cardinal utility. I have no argument against all these positions. However, many economists go from here to deny the use of cardinal utility even where it is essential or at least helpful, such as in social choice, optimal population, choices involving risk, and choices affecting the probability of survival. (On the usefulness of cardinal utility for the last item, see Ng (1992*a*) which shows that the dollar value of life may *increase* spectacularly with age.) This is like insisting that I have to shave off my moustache on the ground that it is unnecessary for eating, while I want to keep it to increase my sex appeal.

Selected almost at random, the following is representative of the modern textbook hostility against utility measurability and comparability. 'There is no way that you or I can measure the amount of utility that a consumer might be able to obtain from a particular good ... there can be no accurate scientific assessment of the utility that someone might receive by consuming a frozen dinner or a movie relative to the utility that another person might receive from that same good ... Today no one really believes that we can actually measure utils' (Miller, 1994, pp. 418, 419). There is at least one counter-example to this confident assertion – the present writer.

Another textbook example (a non-textbook example is Kolm, 1993) on the hostility against cardinal utility is Varian: 'But how do we tell if a person likes one bundle twice as much as another? How could you even tell if *you* like one bundle twice as much as another? One could propose various definitions for this kind of assignment: I like one bundle twice as much as another if I am willing to run twice as far to get it, or to wait twice as long, or to gamble for it at twice the odds ... Although each of them is a possible interpretation of what it means to want one thing twice as much as another, none of them appears to be an especially compelling interpretation' (Varian, 1993, pp. 57–8).

There is in fact an interpretation of cardinal utility that is especially compelling. This is whatever the individual concerned values ultimately. If we abstract away effects on other individuals and sentients, what I ultimately value is my net happiness (i.e. enjoyment minus suffering, including the sensuous as well as the spiritual). On the ground of evolutionary biology, daily experience, and interviews, I have reasons to believe that I am not an exception here but rather quite representative. Since, for myself, it is ultimately net happiness that I want, it has an especially compelling interpretation (for cardinal utility).

I want money but not for its own sake, only to obtain, ultimately, happiness. Thus, I have diminishing marginal happiness of money. For big variations, my willingness to pay twice as much does not indicate twice as much happiness or utility. (The two are the same if we abstract away ignorance, concern for others, and irrational preference. This is so with my definition of irrational preference as preferring something that decreases one's own happiness or welfare, neither due to ignorance nor to a concern for the welfare of others.) Utility here is taken as representing preference which can be cardinal. (See Ng (1979), Section 1.3 for details.) However, as I want happiness for its own sake, if bundle *A* (or anything else) gives me twice as much happiness as bundle *B*, it is perfectly sensible, natural, and informative to say that I prefer (recalling the abstraction of ignorance, etc.) bundle *A* twice as much as bundle *B*.

Even if we re-introduce factors other than personal happiness in the preference function, I have no difficulty (except for imperfect information to be discussed presently) in comparing the intensities of my preference for different pairs of alternatives.

Thus, if I take account of the income or welfare levels of others, there is no problem in allowing for that. For the simple case where both my and the (only) other person's welfare are functions of the log of own income, my preference or utility function could be the log of my income plus alpha times the log of the other person's income, where alpha is a positive number slightly larger than zero. I could also allow for alpha itself to be a function of the income or welfare level of others. (The rationality of doing that may however be queried.) It is true that I often have difficulties knowing the intensity of my preference for an alternative over another. This is due to the lack of information (or lack of perfect memory for past events) as to what my own and other people's welfare values will be under different alternatives. Given this lack of information. I even have difficulties knowing whether I prefer A to B or *vice versa*. Thus, not only the intensities of preference or cardinal utility are made unclear but the ordinal preference or ranking itself is also made unclear. If you put two close enough quantities of water into two containers of different shape, I may have difficulties judging which container has more water. But that does not mean that the volume of water is not a cardinally measurable quantity!

I have also no difficulties saying that my welfare level is positive, zero, or negative. When I am neither enjoying nor suffering, my welfare is zero. Thus, the value of my welfare is a fully cardinal quantity unique up to a proportionate transformation. I am also sure that I am not bestowed by God or evolution to have this special ability of perceiving the full cardinality (both intensity and the origin) of both my welfare and preference levels. In fact, from my daily experience, observation, and conversation, I know that all people (including ordinalist economists) have this ability, except that economists heavily brainwashed by ordinalism deny it despite actually possessing it. This denial is quite incredible. If your preference is really purely ordinal, you can only say that you prefer your present situation (A) to that plus an ant bite (B) and also prefer the latter to being bodily thrown into a pool of sulphuric acid (C). You cannot say that your preference of A over B is less than your preference of B over C. Can you really believe that!

4 THE MEASUREMENT AND INTERPERSONAL COMPARISON OF UTILITY AND HAPPINESS

The majority of economists are not that heavily brain-washed. They believe that cardinal utility is not meaningless. In fact, in his path-breaking model of optimal income taxation, Mirrlees (1971), a Nobel laureate (and his followers), use not only interpersonally comparable cardinal utility, but also a utilitarian social welfare function. However, most economists still doubt the possibility of the measurement of cardinal utility and believe in the meaninglessness or normative nature of interpersonal comparison of utility.

While some economists accept the use of the Neumann–Morgenstern expected utility hypothesis as a valid way of measuring individual cardinal utilities (but cardinal only in a limited sense, as any linear transformation of a utility function is still allowed), others (e.g. Arrow 1951/63, p. 10; Baumol 1977, p. 431) query its relevance to the subjective utility of the neoclassical economists and its relevance to social welfare considerations. Using a set of axioms no stronger than that used in the expected utility hypothesis plus the recognition that individuals are not infinitely sensitive (more on this below), I show that the utility function derived by the Neumann–Morgenstern method is in fact a neoclassical subjective utility function (Ng, 1984a). Hahn (1982, p. 195) and Samuelson (1947, p. 228n) declare their failure to see why social choice (e.g. with respect to income distribution) should depend on individual risk aversion (with respect to income), as will be the case if the N–M utility indices are used. This dependence is straightforward once my (1984a) result is recognised. The degree of risk aversion reveals the degree at which subjective marginal utility of income diminishes. Since social welfare is a function of individual subjective utilities, how rapidly marginal utilities diminish has obviously important effects on social choices that affect individual income levels.

The belief in the non-comparability of utility has a long tradition from the time of Wicksteed and Robbins when they declared that every mind is totally inscrutable to any other mind and that interpersonal comparisons of utility are pure value judgements without any objective basis (see Robbins, 1932). however, the judgement that individual I will be made better off than individual J will be made worse off by the choice of alternative A over B does not imply that A ought to be chosen socially. This is true only with the additional normative judgement that social choice should be guided by the maximisation of aggregate welfare. If the normative judgement is for the minimisation of aggregate welfare (or the maximisation of the minimum utility level), the implication is reversed (or may be reversed depending on relative utility levels). Thus, interpersonal comparisons of utility are at most subjective judgements of fact, not value judgements. (See Ng (1972) for details and for the point that economists are more qualified in making those subjective judgements of fact closely related to their field of study.)

I have also argued (Ng, 1992b) that the belief in the impossibility of interpersonal comparisons of utility is based on the existence of a soul in each person's mind. (However, the existence of souls is not sufficient to ensure non-comparability.) The compelling evidence for the Darwinian theory of evolution, the split-brain experiments and other developments in neurology and psychiatry strongly suggest a materialist (biological/neural) basis of mind, making interpersonal comparison of utility possible at least in principle, if not yet accurately in practice. In fact, I have developed and actually applied a method of happiness measurement that is fully cardinal and interpersonally comparable (Ng, 1996a). This is based on the fact (established by everyday observation and psychological studies) that no one is infinitely sensitive. Thus, Edgeworth (1881, pp. 7ff., 60ff.) regarded it as axiomatic ('a first principle incapable of proof') that the just-perceivable increments of pleasure, of all pleasures for all persons, are equatable. I derived this as a proposition based on some compelling axioms but noted the need to consider different lengths of time (Ng (1975, 1981) where a number of objections are also responded to). It is true that the method of utility and happiness measurement has yet to be improved to make its results more reliable. If economists are not that hostile to cardinalism and interpersonal comparison, perhaps faster advance will be made. (On cardinalism, welfare measurement and comparison, see also Allais and Hagen (1994), Harsanyi (1997), Simon (1974), van Herwaarden et al. (1977), van Praag (1968).)

Recently, Roberts (1997) asked whether it is possible to aggregate the different inter-personal comparisons of utilities made by different individuals into a social or aggregate (misleadingly termed 'objective' by Roberts) interpersonal comparison. He concluded: 'Because opinions themselves are not comparable across the individuals making them, the class of possible aggregation mechanisms is severely restricted. With ... rich in-formation structure of full comparability, the only opinion aggregator is dictatorial' (p. 95). However, he remarks that a way out may be the use of 'some "objective" compari-sons which have an independent existence' (p. 94). The interpersonal comparison out-lined in the preceding paragraph provides indeed one that has an independent objective existence and hence a way of solving the Roberts impossibility.

5 THE ACCEPTABILITY OF MONETARY MEASURES OF WELFARE CHANGES USED BY ECONOMISTS

Despite my emphasis on the more subjective concept of happiness over income, I am more tolerant and less sceptical (especially on certain technical or methodological grounds) of the use of monetary measures of consumer surplus or welfare changes such as the willingness to pay and to accept (or compensating variation and equivalent variation in income), subject to some qualifications mentioned below. In fact, I go further than most economists in advocating the principle of treating a dollar as a dollar and using this to largely solve the paradox of interpersonal cardinal utility. As ex-plained below, this will make it less necessary to make interpersonal comparisons of utility.

The impossibility results of Arrow (1951/63), Sen (1970), Kemp and Ng (1976) and Parks (1976) show the impossibility of reasonable social decisions without interper-sonal comparison of cardinal utility, whether we operate with alternative profiles of individual preferences like Arrow, or go along with Little (1952) and Samuelson (1967) in holding individual preferences fixed. Despite my argument above on the meaning-fulness and feasibility of cardinal utility measurement and interpersonal comparison, I freely admit that the practical difficulties associated with cardinal utility measurement and comparison are an order of magnitude higher than those for ordinal preferences (these also exist and are significant, though ignored by most economists). Thus, a paradox is created: we need interpersonal cardinal utilities but have difficulties meas-uring them. This paradox of interpersonal cardinal utility may be largely (but not completely) solved by using some monetary measure of net benefits (e.g. willingness to pay) to reflect the *intensity* of individual preferences, and then using the unweighted sum of individual net benefits in making social choices (i.e. treating a dollar as a dollar to whomsoever it goes).

The use of the monetary measure for cardinal utility is subject to some qualifica-tions. First, where individual ignorance, myopia, or irrationality are strong, especially if also related to insufficient concern for the welfare of children, strong divergence from individual preferences may be needed. The prohibition of heroin, the fluoridation of water, etc. are justified on this ground. Secondly, where there are important external effects, including environmental effects and relative-income effects, appropriate ad-justments should be allowed for, as discussed above.

Thirdly, there is the well-known inaccuracy of consumer surplus measurement due to the possibly changing marginal utility of money as prices change. Moreover, where some individuals gain and some lose from a change, there is the paradox of Boadway (1974). A positive aggregate willingness to pay (i.e. the compensating variations in income over all individuals sum to a positive figure) does not ensure that the gainers can overcompensate the losers, even given the feasibility of costless lump-sum transfers. This is due to a change in relative prices as compensation takes place, possibly making aggregate willingness to pay not perfectly accurate as it is when based on unchanged prices. (For the explanation why this inaccuracy always goes in the same direction, see Hird (1997).) I have argued (Ng, 1979, pp. 96–100) that both these inaccuracies are trivial for most changes. Where changes in relative prices are not huge, as is true for most specific projects or measures, the Boadway inaccuracy involved is negligible. While aggregate willingness to pay does not correspond perfectly with a potential Pareto improvement, it corresponds closely for most cases. For cases involving big changes in the marginal utility of money, I have advocated the use of marginal dollar equivalent (the number of times the utility change is the multiple of the marginal utility of a dollar) in place of either CV or EV to avoid the inaccuracy of the latter (Ng, 1979, Appendix 4A).[1]

Even with the above qualifications, how can we justify the use of *unweighted* sum of aggregate benefits since a marginal dollar may be worth much more to the poor than to the rich in utility terms? The answer is that this issue of income inequality is better tackled through the general tax/transfer system. However, this system has disincentive effects. Thus, most economists (including myself before I tried to prove that a dollar is *not* a dollar to counter the view of my colleague Ross Parish) mistakenly believe that it is better to shift some of the redistributive burden to specific items such as taxing/subsidising items consumed disproportionately by the rich/poor. Though some *marginal* efficiency costs of distorting choice are created, they are thought to be smaller than the reduction in disincentive effects due to relying less on the progressive tax/transfer system. This belief is incorrect. The reason is that, assuming rational individuals, the disincentive effects are in accordance to the total system of tax/transfer, taxes/subsidies, plus all other redistributive and preferential measures, instead of having a separate and independent increasing marginal disincentive effects schedule for each of the separate measures. A rational person, in their work/leisure choice, does not just ask how much post-tax tax income they can earn, but also has a rough idea of the utility they can get from consuming goods and services purchased from the income. They are trading off the utility of leisure with the utility from work (which consists of the utility from consuming the higher income and the positive or negative utility of work itself). Moreover, the utility of consuming the higher income is affected by whatever specific redistributive or preferential measures are in place. Thus, the preferential treatment against the rich in government expenditure and other areas will *add on* to the progressive tax/transfer system to determine the total disincentive effects. Hence, even if only a marginal amount of specific equality-oriented measures

---

[1] From Hause (1975) to Becht (1995) an increasing group of economists believe in the superiority over the compensation measures and the perfect validity of the equivalent variation as a measure of individual welfare; I show the imperfection of either measure in Ng (1979, Sec. 4.6).

are used, the disincentive effects involved are not just marginal. Thus, for the same degree of equality in real income (utility) achieved, the same degree of distinctive effects is incurred whether we use only the tax/transfer system or use a combination of it and some specific purely equality-oriented system. But the latter alternative has the additional efficiency costs of distorting choice, and is thus inferior. (See Ng (1979, ch. 9), (1984b) and (1996c) for more detailed arguments.)

Using the principle of unweighted aggregate net benefits in making decisions achieves a tremendous simplification in the formulation of economic policy in general and in cost–benefit analysis in particular. This frees us from having to make interpersonal comparisons of utility except in choosing the optimal tradeoff between efficiency and equality in the general tax/transfer system and except where the relevant monetary measures are not available or are untrustworthy due to important ignorance and/or irrationality (such as in the case of hard drugs).

References

Allais, Maurice and Hagen, Ole (1994). *Cardinalism.* Dordrecht: Kluwer.

Argyle, Michael and Martin, Maryanne (1991). 'The psychological causes of happiness.' In *Subjective Well-Being* (eds M. Argyle and N. Schwarz). Oxford: Pergamon.

Arrow, Kenneth J. (1951/1963). *Social Choice and Individual Values.* New York: Wiley.

Baumol, William J. (1977). *Economic Theory and Operations Analysis*, 4th ed. London: Prentice-Hall.

Becht, Marco (1995). 'The theory and estimation of individual and social welfare measures', *Journal of Economic Surveys*, vol. 9. pp. 53–87.

Boadway, Robin W. (1974). 'The welfare foundations of cost–benefit analysis.' *Economic Journal*, vol. 84, pp. 926–39.

Brickman, P., Coates, D. and Janoff-Bulman, R. (1978). 'Lottery winners and accident victims: is happiness relative?' *Journal of Personality and Social Psychology.* vol. 36, pp. 917–27.

Chomsky, N. (1959). Review of *Verbal Behaviour* by B. F. Skinner. *Language*, vol. 35, pp. 26–58.

Easterlin, Richard A. (1974). 'Does economic growth improve the human lot? Some empirical evidence'. In *Nations and Households in Economic Growth* (eds P. David and M. W. Reder). New York: Academic Press.

Edgeworth, F. Y. (1881). *Mathematical Psychics.* London: Kegan Paul.

Frank, Robert H. (1997). 'The frame of reference as a public good.' *Economic Journal*, vol. 107, p. 1832–47.

Hahn, F. (1982). 'On some difficulties of the utilitarian economist.' In *Utilitarianism and Beyond* (eds A. Sen and B. William). Cambridge: Cambridge University Press.

Harsanyi, John C. (1997). 'Utilities, preferences, and substantive goods.' *Social Choice and Welfare*, vol. 14, pp. 129–45.

Hause, John C. (1975). 'The theory of welfare cost measurement.' *Journal of Political Economy*, vol. 83. pp. 1145–82.

Headley, Bruce and Wearing, Alexander (1991). 'Subjective well-being: a stocks and flows framework.' In *Subjective Well-Being* (eds M. Argyle and N. Schwarz). Oxford: Pergamon.

Hird, Tom (1997). 'Individual welfare measurements and price indices: the importance of constancy in the marginal utility of money.' Ph.D. thesis, Monash University.

Kemp, Murray C. and Ng, Yew-Kwang (1976). 'On the existence of social welfare functions, social orderings and social decision functions.' *Economica*, vol. 43. pp. 59–66.

Kolm, S.-C. (1993). 'The impossibility of utilitarianism.' In *The Good and the Economical* (eds P. Koslowski and Y. Shionoya. Berlin: Springer-Verlag.

Little, Ian M. D. (1952). 'Social choice and individual values.' *Journal of Political Economy*, vol. 60. pp. 422–32.

Miller, Roger L. (1994). *Economics Today*. London: HarperCollins.

Mirrlees, James (1971). 'An exploration in the theory of optimal income taxation.' *Review of Economic Studies*. vol. 38, pp. 175–208.

Mueller, Dennic C. (1989). *Public Choice II*. Cambridge: Cambridge University Press.

Ng, Yew-Kwang (1972). 'Value judgments and economists role in policy recommendation.' *Economic Journal*, vol. 82, pp. 1014–8.

Ng, Yew-Kwang (1975). 'Bentham or Bergson? Finite sensibility, utility functions, and social welfare functions.' *Review of Economic Studies*, vol. 42, pp. 545–70.

Ng, Yew-Kwang (1979). *Welfare Economics*. London: Macmillan.

Ng, Yew-Kwang (1981). 'Bentham or Nash? On the acceptable form of social welfare functions.' *Economic Record*, vol. 57. pp. 238–50.

Ng, Yew-Kwang (1984*a*). 'Expected subjective utility: is the Neumann–Morgenstern utility the same as the neoclassical's?' *Social Choice and Welfare*, vol. 1. pp. 177–86.

Ng, Yew-Kwang (1984*b*). 'Quasi-Pareto social improvements.' *American Economic Review*, vol. 94, pp. 1033–50.

Ng, Yew-Kwang (1987). 'Relative-income effects and the appropriate level of public expenditure.' *Oxford Economic Papers*. vol. 39. pp. 293–300.

Ng, Yew-Kwang (1992*a*). 'The older the more valuable: divergence between utility and dollar values of life as one ages.' *Zeitschrift für Nationalokonomic*, vol. 55. pp. 1–16.

Ng, Yew-Kwang (1992*b*). 'Utilitarianism and interpersonal comparison.' *Social Choice and Welfare*, vol. 9, pp. 1–15.

Ng, Yew-Kwang (1995*a*). 'Relative income and diamond effects: a case for burden free taxes and higher public expenditures.' *Economic Papers* (Economic Society of Australia), vol. 4, pp. 29–33.

Ng, Yew-Kwang (1995*b*). 'Towards welfare biology: evolutionary economics of animal consciousness and suffering.' *Biology and Philosophy*, vol. 10, pp. 255–85.

Ng, Yew-Kwang (1996*a*). 'Happiness surveys: some comparability issues and an exploratory survey based on just perceivable increments.' *Social Indicators Research*, vol. 38, pp. 1–27.

Ng, Yew-Kwang (1996*b*). 'Electrical brain stimulation.' Typescript.

Ng, Yew-Kwang (1996*c*). 'The paradox of interpersonal cardinal utility: a proposed solution.' Paper presented to the International Conference on Social Choice and Welfare. Maastricht, June.

Ng, Yew-Kwang and Wang, Jianguo (1993). 'Relative income, aspiration, environmental quality, individual and political myopia.' *Mathematical Social Sciences*, vol. 26, pp. 3–23.

Olds, J. and Milner, P. (1954). Positive reinforcement produced by electrical stimulation of septal area and other regions of the rat brain. *Journal of Comparative Physiological Psychology*, vol. 47, pp. 419–27.

Oswald, Andrew J. (1997). 'Happiness and economic performance.' *Economic Journal*, vol. 107, pp. 1815–31.

Parks, Robert P. (1976). 'An impossibility theorem for fixed preferences: a dictatorial Bergson–Samuelson welfare function.' *Review of Economic Studies*, vol. 43, pp. 447–50.

Portney, P. R. (1990). 'Policy watch: economics and the Clean Air Act.' *Journal of Economic Perspectives*, vol. 4, pp. 173–81.

Robbins, Lionel (1932). *An Essay on the Nature and Significance of Economic Science*. London: Macmillan.

Roberts, Kevin (1997). 'Objective interpersonal comparisons of utility.' *Social Choice and Welfare*, vol. 14, pp. 79–96.

Samuelson, Paul A. (1947). *Foundations of Economic Analysis*. Cambridge. MA: Harvard University Press.

Samuelson, Paul A. (1967). 'Arrow's mathematical politics.' In *Human Values and Economic Policy: A Symposium* (ed. S. Hooki) New York: New York University Press.

Sen, Amartya K. (1970). *Collective Choice and Social Welfare.* Amsterdam: North-Holland.

Simon, Julian L. (1974). 'Interpersonal welfare comparisons can be made and used for redistribution decisions.' *Kyklos*, vol. 27, pp. 63–98.

van Herwaarden, Floor, Kapteyn, Arie and Van Praag, Bernard (1977). 'Twelve thousand individual welfare functions.' *European Economic Review*, vol. 9, pp. 283–300.

van Praag, Bernard M. S. (1968). *Individual Welfare Functions and Consumer Behavior.* Amsterdam: North-Holland.

Varian, Hal. R. (1993). *Intermediate Microeconomics*, New York: Norton.

Veenhoven, R. (1984). *Conditions of Happiness.* Dordrecht: Reidel.

17

TRADITIONAL PRODUCTIVITY ESTIMATES ARE ASLEEP AT THE (TECHNOLOGICAL) SWITCH*

William D. Nordhaus

1 THE ACHILLES HEEL OF REAL OUTPUT AND WAGE MEASURES

The analysis of technological change has made tremendous progress since the development of modern growth theory in the mid-1950s. After an ebb during which macroeconomists did battle over business-cycle theories, interest revived about a decade ago in an effort to fuse the earlier qualitative endogenous technology models of Joseph Schumpeter with the standard neoclassical model. The major developments include evolutionary economics (particularly writings of Richard Nelson and Sidney Winter), the insights surrounding path dependence of technological evolution (especially the work of Brian Arthur), and 'the new growth theory' of Paul Romer and others. All these have deepened our analytical appreciation of the complexities that arise when knowledge is a produced good.

How much have these fireworks illuminated our empirical understanding of the factors underlying economic growth? Not much, as is argued by Verman Ruttan in the introduction of this symposium and Gavin Wright in his discussion of economic history. The standard technique by which we decompose growth into its determinants – growth accounting – has changed little since its development in the 1960s by Edward Denison, Zvi Griliches and Dale Jorgenson, and others.[1] Conventional growth-accounting techniques tell us that real output and real wages have grown steadily for more than a century in the United States and Western Europe. Real incomes in the United States (measured either as real wages or *per capita* GNP) have grown by around 1.5% per annum from 1870 to 1995.[2] Over the last quarter century, measured growth in labour productivity has slowed and real compensation has increased only 0.6% per year while real wages have decreased by 0.2% per year. These are *the Standard Story*.

* The author is grateful for helpful comments by the editor.
[1] See Denison (1962) and Jorgenson and Griliches (1967). Major advances have been made over the last two decades in constructing subindexes and in improving the data.
[2] These data are from Maddison (1982) updated from CEA (1996).

The Standard Story has an oft-forgotten Achilles heel. While it is relatively easy to calculate nominal wages and outputs, conversion of these into real output or real wages requires calculation of price indexes for the various components of output. The estimates of real income are only as good as the price indexes are accurate.

While theorists have been engaged in the fruitful discussion of new approaches to understanding technology, the major revolution in economic growth has come in the measurement of prices. Beginning with work on hedonic price theory, work by index-number specialists and industrial-organisation economists has presented an impressive array of evidence that the Standard Story fails to capture the reality of economic history because the Standard Story fails to measure prices accurately. Part of the difficulty in measuring prices comes from standard index-number measurement problems. But recent developments suggest that an even larger part comes from the inability of stand-ard price measures to capture the extent of quality change as technology leapfrogs from old to new products. Our statisticians must somehow measure the degree of improvement from horse to automobile to jet plane, from Pony Express to telegraph to conventional mail to electronic mail, from quills to carbon paper to Xerox machine, from dark and lonely nights to television to VCRs, from bleeding leeches to penicillin, and from exploratory brain surgery to magnetic resonance imaging. In other words, accurate output measures require price indexes that recognise the vast changes in the quality and range of goods and services that we consume.

Statistical agencies have made great strides in tracking the prices of identical goods in a reliable and timely manner. But constructing price indexes that adequately cap-ture the impact on prices of new technologies, especially radical new inventions, is beyond the practical capability of current techniques.

The purpose of this essay is to sketch out the argument that we may have signifi-cantly underestimated the growth in real output and real incomes. To do this, I present two sets of results. The first is a summary of a study I performed for a small but critical sector, lighting. Lighting is particularly useful because we can compare 'true' price and output indexes in this sector with traditional approaches over long time periods. A second section summarises recent evidence on an apparently unrelated piece of evi-dence – the bias in measuring consumer prices. The bottom line is simple: Because of mismeasurement of prices, the Standard Story significantly underestimates the growth in real output and real wages. If further studies bear out this hypothesis, the growth in productivity and real wages may have been significantly understated since the Indus-trial Revolution.

I begin with a review of the technical issues in measuring prices, focusing on product quality. I then provide an example focusing on the case of lighting, for which data are particularly revealing. After reviewing other research on biases in measuring consumer prices, I conclude with a heretical view about the way that conventional economic statistics may dramatically underestimate the growth in real wages and productivity.

2 PRICE MISMEASUREMENT AND GROWTH BIAS

The major theme of this essay is that conventional measures underestimate the growth of real output and real wages. The reason for this syndrome is that accurate measures of real output require accurate price indexes to deflate nominal outputs and incomes, yet long-term price measures are shaky in the best of cases and worthless in the worst of cases. Construction of accurate long-term price indexes is a Herculean task, and at present we have only suggestive evidence of the magnitude of the long-term bias.

The fundamental issue is not new. Measures of the growth of real output and real wages begin with nominal incomes and outputs and then deflate these using price indexes. Clearly, if the price indexes are defective, then the output measures are equally defective. To take the example of a single commodity, if the price index overestimates the price increase by 1% per year, then this will lead to 'overdeflation', and output growth will consequently be underestimated by 1% per year. For the discussion that follows, I will focus on the US consumer price index (CPI).[3] The CPI is the basis for the detailed price data underlying not only the CPI but also the consumption components of the US national income and product accounts.

Mismeasurement of prices arises for two major reasons: classic index-number problems and problems associated with new products and quality change.[4] Index-number problems arise primarily from using inappropriate weights in construction of the aggregates. For example, the CPI currently uses fixed-weight (Layspeyres) indexes at all levels of aggregation. Current evidence indicates that the CPI overstates price increases by about 0.5% per year because of both trends and volatility in price and changes in outlets and the consequent substitution away from goods whose prices are rising.

A second set of issues on which I will focus here is the difficulty of correctly measuring the value of new products and quality change. This difficulty is most easily understood if we recognise that traditional price indexes measure the prices of goods that consumers buy rather than the prices of the services that consumers enjoy. For purposes of measuring the true cost of living, we clearly should focus on the outputs rather than the inputs. More precisely, we must distinguish between a traditional *goods–price index* that measures the prices of inputs of purchased goods and the more appropriate *characteristics–price index* that measures the (implicit) price of the output.

Some general background in the theory and practice of price measurement will illustrate the difficulty of adjusting price indexes for quality change and new products. There are literally tens of thousands of new products that are encountered by price examiners each year. Some are trivial (involving perhaps a different colour shirt). Many involve routine changes in designs (such as upgrading the compressor on an air conditioner or putting a thermometer in a car). For these two kinds of changes, price examiners have devised a set of techniques for allowing quality change, but there are serious questions about the extent to which the value of quality changes is adequately captured in prices.

The real difficulty comes with new goods or services. Current procedure is to 'link' these goods into the index rather than to reprice the basic category taking account of the quality change. Consider the case of a compact fluorescent bulb. Calculations

---

[3] Most of the issues for the United States, particularly those involving new goods and quality change, arise for other countries as well.

[4] The latter includes not only the issues of new and improved products emphasised in this essay but also the movement to self-service sales, changes in outlets from small stores to discount chains, and the life cycle of fashion apparel.

indicate this new bulb delivers illumination at about one-quarter the cost of the earlier technology. An ideal price index would therefore indicate a fall in the price of lighting devices. Instead, current practice would be to start the new device at the same index level as the old device and track changes in the price of the new device. The same procedure would be used when automobiles replace horses, when computers replace typewriters, or when pharmaceuticals replace surgery. Hence, any major changes in efficiency that occur when radical new consumer products are introduced are simply eliminated under the conventions of current price measurement.

A little algebra will illustrate the problem more clearly. An appropriate measure of the true cost of living would calculate the prices of the useful services delivered by purchased goods and services rather than on the prices of the purchased goods themselves. Say that the underlying utility function is $U(C_1, C_2, \ldots)$, where C_i is the quantity of characteristic i, which might be the quantity of illumination, the health improvements from a medical treatment, the number of bits of information transmitted, and so forth. Service characteristics are produced by purchased goods $(X_1, X_2, \ldots)$, which might be lighting devices, pharmaceuticals, or electronic mail. Service characteristics are associated with goods by the relevant production functions. To simplify, assume that each goods is associated with a single characteristic, so that $C_{i,t} = f_{j,i,t}(X_{j,t})$ is the production function by which good j produces characteristic i at time t.

Given the consumer's budget constraint, we can associate 'hedonic prices' (or shadow prices) with each of the service characteristics. These can be derived from the utility maximisation and are given by $q_{i,t} = p_{j,t}/(\partial C_{i,t}/\partial X_{j,t})$ where $q_{i,t}$ is the shadow price of characteristic i. The characteristic price is simply the price of the good $(p_{j,t})$ divided by the efficiency of the good that is used to deliver the characteristic at time t (given by $\partial C_{i,t}/\partial X_{j,t}$).

Using this approach, we can distinguish traditional price indexes from true price indexes. A *traditional price index*, P_t, measures goods or input prices and is given by $P_t = \Sigma p_{j,t} \zeta_{j,t}$, where $\zeta_{j,t}$ are the appropriate weights on the goods. By contrast, a *true price index*, Q_t, measures the trend in the prices of the characteristic services and is given by $Q_t = \Sigma q_{i,t} \omega_{i,t}$ where $\omega_{i,t}$ are the appropriate weights on the characteristic services.

This discussion shows that traditional prices can go wrong in three ways. The first source of error arises if traditional price indexes use the wrong weights. In this context, this is unlikely to be important, because the shares are simply the expenditure weights; these can be directly observed and are not affected by use of traditional rather than true prices.

The second source of error, quality change, comes because of improvements in the efficiency of a good. If a good delivers more services per unit of the good over time, this will lead to a decline in the price ratio, $q_{i,t}/p_{j,t}$. Third, traditional price indexes can mismeasure prices for new goods if the service–good price ratio is lower for the new good than for the old good. For example, if good $(j+1)$ replaces good j, then a bias arises if the ratio $q_{i,t}/p_{j+1,t}$ is lower than the ratio $q_{i,t}/p_{j,t}$ at the time of introduction of the new good. This new goods problem is particularly severe if new goods are introduced late in their product cycle (as is typical in the CPI).

The second and third problems raise no major theoretical difficulties, but they present severe measurement problems in practice. The problem comes in measuring the characteristic services delivered by different goods and services. A complete reckoning would require measuring such characteristics as the health status associated with different medical treatments, the timeliness and safety of transportation modes, the illumination cast by different lighting devices, and the enjoyment delivered by various forms of entertainment. Few of these characteristics are directly observed in the marketplace, and estimating them requires detailed statistical investigation.

I would go further and conjecture that the measurement problems are most severe for the more radical inventions. Our price indexes can do a tolerably good job of capturing the impact of small innovations. But revolutionary jumps in technology are simply ignored by conventional price and output indexes.

3 RECENT EVIDENCE ON MISMEASUREMENT OF PRICES AND REAL OUTPUT

While the importance of quality change and new products has been recognised in the past, recent research indicates that the quantitative significance of price mismeasurement may require a major reappraisal of the pace of growth of incomes and outputs. We move now to some specific examples of quantitative estimates of price bias.

3.1 An enlightened price of light

Begin with the humble case of lighting. Lighting is a particularly nice example because we have good measures of both inputs and outputs, because there are long-term conventional price indexes of lighting, and because we can actually construct an 'ideal' price index for lighting for two centuries to compare with conventional measures.[5] The example of light allows us to calculate the true price of the characteristic service of lighting (q_i being the price of a lumen-hour) as a replacement for the traditional price index of fuel (p_j being the price of candles, town gas, or electricity) over periods of more than a century.

The history of residential lighting displays meandering improvements from the cave dwellers of some half-million years ago, to fat-burning Paleolithic lamps dating from about 40,000 years ago, through candles and lamps of the seventeenth century. Then, around 200 years ago, revolutionary developments in basic science and technology led to a rapid series of lighting innovations, including town gas, kerosine and other oils, the filament electric bulb of 1879, and the compact fluorescent bulb of the last decade.

The overall improvements in technical lighting efficiency over this period are phenomenal. Illumination or lighting output is measured in 'lumen-hours.' 1,000 lumen-hours are approximately the light cast by a modern 75-watt incandescent light bulb in one hour, or the light from burning a standard candle for about 60 hours. Lighting efficiency is measured as 'lumen per watt.' The first recorded device of the Paleolithic oil lamp is perhaps a tenfold improvement in lighting efficiency over the open fire of Peking man, which represents a 0.0004% per year improvement in efficiency; from the

---

[5] The study on lighting is contained in Nordhaus (1996).

Paleolithic lamps to sesame-oil burning Babylonian lamps represented an improvement rate of 0.01% per year; from Babylonia to the candles of the early nineteenth century I calculate an improvement at the more rapid rate of 0.04% per year. The Age of Invention shows a dramatic improvement in lighting efficiency, with an increase of efficiency from 1800 to 1992 by a factor of 900, representing an annual rate of 3.6% per year.

Economists, of course, are more interested in economic efficiency and prices. What had happened to the true price of a lumen-hour, and have traditional price indexes captured the true price change? One measure of efficiency is simply the labour price of light (which is the inverse of labour productivity). This measures the number of hours required to earn enough to buy a given amount of illumination. Fig. 1 shows the labour price of light from Babylonian times. The number of hours required to pay for 1,000 lumen-hours fell slowly until the nineteenth century. Since 1800, the labour price of light has fallen by a factor of almost 10,000.

Constructing price indexes is a more arduous task. The first step is to derive a 'traditional' or conventional estimate of the price of light. For this purpose, I pieced together a traditional price index back to about 1800 from a variety of sources. This index is constructed by linking together the prices of the fuels that go into lighting. It is clear that this traditional index is only a rough proxy for what might have been used as a price of lighting if the official statistical agencies actually had set about to construct

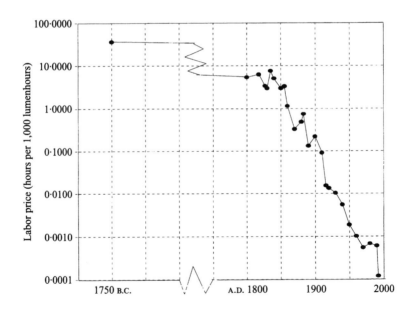

Fig. 1 Labour price of light
Figure shows the number of hours work necessary to pay for 1,000 lumen-hours of illumination. (1,000 lumen hours is approximately the light produced by a standard 75 watt incandescent bulb in about 1 hour.) Note the break in scales between Babylonian times and the last two centuries.
Source: Nordhaus (1996).

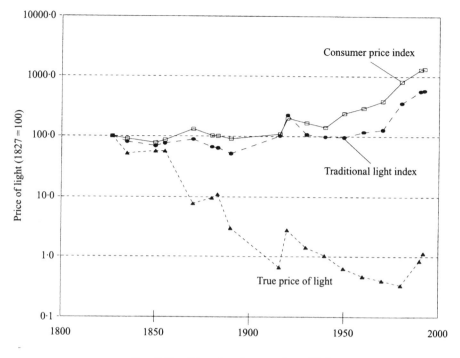

Fig. 2 Traditional and true price of light
Figure shows a traditional measure of the price of light, constructed in conventional price
indexes by linking together the prices of inputs such as candle and electricity prices. The true
price of light examines the price of a lumen-hour, whether that lumen-hour is produced with
candles, whale-oil, or a compact fluorescent bulb.
Source: Nordhaus (1996).

an accurate measure of the price of light. But in this respect, the traditional price of
light is probably a representative price index.[6]

Constructing an ideal or true price requires estimating the price of the service characteristics rather than of the inputs. Unlike many hedonic price indexes, the true price
of light is conceptually simple in that there are objective measures of output, namely
illuminance.[7] To obtain the true price of light, I need only calculations on the efficiency of the lighting device and the price of the fuel. The result of this calculation is
astonishing. Fig. 2 compares the traditional and true price indexes of light along with
the overall consumer price index. The traditional price of light has risen by a factor of

---

[6] It may surprise people to learn that as of 1990 there were only two hedonic price indexes routinely
included in all the price calculations of the US government (these being for housing and for computers).
[7] Clearly, illuminance as measured by lumen-hours oversimplifies lighting services, as it omits other
characteristics such as wavelength, reliability, convenience, safety, and durability. Further, this calculation includes only the marginal fuel cost of lighting for the best-practice technology. These issues are
discussed in Nordhaus (1996).

five in nominal terms since 1800. This is not bad compared to all consumer prices (again, the traditional version), which have risen tenfold over the same period.

The true price of light bears no resemblance of the traditional indexes. As can be seen in Fig. 2, the traditional price of light has risen by a factor of about 1,000 relative to the true price. The two measures are essentially unrelated: the squared correlation coefficient between the changes in the logarithms of the true light price and the traditional price is 0.07. The average annual bias (the rise in the traditional price relative to the true price) is 4.9% per year over the 1850–1992 period.

To summarise, this example shows that for the homely case of lighting, traditional price indexes dramatically overstate the true increase in prices as measured by the price of the characteristic service. The implication is that the nominal spending on lighting has been deflated by a price index that has grown too rapidly: because of overdeflation, the growth in the volume of lighting has been underestimated by a factor of around 1,000 since the beginning of the industrial age.

3.2 Price assessment by the Boskin Commission

Thanks to the dramatic gains in efficiency, lighting is but a tiny slice of consumption spending today. The natural follow up question is whether mismeasurement of prices occurs for other goods and services. This question in turn leads to the issue of the overall bias in the measurement of consumer prices that is currently the source of extensive research.

The most complete assessment of the bias in measuring consumer prices is the recent report of the Advisory Commission on the CPI (the Boskin Commission).[8] This panel of distinguished economists examined the construction of the CPI and concluded that it overstated the actual rate of price inflation by 1.3 percentage points prior to 1996; it projects that the current concept will overstate inflation by 1.1 percentage points over the next few years. The forward-looking bias estimate consists of 0.5 percentage points annually for index-number problems and other technical issues, and 0.6 percentage points annually for new products and quality change. They note that the later number for the most part excludes the bias from new products.

It will be useful to explore the 0.6 percentage point quality bias. The Boskin Commission finds that 0.36 percentage points of the total occurs in six categories. The following lists the top categories and the estimated current upward bias in per cent per year. Professional medical services (3), hospital and related services (3), household appliances (5.6), apparel (1), cars (0.8), and entertainment goods (2).

The following is a montage of results cited by the Boskin Commission that will give some feeling for their estimates. One of the most dramatic examples is in computers, where a hedonic price index for the price of computer performance has over the last three decades risen about 15% per year more slowly than computer unit values. Yet, because the CPI uses 1982–4 consumption weights, the impact of falling computer prices on the CPI is negligible. Robert J. Gordon (1990) conducted a landmark study of quality change in consumer durable equipment. He found a 3.2% per year upward

---

[8] Advisory Commission (1996).

bias for appliances and a 5.9% upward bias for radios and TVs. Jerry Hausman (1996) investigated the value of increased choice of breakfast cereals (e.g. adding Apple Cinnamon Cheerios to Honey Nut Cheerios) and estimated that increased product variety would reduce the trend in the price subindex for cereals by about 0.8% per year.

Of all the sectors, the most daunting problems arise in the health-care sector. Here, prices are almost universally measured as input rather than output prices (e.g. the price of an office visit or hospital stay). Cutler et al. (1996) estimated that a true price index for treatment of heart attacks would rise about 5.5% per year more slowly than the corresponding CPI. Studies of pharmaceuticals have uncovered an upward bias of around 3% per year.

These examples just scratch the surface. They do not include estimates of the bias because of the inadequate treatment of new products. One perennial problem is that new products are introduced late in the product cycle so that much of the improved quality (the decline in the q/p ratio discussed above) has already taken place. For example, in the US air conditioners were introduced into the CPI 13 years after their widespread introduction, and VCRs and computers were not introduced until 1987. An astounding contemporaneous example is the cellular telephone. Calculations by Hausman indicate that as of 1996, the price of cellular phone service has declined by about 90%, and there are more than 45 million subscribers, yet cellular telephones will not be introduced into the CPI until 1998.

The most difficult issues for price indexes involve revolutionary technological inventions like the case of lighting discussed above. These include air conditioning, air service, antibiotics, automobiles, electronic mail, long playing record, nuclear weapons, radio, railroad, rockets, telegraph, telephone, television, and xerography. Traditional price indexes do not even attempt to capture the tectonic shifts that occurred as railroads replaced muddy roads, as telegraph replaced Pony Express, as telephone replaced correspondence, as air conditioning made the deserts habitable, or as medical advances have allowed life expectancy and health status to increase immeasurably. It is worth some reflection even to consider how one might go about measuring the impact of these revolutionary changes on living standards.

This catalogue of potential biases provides some background for the surprising conclusion that the US CPI has an upward bias of 1.1% annually. The Boskin Commission labels its finding as 'conservative' because of the omission of new products and gives a plausible range of the bias of 0.8% to 1.6% per year. Other studies reach roughly similar conclusions, with a lower bound of bias estimates of 0.5% per year and an upper bound of 1.5% per year.[9] In my own work, applying the estimates from the lighting study to all consumer commodities, including guesstimates for the contribution of new products, I estimated the bias might plausibly lie between 0.6 and 1.4% per annum.[10]

It must be emphasised that these are no more than informed hunches. Empirical quality change estimates have been carefully made for only a small fraction of consumer purchases. Moreover, aside from the lighting study, estimates include none of

[9] See Stockton (1995). Advisory Commission (1996). Shapiro and Wilcox (1996)
[10] Nordhaus (1996).

the major revolutionary inventions discussed above. To move beyond hunches to systematic measurement is a worthy challenge for economists.

3.3 The implication of bias in measuring consumer prices

The possibility that consumer prices might be mismeasured by 1 percentage point per
year or more hardly seems worthy of a controversy. Does it really matter that the
inflation rate from 1950 to 1995 averaged 3.1 rather than 4.2%? Actually it matters a
great deal. From a policy perspective, this implies that real compensation has risen
respectably over the last quarter-century whereas most measures indicate real wages
have stagnated. It also implies that indexed government programmes have overcom-
pensated people for movements in the price level. The Boskin Commission estimates
that if over-indexation at their estimated rate continues over the next decade, in 2008
this would add $180 billion to the budget deficit and more than $1 trillion to the U.S.
national debt.

But I would focus here on the implication on the measurement of real output. To a
first approximation, an upward bias in the trend in consumer prices will be reflected
on a percent-for-percent basis in a downward bias in the growth in real consumption.
The reason for this correspondence is that the deflators for nominal consumer expenditures are based on the same components on which the CPI is constructed.[11] To
the extent that the CPI misses the value of improved light bulbs, of new treatments of
heart attacks, of the enhanced value of electronic mail, or of the improved consumer
welfare from the availability of Honey Nut Cheerios to just that extent will the corresponding component of real consumption overlook the quality improvements.

The implication of the price–output duality is that to a first approximation, the
growth in real wages is underestimated by the upward bias in the CPI. Hence, if the
bias has been 1.2% a year, then real US wages from 1959 to 1995 grew by 70% rather
than 10%. Another important implication is for the rate of growth of total factor
productivity (TFP). Estimates of TFP growth for the US private economy have been
around 0.6% per year over the 1973–95 period. Assuming that the bias in the CPI is
representative of the rest of the private economy, true TFP growth has been about
three times the estimated rate.

A final intriguing possibility is that the productivity slowdown since the early 1970s is
a statistical fiction. Is it possible that the bias in measuring prices has so deteriorated in
the Information Age that the productivity slowdown is an illusion produced by defective price data? While this possibility cannot be ruled out, in fact it seems unlikely.
Studies of long-term trends provide no evidence that the bias has increased in recent
years. Indeed, it would be hard to match the pace of revolutionary inventions of the
period from 1875 to 1950 (think particularly of telephone, electricity, radio, automo-

---

[11] The price index for consumption in the US national accounts uses the CPI components for major
sectors and weights these using a Fisher Ideal chain index. It uses production rather than expenditure
weights for consumption. For a very small number of products – computers, airfares, and some components of medical care – the national accounts uses alternative component price indexes. Over the last
decade, the difference between the CPI and the national accounts deflator is less than 0.1% per year.

biles, airplane, and antibiotics). So while productivity growth is more rapid than conventional measures indicate, it has probably slowed in the last two decades.

4 SOME HERETICAL PROPOSITIONS

I conclude with some heretical propositions. I put these forward with an eye to prodding economists and especially economic historians to rethink the Standard Story of the contribution of technology to living standards:

1 Because of the practice of measuring inputs rather than output, we may be overestimating the trend rate of growth of the cost of living. In the one case where we have reasonably accurate measures of output and characteristic prices – lighting – the overestimate is a factor of about 1,000 over the period 1830–1992.

2 Recent evidence for the United States suggests that there is a pervasive overestimate of the rise of consumer prices, with a significant part of that bias coming from inability to measure the value of new and improved goods and services.

3 The consensus of price-index experts is that the US consumer price index has been biased upward by around 1% per year, with the lower end of the range about 0.5% and the upper end about 1.5% per year.

4 The central estimate of the price bias would lead us to revise our estimate of US real wage growth over the period from 1959 to 1995 from 10% to 70% and to increase our estimate of total factor productivity growth by a factor of three.

5 My apostacy stops with the productivity slowdown, however. There is no evidence that the productivity slowdown in the United States over the last quarter century is a statistical illusion. While productivity growth has been understated, it is hard to imagine that true productivity growth has been faster in the last two decades than during the Age of Invention from 1875 to 1950.

References

Advisory Commission (1996). *Toward a More Accurate Measure of the Cost of Living*. Final Report to the Senate Finance Committee from the Advisory Commission to Study the Consumer Price Index. Michael J. Boskin, chairman, December 4, Updated Version.

CEA (1996). U.S. Council of Economic Advisers. *Economic Report of the President*, Government Printing Office, Washington, DC.

Cutler, David, McClellan, Mark, Newhouse, Joseph P, and Remler, Dahlia (1996). 'Are medical care prices declining?' NBER Working Paper no 3750, Cambridge, MA (September).

Dension, Edward F. (1962). *Sources of Economic Growth and the Alternative Before Us*. Committee for Economic Development. New York.

Diewert, W. Erwin (1987). 'Index numbers.' In *The New Palgrave: A Dictionary of Economics*, vol. 2 (eds J. Eatwell, M. Milgate and P. Newman). London: Macmillan, pp. 767–80.

Gordon, Robert J. (1990). *The Measurement of Durable Goods Prices*, Chicago: University of Chicago Press.

Griliches, Zvi and Cockburn, Iain (1994). 'Generics and new goods in pharmaceutical price indexes.' *American Economic Review* (December) vol. 84(5), pp. 1213–32.

Hausman, Jerry A. (1996). 'Valuation of new goods under perfect and imperfect competition. In *The Economics of New Goods* (eds Timothy F. Bresnahan and Robert J. Gordon). Chicago: Chicago University Press for the National Burean of Economic Research.

Jorgenson, Dale W. and Griliches, Zvi (1967). 'The explanation of productivity change.' *Review of Economic Studies*, vol. 34. no. 99 July, pp. 249–80.

Maddison, Angus (1982) *Phases of Capitalism Development,* Oxford: Oxford University Press.

Nordhaus, William D. (1996). 'Do real output and real wage measures capture reality? The history of lighting suggests not.' In *The Economics of New Goods* (eds Timothy F. Bresnahan and Robert J. Gordon). Chicago: Chicago University Press for the National Burean of Economic Research.

Shapiro, Matthew D. and Wilcox, David W. (1996). 'Mismeasurement in the Consumer Price Index: an evaluation.' *NBER Macroeconomics Annual 1996.* Cambridge, MA: MIT Press.

Stockton, David J. (1995). 'The Consumer Price Index and public policy.' (mimeo), Federal Reserve Board.

Part 6

ECONOMISTS, THE WELFARE STATE AND GROWTH: THE CASE OF SWEDEN*

* I would like to thank Tony Atkinson for suggesting the topic of this controversy, and helping me to organise it.

INTRODUCTION

Huw D. Dixon

There is a growing consensus amongst policy makers and some economists that the welfare state is bad for growth, at least in the post-war western European form. One of the most influential bodies to argue for this was the Lindbeck commission, who recently prepared a wide ranging analysis of the options for the future of Sweden.[1] Many of the recommendations of the report have been implemented by the Swedish government. Sweden is an interesting case, since it has often been taken as one of the ideal 'Nordic' models for the welfare state, and has had one of the highest standards of living in the world for some time. If the welfare state is problematic for Sweden, it is likely to be even more problematic for countries such as Italy or the United Kingdom. There are really two key questions here: first, has Sweden's recent economic performance been poor relative to that of other economies?; secondly, how is this related to the welfare state – has the welfare state caused Swedosclerosis, that virulent form of Eurosclerosis.[2]

The origin of this controversy is Walter Korpi's paper, which opens the controversy.[3] Whilst Korpi has several arguments, there are two main points. The first is an empirical one: economists have not been very good at evaluating the evidence, and he believes that the arguments for Sweden's relative decline are very weak. Secondly, he argues that the advice given by economists has not been objective: the diagnosis that the Swedish economy was suffering from 'sclerosis' was an ideological one with little empirical support. It is worth pointing out that Korpi is a Professor of Sociology and Social Policy, and not an economist: he has consistently taken an anti-sclerosis position. He

---

[1] This was first published in 1993 in Swedish, and has since been published in English, Lindbeck et al. (1995) – all citations in Korpi.

[2] Paraphrasing Stähl and Wickman (1993), cited in Korpi.

[3] Although this is Korpi's first publication in English language economics journals, he has been arguing his case in Swedish for some time.

argues that the incentives are against Swedish economists rocking the boat and arguing as he does.

Magnus Henreksen[4] is very much someone who believes that Sweden has faced a sclerosis problem, and his paper outlines in some detail the argument for the proposition that 'relative to other rich countries, the rate of growth has been slow in Sweden for at least a quarter of a century'. In particular, he presents detailed arguments against Korpi's claim that the arguments of the Lindbeck committee and others are based on 'careless analysis'.

Jonas Agell's paper stands somewhat in the middle. He argues that the international cross-section evidence does not indicate that the welfare state is bad for growth. However, despite this he argues that the Swedish welfare state needed reform for a variety of reasons, over and beyond the evidence of Sweden's relative growth performance. He highlights the need to reform the legislation relating to the labour market, unemployment benefit and the deadweight loss due to taxation. The arguments here are standard microeconomic efficiency arguments, what Agell calls the 'bread and butter of a public finance economist'.

Lastly, we have an antipodean comment from Steven Dowrick, zooming out from the exclusively Swedish perspective. I leave it to the reader to draw his or her own conclusions from his comments. Whilst this debate focuses on Sweden, it is of course of much more general relevance. In particular, similar debates are taking place in the corridors of power and the groves of academia in many countries at this moment. Perhaps Sweden's social experiment will be the 1990s equivalent of the Thatcher experiment in the 1980s. In both cases the controversy will continue into the next millennium.

---

[4] Assar Lindbeck was of course asked to reply himself. However, he is writing an article on the Swedish experience for the *Journal of Economic Literature*, and so declined to contribute to this Controversy.

18

EUROSCLEROSIS AND THE SCLEROSIS OF OBJECTIVITY: ON THE ROLE OF VALUES AMONG ECONOMIC POLICY EXPERTS*

Walter Korpi

1 TACKLING THE IRRATIONAL TABOO

Schumpeter once observed that frequently economists, 'not content with their scientific task, yield to the call of public duty and to their desire to serve their country and their age' by acting as policy experts and policy advocates (Schumpeter 1949, p. 346). This raises the issue discussed by Gunnar Myrdal (1958, p. 4) of whether social scientists can be practical and at the same time objective: 'What is the relation between wanting to understand and wanting to change society? How can the search for true knowledge be combined with moral and political valuations?' Myrdal's questions point to serious but rarely discussed issues of objectivity and values when economists and other social scientists become involved in the making of public policy, often in areas of conflict between major interest groups in Western societies (see also Myrdal, 1929, 1958; Blaug, 1992, ch. 5).[1]

In everyday life the roles of the policy expert and the policy advocate tend to merge. This mixing can be understood in terms of Sen's distinction between basic values, supposed to apply under all conceivable circumstances, and non-basic values expected to hold only under specified factual circumstances (Sen, 1970, p. 59). Policymaking is typically concerned with non-basic values. Economists can change the goals and choices of policymakers by changing their views of what the facts are. By acting as policy advisers, many brilliant economists have undoubtedly done excellent service to their

* In the work leading up to this paper I have had valuable discussions with many Swedish economists and sociologists. However, several of them have been wary of being publicly associated with the views presented herein. Therefore, I thank them all anonymously. This work has been supported by grants from the Bank of Sweden Tercentenary Foundation, the Social Science Research Council, and the Council for Research in Humanities and Social Sciences.

[1] In the following discussion, the examples used refer to economists. However, similar problems are of course also found in the other social science disciplines. One example is the debate around R. Herrenstein's and Ch. Murray's book *The Bell Curve* (Goldberger and Manski, 1995).

countries and their times. In this context names such as that of John Maynard Keynes come to many people's mind.

However, it has also been noted that economic policy advisers frequently rely on anecdotal evidence and misleading statistics (Stigler, 1965; Rivlin, 1987; Krugman, 1994). Like bad weather, this situation has typically been accepted as a necessary evil. From the point of view of scientific progress as well as the democratic process, however, the intellectual responsibility of academic policy experts must be increased. With only the threat of losing intellectual credibility as a potential sanction, from time to time they should therefore be required to justify the empirical basis of their policy advice for a scientific audience. A case study on the empirical foundations of policy advice given by internationally prestigious and influential economists can be relevant for alerting the professional community as well as policymakers to problems of objectivity among policy experts. The purpose of this paper is to provide such a case study. The paper thus confronts what Myrdal (1958, p. 4) called 'the irrational taboo' against analysing the influence of values among social scientists.

The case study is of Sweden, where economics professors and other university-affiliated economists have exerted a major influence on public policymaking by claiming empirical data to clearly show that taxation and welfare state policies have resulted in Sweden's economic growth, since about 1970, seriously falling behind that in other comparable countries. These economists have thus claimed empirical support for what I here will refer to as the Eurosclerosis diagnosis, assuming serious negative effects on economic growth of the welfare state, taxation, and many other forms of political interventions into market forces.[2] Their diagnosis was summarised in captions such as '*The welfare state – a threat to employment and growth*' (Henreksen et al. 1994, p. 8, italics in the original) and '*Swedosclerosis – A Particularly Malign Form of Eurosclerosis*' (Ståhl and Wickman, 1993).

In Sweden economics professors have long acted as policy advisers.[3] The establishment of the Nobel Prize in economics in the 1960s greatly enhanced the national as well as the international prestige of Swedish economists. The Sclerosis diagnosis became established in Sweden already in the mid-1980s. Of significance in this process was a series of newspaper articles arguing for this view published in 1985 by Professor Assar Lindbeck.[4] In this context it must be remembered that the majority of Swedish university-affiliated economists have not publicly taken a stand on the Sclerosis hypothesis, but that during the decade up to early 1996 those who did supported it practically unanimously. This group included many of Sweden's most prestigious economics professors. The unanimity among these academic economists was seen by the Prime Minister as strengthening his policy position.[5] Some questioning of the Sclerosis hypothesis, however, came from economists abroad (see Bosworth and Rivlin, 1987).[6]

---

[2] These negative effects have been assumed to be generated, *inter alia*, through tax wedges on capital and labour markets (Barro, 1990; King and Rebelo, 1990; Lindbeck, 1983, 1988).

[3] Cf. Myrdal (1958), p. 237 ff.

[4] The articles were published in Sweden's largest and most influential newspaper. *Dagens Nyheter*. One result of these articles was a debate between Lindbeck and myself (Korpi, 1985*a*, *b*; Lindbeck, 1985; Cf. also Korpi. 1985*c*).

[5] Carl Bildt, Prime Minister 1991–4, in *Svenska Dagbladet*, July 21, 1991.

[6] Cf. also the forthcoming comparative study of Sweden and the United States directed by Richard Freeman and Robert Topel on behalf of the National Bureau of Economic Research.

The academic proponents of the Sclerosis diagnosis have received extensive media coverage. Leading politicians in all the major Swedish parties came to reverse their previous assumptions and have largely accepted the Sclerosis interpretation, which has provided the intellectual underpinnings for major policy changes made since the mid 1980s. A basic theme running through the memoirs of Kjell-Olof Feldt, powerful Minister of Finance in the Social Democratic government 1982–90, was the belief that Sweden's 'fundamental problem was the low growth of productivity and the lack of efficiency in the utilisation of economic resources' (Feldt, 1991, p. 432, cf. also pp. 254, 286–7, 296, 304, 325, 336, 382, 391 and 429).[7] On the basis of such a diagnosis, major structural reforms were initiated. Thus, for example, Social Democratic as well as Conservative–Centre governments have used the assumed low growth as one of the major arguments for the lowering of marginal tax rates, deregulations, and cutbacks in the welfare state. In the Spring of 1991, the Social Democratic government announced that its primary policy goal was low inflation rather than full employment, a position maintained by the following Conservative–Centre and Social Democratic governments.

It goes without saying that political interventions into markets via taxation or in other forms may have negative consequences for economic efficiency and growth. The purpose of this paper is however not to discuss the sign or size of these effects or to evaluate the policies based on the Sclerosis diagnosis. The central question of this paper is instead whether the empirical evidence presented by these Swedish economists warrants the Sclerosis diagnosis upon which they based their policy recommendations.[8] In this context there are two minimum requirements of objectivity. First, policy experts must avoid standard methodological pitfalls and use normal care in analysing empirical data. Secondly, they must take account of comparative growth data from OECD sources and easily available scientific publications in an unbiased way. I begin by discussing the empirical evidence presented in support of the Sclerosis diagnosis. One set of questions concerns methodological problems and care in the analyses of the empirical data. A second set concerns biases in the selection among available evidence of relevance for the Sclerosis hypothesis. In the concluding section, the Swedish experience is discussed in the broader context of the role of values and the problem of objectivity in the social sciences.

2 METHODOLOGICAL PROBLEMS

The evidence advanced by Swedish economists in support of the Sclerosis diagnosis has been almost exclusively based on comparative macro-level growth data.[9] The

---

[7] Kjell Olof Feldt holds a masters degree in economics. In comparison with the previous Social Democratic government, he trebled the number of academically trained economists among the top advisers within the Ministry of Finance.

[8] An assumption in this debate is that within Europe variations in causal factors with a potential growth impact are large enough to make possible meaningful comparisons.

[9] I accept their assumption that if the negative efficiency effects are large, it should be possible to observe them also at the macro-level. The Sclerosis diagnosis should, however, preferably be tested on micro-data. A recent micro-analysis of labour supply effects of taxes and transfers in Sweden reveals negative as well as positive effects but 'does not suggest strong general conclusions' (Gustafsson and Klevmarken, 1993, p. 131).

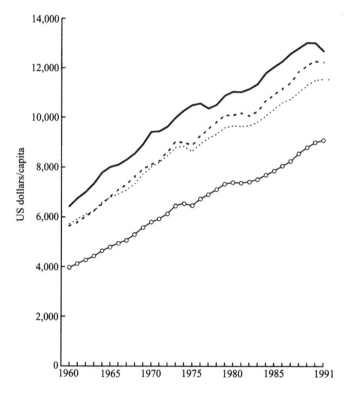

Fig. 1 GDP per capita (1985 prices and exchange rates), 1960–91 in the OECD (- - - -); EEC (—○—); Sweden (—); and six rich western European countries (- - - -)

macro-level effects have been claimed to be large indeed. Often cited as evidence for this position is a paper by Hansson (1984) estimating that as a result of tax wedges on labour supply, in Sweden a marginal increase in taxes by \$1 to finance money transfers to households will create a total cost of \$3–7 (for example, Lindbeck 1985).

Since 1990, Sweden has suffered a severe economic recession. In the concluding section, I will briefly discuss the causes for this economic crisis, which came well after the Sclerosis diagnosis had been established. As a background for the following discussion, let us look at comparative OECD data on GDP growth for 1960–91, data which were available when the Sclerosis diagnosis was established in Sweden. Fig. 1 shows the development of GDP per capita (in 1985 prices and exchange rates) 1960–91 in Sweden, the OECD, and the EEC.[10] The figure also gives the (unweighted) average for the

[10] The source is OECD's *National Accounts*, vol. 1, 1993 and earlier years. The spokesmen for the Sclerosis diagnosis have used OECD data based on 1985 prices and exchange rates. Because of the drastic Swedish devaluations in the late 1970s and in 1982, the 1985 dollar exchange rate is lower than the average exchange rate in 1970 and in 1990.

six European countries (Denmark, France, Germany, the Netherlands, Switzerland, and the United Kingdom) which in 1970 together with Sweden had the highest levels of GDP per capita, and thus also similar starting-points for relative growth in the following period.[11] As in the other OECD countries, growth rates in Sweden declined after the 1973 'oil shock'. In Sweden, however, the decline came two years later than in the OECD. Sweden's absolute advantage over the OECD increased slightly from 1960 to the mid-1970s, then decreased. Its absolute advantage over the EEC and the other six rich countries tended to increase up to 1990.

2.1 GDP growth comparisons

For several years, the only empirical fact advanced as evidence for the Sclerosis diagnosis was a comparison between the percentage growth rate of real GDP since 1970 in Sweden and the OECD (Bergman et al. 1990; Bergman et al. 1991*a*; Henreksen et al. 1992; Henreksen, 1992; Södersten, 1992; Henreksen et al. 1994).[12] Such a comparison indicates, for example, that between 1970 and 1989 the average annual growth of the volume of the GDP was 3.0% in the OECD but only 2.0% in Sweden. However the Sclerosis spokesmen never reported figures in the same table (table 3.1 in OECD's *Historical Statistics*) showing that in the period 1970–89, besides Sweden, other rich West European countries also had percentage growth rates below the OECD average – for example, Switzerland (1.6), Denmark (1.9), the Netherlands (2.3), Germany (2.3), the United Kingdom (2.4), and France (2.7). Since many rich countries with greatly differing types of tax and welfare systems have had growth rates below the OECD average, contrary to what the Sclerosis spokesmen argued the Sweden–OECD comparison can obviously not support the Sclerosis diagnosis.

Subsequently Sweden's relative GDP growth was compared with figures for OECD–Europe, EEC, and the 'Smaller European Countries' as defined by the OECD (for example, Eklund et al. 1993), and was seen as alarmingly low. This type of growth comparisons have also found their way into elementary economics textbooks (Eklund, 1994). However, all the aggregates used in these comparisons include several relatively poor countries, such as Turkey, Greece, Portugal, Spain, and Ireland. Therefore, they have average GDP per capita levels considerably lower than that in Sweden, which in 1970 was one of the richest of the OECD countries. As is well-known, the catch-up/convergence hypothesis predicts that *ceteris paribus*, poorer countries will tend to have higher relative growth rates than richer ones (Abramovitz, 1988, 1990; Baumol, 1986; Baumol et al. 1989, chapter 5; Dowrick and N'gyuen, 1989; Korpi,

[11] The ranking is based on PPP-adjusted GDP per capita. The following comparisons are not significantly changed if we include three non-European rich countries (Australia, Canada, and the United States) in this group.

[12] In spite of the scientific and political importance of the issues raised, the empirical arguments for the Sclerosis diagnosis were generally not presented in scientific works but in newspaper articles and in publications from an influential think-tank sponsored by the Swedish business community, the Centre for Business and Policy Studies (SNS). The following discussion is limited to publications by university-affiliated economists with a more 'scholarly' touch.

1992; Sala-i-Martin, 1994).[13] If we are to make causal interpretations based on comparisons of percentage growth rates among the OECD countries, we must, therefore, in one way or another control for differences in initial levels of GDP per capita between countries.[14]

However, Sweden's Sclerosis spokesmen appear to have been unaware of the catch-up/convergence hypothesis and consistently failed to control for the effects of initial differences in GDP per capita levels on differences in percentage growth rates. In an intellectual somersault they instead used these initial differences to corroborate their diagnosis in terms of absolute growth. Thus they applied the relatively high percentage growth rates, for example, of OECD–Europe from 1970 to 1990 to Sweden's higher initial level of GDP per capital in 1970 and calculated how much higher Sweden's GDP per capita would have been in absolute terms if Sweden's percentage growth rate had been the same as in OECD–Europe. In their presentations they then stated that Sweden lagged behind OECD–Europe in terms of absolute growth of GDP per capita (Henreksen et al. 1992, chapter 7; Henreksen, 1992, chapter 2). Thereby they ignored published OECD data showing that in the period 1970–90, the absolute growth of GDP per capita in Sweden, although being somewhat lower than the OECD average, was in fact higher than in OECD–Europe.[15]

2.2 The Lindbeck Commission

The most prestigious support for the Sclerosis diagnosis was provided by a commission of public inquiry appointed by the government to analyse the background of the deep post-1990 economic crisis and to suggest remedies. The commission was headed by Professor Assar Lindbeck and included four other economists, Torsten Persson (Stockholm), Agnar Sandmo (Oslo), Birgitta Swedenborg (Stockholm), and Nils Thygesen (Copenhagen) as well as a political scientist, Olof Petersson (Uppsala). According to the Lindbeck Commission, because of 'deficiencies in the general economic, social, and political milieu', Sweden's economic growth has seriously lagged behind that in other comparable countries (Lindbeck et al. 1993a, p. 11).[16] In an English summary of this report, the authors argue that 'Sweden's problems are largely due to distorted markets, ageing institutions and ossified decisionmaking mechanisms, which have not

---

[13] Convergence has often been interpreted to imply a decline in the dispersion of absolute GDP per capita levels among countries. Thus, for example Abramovitz (1990, p. 2) writes that '... as the process of convergence went on, the gaps separating laggards from leaders would be smaller ...' However, as I have shown among the OECD countries during the period 1890–1990 although the less rich countries tend to have higher relative growth rates, we do not find a convergence of growth paths in the sense of a decrease in the dispersion of the absolute levels of real GDP per capita (Korpi, 1992). C.f. also Barro and Sala-i-Martin (1992).

[14] This can be done, for example, by regression techniques or in a crude way by limiting comparisons to a group of countries with roughly similar initial GDP per capita levels.

[15] In terms of 1985 prices and exchange rates the total absolute growth of GDP per capita from 1970 to 1990 was $3,622 in Sweden, $4,148 in the OECD, $2,766 in OECD-Europe, and $3,288 in the EEC.

[16] In the English translation of the report, the section on growth problems is somewhat revised (Lindbeck et al. 1995, pp. 8–12. cf. also footnote 21).

been conducive to favourable long-run economic outcomes' and state that 'Sweden's chronic (long-term) problems are revealed in disappointingly low efficiency in both the private and the public sectors' (Lindbeck et al. 1993*b*, p. 220). Based on this diagnosis, the Lindbeck Commission advanced a catalogue of far-reaching policy proposals, which received an extreme media coverage.

The Sclerosis diagnosis made by the Lindbeck Commission stands on only two legs of empirical evidence. One of these is a table giving the ranks of Sweden and the other OECD countries for 1970 and for 1991, in terms of GDP per capita adjusted by purchasing power parities. According to this indicator Sweden drops from third place in 1970 to fourteenth place in 1991 (Lindbeck et al. 1993*a*, p. 13; Lindbeck et al. 1995, pp. 9–10). The most likely symptom of 'chronic, long-term problems' would appear to be a gradual retardation accumulating over the years. By presenting Sweden's relative positions only for 1970 and 1991, the Lindbeck Commission implies but does not show such a gradual decline congruent with its diagnosis.

The full set of OECD data indicate that for the major part of this period, between 1977 and 1990, Sweden's ranking was relatively stable, oscillating between sixth and eighth place.[17] Instead of a gradual decline congruent with the arguments of the Lindbeck Commission, the major drop occurs in 1991, the last year of the series. The annual figures on PPP-adjusted GDP per capita, which the Lindbeck Commission does not refer to although they were found on the same page from which they took their data,[18] indicates that from 1970 up to 1989–90, the Swedish development quite closely follows that in the EEC as well as the average for the six rich European countries (Fig. 2). Sweden's relatively small absolute advantage over the OECD observable in 1970 partly reflects the extreme Swedish growth peak that year. This absolute advantage disappears in 1989 and changes to a slight disadvantage in 1990. Sweden's absolute advantage over the EEC, however, increases somewhat up to 1990.[19] Published OECD data ignored by the Lindbeck Commission thus do not square with its diagnosis of long-term Swedish growth problems.

Furthermore, the Lindbeck Commission runs into the convergence problem without noticing it. Even if an originally rich country maintains the same absolute difference to the OECD average, in relative terms this difference will decrease because of the marked increase in PPP-adjusted GDP per capita levels. Thus while Sweden's position in relation to the OECD average declined by 14 percentage points from 1970 to 1991 (Lindbeck et

---

[17] From 1970 to 1991 the consecutive ranks for Sweden are 3, 4, 6, 6, 5, 4, 4, 8, 8, 7, 7, 8, 8, 7, 6, 6, 8, 7, 7, 7, 8, and 14. These rankings often hide very small absolute differences in GDP per capita. The high Swedish ranking in 1970 is based on the extreme Swedish peak this year, when Sweden registered a growth rate of 5.6 per cent, about twice the postwar Swedish average and twice the OECD average for 1970 (cf. Fig. 1). The relatively high ranks between 1974 and 1976 reflect the fact that in this period the other OECD countries were hit by the growth decline after the first 'oil shock', a decline which only reached Sweden a couple of years later. The Commission, used rankings based on percentages, which yields tied ranks.

[18] Table 2. Part Seven in OECDs, *National Accounts*, vol. 1.

[19] The total absolute increase of GDP per capita in purchasing power parities 1970 to 1989 was $12,400 in Sweden, $12.675 in the OECD, $11,540 in the EEC, and $12,720 in the six rich European countries (OECD. 1993, pp. 146–7). The OECD average is here strongly affected by developments in the United States, Canada, and Japan.

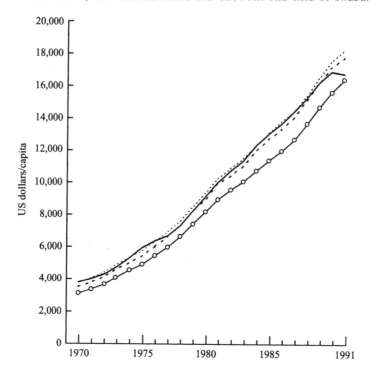

Fig. 2 GDP per capita in purchasing power parities 1970–91 in Sweden (—); OECD (‐‐‐‐);
EEC (—o—); and six rich western European countries (·····).

al. 1995, p. 9), the Commission failed to note that according to their own figures the relative position of, for example, Switzerland fell by 23 and of the United States by 16 percentage points. Here the catch up/convergence effect precludes causal interpretations but they have been frequently made (Henreksen et al. 1992, p. 96; Henreksen, 1992, p. 19; Lindbeck et al. 1993*a*). Thus gives way one of the two legs of empirical evidence presented by the Lindbeck Commission in support for its policy advice.

As a second leg of empirical evidence, the Lindbeck Commission compared productivity increases in Sweden and in the OECD in terms of GDP per employed person in the total economy, that is including the public sector. Sweden still follows early UN recommendations of setting productivity growth in the public sector equal to zero in its national accounts. The Commission failed to take into account well-known facts about Sweden's exceptionally large increase in government employment and selected an indicator which is biased in favour of the Sclerosis diagnosis (Korpi, 1992, chapter 4).[20] Other more comparable productivity indicators do not show the same relative

---

[20] From 1970 to 1990, government employment as a percentage of the labour force increased by 11.1 percentage points in Sweden but only by 1.3 points in the OECD. Several OECD countries (including Germany, Japan, and Norway) assume a positive public sector productivity development in their national accounts. The Swedish Ministry of Finance has also used the decline in the growth of GDP per hour worked in the total economy to argue for a long-term Swedish productivity decline.

decline (cf. below). Thus also the second leg of the Lindbeck Commission's empirical support gives way.[21]

In their English presentation of the Commission's report, the authors attempt to support their diagnosis by the argument that since 1970, Sweden's growth of total output in the manufacturing sector has been below the OECD average (Lindbeck et al. 1993*b*, p. 221; Lindbeck et al. 1995, p. 9; see also Eklund, 1994). Again, however, causal interpretations are unwarranted. In the period 1973–89, the growth rate of manufacturing output in Sweden (1.5 per cent) was not lower than the average for the above-mentioned six rich European countries (1.3 per cent) (Korpi, 1992, pp. 71–3). In this context, the OECD average is pulled up by Japan, North America, and the less rich European countries.[22]

2.3 Careless analyses with systematic errors

A very large part of the claims by academic economists for empirical corroboration of the Sclerosis diagnosis has been based on what, with an understatement, can be called careless analyses. To alert international readers to the rather astounding nature of this carelessness, I will here give one example. In the 1990 yearbook from the influential Centre for Business and Policy Studies (SNS), a group of economics professors and university-affiliated economists presented a table claimed to support the Sclerosis diagnosis. The table depicts the average annual growth rates of GDP per capita for Sweden, the United States, Germany, and the United Kingdom during four time periods during 1870–1973 and two time periods thereafter (Table 1). Under the caption '*Sweden first in the lead and then in the rear*' (italics in the original) the authors summarise the table in the following way: 'Sweden is highest in the growth league in all time periods up to the beginning of the 1970s. Thereafter Sweden falls into the rear' (Bergman et al. 1990, p. 15).

Table 1 GDP *per capita* in four countries 1870–1988 (Average annual percentage change)

	1870–95	*1896–1914*	*1920–39*	*1948–73*	*1974–81*	*1982–8*
Sweden	1.69	2.37	3.17	3.26	1.00	2.31
United States	1.95	1.81	0.84	2.23	1.42	3.22
West Germany	1.36	0.77	3.96	5.44	2.26	2.42
United Kingdom	0.82	0.78	1.38	2.49	0.93	3.06

Source: Bergman et al. (1990), p. 15.

[21] The Lindbeck Commission also pointed to the decline in Sweden's productivity growth in the decades after 1970 compared to the decades before. In the English version of their report they add: 'This is a serious problem regardless of whether productivity growth has fallen more or less than in other countries, and regardless of whether the slowdown in productivity is caused by the same or different factors in Sweden and in the other countries' (Lindbeck et al. 1995, pp. 8–9). However, to support policy recommendations tailored for Sweden, they would have had to show that the causes and/or size of the Swedish slowdown differed from that in other comparable countries.

[22] Calculations based on OECD *Main Economic Indicators* and US Department of Labor, *Monthly Labor Review.*

Quite apart from the minor relevance of the above table for the Sclerosis diagnosis, professors with experience in correcting student papers will quickly note that the summary of the table made by the authors is wrong for four of the six time periods.[23] As has been documented elsewhere, this is but one example of errors appearing time and again in the handling of empirical data by the Sclerosis spokesmen (Korpi, 1992). It is significant that these errors are not random slips, instead they reflect a systematic bias in favour of the Sclerosis hypothesis.

3 BIASED EVIDENCE

The Sclerosis spokesmen have presented a clearly biased selection of available evidence and data of relevance for their diagnosis. In terms of bias in references to published research, one example is sufficient. A survey claiming to 'summarise the most important results' from comparative studies of the effects of public sector size on economic growth in the OECD countries came to the conclusion that 'practically all studies' show this effect to be negative (Henreksen et al. 1994, pp. 47–9). However, in good economics journals it is easy to find studies which do not give clear support for this conclusion, such as publications by Kormendi and Meguire (1985), Ram (1989), Conte and Darrant (1988), Rao (1989), Dowrick and N'gyuen (1989), Levine and Renelt (1992), Levine and Zervos (1993), and Easterly and Rebelo (1993). The Sclerosis spokesmen have not initiated discussions on any of these studies.[24]

Biases in the selection of basic data on economic growth from annual OECD publications are all too easy to demonstrate.[25] Table 2 shows annual percentage increases between 1973 and 1991 of GDP per capita in the OECD countries, ranked according to average growth rates for the period 1973–89.[26] Since the international recession starting in 1990 hit the OECD countries with various degrees of delay, period averages are

---

[23] When I pointed this out, the authors (Professors Lars Bergman, Ulf Jakobsson, Mats Persson, and Hans Tson Söderström) thanked me for drawing their attention to a typographical error. 'The typographical error is that we stated that during all four time periods between 1870 and 1973 Sweden was highest in a group of countries. Our own table clearly indicates that it should have been high (first or second)' (Bergman et al. 1991 b). The editors of *Ekonomisk Debatt*, the leading Swedish-language economics journal sponsored by the Swedish Economic Society, were unwilling to publish a brief rejoinder, where I was to comment that among four competitors the one who comes second is in the middle, not in the lead. Therefore, also the authors' caption (Sweden first in the lead and then in the rear) apparently suffered from typographical errors. It should perhaps have read 'Sweden first in the middle and then in the middle'.

[24] Cf. Agell et al. (1994). The Sclerosis spokesmen have also ignored micro-studies indicating that the negative effects of taxation and social policies on labour supply would appear to be relatively limited (Danziger et al. 1981; Bosworth and Burtless, 1992; Moffit, 1992; Atkinson, 1993).

[25] See OECD's *Historical Statistics and National Accounts*. The level of unreliability of the GDP growth figures is often overlooked. My comparisons indicate that revisions of *National Accounts* generate an average range of variation for the annual estimates of the order of one percentage point. This estimate is based on a comparison of annual figures on GDP per capita growth 1980–4 in OECD's *Historical Statistics* 1982–92.

[26] Since average annual population growth 1960–90 was 0.5 per cent in Sweden and 0.9 per cent in the OECD, growth comparisons should be based on GDP per capita rather than on GDP.

Table 2 Growth of real GDP per capita in the OECD countries 1973–91 (%)

	1973–9	1979–89	1973–89	1990	1991
Norway	4.4	2.6	3.1	1.4	1.4
Ireland	3.3	2.7	3.0	8.7	2.0
Japan	2.5	3.4	3.0	4.9	4.1
Finland	1.9	3.2	2.8	−0.1	−6.9
Italy	3.2	2.3	2.6	2.0	1.2
Canada	2.9	2.0	2.4	−2.0	−3.2
Turkey	2.9	1.9	2.4	6.9	−0.2
Austria	3.0	1.9	2.3	3.3	1.6
Belgium	2.1	1.9	2.0	2.9	3.5
France	2.3	1.6	1.9	1.7	0.6
Germany	2.5	1.6	1.9	3.1	2.4
United Kingdom	1.5	2.1	1.9	0.2	−2.2
Spain	1.1	2.2	1.8	3.4	2.2
Denmark	1.6	1.8	1.7	1.6	1.0
Greece	2.2	1.2	1.7	−1.1	0.5
Portugal	1.3	2.1	1.7	4.2	2.1
Sweden	*1.5*	*1.8*	*1.7*	*0.6*	*−2.4*
Australia	1.5	1.7	1.6	−0.2	−2.7
Netherlands	1.9	1.0	1.4	3.2	1.5
United States	1.4	1.4	1.4	0.2	−2.4
Switzerland	−0.1	1.7	1.0	1.2	−1.0
New Zealand	−0.2	1.2	0.7	−1.3	−1.6
OECD	1.9	1.9	1.9	1.4	−0.4
Six rich European countries*	1.6	1.6	1.6	1.8	0.4

* Denmark, France, Germany, the Netherlands, Switzerland, and the United Kingdom.
  Source: 1973–9: OECD, *Historical Statistics 1993*; table 3.2. 1973–91: OECD, *National Accounts 1993*, vol. 1; Sweden 1990 and 1991, *Revised National Accounts, 1992*.

based on data for the years up to 1989.[27] In 1973–89, the average increase in GDP per capita in Sweden (1.7 per cent) was relatively close to the OECD average (1.9 per cent). Using the comparison with the other six rich European countries as a crude control for the catch-up factor, we find that in this group the unweighted average percentage growth rate (1.6 per cent) was about at the Swedish level. None of the other originally rich European countries had markedly higher growth rates than Sweden, but the Swiss growth rate was lower.

As a result of the international recession, in 1990 and 1991 low or negative growth rates were noted in Sweden, the United States, the United Kingdom, Finland, Greece, Australia, Switzerland, New Zealand and Canada.[28] Partly because of the boom generated by German unification, the onset of the recession was delayed in several of the

---

[27] To decrease the effects of national variations in business cycles, I will follow the convention of using 1973 as a breaking point for time periods. The proponents of the Sclerosis diagnosis have instead used 1970; the year of the extreme Swedish peak in GDP growth (cf. Fig 1)

[28] Sweden's growth rates given here for 1990 and 1991 are revised figures published in 1992.

Table 3 Growth of GDP per capita in purchasing power parities in the OECD countries 1973–91 (%)

	1973–89	1989–91
Norway	9.5	5.6
Ireland	9.4	10.1
Japan	9.4	8.8
Finland	9.2	0.5
Italy	9.0	6.0
Turkey	9.0	7.6
Austria	8.7	5.9
Canada	8.7	1.5
Belgium	8.3	7.2
Germany	8.3	7.0
France	8.2	5.7
United Kingdom	8.2	1.8
Denmark	8.1	6.2
Sweden	*8.0*	*1.7*
Australia	7.8	2.7
Portugal	7.8	9.3
Spain	7.8	8.1
Netherlands	7.7	5.6
Greece	7.7	4.1
United States	7.7	3.0
Switzerland	7.3	4.5
New Zealand	6.9	2.7
OECD	8.2	4.8
Six rich European countries	8.0	5.1

Source: OECD, *National Accounts*, 1993, pp. 146–7.

continental European countries. Growth rates for 1990 and 1991 are therefore not easy to use in a comparative discussion of the Sclerosis diagnosis (cf. below).

As indicated above, Swedish economists have made frequent use of PPP-adjusted GDP per capita figures in their attempt to corroborate the Sclerosis diagnosis (see for example Lindbeck et al. 1993a, b, 1995; Henreksen et al. 1992; Henreksen, 1992). In the period 1973–89, the average annual growth of PPP-adjusted GDP per capita in Sweden (8.0 per cent) was close to the OECD level (8.2 per cent) and the same as the average for the six rich European countries (Table 3).[29] Again, among the six rich

[29] The PPP-adjusted GDP per capita figures must be interpreted with great caution. Not only are they given in nominal rather than in real terms. They also suffer from a very high degree of unreliability. Thus the 1992 OECD revision of the first estimates made in 1985 generated major changes in terms of GDP/capita expressed as a percentage of the OECD average. For the year 1989, the average change for the 24 OECD countries was 5.2 percentage points. For individual countries the maximum change was 13.0 percentage points. For the top 17 countries the rank correlation between the two estimates for 1989 was only 0.70.

Table 4 Growth of labour productivity (output per employee) in the business sector in the OECD countries 1973–89

	1973–9	1979–89
Finland	3.2	3.8
Spain	3.5	3.3
Japan	2.9	3.0
France	3.0	2.6
Belgium	2.8	2.4
Denmark	2.6	2.1
Italy	2.9	2.1
United Kingdom	1.6	2.1
Austria	3.2	2.0
New Zealand	−1.2	1.8
Sweden	*1.5*	*1.7*
Germany	3.1	1.6
Switzerland	0.7	1.6
Canada	1.5	1.4
Netherlands	2.8	1.5
Australia	2.2	1.1
United States	0.0	0.8
Norway	0.3	0.6
Greece	3.3	0.4
OECD	1.4	1.6
Six rich European countries	2.3	1.9

Source: OECD (1991 (49), p. 120)

European countries, markedly higher growth rates than the Swedish one were not found. In 1989–91, however, Sweden's growth was low, at the level of those in the United Kingdom, Finland, and Canada.

For the period 1973–89, OECD figures on GDP per capita percentage growth rates, whether based on exchange rates or PPP-adjusted, thus indicate that Sweden's growth performance has not been far from the OECD average and at roughly the average level of that in the six other originally rich West European countries.

To be of relevance for the Sclerosis Diagnosis, cross-national comparisons of productivity growth should concentrate on the private sector.[30] The Sclerosis spokesmen consistently ignored statistics on productivity growth in the business sector published twice a year in OECD's *Economic Outlook*. These statistics indicate that in the period 1973–89, Swedish labour productivity growth in the business sector has been at approximately the same level as in the OECD (Table 4).[31] Thus in the period 1973–9, the increase in the output per employee in the business sector in the OECD (1.4 per

---

[30] The Sclerosis hypothesis deals with the effects of political measures on the functioning of markets. Productivity in the public sector is of interest in its own right but is very difficult to measure.

[31] This holds true also for the growth of capital productivity and total factor productivity in the business sector.

cent) was about the same as in Sweden (1.5 per cent). In this period Sweden's pro-ductivity growth was, however, lower than the average of the other six rich European countries, something which primarily reflects a specifically Swedish productivity de-crease in 1975–7 (cf. below). Yet it was higher than in the United States and Switzer-land and at about the same level as in Canada and the United Kingdom. In the period 1979–89, Sweden's output per employee increased by 1.7 per cent, that is at about the same rate as in the OECD (1.6 per cent) and the other six rich European countries (1.9 per cent). Again Sweden's labour productivity growth was higher than in the United States and at about the same level as in Germany, Switzerland, Canada, and the Netherlands.

Since the service sector with relatively low productivity growth makes up a smaller proportion of the business sector in Sweden than in many other countries, business sector comparisons introduce some bias against the Sclerosis diagnosis. The interna-tionally most comparable productivity measures refer to the manufacturing sector.[32] However, here problems of data reliability are especially serious.[33] In the Swedish case problems are aggravated by a break in the labour productivity series giving somewhat lower estimates for the period after 1985.[34] Since 1950, Japan has had an exceptionally rapid productivity growth. I will here limit comparisons of period averages to the other ten countries for which comparable data are available, that is Belgium, Canada, Den-mark, France, Germany, Italy, the Netherlands, Norway, the United Kingdom, and the United States.

During the 1973–89 period the average growth of manufacturing productivity per hour worked in the above ten countries was somewhat higher than in Sweden (Table 5). A specific Swedish lag appeared in 1975–7, when policy makers expected the down-turn after the first 'oil shock' to be relatively short and induced manufacturing firms to retain surplus labour. For the period 1973–7 this 'bridging-over' policy thus decreased not only open unemployment but also the labour productivity growth rate (1.5 per cent in Sweden compared to the 3.7 per cent average for the other ten countries). In the following upswing, it facilitated a productivity increase when firms could make use of hoarded labour.

The labour productivity increase in Sweden 1977–9 was at the same level as the average for the other ten countries. Higher increases were evident in Belgium, Italy, the United Kingdom, the Netherlands, and France, comparable or lower growth rates in the United States, Germany, Norway, Denmark, and Canada. For the 1980–9 period, when the main effects of previous labour hoarding should have been exhausted, the Swedish productivity increase was somewhat lower than the ten-country average. Yet it was higher than or at the same level as productivity increases in Denmark, Canada,

---

[32] US Department of Labor, Bureau of Labor Statistics.

[33] A comparison of manufacturing labour productivity figures published in nearby issues of the *Monthly Labor Review* indicates that as a result of revisions, for individual countries for the period 1984–9 estimates on average productivity growth differed by up to 1.2 percentage points and for the period 1979–84 by up to 1.6 percentage points. For single years changes up to 3 or 4 percentage points were noted. Since data quality on capital stocks is likely to be even lower. I will here limit comparisons to labour productivity measures.

[34] For Sweden, the following productivity estimates are from the 1993 revision of *National Accounts*.

Table 5 Growth of productivity in manufacturing per hour worked in ten OECD countries, Sweden, and Japan 1973–89 and 1980–89 (%)

	1973–89	*1973–7*	*1977–9*	*1980–9*
Belgium	5.3	6.3	3.2	4.9
Italy	4.7	4.7	4.7	3.9
Netherlands	4.2	5.3	3.6	3.4
France	3.9	4.6	3.7	3.8
United Kingdom	3.4	1.2	4.1	5.3
Germany	2.7	4.4	2.2	2.5
United States	2.5	1.9	2.7	3.6
Norway	2.3	1.2	2.6	2.9
Denmark	2.2	4.6	1.4	0.6
Canada	1.6	2.6	1.3	2.1
Average	3.3	3.7	3.2	3.3
Sweden	*2.7*	*1.5*	*3.1*	*2.8*
Japan	4.5	4.2	4.6	4.1

Source: U.S. Department of Labor, Bureau of Labor Statistics, December 1991, Sweden: *National Accounts* 1993.

Germany, and Norway.[35] In Sweden, it is thus difficult to discover clear evidence for a long-term labour productivity lag in manufacturing of the type likely to have been caused by distorted market mechanisms.

4 HIGHLY PRECARIOUS OBJECTIVITY

Needless to say like other Western countries, Sweden has had serious economic problems since the early 1970s.[36] Nevertheless, given the relatively large and often unrecognised unreliability in macroeconomic growth measures, throughout the postwar period and up to 1989 Swedish GDP per capita growth appears to have been roughly similar to that in other originally rich European countries. Empirical data available at the time when the Sclerosis diagnosis was established in Sweden thus failed to corroborate such a diagnosis. The lack of empirical support is also evident in recent OECD growth data. Thus for the periods 1960–73, 1973–9 and 1979–89, Sweden's average rate of GDP per capita growth was 3.4, 1.5, and 1.8 per cent compared to 3.5, 1.6 and 1.7 per cent, for the above-mentioned six rich European countries.[37] For the years 1989–93, however,

[35] Especially during the second half of the 1980s, Swedish unemployment rates were very low (below 2 per cent of the labour force), indicating the possibility that also less productive labour was accepted into the labour force. The Swedish figures after 1985 are also affected by the change in the methods used for estimating productivity in the National Accounts.

[36] In this context it must however be noted that during the 1980s, Sweden's labour force participation rates were among the very highest in the OECD and average hours worked per week increased from 36.0 in 1981 to 37.9 in 1990.

[37] OECD, *Historical Statistics*, 1995, table 3.2.

Sweden's growth rate was −1.6 per cent as against 0.6 for the six rich countries.

Is the dramatic decline in Sweden's economic growth after 1990 – a decline which came well after the general acceptance of the Sclerosis hypothesis – a lagged Sclerosis effect? In this context a more realistic alternative hypothesis would appear to be that this marked decline primarily reflects a combination of the international recession and of national economic policies of the late 1980s and early 1990s, some of them inspired by the Sclerosis diagnosis. A tax reform and other political measures increased the household savings ratio by not less than 13 percentage points between 1989 and 1992, thus drastically curtailing domestic demand.[38] Banks and international currency transactions were deregulated and the exchange rate fixed to the ECU. After 1990, the top priority in Swedish economic policy was no longer full employment but instead low inflation. Major financial turbulence was created and mass unemployment reappeared.

Largely borrowing lines of argument from their American counterparts, Swedish economists managed to convince Sweden's political decisionmakers to base their policies on the Sclerosis diagnosis. They were successful in changing the policy goals of successive governments and in 'Turning Sweden Around', to use the English title of the Lindbeck Commission's report. As an example of achievements of economists, who in Schumpeter's words 'yield to the call of public duty and to their desire to serve their country and their age', from an intellectual perspective this exploit is however devalued by the fact that their policy advice was based on empirical analyses which can profitably be used as warning examples in introductory methodology courses. The work of these economists thus shows serious symptoms of an objectivity sclerosis. One can draw one's own conclusions from the fact that among the leading Sclerosis spokesmen, we find members of the Nobel Prize Committee in economics.[39]

Do the problems of objectivity identified above have more general relevance? Arguments similar to those made by Swedish Sclerosis spokesmen since the mid-1980s have been advanced by policy experts at least since the debates on the 'new' English Poor Law of 1834 (Polanyi, 1944). Thus for example, in Sweden in the early 1920s when taxes amounted to only single percentage points of the GDP, the great economist Eli F. Heckscher (1921, p. 55) warned for their serious negative efficiency effects. In the late 1930s, his followers Gustav Cassel and Gösta Bagge produced theoretical arguments for the conclusion that at 15 per cent of GDP the limits of taxation had been reached. A decade later, Colin Clark (1945) raised this upper limit to 25 per cent. Since the early 1980s, the Swedish Sclerosis spokesmen have repeated the old theoretical arguments of Cassel and Bagge (Lundberg, 1985, pp. 8–12). In the OECD countries government receipts have varied from around 20 to around 60 per cent of GDP, but in all of them similar warnings have been sounded by economic policy experts. It can be argued that the negative effects appear with long time lags, but as Lundberg (1985, p.

---

[38] In Sweden the household savings ratio (as a percentage of disposable income) has changed in the following way; 1986: 1.3, 1987: −2.8, 1988: −4.8, 1989: −4.9, 1990: −0.6, 1991: 3.4, 1992: 8.1, and 1993: 7.8.
[39] Thus Professor Assar Lindbeck, the leading Sclerosis spokesman, has been a member of the Nobel Prize Committee from the beginning in 1969 and its chairman 1980–95. Among other Committee members, Professor Lugemar Ståhl has very actively argued for the Sclerosis diagnosis and also Professor Torsten Persson has given it public support.

33) notes, such a statement 'cannot be proved, and it belongs rather to the metaphysics of wishful thinking.'

Although political measures affecting market processes certainly may have negative efficiency consequences, social scientists should be seriously concerned when theoretical arguments are recycled generation after generation without addition of empirical evidence increasing the precision as to the size of these negative effects and the conditions under which they are likely to occur. This recycling indicates that it is difficult for social scientists to make progress on issues concerning the relationships between markets and politics and the relative merits of small versus large governments, areas of recurring conflicts between major interest groups in western societies.[40] For the community of social scientists, objectivity is a collective good. However, in areas of central relevance for conflicts between major socio-economic interest groups, the individual benefit–cost calculus of social scientists is affected by powerful societal interest groups, something which is likely to generate free riding. Myrdal (1958) argued that to decrease the role of values in the social sciences, its practitioners should make their value judgments explicit. This is however not sufficient. Instead, social science progress requires a combination of two factors – theoretical pluralism and empirical work.

In early 1996, the Sclerosis diagnosis which has guided policy making in Sweden since the mid-1980s, is taken as an established fact in the media and is taught in introductory economics courses.[41] Although the empirical evidence in its support must be described as unimpressive, hardly any university-affiliated economists in Sweden have publicly questioned it.[42] To understand the problems of objectivity within the community of social scientists, we have to explain not only the support for the Sclerosis diagnosis but also why only those who agreed with the Sclerosis diagnosis elected to use their time to participate in a debate which was of major scholarly and public importance. The explanations have to be sought not in personal but in structural factors. Thus we can safely assume that no university-related economists among the Sclerosis spokesmen have consciously misled their readers. A hypothesis close at hand is instead that this outcome reflected rational action in a situation characterised by the combination of a dominant theoretical approach assuming major negative effects on economic efficiency of taxation and other political interventions and a relatively homogenous professional reward structure supported by the surrounding society.[43]

---

[40] In areas less central for conflicts of interests, obstacles to social scientific progress are likely to be smaller.

[41] Thus for example, at the Department of Economics, Uppsala University, in 1995 a test question at an undergraduate economics course stated that as a result of its low productivity growth, in the 1970s and 1980s Sweden's economic growth rate had lagged behind that of other comparable countries and asked the students to give the reasons for the low productivity growth.

[42] Sören Wibe, professor of forestry economies at the Agricultural and Forestry University in Umeá, was long a lone dissenter.

[43] An alternative hypothesis that economists who participate in the public discourse on economic policy do not have as good scholarly credentials as those who stay outside would not appear to fit easily with the fact that in the Swedish case, the Sclerosis diagnosis has had its strongest supporters within the Nobel Prize Committee on Economics of the Royal Academy of Science as well as at the Institute for International Economics at Stockholm University, widely held to be the very best Swedish research institute in economics. Even if this alternative hypothesis were correct, there remains the problem of the ethical responsibility of the professional community for important policy recommendations made in the name of the economics discipline.

A rational choice hypothesis makes it possible to understand variations in the willingness to take a stand publicly on the Sclerosis hypothesis. Any eyeball benefit–cost analysis would have indicated that while a Sclerosis supporter could reap the rewards of the dominant professional networks as well as from the dominant media and other societal power structures without exacting factfinding, net benefits of questioning were likely to be clearly negative.[44] I have heard economists indicate that they have experienced considerable risks associated with a questioning of the dominant view.[45] Whether such perceptions were correct or not, the striking lack of public criticism by economists of the factual bases for the Sclerosis diagnosis may indicate that such questioning was not seen as an abstract intellectual issue or a Sunday picnic. The absence of questioning can thus be understood in rational terms. Since the mid-1980s, as a professor of social policy I wrote a score of articles and a book pointing to the lack of empirical support for the Sclerosis diagnosis. This did not dispose the Sclerosis spokesmen to second thoughts but generated instead an openhanded use of *ad hominem* arguments. Up to early 1996, only one paper by established Swedish economists has publicly criticised the Sclerosis diagnosis (Agell et al. 1994). The media greeted this attempt with resounding silence.

In a pluralistic theoretical setting, tendencies to free riding on objectivity could be checked by an attention to empirical data. As underlined by Leontief (1971, 1982), however, in economics empirical studies have been relatively neglected (also Morgan, 1988; Blaug, 1992). From the point of view of objectivity in the social sciences, this is a serious problem. If the verdict between competing hypotheses would be based on empirical data, instead of being a problem the values of social scientists could be harnessed to contribute to scientific progress. When social scientists with different values meet in the analysis of empirical data, their values are likely to generate competition, the virtues of which are not limited to commerce. Such a competition would lead to intensified empirical efforts and social science would benefit. As the more than century-long Sclerosis debate indicates, however, in areas of central relevance for socio-economic conflicts of interest, the conditions for social science progress are – at best – precarious. Given the structure of rewards in Western Societies, where major societal conflicts of interest permeate research areas thin on theoretical pluralism and empirical data, scientific objectivity may easily become a luxury economic man cannot afford.

References

Abramovitz, M. (1988). 'Catching up, forging ahead, and falling behind.' *Journal of Economic History*, vol. 46, pp. 385–406.
Abramovitz, M. (1990). 'The catch-up factor in economic growth.' *Economic Inquiry*, vol. 28, pp. 1–18.

---

[44] Within the relatively small Swedish professional community, the existence of extremely prestigious bodies such as the Royal Academy of Science and its Nobel Prize Committee is likely to provide the base for a wide variety of influences, which need not necessarily be conducive to theoretical pluralism. In this context also the greatly unequal access to the media is of major importance for pluralism within the profession.

[45] Such perceptions were likely to be strengthened by a couple of incidents widely seen as demonstration cases.

Agell, J., Lindh, T. and Ohlsson, H. (1994). 'Tillväxt och offentlig sektor' (Economic growth and the public sector). *Ekonomisk Debatt*, vol. 22, pp. 373–85.

Atkinson, A. B. (1993). 'Conclusions.' In *Welfare and Work Incentives: A North European Perspective* (eds A. B. Atkinson and G. V. Mogensen). Oxford: Clarendon Press.

Barro, R. J. (1990). 'Government spending in a simple model of endogenous growth.' *Journal of Political Economy*, vol. 98 (5), pp. 103–25.

Barro, R. J. and Sala-i-Martin, X. (1992). 'Convergence.' *Journal of Political Economy*, vol. 100 (21), pp. 223–51.

Baumol, W. J. (1986). 'Productivity growth, convergence, and welfare: what the long-run data show.' *American Economic Review*, vol. 76, pp. 1072–85.

Baumol, W. J., Blackman, S. A. B. and Wolf, E. N. (1989). *Productivity and the American Leadership*. Cambridge: MIT Press.

Bergman, L., Björklund, A., Jakobsson, U., Lundberg, L. and Söderström, H. T. (1990). *I Samidens Bakvatten?* (In the backwaters of our age?) Stockholm: SNS.

Bergman, L., Jakobsson, U., Persson, M. and Söderström, H. T. (1991a). *Sverige vid vändpunkten* (Sweden at the turning point). Stockholm: SNS.

Bergman, L., Jakobsson, U., Persson, M. and Söderström, H. T. (1991b). 'Eftersläpning och faktafel' (Falling behind and factual errors). *Ekonomisk Debatt*, vol. 19, pp. 272–3.

Blaug, M. (1992). *The Methodology of Economics or How Economists Explain*. Cambridge; Mass.: Cambridge University Press.

Bosworth, B. P. and Burtless, G. (1992). 'Effects of tax reform on labour supply, investment, and saving.' *Journal of Economic Perspectives*, vol. 6, pp. 3–26.

Bosworth, B. P. and Rivlin, A. M. (eds) (1987). *The Swedish Economy*. Washington, DC: Brookings Institution.

Conte, A. and Darrant, A. F. (1988). 'Economic growth and the expanding public sector.' *Review of Economics and Statistics*, vol. 70, pp. 322–30.

Clark, C. (1945). 'Public Finance and Changes in the Value of Money.' *Economic Journal*, vol. 55, pp. 371–89.

Danziger, S., Haveman, R. and Plotnick, R. (1981). 'How income transfers affect work, savings, and the income distribution.' *Journal of Economic Literature*, vol. 19, pp. 975–1028.

Dowrick, S. and N'gyuen, D.-T. (1989). 'OECD comparative economic growth 1950–1985: catch-up and convergence, *American Economic Review*, vol. 79, pp. 1010–30.

Easterly, W. and Rebelo, S. (1993). 'Fiscal policy and economic growth. An empirical investigation.' *Journal of Monetary Economics*, vol. 32, pp. 417–58.

Eklund, K. (1994). 'Sveriges tillväxtproblem.' In *Marknad och Politik* (ed. B. Södersten). Lund: Dialogos.

Eklund, K., Lindbeck, A., Persson, M., Söderström, H. T. and Viotti, S. (1993). 'Sweden's economic crises, diagnosis and cure.' SNS Occasional Paper No. 42. Stockholm: SNS.

Feldt, K.-O. (1991). Alla dessa dagar . . . J regeringen 1982–1990. (All these days . . . In government 1982–1990). Stockholm: Norstedts.

Goldberger, A. S. and Manski, Ch. (1995). 'Review article: *The Bell Curve* by Herrenstein and Murray'. *Journal of Economic Literature*, vol. 33 (2), pp. 762–76.

Gustafsson, B. and Klevmarken, N. A. (1993). 'Taxes and transfers in Sweden: incentive effects on labour supply.' In *Welfare and Work Incentives: A North European Perspective* (eds A. B. Atkinson and G. V. Mogensen). Oxford: Clarendon Press.

Hansson, I. (1984). 'Marginal costs of public funds for different tax instruments and government expenditures.' *Scandinarian Journal of Economics*. vol. 86, pp. 115–31.

Heckscher, E. F. (1921). *Gammal och ny ekonomisk liberalism*, (Old and new economic liberalism). Stockholm: Norstedt.

Henreksen, M. (1992). *Sveriges tillväxtproblem* (Sweden's growth problem). Stockholm: SNS.

Henreksen, M., Hultkrantz, L., Ståhl, I., Söderström, H. T. and Söderström, L. (1994). *Välfärdsland i ofärdstid* (The welfare state in misfortune). Stockholm: SNS.

Henreksen, M., Jakobsson, U., Persson, M. and Söderström, H. T. (1992). *Tillväxt utan gränser* (Growth without borders). Stockholm: SNS.

King, R. G. and Rebelo, S. (1990). 'Public policy and economic growth: developing neoclassical implications.' *Journal of Political Economy*, vol. 98, pp. 126–51.

Krugman, P. (1994). *Peddling Prosperity. Economic Sense and Nonsense in the Age of Diminished Expectations.* New York: Norton.

Kormendi, R. and Meguire, Ph. (1985). 'Macro-economic determinants of growth: cross-country evidence.' *Journal of Monetary Economics*, vol. 16. pp. 141–63.

Korpi, W. (1985*a*). 'Välfärdspolitik och ekonomisk tillväxt. En jämförande studie av 18-OECD länder' (Welfare policy and economic growth. A comparative study of 18 OECD countries). *Ekonomisk Debatt*, vol. 13, pp. 192–203.

Korpi, W. (1985*b*). 'Välfärdsstatens ekonomiska konsekvenser och Myrdals problem' (The economic consequences of the welfare state and Myrdal's problem). *Ekonomisk Debatt* vol. 13. pp. 444–53.

Korpi, W. (1985*c*). 'Economic growth and the welfare state: leaky bucket or irrigation system?' *European Sociological Review*, vol. 1, pp. 97–118.

Korpi, W. (1992). *Halkar Sverige efter? Sveriges ekonomiska tillväxt 1870–1990 i jämförande belysning* (Is Sweden falling behind? Sweden's economic growth 1870–1990 in a comparative perspective). Stockholm: Carlssons.

Levine, R. and Renelt, D. (1992). 'A sensitivity analysis of cross-country regressions.' *American Economic Review*, vol. 82, pp. 942–63.

Levine, R. and Zervos, S. J. (1993). 'What we have learned about policy and growth from cross-country regressions.' *American Economic Review*, vol. 83, pp. 426–30.

Lindbeck, A. (1983). 'Budget expansion and cost inflation.' *American Economic Review*, vol. 73(2), pp. 285–96.

Lindbeck, A. (1985). 'Välfärd, skatter och tillväxt' (Welfare, taxes and economic growth). *Ekonomisk Debatt*, vol. 13, pp. 204–14.

Lindbeck, A. (1988). 'Consequences of the advanced welfare state.' *The World Economy*, vol. 11, pp. 19–38.

Lindbeck, A., Molander, P., Persson, T., Peterson, O., Sandmo, A., Swedenborg, B. and Thygesen, N. (1993*a*). *Nya villkor för ekonomi och politik* (SOU 1993: 16) (New conditions for economic policy). Stockholm: Liber.

Lindbeck, A., Molander, P., Persson, T., Peterson, O., Sandmo, A., Swedenborg, B. and Thygesen, N. (1993*b*). 'Options for economic and political reform in Sweden.' *Economic Policy*, vol. 17, pp. 219–64.

Lindbeck, A., Molander, P., Persson, T., Peterson, O., Sandmo, A., Swedenborg, B. and Thygesen, N. (1995). *Turning Sweden Around.* Cambridge, Mass.: MIT Press.

Leontief, W. (1971). 'Theoretical assumptions and nonobserved facts.' *American Economic Review*, vol. 61, pp. 1–7.

Leontief, W. (1982). 'Academic economics.' *Science*, vol. 217, pp. 104–7.

Lundberg, E. (1985). 'The rise and fall of the Swedish model.' *Journal of Economic Literature*, vol. 23, pp. 1–36.

Moffit, R. (1992). 'Incentive effects of the U.S. welfare system: a review.' *Journal of Economic Literature.* vol. 30, pp. 1–61.

Morgan. Th. (1988). 'Theory versus empiricism in academic economics: update and comparisons.' *Journal of Economic Perspectives*, vol. 2, pp. 159–64.

Myrdal, G. (1929, 1953). *The Political Element in the Development of Economic Theory.* London: Routledge.

Myrdal, G. (1958, 1970). *Objectivity in Social Research*. London: Duckworth.

OECD (consecutive years). *National Accounts*, vol. 1, Paris: OECD.

OECD (consecutive years). *Historical Statistics*. Paris: OECD.

OECD (consecutive years). *Main Economic Indicators*. Paris: OECD.

OECD (1991). *Economic Outlook*. Paris: OECD.

Polanyi, K. (1944). *The Great Transformation. The Political and Economic Origins of Our Time*. Boston: Beacon.

Ram, R. (1989). 'Government size and economic growth: a new framework and some evidence from cross-section and time-series data: reply.' *American Economic Review*, vol. 76, pp. 281–4.

Rao, V. V. B. (1989). 'Government size and economic growth: a new framework and some evidence for cross-section and time-series data: comment.' *American Economic Review*, vol. 79, pp. 272–80.

Rivlin, A. M. (1987). 'Economics and the political process.' *American Economic Review*, vol. 77, pp. 1–10.

Sala-i-Martin, X. (1994). 'Cross-sectional regressions and the empirics of economic growth.' *European Economic Review*, vol. 38, pp. 739–47.

Schumpeter, J. (1949). 'Science and ideology.' *American Economic Review*, March, vol. 39, pp. 345–59.

Sen, A. K. (1970). *Collective Choice and Social Welfare*. Cambridge: Holden-Day. Inc.

Södersten, B. (1992). 'Myter om den svenska välfärdsstaten' (Myths about the Swedish welfare state). *Svenska Dagbladet*, Dec. 3.

Ståhl, I. and Wickman, K. (1993). *Suedosclerosis – en särskilt elukartad form av eurosclerosis* (Swedosclerosis. A particularly malign form of Eurosclerosis). Stockholm: Timbro.

Stigler, G. J. (1965). 'The economist and the state.' *American Economic Review*, vol. 55, pp. 1–18.

U.S. Department of Labor (1991). 'Output per hour, hourly compensation, and unit labor costs.' Bureau of Labor Statistics (mimeo).

19

SWEDEN'S RELATIVE ECONOMIC PERFORMANCE: LAGGING BEHIND OR STAYING ON TOP?*

Magnus Henreksen

Sweden came out of the Second World War as a very rich country, relatively speaking. A high rate of growth was sustained throughout the 1950s and 1960s and by the end of the 1960s Sweden was the richest country in Europe with the exception of Switzerland. This is no longer the case, which has stirred a lively debate among social scientists.

The debate in Sweden (mostly conducted in Swedish) has taken place at two different levels. On the one hand, there has been a lively discussion whether Swedish economic performance has been weak relative to other comparable countries. On the other hand, a second discussion has focused on whether this (possibly) weak performance can be explained by the fact that the economic structure of Sweden has deviated in key respects from that of other OECD countries.

The purpose of this paper is confined to illuminating the first of these two aspects: Has Swedish economic growth been slow relative to other industrialised countries in recent decades, i.e. is Sweden lagging behind?

In section 1, the Swedish growth record will be characterised in order to discover if and to what extent Sweden has been lagging behind in recent decades. In section 2, I will critically evaluate the assertion made by Walter Korpi in this issue of the *Journal* that Swedish economic growth has, on the whole, been comparable to that of other countries. Section 3 concludes.

1 THE SWEDISH GROWTH RECORD

In the middle of the nineteenth century Sweden was among the poorest countries in Europe. A take-off began in the 1850s, and in the early 1870s, industrialisation based on raw materials provided a base for sustained economic growth which continued largely uninterrupted for one hundred years. Swedish productivity growth was exceptional in the period 1870–1950 compared to other rich countries, and even when the

* I am grateful for useful comments and suggestions from the participants at an IUI seminar. Financial support from the *Swedish Council for Research in the Humanities and Social Sciences* (HSFR) is gratefully acknowledged.

period is extended to 1970, Sweden comes out as having the highest rate of labour, productivity growth among the 16 countries compared by Maddison (1982).

Sweden's growth rate in GDP per man-hour was very close to the average for the 16 countries in 1950–70. If we exclude the extremely war-torn countries Germany and Japan, which disproportionately benefited from a positive catching-up effect, the Swedish growth rate was somewhat above the average for the period 1950–70.[1] A similar picture emerges from a comparison of growth rates for GDP, GDP per employed and GDP per capita for the 1950s and 1960s with averages for OECD and OECD Europe.[2]

Sweden's growth rate began to slow down relative to other countries around 1970. From Table 1 it is clear that the growth rate of GDP in Sweden has been only slightly

Table 1 Average annual growth rate of GDP, GDP per employee and GDP per capita 1970–93 (%)

	GDP	GDP per employed	GDP per capita
Sweden	1.19	1.37	1.14
OECD	2.76	1.73	1.98
OECD Europe	2.43	1.97	1.84

Source: OECD National Accounts, Main Aggregates, Vol. 1, 1995, OECD Labor Force Statistics, 1993.

more than half that of the OECD from 1970 to 1993.[3] For GDP per capita the difference is slightly smaller, the Swedish growth rate is roughly 60 per cent of the OECD rate. Sweden compares most favourably with the two aggregates in terms of GDP per employed. However, this is entirely explained by the extreme fall in Swedish employment in the 1991–3 downturn. In order to facilitate comparability Mexico has been excluded throughout from the OECD aggregate.[4]

The slow economic growth rate in Sweden since 1970 has had a highly significant impact on the Swedish income level vis-à-vis that of other countries. Comparing income levels is known to be more difficult than comparing growth rates across countries. The most suitable method is probably to use the OECD's purchasing-power-parity

---

[1] According to Maddison (1982, p. 212) growth in GDP per man-hour in Sweden averaged 4.20 per cent p.a. in 1950–70 as compared to an average of 4.46 per cent for the average of all countries and 4.08 per cent excluding Japan and Germany.

[2] See Henreksen et al. (1996) for details.

[3] The comparison ends in 1993 for the simple reason that this is the latest year for which complete data are available from the OECD. As far as we can see at this point a further extension forward would not change the comparison decisively to Sweden's advantage. In the latest issue of OECD Economic Outlook (June 1995) the average GDP growth rate is expected to be 2.4 per cent in Sweden and 2.8 per cent in OECD during the 1994–6 period.

[4] This exclusion has been carried out by the Statistics Directorate of the OECD. Thus, indicated data sources have been used except for the aggregate OECD series, which were received directly from the OECD.

Table 2 PPP adjusted GDP per capita in the 20 richest OECD countries, EC and OECD Europe, 1970, 1991 and 1993 (OECD average = 100)

1970		1991		1993	
Rank	Index	Rank	Index	Rank	Index
1 Switzerland	146	1 U.S.	125	1 Luxembourg†	144
2 U.S.	140	2 Switzerland	123	2 U.S.	128
3 *Sweden*	*109*	3 Luxembourg†	118	3 Switzerland	121
4 Luxembourg†	108	4 Germany	111	4 Japan	107
5 Germany	105	5 Canada	109	5 Canada	102
6 Canada	103	6 Japan	107	5 Belgium	102
7 Denmark	101	7 France	102	7 Denmark	101
7 France	101	8 Denmark	99	8 Austria	101
9 Netherlands	100	9 Austria	98	9 Norway	100
10 Australia	99	9 Iceland	98	10 France	99
11 New Zealand	97	11 Belgium	97	10 Iceland	99
12 U.K.	93	12 Italy	95	12 Germany‡	97
13 Belgium	90	12 *Sweden*	*95*	13 Netherlands	93
14 Austria	87	12 Norway	95	14 Italy	92
15 Italy	85	15 Netherlands	93	15 Australia	91
16 Finland	81	16 Australia	91	16 U.K.	89
17 Japan	80	17 U.K.	88	17 *Sweden*	*88*
18 Iceland	75	18 Finland	87	18 Finland	82
19 Norway	77	18 New Zealand	77	19 New Zealand	81
20 Spain	63	20 Spain	92	20 Ireland	73
EC 12	89	EC 12	92	EC 12	90
OECD Europe	83	OECD Europe	83	OECD Europe	81

Note: Mexico is excluded from the OECD average.
† Luxembourg revised its GDP estimate strongly upwards in 1995. According to the new figures Luxembourg had the highest GDP per capita also in 1991. Using the 1994 OECD publication Sweden was slightly ahead of Luxembourg in 1970, while using 1995 data Luxembourg per capita income was 16% higher than in Sweden in 1970.
‡ The large drop in German income in 1993 is explained by the inclusion of eastern Germany. In order to get data for 1970 and 1991 excluding Mexico, the 1994 OECD publication was used for these years.
Source: OECD *Purchasing Power Parities and Real Expenditures.* EKS Results vol. 1, 1995 (for 1993) and OECD *National Accounts, Main Aggregates,* vol. 1, 1994 (for 1970 and 1991).

adjusted measures of GDP per capita. Table 2 shows that Sweden had the 3rd (or 4th, see note of Table 2) highest GDP per capita in the OECD area in 1970, 9 per cent above the OECD average. In 1993 Sweden was ranked 17th with a GDP per capita 12 per cent below the OECD average.

In order to obtain a more complete picture of Sweden's relative performance, it is worthwhile to study the entire time path of income relative to other countries rather than just compare two points in time. In Fig. 1 (left scale) we can see that there is a clear downward trend in Swedish relative income even excluding the 1992–3 reces-

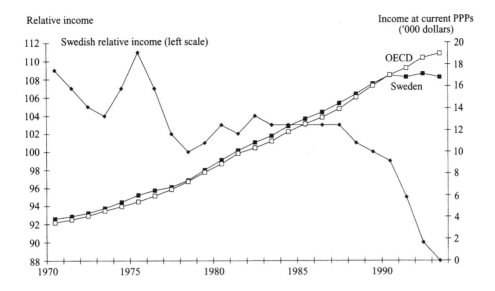

Fig. 1 PPP adjusted GDP per capita in Sweden relative to the OECD average
(left scale, OECD = 100) and nominal PPP adjusted GDP per capita
in Sweden and the OECD (right scale), 1970–93
Source: OECD *National Accounts, Main Aggregates,* vol. 1, 1994 (1970–92 for index series), OECD
Purchasing Power Parities and Real Expenditures. EKS Results, vol. 1, 1995 (1993 for index series)
and OECD *National Accounts* 1960–93, 1995.

sion. At any rate, it should be noted here as well that 1989–90 were extreme boom
years with unsustainable rates of unemployment at 1.4 and 1.5 per cent, respectively.

An important methodological point worth stressing is that consistency should be
maintained between growth and level comparisons. More specifically, is the average
growth rate for GDP per capita in Sweden of 1.14 per cent in 1970–93 when measured
in national real prices (as in Table 1) consistent with the growth rate implied by the
drop in the PPP-adjusted level of GDP per capita presented in Table 2? If indeed GDP
per capita in OECD grew on average by 1.98 per cent from 1970 to 1993 and the
Swedish average income dropped from 9 per cent above the OECD average in 1970 to
12 per cent below this average in 1993, it would imply that the Swedish PPP-adjusted
GDP per capita increased by 1.04 per cent p.a. during this 23-year period. Thus, it
seems that a comparison of growth rates in national currencies is roughly consistent
with the PPP-adjusted level comparisons at two points in time, although it should be
noted that growth comparisons give a slightly more favourable view of the Swedish
development.[5] The reasons for this are unclear – unfavourable terms-of-trade effects
may be part of the answer.

In summation, the analysis in this section shows that the rate of economic growth in

---

[5] The compounded effect of this differential of 0.1 percentage points p.a. is roughly 2.9 per cent on
the GDP level in 1993.

Sweden was comparable to the average of other industrialised countries until the 1960s. But the data on growth and income levels clearly indicate that after 1970 Sweden's economic performance has been far below the average of other OECD countries. The accumulated effect of the slow economic growth has been substantial. In terms of PPP-adjusted GDP level per capita, Sweden now ranks in the lower half among the OECD countries. Thus, it appears quite clear that Sweden has been lagging behind other OECD countries in recent decades. And yet, Walter Korpi, in this issue and numerous other publications, argues vehemently that Sweden's growth performance has been comparable to that of other industrialised countries after 1970 as well. How can he draw this conclusion? In the following section I shall pinpoint and critically evaluate how Korpi is able to present such results.

2 SALVAGING THE NON-LAGGARD HYPOTHESIS

Choosing different combinations of time periods, growth measures, deflators and countries/aggregates to compare with, may convey substantially different impressions when one compares growth across countries. In this section I will attempt to uncover the choices that allowed Korpi to present Sweden as a non-laggard, despite the straightforward evidence to the contrary that I have presented above.

Korpi does concede that Swedish economic performance has been very weak after 1991. But he also claims that the 'Sclerosis diagnosis' was firmly established in Sweden on the basis of OECD data ending in 1991, and that these data did not warrant the conclusion that Sweden was lagging behind. I will deal with this assertion specifically in several instances below.

2.1 Choosing 'propitious' time periods

The relevant issue here is the rate of growth in Sweden relative to other countries in recent decades. Hence, the starting year for a growth comparison should be chosen against that background. 1970 is usually considered a watershed year in this respect. Korpi, on the other hand, chooses to use 1973 as his starting year,[6] and he stops in 1989. Moreover, when he extends the data to 1990–91 these years are presented separately, because the development is seen as exceptional and thus should not influence the long-run averages. This procedure is totally unwarranted: 'the Sclerosis spokesmen' have claimed that Sweden has a long-run growth problem, and hence, as a purely statistical matter, the shorter the time period, the less forceful the critique against it. As Fig. 1 illustrates, Korpi starts his comparison in a year when Sweden had a relatively deep recession (1973) and ends when Sweden had an extreme and unsustainable boom (1989).

---

[6] The reason for using 1973 as a dividing line in many growth comparisons is that the average long-run growth rates were lower after OPEC I. However, here we are not primarily interested in average growth rates across countries, but in the *difference* in growth rate between Sweden and other OECD countries.

Table 3 Average annual growth rate of GDP and GDP per capita 1965–93, 1965–91 and 1970–91 (%)

	GDP			GDP per Capita		
	1963–93	*1965–91*	*1970–91*	*1965–93*	*1965–91*	*1970–91*
Sweden	*1.96*	*2.27*	*1.83*	*1.52*	*1.84*	*1.50*
OECD	3.13	3.27	2.89	2.30	2.43	2.11
OECD Europe	2.82	3.00	2.62	2.19	2.38	2.04

Note: GDP is measured at the 1990 price level and exchange rates (US$).
Source: OECD *National Accounts Main Aggregates* vol. 1, 1960–1993, 1995.

If one does not like 1970 as a starting year, because it is a boom year, then it would be more appropriate to start a few years earlier, say in 1965 when the first signs of an underlying weakness in the Swedish economy appeared, rather than in 1973. By starting in 1965 we get the average growth of GDP and GDP per capita in Sweden, OECD and OECD Europe that are displayed in Table 3. As the reader can see, this extension of the period does not change the general picture. In the same table I also present growth rates for the periods 1965–91 and 1970–91 in order to counter Korpi's claim that no growth lag is apparent before the 1992–3 economic crisis. Even when we use 1991 as the cut-off point, the slow Swedish growth rate is apparent. Furthermore, as already shown in Table 2 above, by 1991 Swedish PPP-adjusted GDP per capita had already fallen to 12th place (shared with Italy and Norway) among the OECD countries at a level 5 per cent below the OECD average.

Thus, this subsection shows that by focusing on the period 1973–89 in the comparisons Korpi has in effect excluded two periods of weak relative performance in Sweden (1970–3 and 1989–93), thereby giving an overly favourable impression of Swedish economic growth.

2.2 Ascribing long-term slow growth to mistakes in stabilisation policy

An implicit assumption underlying the alarm many display regarding Sweden's slow growth performance is that it is a symptom of underlying weaknesses in the economic, political and institutional system (see, e.g., Lindbeck et al. 1994). Korpi, on the other hand, claims that the lag in Sweden's GDP should primarily be ascribed to specific macropolicy mistakes, for example, too much fiscal restraint in 1970–1 and too much monetary restraint (disinflation) in 1990–1. Had these policy mistakes been avoided, the average long-run growth rate would have been much higher, and, consequently, the argument goes, it is quite legitimate to exclude the time periods when these policy mistakes lead to slow or negative growth!

This position is untenable. First, other countries have of course also made policy mistakes, and in order to be consistent these mistakes should also be excluded. Specifically, most European countries went through a period of tight monetary policy and disinflation at an earlier stage than Sweden; should we not then exclude resulting years of slow growth in those countries as well? Secondly, it is perfectly possible that, due to the stabilisation policy pursued, the underlying weaknesses manifest themselves in recurrent crises rather than in a stable negative growth differential relative to other countries. In particular, if there is some leeway in the stabilisation policy to postpone necessary structural changes, recurrent crises appear to be the more likely manifestation of underlying structural weaknesses. In the Swedish case one could mention a series of devaluations in the 1976–82 period, a dramatic expansion of public employment in the 1970s and of transfers in the 1980s, and an unsustainable rate of credit expansion which fuelled the domestic economy in the 1980s.

A look at the data series is also sufficient to show that a macroeconomics recession is not followed by a number of years of above-normal growth leading to a return to the old underlying growth path. Instead the various crises have resulted in a permanent lowering of the GDP level.[7] The same pattern may very well be repeated after the 1991–3 crisis as well (OECD, 1995).

2.3 Appealing to the catching-up effect

By appealing to the catching-up hypothesis,[8] Korpi argues that growth comparisons should chiefly be made with the initially richest countries and not with all OECD countries. This is the justification given for the comparisons made with 'six rich European countries'. Even if we accept the catching-up argument it is hard to see, based on Table 2, why the United States, Luxembourg and Canada are not included. Undeniably, there is plenty of evidence that a catching-up effect was operative in the 1950s and 1960s, but there is also evidence that the catching-up effect is less relevant after 1970 (Abramovitz, 1986; Hansson and Henreksen, 1994).[9] In this case, a comparison limited to the countries with the highest income in 1970 is misleading. At any rate, one should note that catching up concerns a closing of the gap to the leading country, whereas a change in the rank order of countries does not follow from the theory; notably, the theory cannot explain why one of the leading countries had ended up below the average. Thus, the Swedish drop in relative income from 3rd to 17th place after 1970 is not consistent with the catching-up theory.

There is some interesting evidence suggesting that, given the catching-up effect, Sweden performed remarkably well in the 1950s and 1960s, and that this was reversed

---

[7] This is consistent with the main message from the so-called unit-roots literature, see, e.g., the seminal article by Nelson and Plosser (1982) and Mellander et al. (1992) for Sweden.

[8] The catching-up hypothesis maintains that when the productivity level is higher in one or more countries compared to a number of other countries, the latter have the opportunity to embark on a catching-up process by applying superior production techniques transferred from the more advanced economies. Hence, we should expect technologically less advanced countries to grow faster than the technologically leading country(ies). Korpi also claims that the 'Sclerosis spokesmen appear to have been unaware of the catch-up/convergence hypothesis'. Given the number of articles that have been devoted to this issue in the Swedish debate, this statement is no less than outrageous.

[9] This is also consistent with the finding of no absolute convergence in per capita income in a broader data set which includes developing countries, see, e.g., Barro and Sala-i-Martin (1995).

in the 1970s. Dowrick and N'guyen (1989) estimated that Sweden's smaller scope for catching up led, *ceteris paribus*, to a lower rate of growth in GDP per capita during the period 1950–73 compared to the OECD average by approximately 0.8 percentage points. They also try to ascribe differences in growth rates across countries to contributions from increased labour force participation, increased capital deepening and growth in total factor productivity (TFP) after having controlled for the estimated catching-up effect. For Sweden they find that the rate of differential TFP-growth was strongly positive (+0.79 per cent p.a.) in 1950–60, while it turned negative (−0.25 per cent p.a.) in 1973–85.

Furthermore, recent developments in endogenous growth theory (e.g. Romer, 1990, Grossman and Helpman, 1991, and Aghion and Howitt, 1992) also tell us that we should not necessarily expect slower economic growth in rich countries.

Overall, these considerations suggest that a fair evaluation of Sweden's relative growth performance cannot be confined to a comparison with a handful of initially rich countries. Lacking strong arguments to the contrary, the most reasonable comparison is with aggregates of countries as in Tables 1 and 3 above.

2.4 Levels in actual exchange rates rather than PPP-adjusted and absolute rather than relative growth

When comparing GDP levels across countries it is crucial that the conversion makes sense. It is a well-known fact that the use of current exchange rates or exchange rates for an arbitrary year can be grossly misleading when GDP per capita levels are compared. To give the reader a sense of this problem, I compare the levels of GDP per capita in Sweden, Germany and the United States in 1993 at exchange rates for different years in Table 4. It is obvious that the use of current exchange rates gives rise to wide swings in GDP levels. The table also shows that it was not until the great depreciation of the Swedish krona after the conversion to a floating exchange rate system in 1992, which removed the earlier overvaluation of the krona, that comparisons using current rates and PPP rates began to give similar results. Thus, PPP-adjusted compari-

Table 4 GDP per capita in Sweden, Germany and the US in 1993 using different exchange rate conversions (in US$)

	1985 rate	*1990 rate*	*1993 rate*	*PPP rate*
Sweden	*19,228*	*27,949*	*21,246*	*68*
Germany	13,221	24,085	23,546	83
U.S.	24,302	24,302	24,302	100
Sweden/Germany	1.45	1.16	0.90	0.82
Sweden/U.S.	0.79	1.15	0.87	0.68

Note: For the PPP comparison the United States is set equal to too.
Source: OECD *Main Economic Indicators*, September 1994, OECD *Economic Outlook*, June 1995 (for exchange rates) and OECD *National Accounts 1960–93*, 1995.

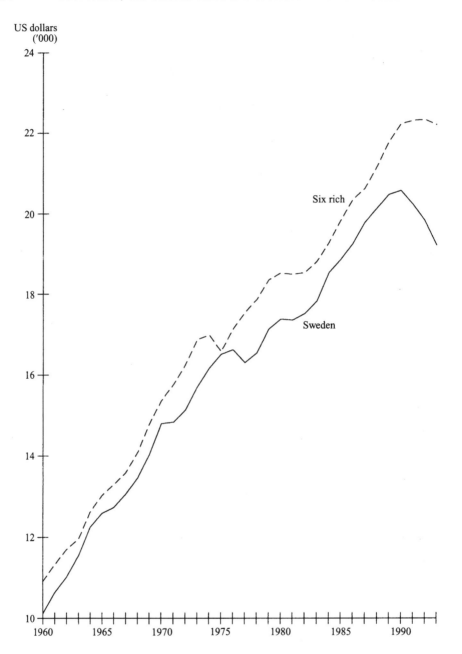

Fig. 2 GDP per capita 1960–93 in Sweden, EC and six rich European countries
(1990 prices and 1994 exchange rates)
Note: Six rich European countries are an unweighted average of Denmark, France, Germany,
the Netherlands, Switzerland and the United Kingdom. The use of 1990 prices does not
influence the level comparisons across countries in any systematic way, since it just determines
the weights applied for the aggregation of GDP components within countries.
Source: OECD *Economic Outlook,* June 1995 (for exchange rates) and OECD *National Accounts
1960–93,* 1995.

sons of GDP levels across countries are the only ones that give consistent and informative results.

Based on his Fig. 1 Korpi draws the conclusion that Sweden's 'absolute advantage over the EEC and the other six rich countries tended to increase up to 1990'. This conclusion is entirely due to the fact that the comparison is made using 1985 exchange rates. In 1985 the US$ peaked and the EMS currencies were very low. The Swedish krona, on the other hand, was tied to a basket of currencies with a disproportionately large weight for the US$. In Fig. 2 I have made the comparison with the 'six rich European countries' using 1994 exchange rates instead. As we can see this reverses all the conclusions. The average income of the 'six rich' is consistently above the level in Sweden and Sweden's absolute disadvantage tends to increase after 1975. This simple exercise just shows that nearly any proposition could be 'proven' by picking exchange rates propitiously, and Korpi has chosen the exchange rate that verifies his proposition.

Therefore, even if the reader were to agree with Walter Korpi that it is reasonable to compare absolute rather than relative growth it is easy to show that absolute growth has been slower in Sweden than among comparable country groups.[10] As shown in Table 2, in 1970 GDP per capita in Sweden was 9 per cent above the OECD average, 31 per cent above OECD Europe and 22 per cent above the EC level, while in 1991 Swedish GDP per capita had fallen to 5 per cent below the OECD average, 14 per cent above OECD Europe and 3 per cent above the EC level. It can be shown mathematically that as long as the average OECD growth rate was below 3.75 per cent p.a. the absolute growth in Sweden was lower than in all three country aggregates, and as we know from Table 3, the OECD growth rate was 2.11 per cent.

When Walter Korpi presents the development of GDP per capita in PPP-terms he does it in a misleading way. In his Fig. 2 he presents the development of PPP-adjusted GDP per capita in Sweden, OECD, EEC and the 'six rich' European countries and comes to the conclusion that 'the Swedish development quite closely follows that in the EEC as well as the average for the six rich European countries'. Korpi presents *nominal* series, which very efficiently trick the eye of the reader. In Fig. 1 I replicate and extend the Korpi curves for nominal PPP-adjusted GDP per capita for Sweden and the OECD (right scale). This is just a different mapping of the previously discussed PPP-adjusted GDP per capita relative to the OECD average, where the OECD average is normalised to 100 (left scale). As the reader can see, the two curves convey very different impressions. The nominal PPP-adjusted GDP seems to show a (roughly) unchanged difference between Sweden and the OECD from 1970 to the mid 1980s, but this implies a falling real difference – and, of course, a deterioration of the relative position (as shown explicitly by the relative income curve).

Finally, it is highly questionable in the first place to expect a lower relative growth rate in initially richer countries, and thus to focus on absolute growth in the compari-

---

[10] Parenthetically, it may be noted that Korpi erroneously maintains that I (Henreksen, 1992) have made comparisons in terms of absolute growth. What Korpi refers to was a calculation of the compounded effect on the GDP level of a certain growth rate differential, a perfectly legitimate exercise, which Korpi labels 'an intellectual somersault'.

sons. It presupposes mechanisms such as a strong catching-up effect, decreasing returns to scale or diminishing returns to capital. As already noted, it is unlikely that the catching-up effect is of much relevance any longer in explaining growth differences across countries at fairly similar income levels. Endogenous growth theory also tells us that when using an extended measure of capital – including physical, human, social and knowledge capital – it is much less likely that there are decreasing returns. As argued by Romer (e.g. 1990), returns may even be increasing, since one component of the extended capital stock, namely knowledge, is nonrival. Romer (1989) also shows that if one takes a very long-run view (beginning in the 1830s) growth rates are increasing rather than decreasing over time, which stands in stark contrast to Korpi's presumption. In short, an evaluation of Sweden's relative growth performance is most appropriately conducted in terms of a comparison of relative growth rates.

2.5 Making inferences about the whole economy from the performance of the (shrinking) manufacturing sector

Between 1970 and 1993 the share of manufacturing in Swedish GDP fell from 26 to 18 per cent of GDP. Korpi makes the point that in the 1977–89 period labour productivity growth in Swedish manufacturing was on a par with the average for ten other countries. From this finding he infers that 'it is difficult to discover clear evidence for a long-term labour productivity lag in manufacturing of the type likely to have been caused by distorted market mechanisms'. This conclusion merits at least two comments. First, 1977–89 constitutes only half the period of interest here;[11] if we consider a longer period Sweden is lagging also in this respect. For the 1970–91 period, labour productivity growth in Swedish manufacturing was 2.9 per cent p.a. compared to an average for the other countries of 3.6 per cent and 3.5 per cent when Japan is excluded.[12] Secondly, what may appear statistically to be a rapid rate of productivity growth is likely to be largely the result of scrapping the least productive production units. Analogously, it may be noted that labour productivity growth has been extremely fast in the rapidly shrinking agricultural sector throughout the postwar period.[13] In short, no conclusions regarding the performance of the aggregate economy can be made by referring to the rate of labour productivity growth in Swedish manufacturing in 1977–89. If anything, the long-run productivity performance in manufacturing gives further credence to the claim that Sweden has a growth problem.

[11] During this particular period Swedish manufacturing was boosted by no less than five devaluations.
[12] US Department of Labor. Bureau of Labour Statistics. August 1994. On the other hand, ironically and somewhat paradoxically, during the 1992–3 recession in Sweden, manufacturing labour productivity grew at almost 8 per cent p.a., resulting in a Swedish labour productivity growth of just 0.1 per cent-points below the eleven country average for the period 1970–93.
[13] It should be remarked that Korpi uses data for Sweden from a different source than the other 11 countries, despite the fact that data for Sweden are reported in that source. In the August 1994 data from the US Department of Labor, the productivity figures reported for Sweden are consistently slightly lower than the ones reported by Korpi.

2.6 Large public sector said to give a negative bias

Another factor claimed to bias the growth figures for Sweden downward is the large public sector, since productivity growth is by definition set to zero in the public sector. Of course there is a risk that the assumption of zero productivity growth in the public sector biases the Swedish growth figures downward.[14] Nevertheless, there are at least two factors working in reverse, and Korpi mentions neither of them. First, the public sector share of GDP has increased since about 1970, which may in itself have contributed positively to registered GDP, because previously unregistered production such as elderly care and child care may have been shifted from households to the public sector faster than in other countries.[15] Second, studies where one has actually attempted to measure public sector productivity show that, at least until the 1980s, an assumption of zero productivity growth in the public sector may have been too optimistic. One study of a large number of central government authorities found a productivity *decrease* of 2 per cent p.a. during the 1960–80 period.[16] In another study of the health sector a productivity decrease of 3 per cent p.a. was found for the same period.[17]

A downward bias is particularly unlikely when comparing the growth rate of GDP or GDP per capita during the period studied by Korpi.

3 CONCLUDING REMARKS

Relative to other rich countries, the rate of growth has been slow in Sweden for at least a quarter of a century. Perhaps the most striking result of this slow growth is that relative income in Sweden fell from 3rd or 4th to 17th place among the OECD countries from 1970 to 1993. Despite this evidence Walter Korpi has argued in numerous publications that those who claim that Sweden has been lagging behind have based their conclusions on 'what with an understatement can be called careless analyses'. Instead he asserts that Swedish growth performance has been on the whole in line with that of other comparable countries.

In this article I have tried to uncover how, against all odds, it is possible to give that impression. It is the result of a number of specific and unwarranted strategic choices

---

[14] In some industrial countries a positive rate of productivity growth is assumed. However, Produktivitetsdelegationen (1991; pp. 115–7) shows that the effect on the Swedish rate of growth is almost negligible if one, as for Germany, were to assume an annual productivity growth rate of 0.5 per cent.

[15] It is also necessary that the increase is larger than the crowding out of private sector activity. In this context it may be mentioned that Rosen (1996) shows that all employment growth since 1963 is accounted for by increased female employment in the local government sector. A large part of these economic activities went unregistered before 1963. To the extent that this was the case, GDP was boosted.

[16] *Statlig tjänsleproduktion. Produktivitetsutvecklingen 1960–1980.* Report 1985: no. 12. Stockholm: Statskontoret.

[17] *Produktions-, kostnads- och produktieitetsutveckling inom offentligt bedriven hälsooch sjukvård.* Report to Expertgruppen för studier i offentlig ekonomi, Ds Fi 1985: no. 3. Stockholm: Liber.

regarding data selection and interpretations of the findings: choosing propitious time periods, appealing to the catching-up effect in order to avoid comparisons with broad averages, focusing on absolute rather than relative growth in some cases and comparing levels by means of arbitrary exchange rate conversions instead of PPP rates, using nominal quantities in order to obscure the real development, interpreting weak long-run performance as the result of isolated policy errors while disregarding errors in other countries, and making unwarranted inferences about overall performance from the performance of subsectors of the economy.

Given that Sweden's key institutions and economic policy have deviated from many other OECD countries in recent decades, it is not surprising that many economists have argued that the slow economic growth may at least partly be explained by this deviation. Korpi dismisses the relevance of their arguments based on his assertion that Sweden has not, in fact, lagged behind. But since there is no convincing basis for Korpi's assertion, the reasons for Sweden's poor growth performance certainly merit close attention. However, this issue is too large to be dealt with in this paper.

Perhaps unwittingly, Walter Korpi shows in his article how important it is that social scientists, when necessary, reveal (or are aware of) their own underlying values. Korpi writes that 'the Sclerosis spokesmen have presented a clearly biased selection of available evidence and data of relevance for their diagnosis'. I hope that this article has convinced the reader that there is no basis for such an allegation; if anything, there may be a basis for the opposite allegation.

References

Abramovitz, M. (1986). 'Catching up, forging ahead, and falling behind.' *Journal of Economic History.* vol. 66, pp. 385–406.

Aghion, P. and Howitt, P. (1992). 'A model of growth through creative destruction.' *Econometrica,* vol. 60, pp. 323–51.

Barro, R. J. and Sala-i-Martin, X. (1995). *Economic Growth.* New York: McGraw Hill.

Dowrick, S. and N'guyen, D.-T. (1989). 'OECD comparative economic growth 1950–85: catching up and convergence.' *American Economic Review,* vol. 79, pp. 1010–30.

Grossman, G. M. and Helpman, E. (1991). *Innovation and Growth in the Global Economy.* Cambridge: MIT Press.

Hansson, P. and Henreksen, M. (1994). 'Catching up in industrialised countries: a disaggregated study.' *Journal of International Trade and Economic Development,* vol. 3, pp. 129–46.

Henreksen, M. (1992). *Sveriges tillväxtproblem.* (Sweden's Growth Problem.) Stockholm: SNS Förlag.

Henreksen, M., Jonung, L. and Stymne, J. (1996). 'Economic growth and the Swedish model.' In *Economic Growth in Europe since 1945* (eds N. F. R. Crafts and G. Tonniolo). Cambridge: Cambridge University Press.

Korpi, W. (1996). 'Eurosclerosis and the sclerosis of objectivity: on the role of values among policy experts.' *Economic Journal,* this issue.

Lindbeck, A., Molander, P., Persson, T., Petersson, D., Sandmo, A., Swendenborg, B. and Thygesen, N. (1994). *Turning Sweden Around.* Cambridge, MA: MIT Press.

Maddison, A. (1982). *Phases of Capitalist Development.* Oxford: Oxford University Press.

Mellander, E., Vredin, A. and Warne, A. (1992). 'Stochastic trends and economic iluctuations in a small open economy.' *Journal of Applied Econometrics,* vol. 7, pp. 369–94.

Nelson, C. R. and Plosser, C. I. (1982). 'Trends and random walks in macroeconomic time series.' *Journal of Monetary Economics,* vol. 10, pp. 139–62.

OECD (1995). *OECD Economic Surveys – Sweden*. Paris.

Produktivitetsdelegationen (1991). *Drivkrafter för produktivitet och välstånd*. (Incentives for Productivity and Welfare.) SOU 1991: 82. Stockholm: Allmänna Förlaget.

Romer, P. M. (1989). 'Capital accumulation in the theory of long-run growth.' In *Modern Business Cycle Theory* (ed. R. J. Barro) Oxford: Blackwell.

Romer, P. M. (1990). 'Are nonconvexities important for understanding growth?' *American Economic Review*, vol. 80, pp. 97–103.

Rosen, S. (1996). 'Public employment and the welfare state in Sweden.' In *The Welfare State in Transition* (eds R. B. Freeman, B. Swedenborg and R. Topel). Chicago: University of Chicago Press.

20

WHY SWEDEN'S WELFARE STATE NEEDED REFORM*

Jonas Agell

According to Professor Walter Korpi the Swedish economy would be in better shape if leading politicians had paid less attention to the advice from an influential group of Swedish academic economists allegedly hostile to the welfare state. Their claim that high taxes and extensive social security programmes have strong adverse effects on aggregate economic performance rested on a politically biased reading of comparative international data. In purporting to show that Sweden had fallen behind other comparable countries (the 'sclerosis diagnosis'), they set the stage for cutbacks in the welfare state, and a major tax reform involving substantially lower marginal tax rates.[1] Apart from creating inequality at a negligible gain in efficiency, the very same reforms may also explain why Sweden ran into a macroeconomic tailspin in the early 1990s. Rather than an instructive case study of the ultimate consequences of a long-term obsession with income equality and social protection, the exceptional economic crisis can be traced to severe macroeconomic policy blunders.

The views of Professor Korpi are quite familiar for anyone that has followed the Swedish debate over the last decade. Supporters of the welfare state applaud Professor Korpi for revealing the ideological bias underlying the evidence presented in support of the sclerosis diagnosis. Some Swedish economists rather thank of him as a modern day Don Quixote, eager to pick a fight with imaginary villains.

Being a Swede, and a professor of economics, I can hardly claim the status of an impartial observer. I certainly believe that Harberger triangles convey information, and I am convinced that most of the recently implemented reforms make sense. Nevertheless, I believe that Professor Korpi raises important issues. Many of the accusations made against the welfare state, in Sweden and elsewhere, rest on evidence which does not survive normal academic scrutiny. In their capacity as policy advisors, academic economists far from always live up to the standards of the seminar room. Speculation and sweeping generalisations are poor substitutes for facts and empirical investigations. Like Professor Korpi, I doubt that very important insights on the harmfulness of

* I would like to thank Susanne Ackum Agell, Per-Anders Edin, Peter Englund, Anders Forslund, Bertil Holmlund, Thomas Lindh and Henry Ohlsson for comments on an earlier draft of the paper. Needless to say, the usual disclaimers apply.

[1] In the following, I follow Professor Korpi in using the term 'sclerosis diagnosis' as a synonym for the proposition that aggregate economic performance of countries with a large welfare state is relatively poor.

the welfare state can be gained from comparative aggregate data. Over the period 1970–90, Swedish economic growth was below the OECD-average. At the same time the public sector was very large. However, as I will return to below, there is no easy way of proving that there is a causal connection from the latter observation to the former. Finally, I also agree that the severe economic crisis after 1991 is caused by macroeconomic factors.

But there are other propositions which I am ready to debate. The idea that the Swedish political establishment was seduced into a strategy of dismantling the welfare state by a handful of economics professors and other university affiliated economists may appeal to those subscribing to grand theories of conspiracy. I believe that reality is a bit duller. The claim that Sweden had fallen behind other comparable countries due to a large welfare state was readily adopted by the Conservative party under the leadership of Mr Carl Bildt, by the business community, and by parts of the press and media. But other power groups, including the dominant Social Democrats, the Liberals under Mr Bengt Westerberg, and the trade unions, remained largely unimpressed. The important motivations for the policy changes singled out by Professor Korpi do not seem to stem from the country tables published by the OECD. In the extensive official inquiry that preceded the major overhaul of the tax system in 1991, one looks in vain for references to the sclerosis diagnosis.

While Professor Korpi may overestimate the persuasive powers of certain economists, I also think that he underestimates the intellectual integrity of the community of academic economists. By the end of the 1980s, it is probably true that a majority of university affiliated economists had come to the conclusion that the Swedish welfare state could no longer deliver what it had promised. But in this process, the simple minded sclerosis diagnosis was of marginal importance. Although Professor Korpi is right in remarking that publications from the Centre for Business and Policy Studies (SNS) gave academic credibility to the sclerosis hypothesis, and that the prestigious report of the Lindbeck Commission (Lindbeck et al. 1994) contains some fanciful passages on the sources of decay in Swedish society, most academic economists advocated change for very different reasons. I will show that the kind of evidence that belongs to the bread and butter of a public finance economist seems to suggest that some parts of the welfare state had expanded to the point where they risking imposing significant deadweight losses.

1 COMPARATIVE GROWTH AND THE SIZE OF THE PUBLIC SECTOR

The simple sclerosis diagnosis rests on two claims. First, Swedish economic growth has been lower than in other comparable countries. Secondly, the poor aggregate growth record is the result of a large welfare state. The first proposition concerns the facts, and the second the question of inference. A qualified international readership would be surprised to learn how much Swedish newspaper space that has been devoted to heated exchanges on what the facts actually look like. No doubt, much of the fuel for this discussion stems from the difficulties inherent to the measurement of GDP and productivity. The statistics available for many countries are deficient; volatile exchange rates and other index number problems make it difficult to create comparable measures of production; countries have different conventions in measuring the size of the public sector and its change in productivity, etc. There is also much scope for disagreement on the choice of sample period, and what we ought to mean by countries comparable to Sweden.

Professor Korpi clearly prefers to view the period after 1991 as too special to be included in his charts. While it is reasonable to attribute the exceptional Swedish bust period to macroeconomic rather than structural factors, the reader should be aware of the fact that average Swedish growth performance looks considerably worse once we extend the sample period to 1994. Also, Professor Korpi builds part of his case on growth comparisons over a period, 1973–89, when the Swedish business cycle was out of line with developments elsewhere. Swedish growth was relatively low in 1970–2, and by ending the sample in 1989, Professor Korpi includes the final year of a prolonged peak in the Swedish business cycle, where many markets showed signs of overheating.

Facts are important, but so is the question of inference. Even if sensible people ought to be able to reach an agreement on the numbers, there is still room for rather different interpretations of observed growth differentials. To my mind, the inference problem is the tricky one. Fig. 1, taken from the recent survey on growth and the public sector by Agell, Lindh and Ohlsson (1995),[2] makes the point.

The upper panel plots the average growth rate of GDP per capita against the average size of tax revenues as a share of GDP – a common, but certainly imperfect, proxy for the extent of government involvement in the economy – for the 1970–90 period for 23 OECD countries. For this particular time period, there is no doubt that Sweden *is* falling behind. Only Switzerland and New Zealand had a lower growth rate, and Sweden lines up with the United States, both countries having an average growth rate of about 1.6 per cent. But it is not easy to detect a very clear relation between growth and the tax ratio. While Sweden combines high taxes and low growth, the tax ratio is relatively low in New Zealand, Switzerland, and the United States. When one adds a bivariate regression line, however, there seems to be a modest negative relation.

Few economists entertain the idea that only taxes matter for growth. According to the catching-up (or convergence) effect, countries which are relatively poor initially have a greater potential for growth. If one estimates a regression equation which includes both the tax share and initial GDP per capita, it is easy to construct the points in the middle panel. These points describe the combinations of growth rates and tax shares which arise after eliminating the growth differentials which in a statistical sense can be attributed to differences in initial GDP. Since the regressions indicate that the catching-up effect is important and significant, countries having a high initial GDP will improve their position. But we can also see that the partial correlation between adjusted growth and the tax share is zero – the bivariate regression line is horizontal.

According to the basic life cycle theory of consumption, countries with a large share of pensioners ought to have a relatively low savings rate. There is also good reason to believe that demographics can be important for a country's aggregate stock of human

[2] A previous version of this paper, cited by Professor Korpi, was published in response to some very definite claims about the link between growth and the public sector in the 1994 macroeconomics annual of the Centre for Business and Policy Studies (SNS).

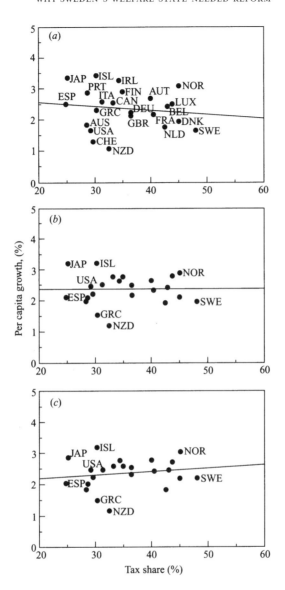

Fig. 1 GDP growth in OECD 1970–90 *vs.* tax shares
Top panel unadjusted. Mid panel adjusted for initial GDP. Bottom panel adjusted for initial
GDP and demography
Source: Agell, Lindh and Ohlsson (1995).

capital (human capital is unevenly distributed across cohorts). Since many growth models imply that savings and human capital formation affect growth, on a temporary or permanent basis, it is worthwhile to account for demographic differences between countries. If one runs a new regression where the proportions of the population at the tails of the age distribution (younger than 15 years, older than 64) are added to the right-hand variables, we arrive at the bottom figure. It is obviously less evident that Sweden is lagging behind. Given her initial conditions, Swedish growth ought to be relatively low. In 1970, Sweden was one of the richest members of the OECD, and the fraction of pensioners was high during the sample period. A friend of a large welfare state may also take comfort from the fact that the regression line now has a positive (but far from significant) slope. When one allows for some alternative explanatory factors, countries with high taxes seem to have a tendency to grow faster than others.

This simple exercise suggests that the advocates of the sclerosis diagnosis have a hard nut to crack. Economic growth depends on many factors, and unless one controls for their influence in a systematic way it is not meaningful to attach value to partial correlations between growth and indicators of the size of the public sector. In recent years there have been many cross-country studies of the link between growth and government size. While some studies claim to have shown that there is a significant negative relationship, it does not seem to survive small, but not implausible, changes in the set of conditioning variables (see also Levine and Renelt (1992) and Easterly and Rebelo (1993)).

In my view, cross-country growth regressions are far from a stage where meaningful answers can be given to questions that would interest policy makers. The problems of data quality loom large, and the results are often difficult to interpret. The estimated regressions are nearly always to be considered as reduced forms, with a loose link to underlying theory. Another problem is reverse causation; it is easy to think of reasons why the size of the public sector might depend on, rather than affect, economic growth. Finally, as noted by Agell, Lindh and Ohlsson, the welfare state '. . . is in fact a microcosm, which includes everything from the choice of tax bases and setting of tax rates to decisions concerning public consumption and social insurance compensation levels. To reduce this multitude of activities to a few aggregate indicators of the public sector, and then proceed to examine the cross-country correlation with economic growth, is a rather peculiar detour' (1995, p. 27). In the end, there is no excuse for ignoring the fine print.[3] After all, microeconomic questions seem to require microeconomic analysis.

2 THE SERIOUS CASE FOR REFORMING THE WELFARE STATE

According to my preferences the welfare state is worth fighting for. A relatively egalitarian income distribution, and the near absence of poverty, are achievements that justify a not so modest cost in terms of lower efficiency. In this section I will try to explain why even a sympathetic observer had reason to worry about certain features of the welfare state, and why policy changes were – and to some extent still are – called for. I should stress from the outset that my discussion will be rather sketchy, and far from exhaustive. The common denominator of my examples is that they have a microeconomic flavour, and that they refer to concrete institutions, rather than the welfare state in the abstract.

[3] See Atkinson (1995) and Slemrod (1995) for discussion.

2.1 Small elasticities, but large tax wedges

According to Professor Korpi, economists have aired similar warnings about the negative consequences of taxation for a very long time. Swedish economists of today essentially repeat the arguments of the great economic historian Eli Heckscher in the 1920s and the internationally acclaimed economist Gustav Cassel in the 1930s. Professor Korpi's position seems to be that economists cry wolf too often.

Table 1 shows the result from a recent attempt at quantifying the marginal efficiency cost due to labour supply distortions of the Swedish tax system.[4] The values of the

Table 1 Marginal excess burden per krona of tax revenue (in %)

	Compensated labour supply elasticity		
	0.05	0.11	0.25
Marginal tax wedge (%):			
62 (average blue-collar worker, 1991)	8.2	19.0	54.7
63 (average earned income, 1991)	8.6	20.1	59.0
70.5 (average blue-collar worker, 1988)	12.7	31.6	121.8
71.5 (average white-collar worker, 1991)	13.4	33.9	139.1
73 (average earned income, 1988)	14.6	37.8	175.0
79 (average white-collar worker, 1988)	22.0	65.3	2,280.0
85.5 (average senior white-collar worker, 1988)	41.0	192.5	–
Tax rate which maximises tax revenue	94.5	89.5	79.5

Source: Agell, Englund and Södersten (1995).

compensated elasticity of labour supply is chosen to reflect the range of findings in recent empirical studies.[5] The highest elasticity, 0.25, might be of relevance for women's labour supply. The intermediate elasticity, 0.11, is typical for many studies of the labour supply behaviour of married prime-age males. The smallest elasticity, 0.05, is taken from a recent panel study on the labour supply of blue-collar workers in manufacturing (Agell and Meghir 1995). An empirical approximation of the marginal tax wedge (the difference between marginal productivity and real take home pay) should account for income, payroll and net indirect taxes, as well as transfers related to in-

---

[4] See Agell, Englund and Södersten (1995). The numbers derive from a simple partial equilibrium model, where a typical worker maximises a single period CES-utility function in leisure and goods consumption subject to a linear tax system. To make life easy, it is assumed that all incremental tax revenue is returned as a lump sum (all income effects are eliminated). The marginal welfare cost per unit of tax revenue is here defined as $\Delta EB/\Delta T$, where ΔEB is the change in excess burden, and ΔT is the change in tax revenue.

[5] For recent surveys, see Aronsson and Walker (1995) and Agell, Englund and Södersten (1995).

come. According to calculations of Du Rietz (1994) and the Ministry of Finance (1992), reported in the table, the average marginal tax wedge for some broad categories of employees was in the range 71–86 per cent in the late 1980s.

My simple point is that small elasticities matter also, if the tax rate is sufficiently high. The logic behind the marginal welfare cost per krona of tax revenue implies that there is a region of tax wedges at which the efficiency cost starts to increase very rapidly. At some level of the tax wedge, an additional tax hike creates additional excess burdens, but little extra tax revenue. Although the table clearly brings out the sensitivity of the results to alternative assumptions, one can hardly rule out the possibility that marginal tax wedges in Sweden were close to that level. The point estimates of labour supply elasticities (not to mention the confidence intervals) reported in a number of recent studies are consistent with the view that the tax wedges of the 1980s had marked negative efficiency effects.

From the perspective of a modern day public finance economist, Professors Heckscher and Cassel may have had a weak case. The excess burden created when the marginal tax wedge is around 20 per cent is negligible by any standard of comparison. But the efficiency algebra looks very different when one adds some 60 percentage points to the tax wedge. In my view, the lower marginal tax wedges which materialised after the major tax reform of 1991 looks like a much less risky proposition.

2.2 Tax arbitrage and levelling the playing field

Efficiency is important, but so is distribution. How could wide political support be gathered for a tax reform which implied much lower marginal tax rates for the rich? The answer, not mentioned by Professor Korpi, is that the reform also included tax hikes, and increased child and housing allowances. People with high income should pay for their lower marginal tax wedges by higher, and more uniform, taxes on capital income. The tax reform act of 1991 was meant to promote efficiency, subject to the constraint of an unchanged distribution of disposable income.

Before the tax reform act of 1991, most economists agreed that the taxation of capital income had two major shortcomings. First, as the tax system treated the returns on different assets in a non-uniform manner, especially in times of inflation, it was feared that investments were channelled to the wrong sectors. Investments in non-corporate assets, and housing in particular, were given a preferential tax treatment. Secondly, the scope for a number of straightforward tax arbitrage operations under-mined the tax base and stimulated borrowing. This spelled bad news for the fisc, and for those concerned about redistribution policy. For several years, the aggregate house-hold sector claimed tax deductions to such an extent that net revenue from taxes on personal capital income was negative. Also, people with high marginal tax rates and high incomes were more prone than others to inflate their balance sheets by purchasing assets with borrowed money (see e.g. Agell and Edin (1990)).

The tax reform implied far-reaching changes in the system of personal capital income. The tax bases were broadened, and all kinds of personal capital income were taxed at a flat rate. Calculations in Södersten (1993) imply that there was a marked reduction in the magnitude of intersectoral tax distortions – the playing field was levelled. But the tax reform also did much to eliminate tax shelters and reduce the incentive to inflate balance sheets. Although it is premature to make a definite statement about long-term distributional consequences, the recent study of Björklund et al. (1995) indicates that the tax reform was approximately neutral with respect to the distribution of disposable income.

2.3 Full compensation, but no monitoring

Sweden has for a long time cared for her citizens through an extensive network of transfer schemes. From an incentive point of view, a striking feature is that many of these programmes including – unemployment insurance, provisions for parental leave, and sickness benefits – presuppose that individuals are active participants in the labour market. This principle of workfare may certainly counteract some of the disincentive effects of marginal tax wedges.

Even so, important issues of policy design remain. In the imperfect world of human beings, it is hard to see how a social insurer can manage without a stick which discourages misuse. A suggestive example is the Swedish system of sickness insurance. Since the early 1960s it became increasingly generous. According to the rules in place by the end of the 1980s, employees were entitled to a 90 per cent compensation level from the first day of reporting sick. Due to supplementary insurance agreements in the labour market, however, many employees had a compensation level of 100 per cent. For the first seven days of sickness leave, a physician's certificate was not required. If individuals ever respond to economic incentives, work absenteeism ought to be widespread in Sweden.

The increase in the average number of sickness days per insured employee from 13 days in 1963 to 25 days in 1988 can hardly be attributed to a deteriorating health status of the population. As discussed by Aronsson and Walker (1995), there was no relationship between average sickness days and the business cycle until the three day waiting period was eliminated in 1967. Since then, however, the relationship has been highly procyclical; an observation which is consistent with the idea that sickness leave has been exploited as a device to smooth work hours over the cycle. Moreover, the timing of increased usage coincides with changes that increased the generosity of the system. Finally, the microeconometric studies of Brose (1995) and Johansson and Palme (1994) suggest that individuals' decisions on sickness leave incorporate economic considerations.

Recent design changes have probably restored the balance. Reforms in 1991 and 1993 lowered the replacement rate, and introduced a waiting period.

2.4 Labour market structure and the welfare state

One common, but possibly somewhat overrated, explanation for the fine Swedish historical unemployment record is that all-encompassing trade unions used to internalise the negative macroeconomic externalities present in wage setting. An important related point is that corporatist collective bargaining may internalise some of the negative incentive effects from high tax wedges and generous benefit schemes. Unions operating at the national level have an incentive to strike wage and employment bargains which mitigate labour supply distortions at the micro level (Summers et al. (1993)). An obvious implication is that changes in bargaining structure may alter the impact on economic behaviour of taxes and benefits.

A conspicuous example concerns the financing of Swedish unemployment benefits. The Swedish system of unemployment benefits has for a long time been run by the trade unions in the form of a number of certified unemployment insurance funds.[6] While part of the financing stems from membership fees, the government has provided large and growing subsidies, financed by general income and payroll taxes. In the 1980s, the government's share of total expenditures on unemployment benefits had risen to more than 90 per cent. After a design change in 1989, the level of membership fees was made independent of the unemployment rate in the area of the specific fund – the marginal cost of unemployment for a single fund was in effect driven to zero.

In an economy with one all encompassing union marginal subsidies on this scale should be of no consequence, since the union recognises that higher subsidies also means higher taxes on labour. However, since the early 1980s, Swedish wage setting has been characterised by a strong tendency towards decentralisation. As industry and local level bargaining have replaced bargaining at the national level, there is a much greater risk for macroeconomic free-riding. The bill for the unemployment consequences of excessive wage deals in a specific sector can be passed on to tax paying workers in other sectors of the economy. A change to a system of unemployment insurance where the members of sector specific unions have to pay some part of the marginal unemployment cost seems long overdue.[7]

2.5 International factor mobility

Is the integrated European market for labour and capital a threat to the Swedish welfare state? The important observation when it comes to capital mobility is that policy makers for a long time have adopted the position that Sweden is a small fish in a big pond of investment opportunities. While the source based corporate income tax is potentially harmful for investment, the effective marginal tax rate has been very low (see OECD (1991)). The mobility of labour and human capital is another story. The Swedish welfare state has to a very large extent built on the ability to tax and redistribute wage income. Even if egalitarian-minded Swedes sometimes complain about the accuracy of redistribution policy, available studies indicate that taxes and transfers have contributed to a dramatic equalisation of income between different socio-economic groups. According to Björklund (1991) the losers have been the highly edu-

---

[6] For an overview of Swedish unemployment insurance, see Björklund and Holmlund (1991).

[7] Although there is a strong theoretical case for some amount of marginal self-insurance (see e.g. Holmlund and Lundborg (1988)). Forslund (1994) is unable to find a significant wage effect from the degree of government subsidisation of unemployment insurance funds. As pointed out by the author, however, his measure of subsidisation captures average rather than marginal aspects of the system. Also, his sample period ends in 1989, i.e. the year when important design changes were implemented.

cated, and those of 'upper-class origin'. It goes without saying that the possibility that these losers choose to vote with their feet in a common European labour market is a chilling prospect for a country that for so long has taken pride in its ability to reduce income differentials.

Clearly, there are a number of informal barriers to international labour mobility. Ties in the form of culture, language and family are important. A striking finding from a recent research project on skill migration in the intra-Nordic labour market (where mobility has been free since 1954) is that labour mobility has been very low, despite minor cultural and language barriers (Pedersen and Schröder (1994) summarise the main findings). But the propensity to migrate increases with the educational level, and there are differences between skill groups when it comes to the motive for migration. Highly educated Scandinavians (e.g. civil engineers and business administrators) are more sensitive to wage gains, while emigrants with little education mainly react to the probability of finding a job.

Historical migration patterns need not be a good guide for the future. As noted by Pedersen and Schröder, one reason for the modest migration flows in the past is that the Nordic countries have many common characteristics, including progressive taxes and compressed wage structures. For many highly educated Swedes, the admission to European labour markets with greater earnings disparities implies a substantially higher return to migration. Another indication of potential future labour mobility is the on-going process of harmonisation of university education and student exchange within the European community. Although the risk of large scale Swedish skill migration seems very small, the potential for increased mobility over the coming years suggests that the efficiency cost of redistribution policy will increase. Some hard choices might wait around the corner.[8]

3 CONCLUDING REMARKS

According to an old joke, an economist should never let the facts stand between him and the right answer. From this cynical perspective, the community of Swedish academic economists ought to be grateful for Professor Korpi's relentless struggle with the statistical problems of international comparisons of aggregate economic performance. Over the years he has identified several instances of careless and misleading data comparisons. No doubt, Professor Korpi has done much to promote a more respectful attitude to the facts. He has done the job that some economist should have shouldered long ago.[9]

---

[8] Sinn (1990) even argues that international labour mobility might spell the 'death of the insurance state'.

[9] Why did no economist sign up for the job of scrutinising the claims of the sclerosis proponents? Professor Korpi suggests that the reason is that the hierarchic structure of Swedish university economics may have put an especially high price on pluralism. Although there might be some truth in this, a more plausible alternative explanation – based on introspection – is that many university affiliated economists never felt at home with the issues. In these days of highly specialised research, few economists find the time to bother very much about claims made in areas outside their own speciality.

But the battleground of cross-country growth comparisons is a strange place to settle the future of the welfare state. In presenting the silly sclerosis diagnosis as *the* case against the welfare state, Professor Korpi ducks the substantive issues. To understand why many Swedish economists became critical of the welfare state during the 1980s, one must look in other directions.[10] While it would be foolish to rule out the influence of a right-wing change in political and ideological attitudes, I believe that 'objective' circumstances were more important. Sound microeconomic theorising and sound econometric evidence suggest that some parts of the Swedish welfare state functioned less well. The best way of defending the welfare state is not to ignore these troublesome pieces of evidence, or to give an incomplete account of the debate among serious academic economists. In the end, such a strategy only serves to strengthen the position of those big thinkers who claim that the government is to blame for all our economic problems.

References

Agell, A. S. and Meghir, C. (1995). 'Male labour supply in Sweden: are incentives important?' Forthcoming in *Swedish Economic Policy Review.*

Agell, J. and Edin, P.-A. (1990). 'Marginal taxes and the asset portfolios of Swedish households.' *Scandinavian Journal of Economics*, vol. 92, pp. 47–64.

Agell, J., Englund, P. and Södersten, J. (1995). *Svensk skattepolitik i teori och praktik. 1991 års skattereform* ('Swedish tax policy in theory and practice. The 1991 tax reform'). Stockholm: Fritzes.

Agell, J., Lindh, T. and Ohlsson, H. (1995). 'Growth and the public sector: A critical review essay.' Forthcoming in *European Journal of Political Economy.*

Aronsson, T. and Walker, J. R. (1995). 'The effects of Sweden's welfare state on labor supply incentives.' Occasional Paper No. 64. Stockholm: SNS.

Atkinson, A. (1995). 'The welfare state and economic performance.' *National Tax Journal*, vol. 48, pp. 171–98.

Björklund, A. (1991). 'Inkomstfördelningens ntveckling' ('The development of the distribution of income'). In *Ekonomi och samhälle i. Skatter och offentlig sektor*, Stockholm: SNS Förlag.

Björklund, A. and Holmlund, B. (1991). 'The economics of unemployment insurance: The case of Sweden.' In *Labour Market Policy and Unemployment Insurance.* (eds A. Björklund, R. Haveman, R. Hollister and B. Holmlund). Oxford: Oxford University Press.

Björklund, A., Palme, M. and Svensson, I. (1995). 'Assessing the effects of Swedish tax and benefit reforms on income distribution using different income concepts.' Forthcoming in *Swedish Economic Policy Review.*

Brose, P. (1995). 'Sickness absence: An empirical analysis of the HUS panel.' Working Paper No. 1995: 12, Department of Economics, Uppsala University.

Du Rietz, G. (1994). *Välfärdsstatens Finansiering* ('The financing of the welfare state'). Stockholm: City University Press.

Easterly, W. and Rebelo, S. (1995). 'Fiscal policy and economic growth. An empirical investigation.' *Journal of Monetary Economics*, vol. 32, pp. 417–58.

Forslund, A. (1994). 'Labor market policies and wage setting: A study of Swedish unemployment insurance funds.' In *Pay, Productivity and Policy. Essays on Wage Behaviour in Sweden*, (ed. B. Holmlund), Stockholm: Trade Union Institute of Economic Research.

---

[10] For an interesting account of the development of the views of Scandinavian economists on the welfare state since the 1930s, see Sandmo (1991).

Holmlund, B. and Lundborg, P. (1988). 'Unemployment insurance and union wage setting.' *Scandinavian Journal of Economics*, vol. 90, pp. 161–72.

Johansson, P. and Palme, M. (1994). 'The effects of economic incentives on worker absenteeism: An empirical study using Swedish micro data.' Working Paper No. 4, The Economic Research Institute, Stockholm School of Economics.

Levine, R. and Renelt, D. (1992). 'A sensitivity analysis of cross-country growth regressions.' *American Economic Review*, vol. 82, pp. 942–63.

Lindbeck, A., Molander, P., Persson, T., Petersson, O., Sandmo, A., Swedenborg, B. and Thygesen, N. (1994). *Turning Sweden Around.* Cambridge: MIT Press

Ministry of Finance (1992). 1992 Medium Term Survey. Stockholm: Allmdnna Frvlaget.

OECD (Organization for Economic Co-operation and Development) (1991). *Taxing Profits in a Global Economy.* Paris: OECD.

Pedersen, P. and Schröder, L. (1994). 'Summary and conclusions.' In *Scandinavians Without Borders – Skill Migration and the European Integration Process.* (ed, P. Pedersen), forthcoming. Amsterdam: North-Holland.

Sandmo, A. (1991). 'Economists and the welfare state.' *European Economic Review*, vol. 35, pp. 213–39.

Sinn, H.-W. (1990). 'Tax harmonization and tax competition in Europe.' *European Economic Review*, vol. 34, pp. 489–504.

Slemrod, J. (1995). 'What do cross-country studies teach about government involvement, prosperity, and economic growth?' *Brookings Papers on Economic Activity*, 1995 (2), pp. 373–431.

Summers, L., Gruber, J. and Vergara, R. (1993). 'Taxation and the structure of labor markets: the case of corporatism.' *Quarterly Journal of Economics*, vol. 108, pp. 385–411.

Södersten, I. (1993). 'Sweden.' In *Tax Reform and the Cost of Capital. An International Comparison*, (eds D. W. Jorgenson and R. Landau), Washington DC: Brookings.

21

SWEDISH ECONOMIC PERFORMANCE AND SWEDISH ECONOMIC DEBATE: A VIEW FROM OUTSIDE

Steve Dowrick

The papers by Korpi, Henreksen and Agell raise important questions both about the Swedish economy and about the way in which evidence on economic growth should be handled in debate on economic policy. I want to comment in particular on the fundamental question of whether the international evidence allows us to judge that Swedish growth has been below par. The papers raise two further questions. On the first – whether growth is inhibited by high taxation and a large welfare state, the hallmarks of the post-war Swedish economy – Agell provides as good an assessment of the cross-country macroeconomic evidence as we can probably hope to get at the moment: unproven. On the final vexed question of whether the structure of the economics profession has been inimical to open debate, I have only a few comments to make.

Let me start with the criteria and method by which we should attempt to assess relative economic performance. This is a methodological minefield. There are numerous paths leading to divergent conclusions. The least we can do is to be explicit about our choices and subject our provisional conclusions to some cheeks for robustness. *What performance measure is relevant?* We could look at GDP or consumption, scaled per head of population or per member of the workforce or per hour worked. *What deflators do we use?* We can reduce measures denominated in local currency to a common unit using exchange rates or using fixed international prices or using utility-based indexes. *Which derivative of the performance measure do we use?* We might want to compare levels or rankings, or we might choose to assess relative rates of growth, or even relative changes in growth rates? *Which time period is relevant?* In particular, comparisons of growth rates are often very sensitive to choice of start and end years when business cycle fluctuations are asynchronous. *What is the reference point for assessing under- or over-achievement?* The definition of par might be either the best performance or average performance, for some group of countries for some period of time. *Finally, what exogenous factors are to be taken into account?* We might wish to control for the influence on our preferred performance measure of a wide range of factors which are extraneous to the policy question under examination.

I will take a brisk jog through this minefield, explaining briefly some of the choices which seem most relevant to the problem in hand but without attempting a full exposition of the problems. The most usual starting place is to choose real GDP per capita as a measure of aggregate performance. This choice is suggested both by data availability for comparative analysis over an extended period and for comparability with a wide range of previous studies – but we should be aware that it is a problematic choice.

The problems of GDP as an economic performance measure, let alone a welfare measure, are well known. Different aspects are discussed in detail in Eisner (1988) and in the Human Development Reports of the United Nations Development Programme (UNDP). For example, UNDP (1994, p. 129) placed Sweden 12th in the 1991 world rankings of real GDP per capita, at just over seventeen thousand dollars. On the other hand, Swedish life expectancy of 78 years places them 4th in the Human Development Index (HDI), significantly above countries such as Germany, the United States and the United Kingdom where life expectancy is two years less. We might of course dispute details of the construction of the HDI,[1] but the weight given to life expectancy relative to GDP measures is intuitively appealing when it comes to judging comparative welfare. It is not unreasonable to suppose that a representative household in Sweden might refuse the offer of a 15% rise in income, their GDP shortfall relative to Germany, if they would thereby have to cut two years off the life expectancy of each member of the family.

Despite the attractiveness of the HDI as an attempt to measure comparative national welfare, it is not yet sufficiently well developed conceptually or statistically to replace GDP as a standard measure of economic performance. Bearing in mind that failure to take account of important factors such as life expectancy probably works against a favourable assessment of the benefits of the large welfare state in Sweden, I proceed to discuss the use of GDP measures.

Henreksen's point that we should examine *real* GDP measures, i.e. that price inflation should be discounted, is obviously reasonable. I follow all three papers in concentrating on measures of real GDP *per capita* as a reasonable starting point for judging overall economic performance, although Korpi is surely right to argue that we should also look at measures of labour productivity and also disaggregate by sector in order to develop a fuller picture.

Korpi and Henreksen present conflicting evidence in their diagrams and figures on comparative GDP performance. Many of the differences are attributable to the choice of appropriate periodisation and to the choice of the 'par' measure – Korpi favouring the average performance of six rich European economics and emphasising rates of growth, Henrekson favouring the OECD average and emphasising changes in rankings. The reason that their respective choices lead to such widely differing conclusions can be gleaned from examination of the growth paths of each of the 24 OECD countries since 1950.

Fig. I shows paths of real GDP per capita, measured in 1985$ at constant international prices up until 1992, using data from the Penn World Tables (PWT). The Swedish GDP line is shown in bold. As a point of reference the UK GDP path is shown by circles and the Australian path by diamonds. The legend lists the countries in decreasing order of 1992 income levels.

This picture must surely be worth at least 10,000 words. Three preliminary observations stand out. First, all countries experienced a slowdown in growth after 1973, so it is hardly surprising that anguished debates about 'what went wrong' have been held throughout the 1980s in each country. Second, countries experience significant year-

---

[1] See Dowrick et al. (1994) for a detailed analysis and proposal of a utility based alternative.

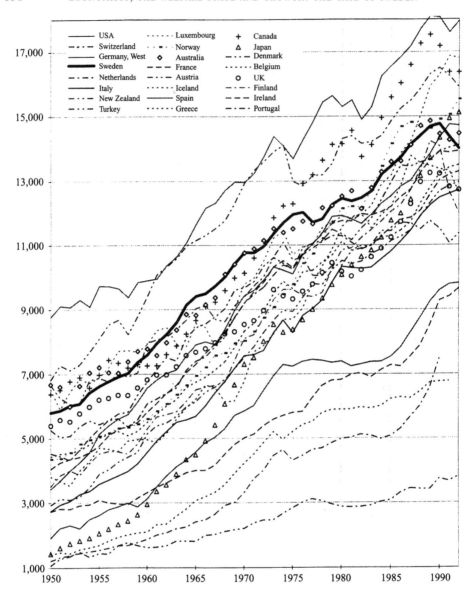

Fig. I Real GDP per capita in $1985 @PPP for 24 OECD countries 1950–92
Source: Penn World Tables, version 5.6 (Summers and Heston, 1991)

by-year fluctuations around their trend growth lines. These business cycle fluctuations are not fully synchronised, particularly in the Swedish case, so comparisons with other countries are very sensitive to the choice of period. Finally, income levels have converged to the extent that by 1990 there was a clearly identifiable group of fifteen fairly rich countries, from New Zealand to Norway with per capita GDP levels in a tight range, $12–15,000. (There are four richer countries – US, Canada, Luxembourg and Switzerland – with GDP per capita above PPP$16,000. The five poorest countries have been catching up but are still below $10,000 per capita.)

The combination of convergence and cyclical fluctuation suggests that we should be wary about placing much emphasis on changes in GDP rankings between a particular pair of years. The 'fairly rich' countries are so close to each other that changes in rankings may reflect the state of the business cycle rather than any significant shift in the trend growth line. For instance, Sweden in the first half of the 1950s lay between 6th and 7th position, rose to third in the 1960s, returned to 6/7th position in the late 1980s and only slipped to 10th position in 1992. The data displayed here go only as far as 1992, but it is evident that the further 1993 slump in Swedish GDP (it fell over 3% in per capita terms) will have prompted a further slide down the rankings. This point is emphasised by Henreksen's table 2 (page 328, this volume) which focuses on the decline from 3rd in 1970 to 17th in 1993. On the other hand, we could emphasise the rise in the Swedish ranking from 7th in 1950 to 6th in 1990. This is a game which is, I know all too well, played vigorously in the context of Australian policy debates. Proponents of change are tempted to pick a pair of years which show a dramatic decline down the rankings, whereas others are tempted to pick on years which show the opposite.

In the context of debates about medium-term and long-term growth, it is obviously desirable that serious attempts should be made to distinguish between cyclical fluctuations and trends. This can be done using a variety of statistical techniques. More simply, all comparisons can be made peak to peak (or trough to trough). Or even more simply we can use a diagram such as Fig. I and let the human eye provide some intuitive decomposition of trend and cycle.

A further cautionary note is important here. These real GDP comparisons are subject to substantial aggregation error. The current standard method for international comparisons is to use the PWT data which aggregate real quantities of goods and services at constant international prices. These purchasing power parity (PPP) estimates are a substantial improvement over comparisons based on exchange rates, as Henreksen correctly points out. There remain, however, substantial problems of substitution bias with this PPP method. When it comes to bilateral comparisons, the international prices may be quite different from those prevailing in either of the two countries in question. It follows that fixed price rankings are not utility-consistent in that a GDP bundle which is revealed preferred to another may be, nevertheless, ranked lower at international prices. Dowrick and Quiggin (1994) find that there is a typical 'aggregation error' of up to 10%. We should really view the GDP lines in Fig. 1 with a ±5% 'error' band around each line. This explains why Henreksen's rankings are different from mine, e.g. he places Sweden 12th in 1991 compared to 8th as shown in Fig. 1. He uses *current* international prices whereas I am using the PWT *constant* (1985) international prices.[2] The point is not that one set of rankings is necessarily superior to the others, but that there is a fundamental indeterminacy in the compilation of all of these

---

[2] This also explains why Henreksen's comparisons do not match up between real (constant price) growth rates and the relative growth rates he infers from the OECD PPP tables. The OECD tables use current PPPs, i.e. a different price vector for each year. The PWT estimates of GDP levels and rates of growth are, on the other hand, consistent because they value GDP at constant international prices.

PPP indexes. For example, revealed preference tests suggest that the Swedish 1990 GDP bundle could be utility-ranked anywhere between 5th and 10th.

The combination of income convergence, asynchronous business cycle fluctuations, and index number aggregation error suggest that we should pay relatively little attention to simplistic comparisons of rankings of GDP levels within the group of fifteen middle-income countries. A sensible assessment would be to note that Sweden was consistently towards the top of the middle-rank group over the four decades up to 1990 before negative growth of 7% over three years saw the ranking plummet towards the bottom of this tightly bunched, fairly affluent group.

Turning to the evidence on comparative growth rates, the problem of timing is the same as that encountered in looking at levels and rankings. Picking a Swedish business cycle slump as a starting point will tend to exaggerate subsequent Swedish growth whilst picking a slump as the end point will tend to understate true trend growth. There is a further major problem. Do we take account of exogenous factors such as technological catch-up? Henreksen and Korpi clearly differ here, with the former preferring to ignore catch-up on the grounds that it is likely to have little explanatory power in recent decades when income levels are already fairly close and that recent theories of growth are capable of predicting divergence rather than convergence.

The important point to be taken from the new growth theory is, however, that initial conditions can matter and should be taken into account when explaining or comparing rates of growth. Whether positive feedback effects dominate over negative feedback is an empirical question, and the answer will no doubt vary for different countries and different periods. Here, we are concerned with the evidence on OECD convergence or divergence over the last twenty years. Fig. 2 plots annual average rates of

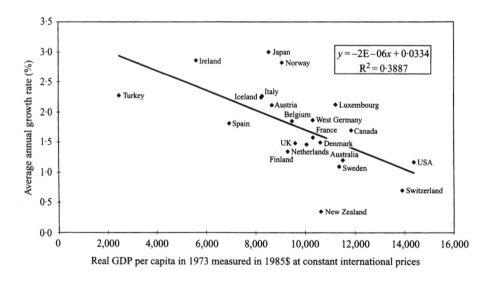

Fig. 2 OECD catch-up: 1973 real GDP and growth 1973–92
Source: Penn World Tables, version 5.6

growth over the period 1973–92 against the starting level of GDP per capita, again using the Penn World Table data which measures everything at 1985 international prices. There is a strong downward trend in the scatter plot, implying faster growth for poorer countries. The simple correlation coefficient is −0.6, implying a high level of statistical significance and a substantial degree of explanatory power.

This evidence of convergence is in line with the standard results in the many empirical results surveyed in Barro and Sala-i-Martin (1995) and is implied by Agell's analysis. Although modern growth theory is certainly capable of explaining divergent growth, there is in fact no evidence that this has been occurring systematically amongst the richer countries of the world over the past half century. Catching-up has in fact been the rule for all but the very poorest countries of the world. Taking account of this effect allows meaningful comparisons between growth rates of countries coming from very different starting points. There still remains the question of which countries should be included in the reference group, but in practice the inclusion of newly industrialising countries makes little difference to econometric estimates of the convergence parameter. What is important, is that assessment of relative growth performance should take account of the initial conditions.

Taking the regression line illustrated in Fig. 2 for OECD countries, Swedish performance appears to have lagged 0.3 percentage points per year compared with the predicted performance of comparably rich countries. Of course examining growth only up until 1990 would make Swedish performance look substantially better. Indeed, my earlier econometric study (Dowrick and N'guyen, 1989) found that taking account not only of catch-up but also of cyclical fluctuations, Swedish growth was actually 0.25 percentage points *above* the OECD average over the period 1973–85. Henrekson refers to this paper but emphasises the rather different finding that residual (multi-factor productivity) growth was 0.25 points below average. The discrepancy is explained by the fact that Swedish investment and employment growth were both substantially higher than average.

Which of these figures is relevant − 0.25 points above or below average − depends, in the context of the debate on the Swedish welfare and tax system, on whether investment and employment are taken as endogenous or exogenous. Treating factor supplies as exogenous, one would take the evidence as one of mild underperformance. On the other hand, treating rapid growth in factor supplies as the result of policy would lead to the more optimistic assessment. On balance, it seems reasonable to conclude that *at least up until 1990* there is nothing in the Swedish growth performance which suggests substantial underperformance.

This assessment of trend growth rates backs up the comparison which was conducted in terms of levels and rankings. It suggests that there is a stiff challenge for the proponents of the 'lagging behind' thesis. It is incumbent on them to explain why Swedish GDP performance was consistently reasonable over forty years and only shows a marked decline after 1990.

When it comes to the question of whether high taxes and welfare spending can be blamed for low growth, I think that Agell's careful evaluation of the evidence is convincing in suggesting that there is little robust evidence for this thesis in comparisons across countries. Indeed, I am tempted to read into his Fig. I some evidence in support of the 'hump-shaped' hypothesis which comes out of Barro's (1990) model of endogenous growth with the provision of a productive public good. If the public good is financed out of distortionary taxation, there comes a point at which the distortionary impact on incentives to invest result in further taxation reducing growth. On the other hand, at low levels of public good provision, tax increases which finance the scarce public good are growth-enhancing. The productive good may be tangible like transport and communications infrastructure, but it may also be an intangible such as income redistribution.

I am less inclined to agree with Agell's assessment that cross-country GDP comparisons are too imprecise to shed any light on the relationship between taxation and growth. The finding that a simple monotonic relationship is not evident in the macroeconomic aggregates is an important result. Agell presents microeconomic estimates of the welfare cost of high Swedish taxes. Such estimates are very important if we are looking at alternative ways of financing a given programme of public expenditure. But these are simply cost estimates, constructed without regard to any possible positive benefits flowing from the expenditures. To measure the trade-off between costs and benefits, we really do need to examine the macroeconomic outcomes using both time-series and cross-country evidence. So for instance, we need to take seriously the cross-country evidence from Easterley and Rebelo (1993) and Persson and Tabellini (1994) who find that growth is stimulated by public provision of infrastructure and by reductions in income inequality. Equally, we need to look at the macroeconomic time-series evidence which tends to back up the suggestion that public infrastructure is productive, such as the evidence presented by Aschauer (1989) for the United States and Berndt and Hansson (1992) for Sweden. Evidence on the distortionary impact of taxation needs to be weighed against these benefits.

The Swedish debate shows that reading the macroeconomic evidence is still a controversial exercise. It is all too easy to select particular measures over a particular period to suit a particular argument. However, academic debate through refereed journals has built up a set of methodological guidelines and empirical analyses which do enable us to tighten the criteria for a more objective assessment of aggregate performance.

References

Aschauer, David Alan (1989). 'Is public expenditure productive.' *Journal of Monetary Economics*, vol. 23, pp. 177–200.

Barro, Robert J. (1990). 'Government spending in a simple model of endogenous growth.' *Journal of Political Economy*, vol. 98 (5:2), pp. S103–26.

Barro, Robert J. and Sala-i-Martin, Xavier (1995). *Economic Growth*, McGraw-Hill.

Berndt, Ernst R. and Hansson, Bengt (1992). 'Measuring the contribution of public infrastructure capital in Sweden.' *Scandinavian Journal of Economics*, vol. 94, Supplement, pp. S151–68.

Dowrick, Steve and N'guyen, DT (1989). 'OECD economic growth 1950–85.' *American Economic Review*, vol. 79, December, pp. 1010–30.

Dowrick, Steve and Quiggin, John (1994). 'International comparisons of living standards and tastes: a revealed preference analysis.' *American Economic Review*, vol. 84 (1), March, pp. 332–41.

Dowrick, Steve, Dunlop, Yvonne and Quiggin, John (1994). 'Social indicators and comparisons of living standards: a revealed preference analysis.' CEPR Discussion Paper No. 312, Canberra: Australian National University.

Easterly, William and Rebelo, Sergio (1993). 'Fiscal policy and economic growth: an empirical investigation.' *Journal of Monetary Economics*, vol. 32(3), December, pp. 417–58.

Eisner, Robert (1988). 'Extended accounts for national income and product.' *Journal of Economic Literature*, vol. 26 (4), pp. 1611–84.

Ministry of Finance (1992). *1992 Medium Term Survey*, Stockholm: Allmdnna fvr laget.

Persson, Torsten and Tabellini, Guido (1994). 'Is inequality harmful for growth.' *American Economic Review*, vol. 84 (3), June pp. 600–21.

Summers, Robert and Heston, Alan (1991). 'The Penn World Table (Mark 5).' *Quarterly Journal of Economics*, vol. 106 (2), pp. 327–68.

UNDP (United Nations Development Programme) (1994). *Human Development Report*. New York: Oxford University Press.

INDEX